Urban Change in Central Europe

The changes Central European cities have undergone since 1989 deserve a complex, interdisciplinary analysis that offers deep insight into the specific nature of the transformation taking place in the region. This book presents a multidimensional and cross-disciplinary case study of Kraków, focusing on the changes taking place in Central Europe over the past three decades.

This book answers the question of how the once neglected city of Kraków has transformed into a thriving global tourist destination, an attractive investment market, and a European leader of shared services. It examines political, socio-economic, cultural, and architectural development of the city against the ongoing processes of post-1989 political and economic transition, European integration, and globalisation. The authors offer a portrait of the evolution in thinking about the developmental resources of the city, accounting for what is broadly construed as culture and heritage. Whereas previous studies have offered only one-dimensional insights into these phenomena, this book highlights the specific characteristics of the transition and identifies the challenges typical of many cities in Czechia, Slovakia, Poland, and Hungary, after the fall of communism.

This book will be valuable reading for academics, researchers, and postgraduate and PhD students of economic geography, urban studies, public management, political studies, sociology, culture and heritage management, and modern history, as well as those with an interest in Central European and transformation issues.

Jacek Purchla is Professor of Humanities and Head of the Department of Economic and Social History / UNESCO Chair for Heritage and Urban Studies at the Kraków University of Economics.

Routledge Advances in Regional Economics, Science and Policy

Designing Smart and Resilient Cities for a Post-Pandemic World
Metropandemic Revolution
Anthony Larsson and Andreas Hatzigeorgiou

Political Geography of Cities and Regions
Changing Legitimacy and Identity
Kees Terlouw

The Economic Geography of the Car Market
The Automobile Revolution in an Emerging Economy
Edited by Bartłomiej Kołsut and Tadeusz Stryjakiewicz

Worker Mobility and Urban Policy in Latin America
Policy Interactions and Urban Outcomes in Mexico City
David López-García

Cities Learning from a Pandemic
Towards Preparedness
Edited by Simonetta Armondi, Alessandro Balducci, Martina Bovo and Beatrice Galimberti

Urban Change in Central Europe
The Case of Kraków
Edited by Jacek Purchla

Clusters and Sustainable Regional Development
A Meta-Organisational Approach
Evgeniya Lupova-Henry and Nicola Francesco Dotti

For more information about this series, please visit: *www.routledge.com/series/RAIRESP*

Urban Change in Central Europe

The Case of Kraków

Edited by
Jacek Purchla

Routledge
Taylor & Francis Group
LONDON AND NEW YORK

First published 2023
by Routledge
4 Park Square, Milton Park, Abingdon, Oxon OX14 4RN

and by Routledge
605 Third Avenue, New York, NY 10158

Routledge is an imprint of the Taylor & Francis Group, an informa business

 The publication was co-financed from the subsidy granted to the Cracow University of Economic – Project nr 54/GGH/2020/POT

British Library Cataloguing-in-Publication Data
A catalogue record for this book is available from the British Library

Library of Congress Cataloging-in-Publication Data
Names: Purchla, Jacek, editor.
Title: Urban change in Central Europe : the case of Kraków / edited by Jacek Purchla.
Description: Abingdon, Oxon ; New York, NY : Routledge, 2023. | Series: Routledge advances in regional economics, science and policy | Includes bibliographical references and index.
Identifiers: LCCN 2022020723 (print) | LCCN 2022020724 (ebook) | ISBN 9781032180793 (hardback) | ISBN 9781032180809 (paperback) | ISBN 9781003252757 (ebook)
Subjects: LCSH: Urbanization—Poland—Kraków. | Economic development—Poland—Kraków. | Place marketing—Poland—Kraków. | Kraków (Poland)—Economic conditions. | Kraków (Poland)—Social conditions.
Classification: LCC HT145.P7 U727 2023 (print) | LCC HT145.P7 (ebook) | DDC 307.7609438/62—dc23/eng/20220506
LC record available at https://lccn.loc.gov/2022020723
LC ebook record available at https://lccn.loc.gov/2022020724

ISBN: 978-1-032-18079-3 (hbk)
ISBN: 978-1-032-18080-9 (pbk)
ISBN: 978-1-003-25275-7 (ebk)

DOI: 10.4324/9781003252757

Typeset in Bembo
by codeMantra

Contents

List of figures vii
List of tables xi
List of contributors xiii
Preface xvii
Acknowledgements xix

Introduction 1
JACEK PURCHLA

1 **Kraków 1989 and since** 5
JACEK PURCHLA

2 **Civil society: From "Solidarity" to urban activism** 17
DOMINIKA HOŁUJ

3 **Municipal self-government: 1990–2019** 32
DOMINIKA HOŁUJ

4 **Kraków in the face of the transformation: The economic life of the city** 48
KRZYSZTOF BROŃSKI

5 **Kraków: An eventful city** 69
JOANNA SANETRA-SZELIGA

6 **Kraków spatial development after 1989** 86
MICHAŁ WIŚNIEWSKI

7 **Kraków and its region: Mutual relations after 1989** 109
PIOTR MIODUNKA

8 **Kraków architecture and globalisation** 132
MICHAŁ WIŚNIEWSKI

9 **Kraków culture heritage: On the way to globalising the national potential** 156
ANDRZEJ LASKOWSKI

10 **Kraków: A creative city** 182
JOANNA SANETRA-SZELIGA

11 **Kraków's metropolitan functions** 204
JACEK PURCHLA

Afterword – Kraków: Dialectics of history and change 217
ROBERT PYRAH

Names Index 227

Subject Index 233

Figures

3.1 Revenue and expenditure from Kraków's municipal budget in 1991–2019 (in millions of PLN) 35
3.2 Area of the city covered by the local zoning plans in 2003–20 (in percentage) 41
3.3 The number of "conditions of development" permits issued in 2003–20 (in 1000s) 42
4.1 Employment in Kraków in 1995–2018 52
4.2 Unemployment rate in Kraków in 1991–2020 53
4.3 The structure of employment in business service centres in Kraków in 2020 59
4.4 Tourists in Kraków in 2005–19 63
5.1 Number of MICE events in 2013–20 in Kraków 77
5.2 Organisation of art, entertainment, and sports mass events in Kraków 81
6.1 Galeria Krakowska shopping centre, 2006 90
6.2 Rondo Ofiar Katynia roundabout, 2011 92
6.3 Osiedle Avia residential estate, 2017 97
6.4 Galeria Bonarka shopping centre with the surrounding office blocks, 2009 99
6.5 Campus of the Jagiellonian University in Pychowice, since 2000 103
7.1 Changes of administrative divisions around Kraków after 1989 110
7.2 Changes of the concept of the Kraków Metropolitan Area in the 21st century 113
7.3 Kraków Metropolitan Area in 2021 115
7.4 Population density in the counties surrounding Kraków in 1998–2020 115
7.5 Population of Igołomia-Wawrzeńczyce and Zielonki communes in 1985–2020 116
7.6 Suburbanisation of areas to the north of Kraków, the example of Zielonki commune: in the mid-1990s (above) and currently (below) 117

7.7 Suburbanisation of areas to the north-west of Kraków, the example of Zabierzów and Wielka Wieś communes: in the mid-1990s (above) and currently (below) 119
8.1 Resurrectionist Seminary, designed by Dariusz Kozłowski, Maria Misiągiewicz, and Wacław Stefański, 1984–96 134
8.2 Manggha Museum of Japanese Art and Technology, designed by Arata Isozaki, 1994 135
8.3 The Gate to the City of the Dead, Batowice Cemetery, designed by Romuald Loegler, 1998 137
8.4 Plac Bohaterów Getta/Ghetto Heroes Square, designed by Piotr Lewicki and Kazimierz Łatak, 2005 139
8.5 Małopolska Garden of Arts, designed by Krzysztof Ingarden and Jacek Ewý, 2013 146
8.6 Centre for the Documentation of the Art of Tadeusz Kantor, Cricoteca, designed by Piotr Nawara, Agnieszka Szultk, Stanisław Deńko, 2014 147
8.7 Polish Aviation Museum, designed by Bartłomiej Kisielewski and Pysall Ruge Architekten, 2010 148
8.8 KÄRCHER Cracovia Centennial Hall with the Sports Centre for the Handicapped, designed by Piotr Lewicki and Kazimierz Łatak, 2018 149
9.1 Centre of Kraków with the area entered on the original UNESCO World Heritage List in 1978 and its buffer zone established in 2011 158
9.2 The degraded historical developments in ul. Kanonicza in 1978. From the documentation of former PP PKZ (currently in the WUOZ Kraków Archive), Negative No. 21900/A 160
9.3 The same historical developments in ul. Kanonicza after restoration. Current state 160
9.4 Large-size commercials on the façades in the north-western corner of the Main Market Square before the regulations of the Stare Miasto Culture Park came into force 163
9.5 Centre of Kraków's Kazimierz district: the eastern face of ul. Szeroka in 1985 165
9.6 A current view of the same area in Kazimierz, with filled-in urban tissue, extension of the house at No. 17, and plentiful new architectural detail 166
9.7 A panorama of Wawel from Krzemionki Zakrzowskie Hill, with the "extra" tower of the former NOT skyscraper (currently Unity Tower) in the background 170
9.8 The pressure from tourist and commercial signage in Kraków's Royal Route (ul. Floriańska) before the introduction of the Culture Park Stare Miasto 173

9.9 The deserted Royal Route (ul. Floriańska) during lockdown, early April 2020 174
10.1 Creative city of polycentric structure 184
10.2 Composition of the creative class in Kraków (2010) 185
10.3 Culture and creative industries in Kraków, by domain 192
10.4 Culture and creative industries in Kraków (2021) (%) 192
10.5 Creative Cities Index: Kraków in comparison with other cities 195
10.6 The Creative Cities Monitor: Kraków's scores 196

Tables

4.1 Business entities in Kraków by ownership, 1991–2019 51
4.2 Legal status of entities running business in Kraków in 2005–20 51
5.1 Relation between a city and events – two approaches 71
7.1 Access to selected elements of infrastructure in Kraków and Tarnów regions in 1990 112
7.2 Cities and communes of the KMA (excluding Kraków, in the administrative borders from 2003 to 2018 with positive migration balances in 1988–2020) 114
10.1 Cultural institutions in Kraków (including those run by the municipality) 187

Contributors

Krzysztof Broński has a PhD in economics (1992). He is a Professor in the Department of Economic and Social History / UNESCO Chair for Heritage and Urban Studies at the Kraków University of Economics. He is the deputy dean of the Faculty of Economics and International Relations (2008–16) and of the Faculty of Economics and Public Administration (2016–19). He is the president of the Board of the Pedagogical University of Kraków (2019–20). His research interests include urbanisation in Central Europe in the 20th and 21st centuries, social and economic development of Kraków and Galicia, and cultural heritage management.

Dominika Hołuj has a PhD in economics (2011). She is an Assistant Professor in the Department of Economic and Social History / UNESCO Chair for Heritage and Urban Studies at the Kraków University of Economics. Her research interests include urban studies, local government and governance, and public participation in cultural heritage management. She has authored over 30 scientific papers and a monograph on the role of local government in the development of the metropolitan functions of Kraków. She is a member of expert teams dealing with cultural heritage and local development issues (OECD, National Heritage Institute [NID]). She previously worked for the Regional Chamber of Audit, the public institution supervising the legal aspects of finance in Polish local government.

Andrzej Laskowski is an art historian with a PhD in humanities (2005). He graduated from Jagiellonian University and is an Assistant Professor in the Department of Economic and Social History / UNESCO Chair for Heritage and Urban Studies at the Kraków University of Economics. He is the head specialist at the Kraków branch of the National Heritage Institute (NID). His research interests extend to the history of architecture and urban development, cultural heritage protection, and the art of stained glass making in south-eastern Poland in the 19th and 20th centuries. He is the author and editor of numerous works, articles, and books, notably *Jasło W Dobie Autonomii Galicyjskiej: Miasto I Jego Przestrzeń* (2007) and *Budując System: Ochrona Zabytków Sakralnych W Diecezji Tarnowskiej Na Przełomie XIX i XX wieku* (2020), and co-author of a monographic work on the wooden parish church in Binarowa which is listed on the UNESCO World Heritage List (2004). He is the winner of two competitions organised by the General Heritage Preservation Officer and the Heritage Conservation Society.

Piotr Miodunka has a PhD in history (2010) and an MA in law. He is an Assistant Professor in the Department of Economic and Social History / UNESCO Chair for Heritage and Urban Studies at the Kraków University of Economics. His research interests include the social and economic history of Poland, historic demography, and history of cities. He is a co-author of the book *Krakow: An Ecobiography* and the author of a monographic book analysing small town communities in southern Poland from the late 16th to the 18th centuries.

Jacek Purchla is a Professor of Humanities and a member of the Polish Academy of Arts and Sciences. He is the president of the board of Jagiellonian University and the head of the Department of Economic and Social History / UNESCO Chair for Heritage and Urban Studies at the Kraków University of Economics. He is also the head of the Research Institute for European Heritage at the International Cultural Centre. He is the founder of the International Cultural Centre in Kraków and its director from its inception in 1991 up to 2018. He advised the European Commission in the European Heritage Label project. Since 2015, he has been the president of the Polish National Commission for UNESCO. In 2016–17, he was the president of the UNESCO World Heritage Committee. Since 2018, he has been the vice president of Europa Nostra. He specialises in urban studies, social and art history, and the theory and protection of cultural heritage. He is the author of over 500 academic works, including many books published in numerous languages.

Robert Pyrah is a historian focusing on questions of history, memory, and identity post-Habsburg East-Central European history (especially Poland, Austria, and West Ukraine). He is a research fellow at Oxford Brookes University and a member of Wolfson College, University of Oxford. Dr. Pyrah is the author of *The Burgtheater and Austrian Identity* (Oxford, 2007), co-editor and author of a number of articles and edited volumes on the region, and co-host of the influential podcast: 'Pseudoscience, Fake News, and How to Fight Back', including an interview with Timothy Garton Ash (https://shows.acast.com/pseudoscience).

Joanna Sanetra-Szeliga has a PhD in economics (2017). She is an Assistant Professor in the Department of Economic and Social History / UNESCO Chair for Heritage and Urban Studies at the Kraków University of Economics and consultant at the Statistical Office in Kraków. She has experience in working for public administration, the cultural sector, and the non-governmental sector. She is a researcher and the author of several publications on the socio-economic potential of culture, the use of heritage in innovation and diplomacy, and the impact of mega events on historical cities.

Michał Wiśniewski has a PhD in art history (2010) and an MA in architecture (Kraków University of Technology). He works as an Assistant Professor in the Department of Economic and Social History / UNESCO Chair for Heritage and Urban Studies at the Kraków University of Economics. He is the head of the Educational Department – The Academy of Heritage at the International Cultural Centre in Kraków. His research interests include the history of architecture, urban studies, and cultural heritage management.

Preface

This book is about the contemporary urban development processes in Central European countries and the unprecedented scale and speed of their development. The change that Central European cities started to go through in the wake of the political transformation of 1989 deserves a complex interdisciplinary study that makes it possible to grasp the specific nature of the transformation taking place in the region, including its challenges and problems. Kraków – a metropolitan centre in southern Poland, the historic capital of the country, a cultural and scientific hub with a population of a million, and a top tourist destination (14 million tourists in 2019) – focuses on the rapid liberalisation of the market, deindustrialisation, and globalisation like a lens. As previous studies only offered "one-dimensional" insights into these phenomena, and attempts at broader comprehension have only come in the form of articles, an in-depth, complex, empirical analysis has been lacking.[1] This book offers a multidimensional and interdisciplinary case study of Kraków, focusing on the changes taking place in Central Europe in the past 30 years rather than on the phenomenon of the city itself.

Urban Change in Central Europe: The Case of Kraków is a book that stems from many years of research into the history and development of cities by the faculty of the UNESCO Chair for Heritage and Urban Studies at Kraków University of Economics. It is a multidimensional cumulative case study of Kraków, composed of research conducted using different methodologies that range from literature research, via statistical analysis, interviews, and observations to comparative studies. The nature of the research on the city expands very quickly, which is also one of the reasons why the faculty of Kraków's UNESCO Chair represents fields as diverse as economics, law, art, art history, architecture, and urbanology. The synergy of insights helps us investigate better the phenomenon of being a metropolis, and Kraków is our natural laboratory for urban studies.

1 The few exceptions include an intriguing and synthetic insight into post-communist cities in *Transformation of Cities in Central and Eastern Europe: Towards Globalization* ed. by F.E. Ian Hamilton, Kaliopa Dimitrovska Andrews, Nataša Pichler-Milanović published in 2005 (United Nations University Press, Tokyo – New York – Paris).

Being a complex process, a contemporary city calls not only for the skilful analysis of long-lasting phenomena but also for an interdisciplinary approach. For the modern skillset of an urbanologist needs to integrate very different scientific disciplines that are capable of investigating various aspects of urban development phenomena as well as synthesising them. To the best of the authors' knowledge, no such work has yet been written: not only about Kraków, but also about any other major city of the region. For this reason, I find the uniqueness and unquestioned potential of showing the problems of Central European cities to a wider range of readers in Europe and across the world a particular advantage of this publication.

Professor Jacek Purchla, PhD
UNESCO Chair for Heritage and Urban Studies
Institute of Spatial Management and Urban Studies
Kraków University of Economics

Acknowledgements

As the editor of this book, I would like to express my indebtedness to Piotr Krasnowolski, a real master of Polish–English translations, especially for his extreme dedication to the final touches on the language of *Urban Change in Central Europe*. I would also like to appreciate the contribution of Dr Lucyna Kępa, who provided assistance in organisational and logistical matters.

Last but not least, together with the contributors, I address my special gratitude to the Kraków University of Economics for the financial support to this publication.

Jacek Purchla

Introduction

Jacek Purchla

The specific experience of the Central European nations results not only from the lesson of communism, but also from the abrupt change after 1989, whose dynamics and complexity is usually subsumed under the fashionable term "transition". Now, 30 years after the fall of communism in Central Europe, the ideal moment has come to reflect more extensively on the nature of that transformation.

How did it happen that the previously isolated, polluted, and neglected city of Kraków transformed in the last 30 years into a thriving global tourist destination, an attractive investment market, and a European leader in shared services? Kraków's experience is a perfect illustration of the transformations in many Central European cities that share the common experience of having gone through communism followed by a rapid transition in the last 30 years. The speed, depth, and multidimensional character of transformation intertwine with the processes of European integration and globalisation.

The laboratories of this multidimensional change have been primarily the major Central European cities. An extremely interesting example of this is Kraków: the ancient royal capital city of Poland. Situated between Warsaw, Berlin, Prague, Bratislava, Vienna, and Budapest, it is the only larger city that developed metropolitan functions in its history but plays no significant political function today.

After 1989, Kraków exploited the historical moment primarily as the opportunity for a significant change that furthered its development: a change that must be considered a particular success. Moreover, it is the nexus and resultant of phenomena that run far beyond the borders of Kraków and create an entirely new social and political reality throughout Central Europe. This post-1989 "defrosting of the fridge", the breaking out of the isolation and stagnation that engulfed Kraków in the decades of communism profoundly changed the rules of the game known as the city. It also meant changing the idea of the city! In almost no time at all, Kraków, stifled by the corset of totalitarian systems for five decades, turned into a liberal city. Central Europe's watershed year, 1989, allows us to look again at assorted meanings of the city: as a process, as a function, as an idea, as a form, and as a mirror of our civilisation. In the last 30 years, Kraków has become a true laboratory of change!

DOI: 10.4324/9781003252757-1

The purpose of this book, *Urban Change in Central Europe: the Case of Kraków*, is to grasp the specific characteristics of the change and identify the challenges characteristic not only for Kraków, but also for many cities of Czechia, Slovakia, Poland, and Hungary after the fall of communism, to situate the object of the analysis in a more extensive international academic discourse, and to join the debate about the changes taking place in the region's cities. A measure of development of these cities is the speed and complexity of the changes they are undergoing. A particular characteristic of the contemporary urban development processes in the countries of Central Europe is the previously unencountered speed and scale of development. Rapid transformations of the culturescape of our cities, frequently coming in the form of degradation, result from rapidly progressing market liberalisation and decentralisation. This is also the reason why the change that Kraków has undergone after 1989 is a phenomenon that has grown to deserve a complex and interdisciplinary analysis that this book provides.

The complexity of the problem is investigated from multiple perspectives: political, economic, social, civil, spatial, and cultural. Politics is the determining factor for the non-linear development of cities. The Kraków experience reminds us that the city is a long-lasting process. It clearly demonstrates how political systems and ideologies have governed the shape of city-building processes. Decisive for the success of the city are both "big" and "small" politics. What comes to the fore in the history of Kraków in this area is the role of political breakthroughs. The change in the rules of the game of the city, the rapid transition from a totalitarian system and command economy to a liberal model in the wake of the watershed of 1989 resulted in a rapid and multidimensional change. The next milestone on Kraków's path of opening to the world was 1 May 2004: Poland's accession to the European Union. This is how the political change of 1989–90 determined the future shape of our city's development. At the same time, the case of Kraków of 1990 was still to provide a particularly educational chapter in the history of the Polish democratic revolution.

The analysis of the city's economic transformation reveals the changes that, in the 30 years, have turned Kraków into one of the most economically attractive cities of the region. A mature labour market made it possible to bring the most advanced processes into the city.

This book asks the fundamental question about the metropolitan functions of Kraków. It is primarily a question about the place of Kraków in Europe's settlement network and the change that the city must undergo to enhance its competitiveness. We emphasise that what plays a profound role in releasing creativity and innovation is a mix of cultural, educational, research, and information functions. The new city development strategy formulated in 1990 strongly emphasised a return to the original functions of Kraków, that is, a metropolis of education and culture, and the need to open to the world. The Kraków case also reveals clearly how significant cultural heritage, remembrance, and identity are for the development of the city. This book shows the evolution in the perception of the developmental resources of the city, now accounting for what is broadly construed as culture and heritage. Kraków, from the 19th century the spiritual capital of Poland, is the only European city to have been inscribed on the original UNESCO World Heritage List (1978). Little wonder then that the recognition of culture heritage as a factor favouring development and heritage management has been a significant element of the city's policy and has changed significantly over the years. After 1989, local government was reinstituted in post-communist cities and was entrusted with significant challenges related to the creation of a new vision of development, and management of the rapid change. The past three decades have been marked by a growth in civil society in the region: a trend that has not bypassed Kraków, with its grassroots urban movements, municipal activism, and more extensive involvement of locals in the creation of the city. A separate part of the publication discusses the relationships between the city and the entire metropolitan area and region. The subject of Kraków's metropolitan functions is also investigated in the context of changes in the Central European settlement network. Urban planning and the questions of Kraków architecture are also important subjects covered by this book.

Questions about the phenomenon of Kraków concern its demographic potential, population structure, functional model, spatial arrangements, and relationships with the region, as well as the strategic goals for development and competitiveness. Searching for the answers to the question about the place of Kraków in the settlement network of Central Europe stimulates multithreaded reflections that bring to the fore the question of the metropolitan nature of Kraków.

Politics significantly changed the hierarchy of Central European cities in the 20th century. This is also true of the map of Poland and Kraków itself. The historical polycentrism of the network of Poland's largest metropolises is being destroyed by the hypertrophy of Warsaw's central functions. For the unitarian state kills the "noncapital" metropolises. As a "politically incompatible" city, Kraków has sought its own path of development and its own place in the settlement network, and still does. In these quests, a special role is played by memory and myth. In this aspect, it is not only *prastary Kraków, rodzic polskiej potęgi* ("primordial Kraków, the begetter of the Polish power") but also Kraków – the heir of the myth of Galicia. The power of that myth and its significance for the city also make Kraków a member of the network of most important metropolitan hubs of Central Europe. And for Kraków, that idea of Mitteleuropa as some call Central Europe, is still an untapped opportunity.

Research into the history and development of cities has held a special place in the research undertaken by the faculty of the UNESCO Chair for Heritage and Urban Studies at the Cracow University of Economics for over five decades. Kraków has remained a special field of interest for several generations of the faculty chair. The city's historical and present developments provide urban researchers with unlimited options for interpretation. We treat the city as the fruit of long-lasting processes and the resultant of the interaction of various phenomena. The form of the city, its shape, is a particular summa of civilisation development. So, Kevin Lynch, a classic of modern "urbanology", was right to emphasise that cities are more than just form and the functions they currently play; they are also the ideas and the values that people associate with them.

1 Kraków 1989 and since

Jacek Purchla

1989

The fight of the nations of Central Europe against Soviet domination, which ended in victory in 1989, was not only the fight against communism as a system but to the same extent, the fight for a return to the Euro-Atlantic civilisation. Communism denied the tradition of Central Europe and its civilisational achievements. That was also true of the region's metropolises. It is no coincidence that in the 1980s, the American economist Jane Jacobs devoted a separate comment to the cities of Central Europe in her classic book *Cities and the Wealth of Nations: Principles of Economic Life*. She wrote:

> when the Soviet Union took under its economic control Gdańsk, Warsaw, Cracow, Prague, Bratislava, Budapest, part of Berlin and other cities of East Germany, it acquired an additional supply of cities' earnings to drain for transactions of decline. The chief trade-off for these cities has been export work destined for inert economies in the Soviet Union. Far from continuing to develop, the economies of these cities have been arrested.
>
> (Jacobs, 1986, p. 200)

In this way, communism was a civilisational shock that the nations of Central Europe rejected. The symbol of the pursuit to reject the Soviet system imposed in 1945 was the Solidarity movement.

In the late 1980s, the long-lasting and profound crisis of communism in Poland – reinforced by the introduction of martial law by General Wojciech Jaruzelski in 1981 – gave no hope for change. The system seemed impregnable, and the presence of the Red Army with 60,000 soldiers of the so-called Soviet Army's Northern Group of Forces in Poland and many more around the country (26 Soviet divisions stationed in the GDR alone) meant that any ideas of "Finlandisation" were a utopian dream. In that sense, the events of the Polish spring of 1989 that initiated the breakdown of the post-war division of Europe came as a surprise, even to the opposition gathered around Solidarity that had been hardened by the years of resistance to the regime. Leaving aside the vividly debated question about the degree to which the process of rushed

DOI: 10.4324/9781003252757-2

decomposition of communist power and dismantling of the system that was initiated in Poland on 4 June 1989 was connected to the severance from the "external empire" that Gorbachev intended in the Perestroika scenarios, it is clear that the developments in 1989 were a major surprise for the actors on that stage. Jerzy Turowicz, editor-in-chief of *Tygodnik Powszechny* (literally: "the Catholic weekly", the only magazine officially published by the opposition between East Berlin and Vladivostok, published in Kraków since 1945) and one of the key figures of the Polish democratic opposition (a participant of the Round Table) made the following *post facto* comment: "in 1989 freedom dropped on our heads like a brick from the roof". What proved to be an efficient way of abandoning communism was compromise. Nevertheless, its price is one of the most hotly discussed political questions in contemporary Poland (Purchla, 2018, pp. 171–172).

The discussions concerning the nature and the impact of the breakthrough of 1989 divide the Polish political stage even today, sometimes brushing alongside both science and political fiction. For is it not pure speculation to claim that the Polish Round Table – and in its wake, the "contract election" of 4 June 1989 – were unnecessary concessions towards the regime on behalf of a faction of the Solidarity opposition, as communism would have disintegrated sooner or later anyway? The proponents of that theory fail to remember that at the threshold of 1989, no one, not even in their wildest dreams, could have foreseen such a rapid pace of disintegration of the communist system in Poland or the peaceful character of that essentially bloodless revolution (Borowiec, 2013; Matyja, 2013, pp. 45–210).

The spectacular victory of the Solidarity camp in the elections on 4 June 1989 was a true watershed in the history of Poland. Yet in the latest history of Kraków, it opened a turbulent transitional period, fraught with consequences. Following the Round Table elections and the appointment of the government by Tadeusz Mazowiecki in September 1989, Kraków gained a powerful political representation in Warsaw (Dudek, 2016, pp. 9–57). In the meantime, both the political and administrative power in the city remained in the hands of the representatives of the *ancien régime*. For many long months in late 1989 and early 1990, that was the essence of the Kraków paradox of "joy from reclaiming the good old fleapit".[1]

The Mazowiecki government reforms and their aftermath

At the time, what still distinguished the position of Poland from the "stable" situation of the Czechs, Slovaks, Hungarians, and the GDR Germans in a Europe that was, after all, still divided by the Iron Curtain, was economic disaster. In the autumn of 1989, Poles not only witnessed empty shelves in the shops, a sight they had become used to in the years of communism and especially of martial law, but they also came face to face with galloping inflation. The collapse of the market, a profound crisis of the state budget, and high foreign debt were the principal problems that the government of Tadeusz Mazowiecki had to face (Krasowski, 2012, pp. 74–75). People from "the Mazowiecki draft" wrote a particular chapter in history, and the determination they showed in seeking a way out of the dead end of late 1989 and early 1990 is the key point worth remembering today. For them, the mission of conducting the painful transformation was more important than their own political future. It is to them that Poland owes embarking on the radical reforms whose direct social impact sentenced the reformers to imminent political defeat. Leszek Balcerowicz's harsh economic reforms, approved by the contract Parliament in 1989–90, allowed Poland to leave the profound collapse behind and move from a centrally managed to a free-market economy, yet to this day, they remain the object of contestation for numerous social groups and are politically instrumentalised by populists (Krasowski, 2012, pp. 76–88). However, that was the only moment for the legal enforcement of the profoundly new rules of the game. Tired of the long-lasting crisis of communism, society had relatively low expectations. At a session of the Polish Parliament on 17 December 1989, Balcerowicz remarked that "we need to put an end to this game of pretence, in which people pretend they work and the state pretends that it pays" (Krasowski, 2012, p. 82).

The main goals of the Balcerowicz Plan included:

- introducing internal convertibility of the złoty (Polish currency)
- balancing the state budget and exercising control over monetary policy
- retaining stable currency exchange rates
- combating inflation
- quick privatisation.

No one, not even Leszek Balcerowicz himself or the foreign experts, knew what the reaction of economy to the introduction of this plan would be. A rapid change in the rules of the game left the people on the street disoriented and incapable of identifying their group interests in this transition period (Dudek, 2016, pp. 67–74).

The first reforms of 1989–90 initiated a clear transformation of the democratic forces in Poland. The Solidarity camp evolved from the mission of preaching truth and morality to fighting for power, bickering about the vision of the state, building democracy and entering the path of development, developing a new society, and creating a new place for Poland in the world. The new political perspective was to denote a complete takeover of power and the final dismantling of the system that was still under the control of the apparatus composed of the party, the military, and the police. With the reinforcement of the rule of Solidarity in Warsaw, the asymmetry between "the reforming centre" and the provinces still dominated by the *ancien régime,* continued to expand.

For these reasons, the crucial political task of the Mazowiecki government, apart from economic reforms, was the reconstruction of local government. In

January 1990, the Prime Minister spoke in Parliament about the fundamental course of the reform of the state, and announced that the territorial government elections would be brought forward to April 1990. As the process of development of civil society had been severed by the introduction of martial law, the self-governments of 1990 provided a fundamental step on the path to breaking communism. It was the reform of the local authorities that dotted the i's and crossed the t's in the final victory of the Polish revolution of 1989–90. And it was also that particular reform that revealed the lack of our readiness for the freedom that "dropped on our heads" so suddenly.

Somewhere in 1989 and 1990, egoism of particular groups emerged in the place of solidarity. With the change of the system, the old division into the evil "commies" and the good "solidarity" community began to be replaced with the class division that is natural for capitalism. Galloping inflation and unemployment elicited by Balcerowicz's reforms only boosted ordinary people's frustrations. The fear of an outbreak of the "fury of the people" was already uppermost in the politicians' minds in 1990, yet at the same time, the contemporary political elites (which were actually true elites) were absolutely convinced that there was no other way. The exceptional aspect of that period of transition was vested in the freezing of the natural political mechanisms and the reform being legally enforced by the "sages and authorities". This allowed a change that was both quick and efficient. It was the particular enlightened rationalism of the elites that allowed the arbitrarily selected method to be considered not only to be good, but also to be the only option. The same strategy was applied to the launch of the local self-government reform. It was obvious that its introduction was forced by political developments. The local elections and Solidarity's takeover of power in the regions became a burning necessity in late 1989 and early 1990. That operation was not to be only limited to the introduction of their own people to the existing territorial structures, as its overarching goal was the attempt to build an entire system of territorial self-government in only several months, from square one, and "on the fly": a system that had no place in the former centralised model of a communist state (Purchla, 2018, p. 76). And that was to be the true democratic revolution!

The local authorities' revolution

The prelude to this "revolution" was the Local Governments Act of 8 March 1990, which intended to provide a particular constitution for local government. Its drafting followed discussions and disputes that clearly revealed not only the scale of the fundamental problems that had to be solved to crack communism, but also the weaknesses and the lack of preparedness of the Polish political elites to face the challenge (Stępień, 2020, pp. 167–197). The authors of the act entirely ignored, for example, the question of classifying the communes, and prepared the new legal frameworks with the needs of a commune with a population of about 10,000 people in mind. That is why the "new constitution" failed to account for the scale and specific needs of metropolitan centres, not to mention the extent of their collapse and the systemic crisis that had overwhelmed them by the late 1980s. The weak competences of local governments were a profound drawback of the model, as it was they who – particularly in the main cities – were to assume responsibility for the management of unhealthy organisms that required shock therapy. Yet already at the outset, they were bereft of the strong executive power that would be needed to address the scale of the challenge. It was further sapped by the Competence Act of 17 May 1990, that, even then, could be construed as a "reaction of the bureaucrat lobby" to the ideas of local government. That was essentially a manifestation of a lack of trust in local government by the centralised state that was announced just ten days before the local government elections: a distinct change in the rules of the game while the match was already underway. Thus, on the one hand, the Mazowiecki government fuelled great civil expectations concerning local government from the autumn of 1989, and on the other, it weakened its power even before it was established. The mutually contradictory signal that at the time went unnoticed by public opinion is a good illustration not only of the conflicts that were growing during the transition, but also the characteristic context of the birth of local government in Poland in 1990 (Purchla, 2018, pp. 177–178).

Nonetheless, initially there was enthusiastic euphoria. On 27 May 1990, the first fully democratic elections in post-war Poland were held: these were the elections to the local governments of the new communes and it was the last time that the Solidarity Citizens' Electoral Committee came first. Subsequent elections to territorial authorities in 1994 would be dominated by political parties with clearly defined programmes. The national turnout at the polls on 27 May 1990 was 42.3%, and was higher in large cities: in Kraków, it reached 49.23%, in Wrocław – 44.25%, and in Poznań – 42.6%. At the time, most Poles thought of local government as a "trinket"; something entirely new and mysterious (Nowakowski, 2010, p. 70). For many, it meant being a citizen. The strategy of the new political opening was based on the idea of authorities growing from the ethos of Solidarity, and concentrated around the citizens' (or civic) committees that had been undergoing a clear internal evolution since the contract election of June 1989.[2]

Communism in Kraków finished on 27 May 1990!

In May 1990, the civic committees also achieved such spectacular success for the last time, as they won 44.3% of votes on the national level. Out of 262,846 voters in Kraków, as many as 188,963 (that is 71.89%) supported the Kraków Solidarity Civic Committee. It should be pointed out that in 1990, Kraków did not exist as a city in the legal and systemic sense! It was a "metropolitan region" (or metropolitan voivodeship: *województwo miejskie*), one of three along with Warsaw and Łódź. Before the reform of the territorial authorities, the Mayor of Kraków was in fact the governor or voivode (*wojewoda*) on behalf of the government, exercising centralised power both over the city (at the time divided into four large districts, each with a population of roughly 200,000 people) and the "hinterland" with a radius of around 40 km from the municipal hub. The separation of Kraków from the rest of the region to create a new municipal community on 27 May 1990, the unbundling of the functions of the new mayor – now the head of a large city and of the newly established local government – from those of the former governor/mayor, and the later spinning off of the Kraków Municipal Office from the single huge office of state administration (which was the governor's office), were extraordinary tasks whose implementation only started in Kraków in June 1990, i.e., immediately after the election. No other Polish city had to perform such tasks at the time. In Gdańsk, Poznań, and Wrocław, the regional and municipal offices had already been clearly separated in the previous administrative system, while the governor-mayors of the "metropolitan regions" analogous to Kraków, that is Warsaw and Łódź, with a Solidarity mandate had already claimed their posts earlier (in January and February 1990, respectively) and therefore had had time to conduct those complicated separation operations before the election of 27 May, and prepare a new apparatus for exercising power by the new local government. The Act on Local Governments written for the needs of a small commune did not account at all for the specific needs of Kraków in 1990. Even the semantic controversy around the mayor-governor (*prezydent-wojewoda*) became a major element of the complex game for the local government in Kraków in the first months and years of its operation (Purchla, 2018, p. 161).

Kraków's late start with democracy in May/June 1990 was caused by factors that included the spectacular defeat of the local Civic Committee early in February. The attempt to have a Solidarity candidate assume the post of mayor (of the Kraków Region) failed, unlike in Warsaw and Łódź. Professor Ryszard Gryglewski, nominated to the post by Solidarity back in late 1989, generously took on designing the new programme for Kraków, working with a group of the Civic Committee's experts and conducting extensive consultations with the community to prepare the city for the new era of local government. Professor Gryglewski openly maintained that, should he become mayor, he would conduct profound personal changes in the office under the banner of decommunisation. That was reason enough for the then National Council, whose mandate only expired in May, not to give him the necessary support. Needless to say, the Council was nearly entirely composed of representatives of the *ancien régime*. On the one hand, the "torching" of Ryszard Gryglewski proved the political naïveté of the Civic Committee leaders, and, on the other, was a sign of the power and determination of the communist nomenclature, who in this way gained four precious months to settle their own affairs and block changes in Kraków. Professor Gryglewski, a pharmacologist of global renown and rector of the Medical Academy, had been removed from the post by the regime during martial law and was one of the fundamental authorities on which Solidarity endeavoured to build a civic democracy. The natural need to look for authority – "the beautiful people" – in the face of the void that developed after the dismantling of the past political system became the crux of a series of "beauty contests" for the leaders of the future local government, and the foundation of dialogue with the people. Although it "failed" in February, the model became the basis of the major victory of the Kraków Citizens' Committee in the election of May 1990. The Committee secured 73 out of 75 seats in the new Kraków Municipal Council, with the remaining two newly elected councillors representing the Confederation of Independent Poland (KPN, a party that clearly positioned itself to the right of Solidarity) (Chwalba, 2004, p. 460).

Wojna na górze

Kraków's belated entry into democracy coincided with the start of *wojna na górze* – the War of Leaders – which had a strong influence on the rapid political destabilisation of the Kraków Municipal Council right at the threshold of its first term. Kraków was the first place where the mental rift and the division into "liberal Poland" and the "Poland of solidarity" became visible. In this way, Kraków was a step ahead of the later political split of "post-solidarity" Poland. Unlike Wrocław, Kraków had no extensive alliance for the elections in the spring of 1990, nor did it evolve a model of cooperation with the authorities of the Solidarity trade union. In Kraków, there were in fact already two cities in 1990: the "old" Kraków and Nowa Huta. As much as both Kraków and Nowa Huta were brothers-in-arms under the banner of Solidarity against Jaruzelski's regime back in the 1980s, the animosities between the "old" and "new" Kraków became evident in 1989–90 in the Civic Committee.

The powerful divisions in the Kraków Civic Committee were visible in the discussion about the future constitution of the municipality and its new division into districts. The question "one Kraków or four?" was asked publicly at the time, an absurd situation that arose from the ambitions of the district committees. Some dreamt of turning their districts into autonomous communes, with Kraków being no more than a loose federation. This example illustrates not only the ignorance of part of the nascent political class but also the intensification of conflicts within the Solidarity camp. In the spring of 1990, the confusion in the Civic Committee in Kraków, which was now more of a *levée en masse* of the opponents of communism, and the weakness of its political leadership, led to the discords that were further aggravated by the mistrust between the activists of the Steelworkers Worker Committee and the Kraków intelligentsia. It must be remembered that the martial law transformed Nowa Huta into a battlefield of sorts. The time of Solidarity in 1980 and 1981 had already proved that this proletarian stronghold was especially dangerous for the communist reign. The Lenin Steelworks in Nowa Huta, next to the Gdańsk Shipyard, became one of the strongest mainstays of the new movement, and its strike in 1988 was one of the reasons why

Jaruzelski's regime started talks with Solidarity, which ended in the Round Table agreements a year later. Therefore, it is no coincidence that the Nowa Huta activists openly spoke of their ambitions to govern Kraków (Purchla, 2018, pp. 160–167).

The confrontation of "old" and "new" Kraków came just several days after the triumphant victory of the Civic Committee in the local election. With 73 seats held by its representatives, the City Council elected its first mayor backed by Solidarity with just 40 votes in support! Jacek Woźniakowski – a member of the Citizens' Committee aligned with Lech Wałęsa, a participant of the Round Table negotiations and an eminent intellectual and oppositionist – seemed the dream candidate for mayor "of all Cracovians". He met more than just the criterion of authority. His intellectual potential, command of foreign languages, and international contacts were a symbol of Kraków opening to the world. What seemed to be another strong suit of the new mayor was the fact that he hailed from the milieu of *Tygodnik Powszechny*, was close to the Kraków circles of John Paul II, and had long been friends with Prime Minister Mazowiecki and his political corps (Purchla, 2018, p. 281).

Nevertheless, the theoretically universal, powerful community mandate for the new mayor quickly proved to be an illusion in the face of the War of the Leaders proclaimed by Lech Wałęsa in June 1990. Faced by the political confrontation mounting within Solidarity, a mayor-intellectual was doomed to failure (Krasowski, 2012, pp. 104–263). Even more so as Woźniakowski himself became a party in the conflict. In October 1990, amidst the continuing dog-eat-dog presidential campaign, as harsh emotional political divides were being revealed between the partisans of Wałęsa and Mazowiecki, Jacek Woźniakowski decisively took the side of Prime Minister Mazowiecki who then launched his presidential campaign from Kraków not without reason.

The was no more acceptance for the "patriarchal" model of exercising power in Kraków by the local government in 1990. The division that became apparent during the election of the mayor culminated in 1990–91 in the open questioning of the leadership of the elites by the majority of the Council! The process was unavoidable, yet in Kraków, it was sped up by the alienation of those elites. The position taken by Jacek Woźniakowski added a political dimension to the internal conflict in Kraków's local government, entangling it directly in the War of the Leaders. In this way, in the autumn of 1990, Kraków was the first to enter the path of political crisis, which resulted in the removal of Jacek Woźniakowski from the post of the Mayor of Kraków on 11 January 1991. The "Kraków conflict", which coincided with the fall of Tadeusz Mazowiecki's cabinet, was an evident harbinger of a new phase in Polish democracy. It was when the mental rift, the division into "liberal Poland" and "Poland of solidarity", manifested itself in Kraków with all its might. This is how, already in late 1990 and early 1991, Kraków anticipated the later political divides of the former Solidarity camp at the national level. The democracy being born at the time provided the first opportunity to verify the political effects of Kraków's particular bipolarity after the fall of communism. For democracy quickly revealed the social complexity and variety of the city. In the 40 years of the People's Republic, that is during communism, the city expanded quickly with Nowa Huta becoming the symbol of the radical change of the function and social structure of Kraków. In the 1980s, the "old" Kraków and Nowa Huta were an important centre of Polish democratic opposition and the role model for the synergy of solidary actions of intellectuals and steelworkers. However, there had been no mechanism to verify the citizens' attitudes and beliefs before 1989 (Purchla, 2018, p. 182).

It was already the crisis of June 1990 related to the controversy surrounding the election of the Mayor of Kraków and his deputies by the theoretically homogeneous Solidarity camp with an overwhelming majority in the City Council that clearly showed that the time of the authorities' rule in Poland was over. Moreover, it quickly became apparent that the first local governments of large cities were given weak competences, and their power was entangled in ad hoc political squabbles. As large cities suffered a deep crisis, instead of strengthening the executive power of their mayors, steps were taken in the opposite direction. Gordon Smith mentions three conditions for the development of democracy: stability, representation, and efficiency of governance. None of the three was fulfilled during the establishment of Kraków's local government (Purchla, 2018, p. 182)!

"Democracy is local"

The city was mired in a systemic crisis but managed nonetheless to gradually clamber out of the decline. The first changes were of a symbolic nature. The settlement of scores with the previous era in Kraków primarily boiled down to spectacular gestures including the removal of the monuments to Lenin and Soviet Marshal Ivan Konev, and of the obelisk of gratitude to the Red Army on plac Wolności (i.e., "freedom square" now renamed to plac Inwalidów – "the square of the war veterans"). The "decommunisation" of space and the "amendment" of its semantics meant changes to the names of numerous streets and squares. In the historical city centre that led to a natural return to the names from the late 19th and early 20th centuries that were very much alive in the collective memory. One of the victims of the "peaceful revolution" was the Lenin Museum that was visited – not without great piety – by Mikhail Gorbachev back in 1988. The headquarters of the Regional Committee of the Polish United Worker Party (PZPR) that was disbanded in January 1990 and became home to the Academy of Music. In fact, that symbolic act of transferring the seat of the Communist Party to the service of culture and education was where the settling of political scores in Kraków ended (Chwalba, 2004, p. 460).

After 1989, Kraków primarily used the historical moment as an opportunity for a significant change in favour of growth. It cannot be denied that this change was a success. Moreover, it is both the combination and the result of phenomena that continued far beyond the borders of Kraków and created an entirely new social and political reality throughout Central Europe. The particular "defrosting of the fridge" that occurred after 1989, the breaking of the isolation and stagnation that Kraków had been stuck in for the decades under communism, profoundly changed the rules of playing the game of cities. It also meant a change in the very idea of the city! In a very short time, Kraków, suffocated for half a century by the corset of totalitarian systems, turned into not only a democratic but also a self-governing city! For, as Alexis de Tocqueville wrote, "democracy is local".

Rapid property changes in Kraków had already begun in 1990. They resulted both from the specific circumstances of the city after the period of communism and from the conscious policy of the first local governments. The city that escaped wartime destruction was more than just a symbol of continuity. Kraków was the only major municipal centre in Poland that retained the pre-war structure of ownership throughout communism. When the compulsory administration of real estate by the state was abolished in 1990, property owners regained their full rights and titles to their properties. This rapidly changed the previous arrangement and the way in which Kraków's city centre functioned. The return of real estate from compulsory state administration, consistently carried out by the city authorities from 27 May 1990, stimulated the development of free-market mechanisms and breathed life into the historical centre.

Standing on the opposite end of the spectrum were the colossal state industrial complexes, notably the Lenin (now Tadeusz Sendzimir) Steelworks. In the 1990s, they either underwent rapid reductions in production and employment, as was the case with the steelworks, or gradual liquidation, such as at the Solvay Soda Works, the Bonarka chemical works, Telpod, the Miraculum cosmetics plant, the Wytwórnia Sprzętu Komunikacyjnego rolling stock factory, Krakowska Fabryka Aparatury Pomiarowej manufacturers of measurement equipment, the Zakłady Zieleniewskiego metalworks, the Wawel confectionery makers, Stomil rubber works, Kraków Meat Processing Plant, and the Kraków Brewery. With the liquidation of industrial facilities, many of them sources of environmental pollution, attractive plots became available for development. The final bankruptcy of the command-and-control economy meant stopping the city sprawl, the fall of the industrial system of large-scale construction using prefabricated elements, and last but not least – the demographic stabilisation of Kraków and the rapid development of the services sector of its economic model. Kraków was lucky to avoid a range of negative phenomena and social tensions that affected many other industrial centres in the wake of deindustrialisation, depopulation, and structural transformation. Decisive for this were the heterogeneous functions of the metropolis, its cultural and intellectual potential, and the power of the Kraków brand (Purchla, 2019, pp. 285–286).

The city's new development strategy proposed by the reborn local government in 1990 strongly emphasised Kraków's return to its original functions – as a metropolis of learning and culture – and the need to open to the world.

Already in late May and early June 1991, Kraków hosted a symposium of the Conference on Security and Cooperation in Europe (CSCE). The decision to hold the first major meeting of the East and West after the end of the Cold War and devoted to cultural heritage nowhere else but in Kraków also had its symbolic dimension. It returned the city inscribed on the UNESCO World Heritage List to the cultural map of Europe. It was precisely culture and heritage that was to become Kraków's powerful advantage both in its opening to the world, and in stimulating its structural transformation in its capacity as a place of meetings and dialogue. It was no coincidence either that in 1992, as the first city of the "recent East", Kraków hosted European Cultural Month, a notable festival organised under the auspices of the European Communities (Purchla, 2019, p. 286).

Local government: catalyst of change

Despite the two false starts in 1990, the reborn local government became the main catalyst of fundamental changes in Kraków. Local government meant a profound systemic and constitutional change that, in a way, took place on the fly as the Polish democratic revolution gained momentum. The change followed several decades of communist diktat and the command-and-control economy. Local government quickly became one of the foundations and engines of the Polish transformation, which was especially visible in cities like Kraków as they regained sovereignty after decades of incapacitation. At the same time, the story of post-1990 Kraków provides an instructive chapter in the history of the Polish democratic revolution. It also goes without saying that the political watershed of 1989–90 in Poland radically altered the rules of "playing the city game" and determined the further path of transformation and course of development of Kraków.

Bibliography

Borowiec, P. (2013) *Czas polityczny po rewolucji. Czas w polskim dyskursie politycznym po 1989 roku*. Kraków: Wydawnictwo Uniwersytetu Jagiellońskiego.

Chwalba, A. (2004) *Kraków w latach 1945–1989*. Dzieje Krakowa, Vol. 6. Kraków: Wydawnictwo Literackie.

Dudek, A. (2016) *Historia polityczna Polski 1989–2015*. Kraków: Wydawnictwo Znak Horyzont.

Jacobs, J. (1986) *Cities and the Wealth of Nations: Principles of Economic Life*. New Orleans, LA: Pelican.

Krasowski, R. (2012) *Po południu. Upadek elit solidarnościowych po zdobyciu władzy. Historia polityczna III RP. Lata 1989–1995*, Vol. 1. Warszawa: Czerwone i Czarne.

Krasowski, R. (2014) *Czas gniewu. Rozkwit i upadek imperium SLD. Historia polityczna III RP. Lata 1996–2005*, Vol. 2. Warszawa: Czerwone i Czarne.

Kuczyński, W. (2010) *Solidarność u władzy. Dziennik 1989–1993*. Gdańsk: Europejskie Centrum Solidarności.

Kulesza, M. (2008) *Budowanie samorządu. Wybór tekstów ze "Wspólnoty" 1990–2007*. Warszawa: Municipum.

Matyja, R. (2013) *Rywalizacja polityczna w Polsce*. Kraków–Rzeszów: Ośrodek Myśli Politycznej.
Nowakowski, R. (ed.) (2010) *"Gra o miasto". W 20. rocznicę odbudowy samorządu w Polsce*. Wrocław: Wydawnictwo Naukowe Dolnośląskiej Szkoły Wyższej.
Purchla, J. (2009) "Das Wunder von 1989 aus der Sicht eines Krakauers", *Der Donauraum. Zeitschrift des Institutes fur den Donauraum und Mitteleuropa*, 49 (3–4), pp. 307–318.
Purchla, J. (2018) *Miasto i polityka. Przypadki Krakowa*. Kraków: Universitas.
Purchla, J. (ed.) (2019) *Kraków. History & Art*. Kraków: International Cultural Centre.
Purchla, J. (2020) "27 maja 1990 roku skończył się w Krakowie komunizm!", *Casus*, 96/97, pp. 94–97.
Regulski, J. (2000) *Samorząd III Rzeczypospolitej. Koncepcje i realizacja*. Warszawa: Wydawnictwo Naukowe PWN.
Stępień, J. (2020) *Samorząd wolności*. Warszawa: Wydawnictwo Nieoczywiste.
Woźniak, M.G. (2011) *Gospodarka Polski 1990–2011. Transformacja. Modernizacja. Droga do spójności społeczno-ekonomicznej. Transformacja*, Vol. 1. Warszawa: Wydawnictwo Naukowe PWN.

Notes

1 A travesty of a famous quote from *General Barcz*, a political novel published by Juliusz Kaden-Bandrowski in 1923. It described, in no uncertain terms, the particulars of the problems Poland faced in 1918, having regained independence after over a century of being partitioned by the neighbouring powers.

2 The first partially free Parliamentary election in post-war Poland was held on the power of a political contract between the authorities of the communist People's Republic of Poland and a part of the anti-Communist opposition on 4 June 1989. The contract resulted from the Round Table negotiations and involved a package of decisions concerning both the fundamental reorganisation of the highest state organs (introduction of the second house of the parliament (Senate) and of the office of the President of the People's Republic of Poland) and the drawing of election rules for the coming election. It was agreed that all the seats in the Senate and 35% of seats in the Sejm, being the lower house of the Polish Parliament, will be available to anyone in fully free elections, while the remaining 65% of the seats in the Sejm were reserved to the governing communist party (PZPR) and its satellites. Communists believed that in this way they had a controlling majority, sufficient for running the current affairs of the state but practically insufficient if voting any changes of constitutional character, as those called for two-thirds of the votes.

The results of the election of 4 June 1989 were an utter defeat of the communists. Candidates of Solidarity Citizens' Committees won 160 out of the 161 seats available to them, and 92 out of the 100 Senate seats (it may be interesting to note that all the candidates of the Solidarity (opposition) who failed to secure themselves a seat made it to the second round). The victory of Solidarity opened a new period in the latest history of Poland and significantly contributed to the collapse of communism in Central Europe.

2 Civil society

From "Solidarity" to urban activism

Dominika Hołuj

The chapter presents the process of development of Kraków's civil society in the democratic system after 1989. It considers the local circumstances of that development, and external ones that determine the possibility of undertaking social activity. Historical circumstances have been considered extremely important in the case of Kraków. The social potential developed in the active anti-system opposition after the Second World War became part of the driving force of the revolution of 1989. For that reason, the chapter opens with a brief description of the effects of the city's post-war grassroots opposition against the communist government.

Cracovians vs. post-war public authorities

A high degree anti-system activity was characteristic of the post-war population of Kraków (Weigle and Butterfield, 1992; Walicki, 1996; Purchla, 2000). The city was already emphasising its anti-systemic position in 1946, with student protests against the new authorities and the results of the popular referendum that were shattering for the communist authorities (Purchla, 2000, p. 196). Even though the citizens were stripped of the right to govern and organise themselves (local self-government was liquidated and social organisations were liquidated), some people in Kraków never ceased to be active. That need for grassroots activity was profoundly and deeply rooted in the local community and found various outlets, e.g., in the organisation of numerous associations and foundations of 19th-century origins. Importantly, despite the wartime damage and losses, Kraków of 1945 was the only major urban centre symbolised by a continuity of the social tissue. The surviving human capital (intelligentsia, bourgeoisie) was additionally augmented by the refugees and repatriates who began arriving here during the Second World War (Purchla, 1996, pp. 124–126). In this way, a powerful local base for social activity had already developed here by the beginning of the post-war period. It was later reinforced further by the influx of new people who settled in Nowa Huta – the worker's district developed on a greenfield site, whose population the communists expected to provide a "counterbalance" to the "old, bourgeois-cum-intelligentsia" in Kraków. That plan failed, and

DOI: 10.4324/9781003252757-3

the workers, along with the traditionally socially active citizens, provided an important force for the opposition. It was the Catholic Church that provided a link between those seemingly dissimilar groups (Frentzel-Zagórska, 1990). The Church used to be the substitute for the state earlier in the history of Poland, as it preserved cultural values and symbols. Now, with its charismatic leaders – Cardinals Adam Sapieha and Karol Wojtyła (later Pope John Paul II) – it became a direct rival of the government in the fight for the Polish soul (Purchla, 2000, p. 222). The Church ran pastorship groups for workers, youth, and students (Kraków boasted the largest number of the latter in Poland) and at times, they provided the only spaces for free discussion (Chwalba, 2004, pp. 368–374). Moreover, the Church organised social assistance and published independent magazines (*Tygodnik Powszechny* weekly, *Znak* monthly) that were formative for the contemporary intelligentsia. Cooperation of the Church with that group resulted in the legal activity of the Club of Catholic Intelligentsia (Polish: Klub Inteligencji Katolickiej, KIK). From 1976, the Club cooperated with the Workers' Defence Committee (Polish: Komitet Obrony Robotników, KOR), providing support for the repressed and developing analyses of the current problems.

Academics and students developed a self-education movement to rectify the false information being taught in the official curricula. In 1977, Kraków became home to Poland's first independent student organisation since Stalinist times (the Student Committee of Solidarity [SKS]), and in 1979 – the worker-oriented Christian Worker Community (Polish: Chrześcijańska Wspólnota Ludzi Pracy, ChWLP, Buchowski, 1994, pp. 136, 138). In 1980, all such groups joined together to create the first independent trade union in the Eastern Bloc: the Solidarity Independent and Self-Governing Trade Union (Polish: NSZZ "Solidarność", Friszke, 2014). The Kraków district of Nowa Huta was one of the key centres for Solidarity, as 37,000 out of the total number of 40,000 employees of the steelworks joined as members. By the spring of 1981, Solidarity in Kraków counted 150,000 members (Chwalba, 2004, pp. 393–394, 564).

Kraków often proved its opposition against the authorities: hunger strikes, election boycotts, and strikes were organised both as part of national campaigns and in response to local events, such as the murder of a student and activist of the Workers' Defence Committee by the Secret Police (SB), and the government's refusal to allow the construction of a church in Nowa Huta.

With the regime becoming weaker, during a period known as "the Carnival of Solidarity" (i.e., 1980–81), the legality of instituting legal social organisations was reinstated. In Kraków, these organisations would undertake activities connected to cultural heritage (e.g., the Citizens' Committee for Saving Kraków [Polish: Obywatelski Komitet Ratowania Krakowa, OKRK]; the Committee for the Care for the Józef Piłsudski Mound operated by the Society of Friends of Kraków History and Heritage [Polish: Towarzystwo Miłośników Historii i Zabytków Krakowa, TMHiZK]), and to ecology. Kraków is where the first national environmental organisation in the Eastern

Bloc developed, the Polish Ecological Club (Polski Klub Ekologiczny, PKE), which successfully achieved the discontinuation of the exceedingly harmful production of aluminium in Skawina, a town neighbouring Kraków.

The social, political, and economic breakthrough of 1989

The end of the 1980s was a social, political, and economic watershed in Poland as well as the entire Eastern Bloc. It was achieved in various ways, from a bloody deposition of a dictator to a peaceful transfer of power, the latter being the case in Poland. In fact, it was the way the change was effected that started the disintegration of the Polish opposition, which had previously appeared to be a monolith cemented by a common purpose. The first dilemmas and decisions during the time of transition also divided civil society in Kraków. Some would consider the peaceful transition – with negotiations rather than fighting, and without dramatic settlements – a mistake, which provided the germ of the lasting conflict with those who found the peaceful solution a symbol of the success of society, as it led to the goal without losses or casualties.

In 1989, the effect of the work of the Polish Round Table – whose participants on the side of the democratic opposition included Cracovians from the Club of Catholic Intelligentsia, *Tygodnik Powszechny*, *Znak*, and the Solidarity Trade Union from the Lenin Steelworks – was the announcement of the first partially free parliamentary election on 4 June 1989, which became the symbol of the systemic transition (Dudek, 2016, pp. 26–27). A significant development for the local community was the reactivation of self-government at the commune level in 1990, as it initiated the process of decentralisation of power.

The decision to conduct a partially free election meant that the community had to draft lists of candidates for the positions of MPs and senators. These were populated by the opposition, whose electoral campaigns were supported by the local citizens' committees (aka civic committees, in Polish – *komitety obywatelskie*). They operated without any assistance of the authorities, in a situation where legal solutions were developed on an *ad hoc* basis, and with no experience and/or knowledge of how the structures of democratic states operate. The enthusiasm elicited by the change that was taking place triggered a major social response in the fulfilment of that mission ("all these functions were fulfilled on a voluntary basis, without any remuneration or reimbursement. Despite this, there was no problem in finding people eager to work. Something that is hard to encounter today, 20 years later.") (Grela, 2009, p. 52).

The election proved to be a success for the democratic opposition, and the citizens' committees could use this experience to organise the campaign ahead of the first election for territorial self-governments in 1990. Yet that success came at a price. The takeover of power by the opposition meant that they started to fulfil public functions in the capital, and therefore cease to work for the local community (Bernhard, 1996, p. 313; Brannan, 2003). On the other hand, the takeover of power also meant assuming responsibility for the completion of the transformation. From being members of a civil, anti-governmental movement, the opposition came to hold the power (Ost, 1990, pp. 199–202). Previously, the basis for the fight against the regime was the general need for democratisation, without any detailed plans for reforms. The new authorities lacked knowledge and experience at a time when problems riding on the back of the economic transformation quickly emerged: inflation, drastic supply shortages, and unemployment, which forced many to focus on private problems (Garton Ash, 2000, pp. 395–402). The new authorities were blamed for the new problems and disillusion resulting from the unrealistic expectations concerning the pace of the improvement of the standard of life and the solving of problems that had built up over decades (Buchowski, 1994, p. 141; Michnik, 2000, pp. 81–99). The same phenomenon also affected the local authorities. The Civic Committee for the Dismissal of the Kraków Municipal Council was incorporated as early as 1992. It charged the Council with the inability to make decisions, blamed it for the catastrophic condition of the institutions of culture, health care, and education, and accused it of tacit agreement to the degradation of the natural environment. Tens of thousands of signatures were collected in support. The municipal government was believed to be guilty of long-term neglect in city governance. In the following years, both Kraków and Poland were affected by the waves of strikes by professional groups (e.g., healthcare, education) who were dissatisfied with the results of the transformation and the reforms that were introduced. Moreover, the dissimilar visions of how to conduct the transformation split the new governments into a variety of opposing factions, which also reflected the breakup of society (Krasowski, 2013). At the same time, the antagonism between those in government and those who continued to hold trade union posts manifested more strongly (Fowkes, 1999, pp. 54).

The low turnout at the first elections (around 60% both in Poland and in Kraków) was an important issue that did not bode well for the whole post-1989 period (Chwalba, 2004, p. 455). It resulted from the post-war experience, when citizens were forced to vote and saw the results being doctored. Lack of participation can be considered a reaction to such practices and the application of "the right to nonparticipation" (Chmielewska-Szlajfer, 2019). The community grappled with the problems of transition, which made it focus on private matters (Smolar, 1996, p. 24). In the parliamentary election in 1993, turnout was around 52% both in Poland and in Kraków, and subsequently fell even lower to 48% (1997). The turnout in Kraków was much higher, as it reached 54.48%. With time, that split became a characteristic feature of voter turnout in Poland. Similarly, the turnout at the local and regional elections must also be considered to be disappointing. From 49.2% in 1990, it dropped significantly to 29.5% in the next election (1994), before returning in 1998 to the – still unsatisfactory – level of 41.2% from the beginning of the decade (Urząd Statystyczny w Krakowie, 2009).

The election of the territorial authorities conducted on 27 May 1990 was the first fully free election organised in Poland in decades. The reform of territorial authorities was the last of the significant solutions ratified in the early 1990s that increased the influence of communities on public affairs. At the same time, the new legal acts imposed at that time were subjected to no civil consultations whatsoever. The general legitimacy the government received in the free election was considered a sufficient mandate for acting independently, which stemmed both from the huge time pressure on the new government (all key elements of the state's political and economic system needed quick and simultaneous reforms) and from the need to focus on conducting active foreign policy to shape the new place of Poland on the geopolitical map of Europe.

Consultations, mostly of a limited extent, with key players and not with the community, were accepted. The Constitution of the Republic of Poland from 1997 might have recognised the right of the authorities and society to act together, yet it was only in the following years that the legislation was introduced that fine-tuned the tools and procedures that opened the path to participation. With respect to such actions by the central authorities, it must be emphasised that the idea to consult the activities of the municipal authorities with the borough (district) councils, which were already set up in 1991, was born in the Kraków self-government at a relatively early date (Urząd Miasta Krakowa, 1996). Possibly considered insufficient from today's perspective, it was a rare practice in those circumstances. The self-government was also where the policy of informing society about the steps undertaken by the authorities was carried out most fully: in 1996, Kraków set up one of Poland's first official city websites.

Civil organisations in the 1990s

The law on associations was passed in 1989 and the act on foundations was changed in 1991. That was just the start of developing legal frameworks for civil activity yet acts of law of fundamental importance would only be introduced in the following decade, as in the 1990s priority was given to legislation concerning economic matters (Juros et al., 2004). It was only in 1997 that a general clause on the participation of the community in governance made it into the new Constitution of the Republic of Poland of 2 April 1997.

Despite these unfavourable legal circumstances, in the early 1990s, non-governmental organisations flourished in Poland (and in Kraków). At the time, the city was home to 321 foundations, 893 societies and associations, and 81 civil organisations, which accounted for around 5% of all civil society entities in Poland (Urząd Statystyczny w Krakowie, 1998, p. 224). Many of these were organisations that had operated since the 1980s and whose total know-how and experience could only now be fully put to use, as was the case with the Polish Ecological Club. In 1989, it participated in the work of the Sub-Team for Ecology at the Round Table, which resulted in Kraków being recognised as seriously threatened with ecological disaster and awarded the status of a protected city. Already in the 1990s, the experience of the Club made it possible to emphasise the need to monitor new environmental threats after the social, political, and economic transformation (Juchnowicz, 1990, p. 255).

The professional self-governments also organised themselves anew in the 1990s, and bodies supporting economic and social initiatives emerged. They gradually took over the tasks that, for historical reasons, had to be carried out by the state and, albeit informally, the Catholic Church. Organisations working in education (e.g., the Society for Supporting Economic Initiatives [Polish: Towarzystwo Wspierania Inicjatyw Gospodarczych]), history and cultural heritage (e.g., First Marshal Józef Piłsudski National Remembrance Society [Polish: Towarzystwo Pamięci Narodowej im. Pierwszego Marszałka Józefa Piłsudskiego], Association of Home Army Soldiers [Polish: Stowarzyszenie Żołnierzy Armii Krajowej], Foundation of the Centre for the Research and Documentation of the Fight for Independence [Polish: Fundacja Centrum Dokumentacji Czynu Niepodległościowego, FCDCN]), and supporting self-governments (e.g., Małopolska Institute of Local Government and Administration (Polish: Małopolski Instytut Samorządu Terytorialnego i Administracji, MISTiA), a regional centre of the Warsaw-based Foundation in Support of Local Democracy that operates to this day as one of the leading non-governmental organisations in Małopolska) developed during this time. The Polish Academy of Arts and Sciences (Polish: Polska Akademia Umiejętności, PAU), suspended in Stalinist times, was now reactivated.

The process of gathering funds by civil society was far harder than the registration of its organisations. That was partially due to the post-war curtailment of legal activities related to what is generally understood as charity. Although charitable campaigns were organised, the lack of habit or internal imperatives to participate in them was striking. The question of society's poor financial potential was also not insignificant, as the new middle class was only just forming. Worth mentioning in this context was the decision of the film director Andrzej Wajda to donate the 1987 Kyoto Prize of $400,000, awarded to him by the Inamori Foundation, to the construction of the exhibition centre for the collection of Japanese art gathered by Feliks Manggha Jasieński and the creation of a place where the Polish and Japanese cultures could meet. Thanks to this individual initiative, which was supported by various institutions and individuals, the Manggha Centre of Japanese Art and Technology opened in Kraków in 1994.

After the election campaigns of 1990 and 1991, the citizens' committees continued their operation and focused their activity on organising civil movements in the districts. The committees drafted diagnoses and discussed systemic concepts, for example, of the division of the city into ancillary units (districts). Once these were formally established, they took over some of the matters that the committees had previously dealt with. In this way, they remained a non-systemic voice of the local communities, and as such, they organised protests against the activities and shortcomings of the authorities, for example, the chaotic development and unlimited deployment of ugly advertisements in public space (Dzierżanowski, 2009, pp. 26, 29). The activists' local endeavours quickly led them to experience the limited potential of effective action, which was also influenced by waning social engagement.

One remarkable phenomenon was the establishment of schools by civic educational associations and religious associations. There were 22 such schools operating in Kraków in 1996 (Urząd Statystyczny w Krakowie, 1998, p. 113), and they accounted for only 3% of all schools, yet their operation was the embodiment of the idea of pluralism in the methods of carrying out public tasks. Activists wanted schools with a more democratic internal organisation, custom-made curricula, and proprietary methods of teaching. Unfortunately, they soon had to limit the scope of planned innovation thanks to the regulations that required the imposed curricula to be kept, and by financial problems (Berkowicz, 2019, pp. 53–57). The freedom to act yet again proved to be more difficult to achieve in practice than idealistically assumed.

Towards a European civil society

The 2000s brought a range of changes in the options for conducting civil activity. The central government created a framework for cooperation and financial support (2001: Act on access to public information; 2003: the first legal act fully devoted to civil activity – Act on public benefit and volunteer work). With time, the civil activity of people with no experience in organisations opposing the previous system also developed, assuming forms closer to what was known in Western democracies. At the same time, the falling levels of enthusiasm for working in citizens' committees made it hard for them to "rejuvenate" their staff (Skrzyńska, 2009, p. 142). Young people in Kraków would rather carry out their own initiatives and make use of the new tools for participation. These activists would rather be energised by the new legal frames of operation and support from the European Union (financial and ideological, as the EU emphasised that the formal recognition of the significance of the establishment of civil society is a particular declaration of belonging to European culture) (Makowski, 2008, pp. 73–95).

However, one of the most fundamental indicators of general involvement, that is exercising the passive right to take part in elections, did not change. The low turnouts resulted from a lack of interest in politics, failure to recognise the significance of participation, mistrust of the candidates, and the absence of a viable alternative, and therefore could have been recognised as a symbolic renouncement of electoral rights (Panicz, 2011, p. 116). With certain exceptions, post-2000 turnouts at the polls followed the pattern seen in the 1990s. Participation in elections only rose significantly at historical moments. The turnout for the EU referendum in 2003 (Kraków – 67%, Poland – 59%) reflected the general enthusiasm for a symbolic "return to Europe". Similarly, the elections to the Parliament and Senate in 2019 with the highest post-1989 turnout (Kraków – 71%, Poland – 61.74%) resulted from the national mobilisation of the partisans on both sides of the political stage (of the conservative right wing – to preserve power, and of the liberals – perceiving the need for a quick change in the governing party, or "emergency voting for democracy"). That impulse also influenced a higher turnout in the 2019 European Parliament election (Kraków – 47.89% and Poland – 45.68%), compared with 2014 when only 25.74% of voters in Kraków and 23.83% in Poland turned out at the ballots. In 2018, the turnout to the local and regional elections exceeded 58% (with the results from 2002, 2006, 2010, and 2014 ranging between 35% and 43%) (Urząd Statystyczny w Krakowie, 2009, 2019; Państwowa Komisja Wyborcza, no date).

Civil organisations after 2000

The second decade after the transformation resulted in another rise in the number of associations in Kraków (1,700 in 2001, compared with around 3,600 in 2005). Even though the number was on the rise, many organisations quickly discontinued their activity. The lack of formal deregistration meant that the Statistics Poland (Urząd Statystyczny) data less accurately depicted the real number of active entities. It is estimated that only 70% of the registered entities are genuinely active in Poland, which was corroborated in Kraków by the verification of active associations performed by the Municipality of Kraków: in 2017, Statistics Poland reported around 6,900 organisations, and the Municipality of Kraków – only around 4,900 (Urząd Statystyczny w Krakowie, 2019; Urząd Miasta Krakowa, 2020). In the same year, there were approximately 1,650 foundations registered in Kraków, which, together with the societies and associations, accounted for around 5.5% of all such organisations nationwide. For every 1000 residents there were on average nearly twice as many such organisations in the city (5.9/1000 residents) than in the country (3.2/1000 residents) (Stowarzyszenie Klon/Jawor, 2018). In this aspect, Kraków follows the national trend: civil entities more often develop in large cities with greater social capital. Many of them are established by people and institutions from the world of academia and culture (for example, a foundation to take care of the literary heritage of Wisława Szymborska, promote Polish culture, and support the ideas of tolerance was set up in 2012 to fulfil the last will of the Nobel Prize winner). It is worth noting that important informative and educational activities are carried out as initiatives of Kraków civil organisations: for example, Świat Ma Sens Foundation (literally: "the world makes sense") carried out a major national social media campaign encouraging young Poles to participate in the elections.

Territorial authorities: towards full participation in decision-making

The 2000s brought about significant development in the possible forms of participation in the activity of local and regional authorities, even if they were mostly of a consultative character. An important change came with the introduction of a legal right for the community to be informed about the activities of public authority bodies. The need for extensive access to information was substantiated by the growing numbers of visits to the online Public Information Bulletin of the Municipal Office, with 5.7 million visits in 2004 and 161.8 million in 2019 (Urząd Miasta Krakowa, 2005, 2020). Public consultations became a popular tool of urban democracy. The Kraków authorities began to organise them in 2002, and now organise several dozen a year.

Since 2014, the municipality has allocated funds for citizens' projects as part of the participatory budgeting process. Every year, residents of Kraków submit hundreds of projects (over 600 in 2014–18, and as many as 949 in 2019). The emergence of this tool, known worldwide, must be considered a good change despite its lack of significance in the completion of major capital-intensive projects due to the low value of the allocated funds allocated (only PLN 12.5 million in 2018, in contrast Łódź allocated PLN 50 million and Katowice – PLN 31.5 million). Although the value of the funds allocated to Kraków's participatory budget grew to PLN 30 million in 2019, that only resulted from the introduction of legal minimum thresholds for such budgets. Another weak point was the procedure applied in 2014–19 for selecting projects, which was limited to voting without prior debate. Over the several years that the tool functioned, it can be seen that the problems of implementation also lie on the civil side. The lack of experience in submitting applications generated a large group of projects that were rejected each year at the stage of formal and content verification (46% in 2017). A similar phenomenon is also observed in other Polish cities. Participatory budgeting attracts very low numbers of voters (5–10%), although in this aspect, Kraków compares poorly with other Polish cities. On the other hand, paradoxically, the tool was indicated by the local community as the most recognisable form of participation (Hubert, Latko, and Chlebicki, 2021, p. 11). So the low numbers of voters are not the result of the poor promotion of the tool but from a conscious refusal to participate. It should be added that younger people (under 40s) are the dominant both those submitting projects and those voting for them (Olechowski, 2015, p. 42).

General regulations that allowed submitting petitions might have been in force in the 1990s, yet it was only in 2015 that an act that governed the details of the procedures for submitting and investigating them was introduced. In 2015–19, as many as 4,639 petitions were submitted to the Kraków authorities. Many of them concerned municipal investments, ecology, and public security. Especially thought-provoking was the residents' long fight to have the Las Borkowski woods, with its precious natural resources, purchased by the city to save the area from development. In 2019, after a few years of petitions, the municipality conceded to the civil demand.

From 2012, the people of Kraków have also been able to start initiatives intended to turn into resolutions, even though this is an option hardly ever resorted to. Only four draft citizens' resolutions were submitted in 2012–19, mostly concerning local matters but they also echoed changes in law at the national level, for example, the idea of having the municipality finance in vitro procedures after the National Health Fund stopped funding them.

What is important is that long-term forms of cooperation also developed in the relationship between the public authorities and the local community. The municipality formally approved the first principles of cooperation with non-governmental organisations in 1999. That cooperation has now developed into a permanent element for carrying out public tasks. Systems for informing and consulting plans and activities are in operation, civil advisory teams do their work, and public organisations are supported by local authorities. This cooperation also has a financial dimension, consisting of the commissioning of public tasks and support in completing them. In 2019, the municipality fully financed 807 tasks carried out by civil organisations.

From trade union strikes to urban movement protests

With time, the specificity of contestative participation changed. The first wave of strikes mostly articulated the problems of professional groups as they were co-organised by trade unions. What became dominant over time was civil opposition of spontaneous and informal character developed mostly by younger people – the so-called new urban movements (Hubert, Latko, and Chlebicki, 2021, p. 7). The number of public gatherings rose significantly from 107 in 2011 to 842 in 2019 (Urząd Miasta Krakowa, 2020, p. 88). The identity of Cracovians is shaped through the processes of transformation, globalisation, and European integration. The protesters are linked by their views, a hierarchy of needs, and life goals, as well as belonging to an urban culture (van Amersfoort, 2005, pp. 398–399; Galent and Kubicki, 2010, p. 211).

One of the early informal group protests was directed against the lack of civil consultations around the introduction of ACTA in 2012. Mass demonstrations were organised in many cities, with the largest, gathering 15,000 people, marching through the streets of Kraków. Civil opposition was already alive at the time of unfettered online communication that allows residents to join spontaneous groups of shared interests that transform emerging emotions into instant reactions, rather than build programmes or institutions (Castells, 2012). An opposition of a similar tenor and manner of self-organisation concerned the Kraków's application to host the 2022 Winter Olympic Games. The activists emphasised that the city authorities made the decision without extensive consultations with the people. The main organiser of the protests was the informal initiative "Kraków Przeciw Igrzyskom" (literally: "Kraków against the games"), which later transformed into the Miasto Wspólne association. Another group, "Kraków wart jest Igrzysk" (literally: "Kraków is worth the games"), constituted itself in parallel and gathered the proponents of the event, although it shared its opponent's view that a public discussion concerning its organisation is necessary. The protests resulted in the municipality announcing a referendum in which the residents rejected the idea of organising the event, with 69.72% of votes against. In the public eye, this was considered "punishment" of the city authorities for ignoring the need for civil debate.

Like in other Polish cities, the spontaneous demonstration of locals in Kraków increasingly often results from the mounting global and national problems generating local consequences. The people of Kraków manifest their "right to the city" (Lefebvre, 1967; Harvey, 2008) by opposing the social, environmental, and spatial consequences of a neoliberal economy (e.g., the Kraków Smog Alert is a movement that opposes environmental degradation), the destruction of natural resources, and the excessive commercialisation of space (e.g., protests of people from the Czyżyny district against the construction of a dysfunctional residential complex, or the protest against the demolition of the modernist building formerly housing the Cracovia Hotel). The manifestations are also a reflection of the community's needs. The Kraków Critical Mass organised in 2014–15 saw cyclists blocking the streets by moving in a large number along an established route to draw attention to the need for the development of infrastructure for cycling. This is another example of a grassroots movement that after several years of operation became registered as the Kraków Miastem Rowerów (Kraków City of Bicycles) Association. Another group of civil protests were those against the planned public investments deemed burdensome for society, such as the construction of the plant for thermal processing of waste and the crematorium.

Some manifestations in Kraków were organised as artistic happenings. One of the first (2011) challenged the plan to develop the recreational area of Zakrzówek. The civil campaigns of the Modraszek Kolektyw (which drew its name from the protected common blue butterfly found in the area) included the "congresses of blue butterflies" for which the participants dressed as butterflies, and the campaign of donning blue butterfly's wings and posing on Kraków's most famous monuments. In 2014, artist Cecylia Malik co-organised a parade titled "Chciwość Miasta" (the greed of the city) to protest the idea of demolishing the modernist Cracovia Hotel. Participants dressed in golden costumes and marched across the city with the effigy of a golden idol on a shopping cart. In 2017, she organised the "Mothers at the Felling Site" happening, with women breastfeeding children on the stumps of freshly felled trees, to address the law liberalising the procedures of tree felling. After the first event in Kraków, editions were organised around the country.

Conflicts arising from the policies of the central power that destroys the democratic mechanisms in Poland and the opposition to "moving Poland away from Europe" (demonstrations in defence of the Polish Constitution and of independent courts, etc.) have intensified in recent years. Kraków has also been the stage for protests related to the reduction of women's rights to legal abortion (the "Black Protests"). The expanding catalogue of conflict on the authorities–community axis, based on the clash of worldviews, has become clearly visible.

The low effectiveness of protests organised by informal groups prompts their registration as organisations, e.g., associations (*stowarzyszenie*). These become visibly politicised with time. In 2018, members of the Kraków dla Mieszkańców Association were elected to the Kraków Municipal Council. Similar phenomena took place in other Polish cities. The activists emphasise that by formalising, and later politicising, their activity, they increase the possibility of attaining their goals or obtaining financing.

Conclusion

The history of civil society in Kraków in the last 30 years is an excellent way of portraying the history of civil actions that Poles took after 1989. In a way, it is also peculiar, as it is based on the long-term experience of local activists who provided the founding capital for civil society at the time of transformation.

Two main phases can be clearly seen over the 30 years in question. The first decade of the systemic change, harder to achieve than was assumed, was characterised by a range of gaps in the legal and organisational support of civil society by the public authorities. That was a time of intensive learning about the new reality, which also shaped the activists' working environment. As much as it must be recognised that the community implemented the main functions of civil society (integrative, socialising, controlling, and protective) in different fields from the beginning of the transformation, their scope could have been wider. The reason for this was the quality of the social capital (a relatively small group of active locals, even though still statistically bigger than on the national scale, and the predominance of reactive participation over longer-term civil work). On the other hand, it was the aftermath of the limitations generated by the system for financing of non-governmental organisations and the low expectations of the public authorities regarding the community, among other things. The legal foundations for the operation of social activism were lacking, as was the willingness of the public authorities to cooperate with the community, i.e., the circumstances necessary to make use of the potential vested in the community (Arato, 1981; Putnam, 1995).

A new civil power began to develop more clearly after 2000: a new generation of participating citizens who followed the global trends of the emergence of "the right to the city". The processes of globalisation and, in the case of Poland, accession to the European Union only intensified those needs and expectations. Over time, the catalogue of participative activities developed but the expectations of society are still greater than the capacity for actual cooperation. That is why society must formalise and politicise its activities if it is to carry out significant changes. In other words, if it wants to "fight" politicians, it must become a part of that group itself. In this aspect, the 30-year history of the functioning of Kraków (and Polish) civil society has, in a sense, come full circle.

Bibliography

Arato, A. (1981) "Civil Society against the State: Poland 1980–81", *Telos*, 47, pp. 23–47.

Berkowicz, A. (2019) *Historia powstania krakowskich szkół niepublicznych na tle zmian w zarządzaniu w edukacji polskiej po roku 1989*. Kraków: Wydawnictwo UJ.

Bernhard, M. (1996) "Civil Society after the First Transition: Dilemmas of Post-communist *(sic)* Democratization in Poland and beyond", *Communist and Post-Communist Studies*, 29/33.

Brannan, T. (2003) "From 'Antipolitics' to 'Anti-Politics': What became of East European 'Civil Society'?", *Working Paper Series*, 03–41.

Buchowski, M. (1994) "From Anti-Communist to Post-Communist Ethos: The Case of Poland", *Social Anthropology*, 2(2), pp. 133–148.

Castells, M. (2012) *Networks of Outrage and Hope – Social Movements in the Internet Age*. Chichester: Wiley.

Chmielewska-Szlajfer, H. (2019) *Reshaping Poland's Community after Communism: Ordinary Celebrations*. Cham: Palgrave Macmillan.

Chwalba, A. (2004) *Kraków w latach 1945–1989*. Dzieje Krakowa, Vol. 6. Kraków: Wydawnictwo Literackie.

Dudek, A. (2016) *Historia polityczna Polski. 1989–2015*. Kraków: Wydawnictwo Znak Horyzont.

Dzierżanowski, L. (2009) "XX-lecie ruchu komitetów obywatelskich 1989–2009", [in:] Jurczak, M. (ed.) *Ruch Komitetów obywatelskich w osiedlach krakowskich 1989–2009. Przyczynek do historii*. Kraków: Komitet Obywatelski Miasta Krakowa, pp. 11–29.

Fowkes, B. (1999) *The Post-Communist Era Change and Continuity in Eastern Europe*. Hampshire: Macmillan Press.

Frentzel-Zagórska, J. (1990) "Civil Society in Poland and Hungary", *Soviet Studies*, 42/4.

Friszke, A. (2014) *Rewolucja Solidarności. 1980–1981*. Kraków: Znak Horyzont, Instytut Studiów Politycznych PAN, Europejskie Centrum Solidarności.

Galent, M. and Kubicki, P. (2010) "An Invisible Revolution. How the Urban Way of Life Is Transforming the Identities of Poles", [in:] Góra, M. and Mach, Z. (eds.) *Collective Identity and Democracy: The Impact of EU Enlargement*, ARENA Report 4/10. Oslo: University of Oslo, pp. 205–248.

Garton Ash, T. (2000) "The Conclusion", [in:] Antohi, S. and Tismaneanu, V. (eds.) *Between Past and Future: The Revolutions of 1989 and Their Aftermath*. Budapest: Central European University Press, pp. 395–402.

Grela, J. (2009) "Osiedlowy Komitet Obywatelski Dębniki-Zakrzówek – 20 lat historii", [in:] Jurczak, M. (ed.) *Ruch Komitetów obywatelskich w osiedlach krakowskich 1989–2009. Przyczynek do historii*. Kraków: Komitet Obywatelski Miasta Krakowa, pp. 47–88.

Harvey, D. (2008) "The Right to the City", *New Left Review*, 53 Sept/Oct 2008.

Hubert, W., Latko, P. and Chlebicki, M. (2021) *Społeczeństwo obywatelskie w Krakowie. Raport z badania*. Kraków: Fundacja Socjometr Laboratorium Rozwiązań Społecznych.

Juchnowicz, S. (1990) "Źródła patologicznej urbanizacji i kryzysu ekologicznego obszaru Krakowa", [in:] Gumińska, M. and Delorme, A. (eds.) *Klęska*

Ekologiczna Krakowa. Przyczyny. Teraźniejszość. Perspektywy ekorozwoju miasta. Kraków: Wydawnictwo UJ, pp. 248–255.

Juros, A. et al. (2004) "From *Solidarity* to Subsidiarity: The Nonprofit Sector in Poland", [in:] Zimmer, A. and Priller, E. (eds.) *Future of Civil Society*. Wiesbaden: Springer Fachmedien, pp. 557–599.

Krasowski, R. (2013) *Po południu. Upadek elit solidarnościowych po zdobyciu władzy.* Warszawa: Wydawnictwo Czerwone i Czarne.

Lefebvre, H. (1967) "Le droit à la ville", *L Homme et la société,* 6.

Makowski, G. (2008) "Nowe płaszczyzny dialogu obywatelskiego między władzą i organizacjami pozarządowymi w Polsce", [in:] Makowski, G. and Schimanek, T. (eds.) *Organizacje pozarządowe i władza publiczna. Drogi do partnerstwa.* Warszawa: ISP, pp. 73–92.

Michnik, A. (2000) "Independence Reborn and the Demons of the Velvet Revolution", [in:] Antohi, S. and Tismaneanu, V. (eds.) *Between Past and Future: The Revolutions of 1989 and Their Aftermath.* Budapest: Central European University Press, pp. 81–99.

Olechowski, M. (2015) *Ewaluacja drugiej edycji Budżetu Obywatelskiego w Krakowie.* Warszawa-Kraków: PBiIS "Stocznia".

Ost, D. (1990) *Solidarity and the Politics of Anti-Politics: Opposition and Reform in Poland since 1968.* Series: Labor and Social Change. Philadelphia, PA: Temple University Press.

Panicz, U. (2011) "Frekwencja wyborcza a stan polskiej demokracji", *Refleksje,* 4(2011) jesień-zima.

Państwowa Komisja Wyborcza (no date) *Obwieszczenia o wynikach wyborów.* Available at: https://www.pkw.gov.pl/wybory-i-referenda/ (Accessed on: 9 July 2021).

Purchla, J. (1996) *Kraków – prowincja czy metropolia?* Kraków: Universitas.

Purchla, J. (2000) *Cracow in the European Core.* Kraków: Międzynarodowe Centrum Kultury.

Putnam, R.D. (1995) "Bowling Alone: America's Declining Social Capital", *Journal of Democracy,* 6(1), pp. 65–98.

Skrzyńska, B. (2009) "Zwierzyniecki Komitet Obywatelski 1989–2009", [in:] Jurczak, M. (ed.) *Ruch Komitetów Obywatelskich w osiedlach krakowskich 1989–2009. Przyczynek do historii.* Kraków: Komitet Obywatelski Miasta Krakowa, pp. 121–155.

Smolar, A. (1996) "Civil Society after Communism: From Opposition to Atomization", *Journal of Democracy,* 7(1), pp. 24–38.

Stowarzyszenie Klon/Jawor (2018) *Kondycja organizacji pozarządowych.* Available at: https://api.ngo.pl/media/get/108904 (Accessed on: 27 September 2021).

Urząd Miasta Krakowa (1996) *Raport o stanie miasta 1995.* Available at: https://www.bip.krakow.pl/zalaczniki/dokumenty/n/71886/0/karta (Accessed on: 10 September 2021).

Urząd Miasta Krakowa (2005) *Raport o stanie miasta 2004.* Available at: https://www.bip.krakow.pl/?dok_id=2032 (Accessed on: 20 September 2021).

Urząd Miasta Krakowa (2020) *Raport o stanie miasta 2019.* Available at: https://www.bip.krakow.pl/zalaczniki/dokumenty/n/287199/karta (Accessed on: 11 September 2021).

Urząd Statystyczny w Krakowie (1998) *Rocznik Statystyczny Krakowa,* Kraków: Urząd Statystyczny w Krakowie.

Urząd Statystyczny w Krakowie (2009) *Rocznik Statystyczny Krakowa,* Kraków: Urząd Statystyczny w Krakowie.

Urząd Statystyczny w Krakowie (2019) *Rocznik Statystyczny Krakowa*, Kraków: Urząd Statystyczny w Krakowie.

van Amersfoort, P. (2005) "European Civil Society", *Asia Europe Journal*, 3, pp. 395–402.

Walicki, A. (1996) "Totalitarianism and Detotalitarization: The Case of Poland", *The Review of Politics*, 58(3), pp. 505–530.

Weigle, M.A. and Butterfield, J. (1992) "Civil Society in Reforming Communist Regimes: The Logic of Emergence", *Comparative Politics*, 25(1), pp. 1–23.

3 Municipal self-government 1990–2019

Dominika Hołuj

The political watershed of 1989 reorganised the goals, priorities, and instruments of both the economy and public authorities. The process of decentralisation of the latter was initiated first by the reactivation of local government (1990), and a decade later by the establishment of governments at the supralocal and regional levels (1999) (Swianiewicz, 2003, p. 286; Marcou and Wollmann, 2009, pp. 133–135, 140). When the Act of 8 March 1990 on territorial self-government came into force, the communes became new and active participants in civil and economic life at the local level, and also representatives of the residents' interests. Five state monopolies were broken up: political (the first elections to the local authorities were held in 1990), public government (decentralisation), public ownership, public finance, and public administration (Regulski and Drozda, 2015, p. 9). The autonomy of local government was reinforced by the Constitution of the Republic of Poland on 2 April 1997, whose Article 171 limited the options for state intervention into the activity of local governments to only the assessment of legality of their operation (*Konstytucja Rzeczpospolitej Polskiej*, 1997). However, the profound significance of the systemic change clashed with the legal and financial circumstances of the functioning of the reactivated local authorities. This chapter presents the activities undertaken by the Municipality of Kraków (*gmina miejska Kraków*) in 1990–2019, and accounts for the key achievements as well as the circumstances that influenced the possibility of carrying out the development plans. The analysis is based on the material and data made available by the municipality, and sources from the literature.

Dysfunction of the state policy towards cities after 1989

Knowing the glorious tradition of operation of the local government in Kraków that dated back to the 19th century, the city could have expected that the local community would again be able to take over the responsibility for the functioning and development of the city. The optimism accompanying the development of the foundations for the empowerment of local communities, which were reflected in the first daring electoral programmes from 1990, was fairly quickly dampened. On 17 May 1990, just before the

DOI: 10.4324/9781003252757-4

first elections to territorial governments held on 27 May 1990, the so-called Competence Act was passed. It limited the tasks of the commune to matters concerned with only the communal economy and administration (Regulski, 2000, pp. 110–111; Kulesza, 2008, p. 35). The central government entrusted local tasks to the communes so that it was able to focus on national issues, at the same time transferring part of the costs of transformation to the local authority (Levitas, 2018, p. 7).

The unification of the range of matters entrusted to the local governments that took place in 1990 hit major cities in particular, as they have developmental, infrastructural, and institutional needs that are significantly different from those that determine the functioning of a rural commune. For Kraków, a municipality with an especially powerfully developed cultural function, depriving it of influence on the functioning of the key institutions representing this function was particularly painful. The disproportion between the expectations and the competences it received was only partly removed later on. Although municipal communes would assume successive tasks over time, e.g., in healthcare, welfare, road management, education, and culture, their handover was not always accompanied by an increase in revenue for the local budget that was proportional to the new competences (Misiąg, 2001, pp. 99–100).

Another difficulty was the need to build the hierarchy of civil servants from scratch. Moreover, the lack of experience and knowledge of the practical functioning of territorial authorities was another drawback (Sakowicz, 2017, pp. 349–350). The problems were aggravated by the difficulties of a time of social and economic transition, and the protracted process of taking over state property. Moreover, it often happened that the units the city took over operated with no recourse to any economic principles, which was a legacy of the previous system. Less wealthy communes were incapable of providing them with appropriate co-financing, and restructuring took time (Unia Metropolii Polskich, 1991). The recently elected members of the local government were quickly burdened with responsibility for many years of neglect and dysfunctions in the development of the city, even if they were not their fault. The difficulties contributed to increasing antagonism between the residents, civil servants working for the local governments, and the city authorities, as well as between the local executive and legislative powers (Hołuj, 2015, pp. 14–15).

An important extension of the scope of operation of governments at the community level took place in 1999 when the supralocal level of territorial authorities – the county (*powiat*) – was set up. In large cities, it was connected at the level of the commune, developing into units known as "cities with county rights" (Polish: *miasto na prawach powiatu*) (European Committee of the Regions). That status was granted to Kraków and was accompanied by additional tasks that needed to be carried out. Unfortunately, the central power again entrusted competences without ensuring adequate additional revenue sources to cover the costs of carrying them out. It should also be added that the weakness of the reform of 1999 became manifested not only in the legal and financial construction of the counties, but also in the fragile structure of the new regions. Kraków became the capital of the Małopolska Region; one of the 16 new regions (or voivodeships, Polish: *województwa*). The eventual number of regions was nearly double the optimum number suggested in experts' reports. This resulted from the political pressure from smaller cities, and for large centres such as Kraków, it meant a reduced capacity for absorption of EU funds designed for the development of the regions and their capital cities (Kukliński and Swianiewicz, 1990, pp. 32–33).

Generally speaking, over 30 years, cities like Kraków have not seen a constitutional revolution that would make them fully capable of managing both the endogenous and the external functions, metropolitan ones included. Recognising the need to cooperate in these functionally and spatially consistent areas, the authorities of individual local government units often embarked on *ad hoc* voluntary cooperation. One such example is the Council of the Kraków Metropolitan Area (Krakowski Obszar Metropolitalny), gathering representatives of 52 territorial units, that constituted itself in 2007. The eagerness to carry out the goals of EU policy towards metropolitan areas has resulted in the development of federations of local authorities since 2014 (Kaczmarek and Ryder, 2015, pp. 20–21). That was when Kraków, together with 14 neighbouring communes, set up the Metropolia Krakowska Association (Stowarzyszenie Metropolia Krakowska). The effect of its cooperation was the implementation of the Integrated Territorial Investments (ITIs), key public tasks whose spatial scope exceeds the borders of individual administrative units. Nevertheless, it still remains an improvised solution rather than a long-term strategic cooperation.

A significant barrier in conducting local developmental policies by municipalities after 1990 was not only the failed and unfinished decentralisation reform. Another factor was the purposeful activity of central authorities and public entities that curtailed the full use of the internal potential of the centre, as well as the acquisition of external resources for development. An example of such an act is the blocking of the development of the airport in Balice near Kraków that lasted for many years, a policy that was also aimed at other cities. That limitation was only removed by Poland's accession to the European Union.

Municipal finances

In the early 1990s, Kraków's local government grappled with budgetary instability generated by the issues of its target revenue structure, as well as with the list of tasks (i.e., the structure of expenditure) that was only being decided. The first budgets were very low (Figure 3.1). Nonetheless, they grew in the following years, even if the local governments continued to operate while facing the lack of stability in financing and the scope of the tasks to be conducted. That made long-term financial planning especially difficult.

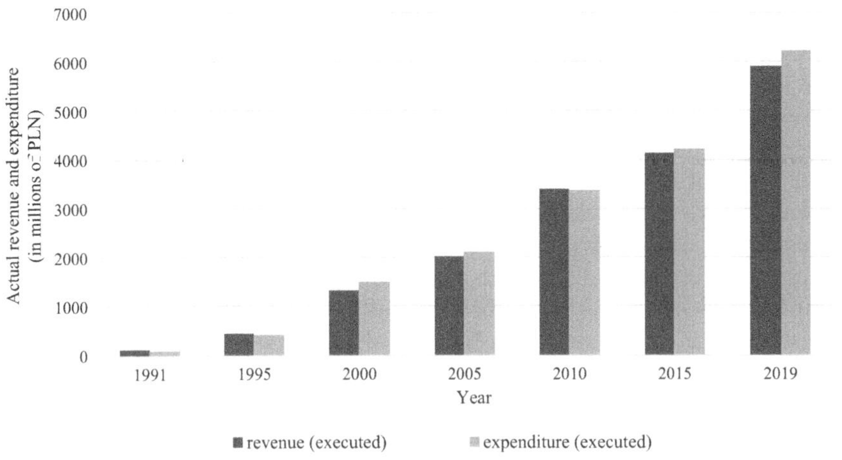

Figure 3.1 Revenue and expenditure from Kraków's municipal budget in 1991[1]–2019 (in millions of PLN).

1 In 1995 Poland underwent a currency reform (denomination). To keep the data from 1991 to 2019 comparable, recalculation of the values of both revenue and expenditure for 1991 accounts for the denomination conducted in 1995.

Source: Own study based on: Prezydent Miasta Krakowa, 1992, 1996, 2001, 2006, 2011, 2016, 2020.

Additionally, after 1999, the "commune revenue" dominated the budgetary structure as the "county part" only held a 20–25% share of the total in the general budget in 1999–2019. Thus, on the one hand, the reform that introduced counties added competences to the cities, but on the other, it weakened their financial potential (Wollmann and Lankina, 2003, p. 111).

In 1991–2019, the city's own revenue – which included local taxes and fees, revenue from property, and the share in personal and corporate income tax – accounted for 50–70% of the budget. Kraków only had a limited influence on defining tax levels due to the statutory limitations on local taxation. The local government could operate a policy of attracting investors and supporting the local economy, yet even that policy could not fully translate into increasing the share of income tax revenue. That resulted from the particulars of the tax redistribution system and the operation of compensation mechanisms that made the relatively wealthier units of local government give up some of their revenue in favour of the less wealthy ones. The purpose behind the mechanism was to equalise the level of wealth between such units on the national scale. The share of subsidies and grants in the area in question was at approximately 30%, growing incidentally to 50%; however, these were the funds whose value is defined by the generally applicable laws and not by the local policy of the local government. These are transfers mostly from the state budget, some of which are only allocated for specific tasks. Moreover, such flows were underestimated for the needs they were supposed to cover, a fact that was material in the comparison of the expenditure on education to the value of educational subsidy.

With time, the increasing level of revenue made it possible to increase the expenditure gradually. Its structure was nonetheless still dominated by current expenditure, which in 1991–2019 ranged from 73% to 85% of the total. Most of that accounted for obligatory tasks such as managing public schools, hence there was hardly any option to change their level, let alone reduce them, especially in the face of ever-growing expectations of the community concerning the standards and scope of the public services. The remaining expenditure (approximately 15–27%) was on property, including investments. It should be emphasised that what had a bearing on the increase of the budget, other than the rising revenue, was the gradual repayment of debt by the city and the acquisition of non-refundable external financing, accounting for 1–3% of the budget revenue. As for debt financing, Kraków's authorities made a strategically justified decision that the funds obtained in this way would only be used to speed up the implementation of the investment programme. Due to the significant delays in investments in the city, the accumulated debt was growing rapidly, and at the end of 2019, it amounted to PLN 3.07 billion. Eager to speed up the reduction in the civilisation backlog, the city authorities actually had no other option for action, given that there were no regulations to allow them to carry out public tasks successfully in the form of public–private partnerships for the most of the period in question (Sześciło and Kulesza, 2012, p. 487). The use of external returnable funds sped up the investment programme by two decades (Hołuj, 2015, p. 56).

A study of the condition of finances of the Municipality of Kraków in 1990–2019 highlights a number of key aspects that had an impact on the condition of the local budget. The first were the repeated changes in the scope of the tasks to be conducted and competences in the 1990s, which resulted from the central powers' experiments on the finances of large cities. The main problem in this case was the (at times dire) underfinancing of the entrusted tasks, which violated the constitutional principle of balance between the new tasks and the provision of additional sources of revenue. (*Konstytucja Rzeczpospolitej Polskiej*, 1997, art. 167). This can be illustrated by the disparity between the cost of carrying out the new tasks that Kraków took over from the central powers in 1993, which was estimated at PLN 93 million[1] and was also the amount contracted with the government, and the PLN 77.5 million it eventually received,[2] while in addition being forced to pay the debts of the units it took over, as their financial position was dramatic. In 1994, the municipality allocated the entire budgetary surplus from the previous year to that process (Hołuj, 2015, p. 41).

The next collapse of the system of commune financing came with the establishment of the city with county rights, that is, with the reform of 1999. Since that moment, the budget of Kraków has consisted of two parts: that of the commune and that of the county. An analysis of the proportions between them in the budget revenue and expenditure reveals that the tasks of the county are often financed from the surplus obtained from "commune" revenue, and that the "county" part accounts for a low share of the total (approximately 25%).

Creating conditions for social and economic development

The systemic transformation changed the roles and scope of intervention of the public authorities into the economy, shifting them from central planning to coordinated activities and the development of conditions for the operation of commercial entities (Jarosz, 2018, p. 689). The local government also had its input into this process, as it had already started to focus its activities on the development processes in the city from the first years of its operation. The goals of the development policies were initially contained in the plans of development spanning several years and were later included in every subsequent city development strategy. The first was adopted in 1999, and the following in 2005 and 2018. Actually, each defined the main courses of activity of government as the care for the quality of life in the city and the development of Kraków's metropolitan functions (as the centre of culture, science, and tourism). Moreover, the last two strategic documents additionally emphasised the significance of partnership in the governance of the city. The degree of achieving this last goal was presented more extensively in the chapter devoted to civil society in Kraków.

In the period in question, local authorities could make a direct impact on the development processes only to a limited extent. They focused on the development of conditions for the operation of economic entities and communities (implementation of the investment policy, together with promotion and image-building). Moreover, the channelling of the social and commercial activities in the space of the city (spatial policy) became an important role of the local government.

Promotional and image-building activities

In fact, in the early 1990s, Kraków's local government began to act as the host of the city and a promoter of its potential. With time, these activities were expanded, which resulted from a certain stabilisation in the functioning of the commune and also from the emergence of new options for promotion and image-building due to Kraków's opening to Europe after 2004. In carrying out their duty to create the city's brand, the municipality conducted multichannel activity, embarking on the search for investors, promotion of the tourist potential, supporting the research and academic functions of the city, and developing the Kraków brand, e.g., as a destination for congresses and other business tourism events.

Activities aligned with what is broadly understood as "city marketing" also encompassed the development of appropriate administrative structures.

The Investors and Innovative Economy Support Centre and Convention Bureau (one of only seven operating in Polish cities at the moment of its establishment) were launched. Programmes for the support of commercial activities by recommending businesses that guaranteed high-quality services were implemented. Such actions gained special significance when the quality of a specific commercial offer dropped dramatically due to external circumstances (e.g., when the legal obligation to pass the state examination for a tourist guide was removed in Poland in 2014).

Due to the limited direct impact on the commercial sectors of economy, the main task of the commune was to increase the recognition of the city, and the skilful highlighting of its varied potential. This became even harder, especially after joining the EU, as new threats have emerged alongside new options for development, for example, those related to the development of mass tourism. In the actions undertaken in the 2000s, the local government did not undertake any due diligence in choosing the subjects and methods of building messages about the city. The campaigns promoting Kraków as a tourist destination instrumentalised its most valuable resources. Heritage became a beautiful backdrop for entertainment tourism as the successive record number of visitors in the city became the yardstick of success. It was overlooked that the rapid development of tourism only generated income for a certain narrow group of people or entities, while the costs, that is the negative external effects that were generated, were borne by all the residents. In recent years, the priorities were reoriented as a result of a reflection connected to the observation of these negative phenomena. The focus is increasingly on the quality and not the quantity of visitors, and more sustainable forms of tourism are promoted, as well as those connected to the economic and cultural potential of the city, such as festival, business, and pilgrimage tourism. There is also a greater focus on research into tourist traffic. The consideration of the city's values and their promotion is run over longer time frames than just a single marketing campaign. The endeavours of the municipality to change the structure and purposes of the visitors to the city have become easier, thanks to the greater knowledge and awareness of the consequences of frequent record-breaking numbers but also thanks to the significantly improved range of offered infrastructure (ICE Kraków Congress Centre, Tauron Arena Kraków events and sports hall) and culture (culture festivals and development of cultural institutions) in the city.

Investment policy

Due to the low revenue and a range of legal, and organisational- and competence-related problems, the commune did not carry out major investments in the early 1990s, especially any of metropolitan significance. Activity was only limited to the implementation of the plans prepared before the breakthrough of 1989 (e.g., redevelopment of the new transport centre) and the completion of urgent investments that helped improve the quality of life in the city (these included the construction of the Kujawy Wastewater Treatment

Plant, construction of communication hubs, preparation for the construction of bridges, and the construction of the rapid tram). The structure of investment expenditure was dominated by the forms that assured improvement in the quality of public services provided as part of municipal management (approximately 50% of all the investment expenditure in 1994) and other basic services for the residents (e.g., education). It was only late in the 1990s that the local government embarked on the implementation of an investment programme that stepped beyond the endogenous functions, which coincided with the commune's adoption of the first development strategy (1999). The city quickly realised the necessity of implementing long-term investment programmes related to the need to connect development areas. Investments also began on the premises of institutions of culture, so important due to the significance of that metropolitan function. These included the adaptation of the former tram (light railway) depot in Kazimierz district for the Museum of Municipal Engineering, and refurbishment of the Ludowy Theatre, the Krzysztofory Mansion, and the Bunkier Sztuki Contemporary Art Gallery.

From the 2000s, the implementation of the investment plans accelerated, which was the result of the preparatory and design work conducted in the previous years, and also of the significant increase in the commune's revenue and the availability of the non-returnable investment financing from the European Funds. The city's investment budget amounted to approximately PLN 270 million in 2000; in 2005, it was under PLN 350 million; and in 2010 and 2015, it was on a similar level of PLN 560 and 580 million, respectively, before reaching PLN 845 million in 2019.

From 2000, the city has divided investment into a "programme" category, that is satisfying the needs of the residents, and a "strategic" category, that is related to the development of the metropolitan infrastructure. The largest share of the strategic investment budget was allocated to projects related to transport, followed by those covering municipal and sports infrastructure. The significant municipal investments into road and transport infrastructure include the construction of the successive stages of the Kraków rapid tram system, development of the key ring road and radial connections in the city and on the borders of Kraków with the neighbouring communes, and investments aimed at improving the quality of municipal transport. Moreover, a construction programme for underground and ground-level car parks was launched. As far as sports infrastructure is concerned, the city made a special investment into the organisation of UEFA Euro 2012 European Football Championship, with investments that covered the extension and modernisation of stadium infrastructure. In 2000–19, the city also conducted several further investments related to the development of the metropolitan potential of the centre, namely the construction of:

- the sports hall in Czyżyny
- the Kolna Sports and Recreation Complex with the whitewater canoeing slalom course

- the construction of the Cracovia 1906 Centennial Hall and Sports Center for the Disabled.

The largest municipal investments in cultural infrastructure conducted after 2000 have been:

- the development of a cultural centre in the Kazimierz district known as Kwartał św. Wawrzyńca (the Quarter of St Lawrence) being the extension of the investment related to the Museum of Municipal Engineering carried out back in the 1990s
- the establishment of the Museum of Contemporary Art in Kraków (MOCAK) and of the museum commemorating the place of the former Oskar Schindler's Factory on ul. Lipowa in Zabłocie district
- the modernisation and overhaul, with elements of conservation/under supervision of conservation officers, of the Krzysztofory Mansion being the headquarters of the Museum of Kraków that included its adjustment to the tasks of a modern multifunctional museum building, opening of a tourist route below the surface of the Main Market Square
- modernisation of the Home Army Museum
- adaptation of the workshops of the Mechanical Schools at os. Szkolne 25 for the purposes of the Łaźnia Nowa Theatre.

Another municipal investment of a metropolitan character was the construction of the ICE Kraków Congress Centre by the Rondo Grunwaldzkie roundabout.

Other investments improving the quality of life of the residents of Kraków certainly include those into the modernisation of healthcare, welfare and inpatient facilities, improvement of public security, increasing safety of road traffic, flood protection, construction and modernisation of local roads, construction of a system of cycle paths, modernisation of municipal transport infrastructure, protection and development of municipal green areas, and the construction and modernisation of educational facilities and of sports and recreation premises of local significance.

In the post-1990 period, the Municipality of Kraków conducted investments directly from the municipal budget and through the municipal utilities, and later also through public–private partnerships (which included the construction of a cemetery and an underground car park). This latter did not develop to its full potential as it has been stymied by the low quality of the legislation regulating it. The municipality only managed to complete the first public–private investment in 2005.

Due to the spatial span of the investments and their supralocal significance, the local authority prepared and carried out some investments in partnership with other public entities, notably the Government of the Małopolska Region, the General Directorate for National Roads and Motorways (GDDKiA) and the Polish State Railways (PKP). An example of such a task was the construction of elements of Kraków's ring road that crossed some communes around the city. Activities aimed at the acquisition of EU funds for the Integrated Territorial Investments mentioned above were made as part of the cooperation within the Kraków Metropolitan Association. They will result in the construction of the Fast Commuter Railway (SKA) and a system of Park & Ride car parks with integrated exchange hubs.

Spatial planning

The local authorities that were reactivated in 1990 took over the duties in the scope of spatial planning within the city, having at their disposal the local general zoning (spatial management) plan (*Miejscowy plan ogólny zagospodarowania przestrzennego*) that was drafted in 1988. With time, the process of adjusting its assumptions to the new social and economic conditions began. In 1994, the local general zoning plan (*Miejscowy plan ogólny*) was adopted on the grounds of the Act of 12 July 1984 on Spatial Planning. The new Act on Spatial Planning (from 7 July 1994) ruled that plans such as the one adopted in Kraków in 1994 would be obsolete after the end of 1999 (although their validity was later extended to the end of 2002). However, the work on updating the municipality's spatial planning policy was progressing so slowly that in 2003, when all the topical plans adopted before 1994 became null and void, the city only had less than 2% of its area covered by such plans (Figure 3.2). Moreover, work on approximately 70 such new plans was discontinued as it was pointless. The crisis in planning quickly generated rapid growth in the number of developments based on one-off administrative decisions (known as *warunki zabudowy*, literally "conditions for development") that failed to account for a broader planning context, which is required in the case of the decisions based on the local zoning plans (Figure 3.3). Altogether, in 2003–20, the municipality issued approximately 56,500 such "conditions for

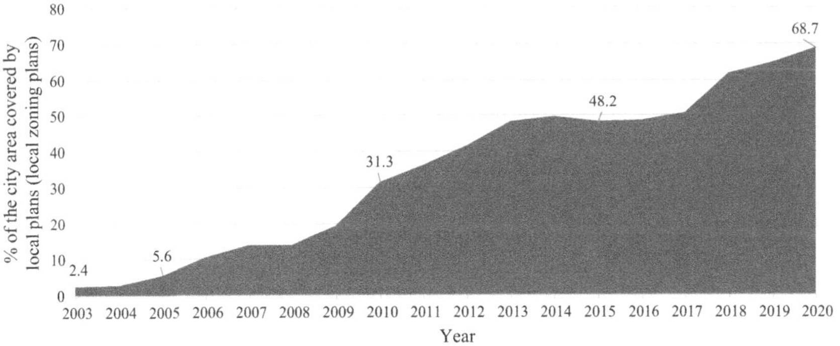

Figure 3.2 Area of the city covered by the local zoning plans in 2003–20 (in percentage).
Source: Own study based on Urząd Miasta Krakowa, 2004–21.

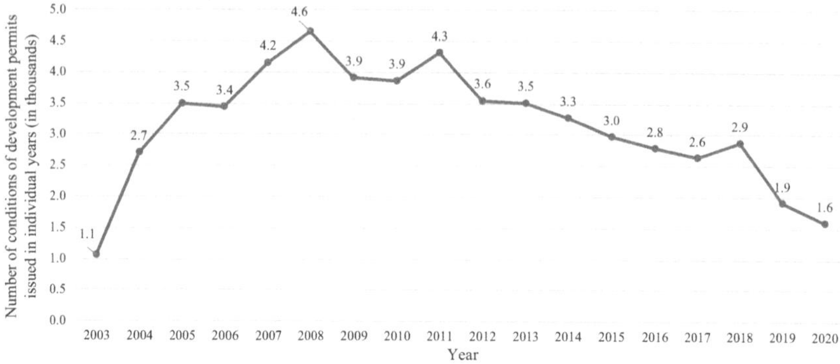

Figure 3.3 The number of "conditions of development" permits issued in 2003–20 (in 1000s).

Source: Own study based on Urząd Miasta Krakowa, 2004–21.

development" decisions whose legal construction did not guarantee the consistency of their provisions with the municipality's general spatial planning policy contained in the "Study of the Courses and Conditions of Spatial Management" (*Studium uwarunkowań i kierunków zagospodarowania przestrzennego*).

The weakness of the systemic solutions that the local government has at its disposal, as well as the reality of private property dominating in the city, resulted in a highly turbulent process of adopting the local zoning plans that was initiated after 2003. The conflicts were generated by the various, often opposing, interests that are especially visible in the most valuable areas of the city. Furthermore, the process proved to be highly time-consuming and loaded with uncertainty, as it was not certain whether a plan once adopted would perhaps be rendered invalid by an organ of state administration through a review of the legality of the decisions of the local law.

Several years after the crisis of 2003, the municipal government had only managed to adopt local zoning plans covering around 69% of the city. However, it must be noted that just the approval of a plan (oftentimes after many years of absence) did not guarantee the rational management of the space, as the area covered by the plan had, in many cases, already been affected by changes depreciating the functionality of the space, with a negative impact on the quality of life of its residents, and also resulting in the loss of real estate reserves designated earlier (before 2003) for significant public investments, due to the significant procedural delays. A broader treatment of the deficiencies of the municipal spatial planning policy as well as the issues related to the application of forms of landscape protection other than the local zoning plans are discussed in the chapter "Urban development of Kraków after 1989".

Summary

Poland was the first country of the former Eastern Bloc to ratify (in 1993) the European Charter of Local Self-Government of 1985, which declared the course of the changes that would take place in the system of division of power. Now, after 30 years of the functioning of such local self-government in major Polish cities, one can clearly see that none of the systemic reforms gave those municipal centres, Kraków included, any legal solutions that would guarantee complete fulfilment of the principles and standards defined in the Charter. Although in general terms Poland achieves very good results in the studies of systems of local self-government in European countries, as it is counted among the countries with the highest local autonomy (Ladner et al., 2019, p. 337), such studies treat all local governments as a homogeneous group without breaking them down into types and units. At that level of granularity, the problems of municipal communes became blurred, because as much as granting local government autonomy is one of the *sine qua non* conditions for the start of their activity that condition is far from being sufficient, especially in major centres. The two further factors are the development of civil participation, described in the chapter titled "Civil society. From 'Solidarity' to urban activism", and circumstances determining the efficiency of activity of the local authorities (Stewart and Greenwood, 1995).

Especially significant for the assessment of efficiency were the circumstances determining it independently of the local governments. In the history of the last three decades, one can find examples of external influence that depreciate and reduce efficiency, and those that increase it significantly, such as accession to the European Union (Swianiewicz, 2011, pp. 501–502), which not only opened up financial opportunities for the large cities, but first and foremost changed their strategic situation. For Kraków, a city of high potential for the development of tourist (and business) functions, the liberalisation of international traffic changed the city's strategic position. Facing these new circumstances, the local government assumed the role of promoter of the city's civil and economic resources, provider of infrastructure, and regulator of the conditions of operation and investment in the city. However, the local government did not avoid making mistakes, which resulted in the development of entertainment tourism, for example. A reflection concerning threats connected to the mass tourism has long been lacking. In this sense, Kraków became a peculiar victim of its own success. The local government did not act as the radical moderator of the freedom of the economy when it hurt both the historic and community resources of Kraków (e.g., causing the gentrification of its centre). Nonetheless, it must be noted that the city actually had limited options for taking actions towards focusing and improving the quality of activity of the commercial sector.

In pointing to the circumstances that have a destructive impact on the efficiency of local self-government in major Polish cities, one needs to recognise the low quality of legislation and its frequent changes (Regulska, 2009, p. 553) as it exacerbates the uncertainty of action and favours the creation of unclear administrative procedures potentially generating corruption, such as in the case of the decision on the forms and parameters of spatial management. Another circumstance is the long-term exploitation by the state of the development potential of large urban centres to reduce the problems that the central authorities encountered, including steps such as allocating inadequate revenues to local governments while entrusting them with new competences, which also increased the dependency of such governments on central sources of financing (Hughes, Sasse, and Gordon, 2001, p. 157; Hausner et al., 2013, p. 81). The development of centralism only highlighted the consequences of the phenomenon. In a way, Warsaw began to develop at the expense of other major cities not only by focusing authority on a single centre, but also by pulling development resources from other cities (the location of key offices and institutions made the capital the country's most attractive labour market). That also attracted investments to Warsaw, which meant removing the new tax and revenue base from other regions and cities.

Reduction of the role of major cities also meant ignoring the voices of their local government and failing to treat them as equal partners in the discussion on the creation of development strategies for the state and its key cities. Over time, this became increasingly burdensome due to the growing needs and specific problems of these centres and their metropolitan areas. Efficient mechanisms for reducing problems and the financial consequences of the coexistence of a major city like Kraków and the neighbouring communes forming a part of its functional area were missing. Following their own development policies, the local authorities of the communes in that area often carried them out for reasons contradictory to those that Kraków defined for itself. That became manifested in the lack of continuity of spatial planning on the scale of the metropolitan area, and in the transport dysfunction in the area of commuting. Currently, the most formalised form of cooperation is the association, whose actions are of a limited and focused rather than a strategic character. A permanent regulation of the status of metropolitan areas is missing, while the operation of lasting solutions adjusted to the specific functional and spatial structure in urbanised areas is one of the key challenges for contemporary decentralisation (Hausner et al., 2013, p. 81; Ros-Tonen, Pouw, and Bavinck, 2015, p. 98). Some 30 years into the process, the lack of completion and pathological subsidiarity are still problems (Illner, 2000, pp. 396–397) that have further intensified in recent years due to the anti-local government policy of the ruling party (Council of Europe, 2019). A good example is the programme intended for economic recovery after the COVID-19 pandemic, which was constructed to encumber the budgets of local governments and direct some of their revenue to the State Treasury. Kraków estimates the resulting losses at a level of approximately PLN 500 million a year.

Bibliography

Council of Europe (2019) *Local and regional democracy in Poland, 36th SESSION Report,* Committee on the Honouring of Obligations and Commitments by member States of the European Charter of Local Self-Government (Monitoring Committee), Strasbourg: The Congress of Local and Regional Authorities.

European Committee of the Regions. *Division of Powers – Poland.* Available at: https://portal.cor.europa.eu/divisionpowers/Pages/Poland.aspx (Accessed on: 25 February 2022).

Hausner, J. et al. (2013) *Narastające dysfunkcje, zasadnicze dylematy, konieczne działania. Raport o stanie samorządności terytorialnej w Polsce.* Kraków: Małopolska Szkoła Administracji Publicznej.

Hołuj, D. (2015) *Samorząd Krakowa wobec wyzwań metropolitalności.* Kraków: Wydawnictwo Uniwersytetu Ekonomicznego w Krakowie.

Hughes, J., Sasse, G., and Gordon, C. (2001) "Enlargement and Regionalization: The Europeanization of Local and Regional Governance in CEE States 145", [in:] Wallace, H. (ed.) *Interlocking Dimensions of European Integration.* Houndmills: Palgrave Macmillan, pp. 145–178.

Illner, M. (2000) "Issues of the Decentralization Reforms in Former Communist Countries", *Informationen zur Raumentwicklung*, 7/8, pp. 391–401.

Jarosz, A. (2018) "The Formation of Local Self-government during the System Transformation Period in Poland and the Former GDR: A Comparative Study", *Polish Political Science Yearbook*, 47(4). Available at: https://doi.org/10.15804/ppsy2018407 (Accessed on: 2 September 2021).

Kaczmarek, T., and Ryder, A. (2015) "Top-Down and Bottom-Up Metropolitan Integration in Poland", [in:] Buček, J., and Ryder, A. (eds.) *Governance in Transition.* Dordrecht: Springer. Available at: https://doi.org/10.1007/978–94–007–5503-1_2 (Accessed on: 14 September 2021).

Kukliński, A., and Swianiewicz, P. (1990) "Polskie województwo. Doświadczenia i perspektywy", [in:] Kukliński, A., and Swianiewicz, P. (eds.) *Polskie województwo. Doświadczenia i perspektywy.* Warszawa: Uniwersytet Warszawski, pp. 9–38.

Kulesza, M. (2008) *Budowanie samorządu. Wybór tekstów ze „Wspólnoty" 1990–2007.* Warszawa: Municipum.

Ladner, A. et al. (2019) *Patterns of Local Autonomy in Europe.* London: Palgrave Macmillan.

Levitas, A. (2018) "Local Government Reform as State Building: What the Polish Case Says about 'decentralisation'", *Zarządzanie Publiczne/Public Governance*, 3(45), Kraków: Uniwersytet Ekonomiczny w Krakowie, pp. 5–25.

Marcou, G., and Wollmann, H. (2009) "Europe", [in:] Marcou, G. (ed.) *Decentralization and Local Democracy in the World: First Global Report by United Cities and Local Governments,* Barcelona: World Bank and United Cities and Local Governments, pp. 127–165.

Misiąg, W. (2001) *Finanse publiczne w Polsce 1989–2001. Studium transformacji.* Warszawa: Instytut Badań nad Gospodarką Rynkową.

Prezydent Miasta Krakowa (1992) *Sprawozdanie z wykonania budżetu miasta Krakowa za rok 1991,* Kraków: Urząd Miasta Krakowa.

Prezydent Miasta Krakowa (1996) *Sprawozdanie z wykonania budżetu miasta Krakowa za rok 1995,* Kraków: Urząd Miasta Krakowa.

Prezydent Miasta Krakowa (2001) *Sprawozdanie z wykonania budżetu miasta Krakowa za rok 2000,* Kraków: Urząd Miasta Krakowa.

Prezydent Miasta Krakowa (2006) *Sprawozdanie z wykonania budżetu miasta Krakowa za rok 2005,* Kraków: Urząd Miasta Krakowa.

Prezydent Miasta Krakowa (2011) *Sprawozdanie z wykonania budżetu miasta Krakowa za rok 2010,* Kraków: Urząd Miasta Krakowa.

Prezydent Miasta Krakowa (2016) *Sprawozdanie z wykonania budżetu miasta Krakowa za rok 2015,* Kraków: Urząd Miasta Krakowa.

Prezydent Miasta Krakowa (2020) *Sprawozdanie z wykonania budżetu miasta Krakowa za rok 2019,* Kraków: Urząd Miasta Krakowa.
Regulska, J. (2009) "Governance or Self-Governance in Poland? Benefits and Threats 20 Years Later", *International Journal of Politics, Culture, and Society*, 22/537. Available at: https://doi.org/10.1007/s10767-009-9080-x (Accessed on: 14 September 2021).
Regulski, J. (2000) *Samorząd III Rzeczypospolitej. Koncepcje i realizacja.* Warszawa: Wydawnictwo Naukowe PWN.
Regulski, J., and Drozda, J. (2015) *Polish Experiences in Building Local Government and Democracy: A Useful Tool for Others?* Washington, DC: The World Bank, International Bank for Reconstruction and Development.
Ros-Tonen, M., Pouw, N., and Bavinck, M. (2005) "Governing beyond Cities: The Urban-Rural Interface", [in:] Gupta, J. et al. (eds.) *Geographies of Urban Governance Advanced Theories, Methods and Practices.* Cham: Springer, pp. 85–105.
Sakowicz, M. (2017) "Rebirth of Local Government in Poland: 25 Years of Decentralization Reform", [in:] Ruano, J., and Profiroiu, M. (eds.) *The Palgrave Handbook of Decentralisation in Europe.* Cham: Palgrave Macmillan, pp. 349–350.
Sejm Rzeczpospolitej Polskiej (1997), *Konstytucja Rzeczpospolitej Polskiej*, 2 April 1997 (*Journal of Laws* 1997 No. 78 item 483), art. 167, 171.
Stewart, J., and Greenwood, R. (1995) *The Purpose and Character of Local Government.* Birmingham: University of Birmingham.
Swianiewicz, P. (2003) "Reforming Local Government in Europe Closing the Gap between Democracy and Efficiency", [in:] Kersting, N., and Vetter, A. (eds.) *Reforming Local Government in Europe Closing the Gap between Democracy and Efficiency.* Wiesbaden: Springer Fachmedien, pp. 283–307.
Swianiewicz, P. (2011) "Poland: Europeanization of Subnational Governments", [in:] Hendriks, F., Lidström, A., and Loughlin, J. (eds.) *The Oxford Handbook of Local and Regional Democracy in Europe.* Oxford: Oxford University Press, pp. 480–504.
Sześciło, D., and Kulesza, M. (2012) "Local Government in Poland", [in:] Moreno, A.M. (ed.) *Local Government in the Member States of the European Union: A Comparative Legal Perspective.* Madrid: Instituto Nacional de Administración Pública, pp. 485–504.
The European Charter of Local Self-Government (1985) European Treaty Series, No. 122, Strasbourg.
Unia Metropolii Polskich (1991) *Memoriał w sprawie ratowania wielkich miast polskich.*
Urząd Miasta Krakowa (2004) *Raport o stanie miasta 2003.* Available at: https://www.bip.krakow.pl/?dok_id=2033 (Accessed on: 21 July 2021).
Urząd Miasta Krakowa (2005) *Raport o stanie miasta 2004.* Available at: https://www.bip.krakow.pl/?dok_id=2032 (Accessed on: 21 July 2021).
Urząd Miasta Krakowa (2006) *Raport o stanie miasta 2005, II. Zagospodarowanie przestrzenne.* Available at: https://www.bip.krakow.pl/zalaczniki/dokumenty/n/53774/0/karta (Accessed on: 21 July 2021).
Urząd Miasta Krakowa (2007) *Raport o stanie miasta 2006, II. Zagospodarowanie przestrzenne.* Available at: https://www.bip.krakow.pl/zalaczniki/dokumenty/n/56539/0/karta (Accessed on: 21 July 2021).
Urząd Miasta Krakowa (2008) *Raport o stanie miasta 2007, II. Zagospodarowanie przestrzenne.* Available at: https://www.bip.krakow.pl/zalaczniki/dokumenty/n/59688/0/karta (Accessed on: 21 July 2021).

Urząd Miasta Krakowa (2009) *Raport o stanie miasta 2008, II. Zagospodarowanie przestrzenne*. Available at: https://www.bip.krakow.pl/zalaczniki/dokumenty/n/65689/0/karta (Accessed on: 21 July 2021).
Urząd Miasta Krakowa (2010) *Raport o stanie miasta 2009, II. Zagospodarowanie przestrzenne*. Available at: https://www.bip.krakow.pl/zalaczniki/dokumenty/n/72768/0/karta (Accessed on: 21 July 2021).
Urząd Miasta Krakowa (2011) *Raport o stanie miasta 2010, II. Zagospodarowanie przestrzenne*. Available at: https://www.bip.krakow.pl/zalaczniki/dokumenty/n/81421/karta (Accessed on: 21 July 2021).
Urząd Miasta Krakowa (2012) *Raport o stanie miasta 2011, II. Zagospodarowanie przestrzenne*. Available at: https://www.bip.krakow.pl/zalaczniki/dokumenty/n/94033/karta (Accessed on: 21 July 2021).
Urząd Miasta Krakowa (2013) *Raport o stanie miasta 2012, II. Zagospodarowanie przestrzenne*. Available at: https://www.bip.krakow.pl/zalaczniki/dokumenty/n/108699/karta (Accessed on: 21 July 2021).
Urząd Miasta Krakowa (2014) *Raport o stanie miasta 2013, II. Zagospodarowanie przestrzenne*. Available at: https://www.bip.krakow.pl/zalaczniki/dokumenty/n/81421/karta (Accessed on: 21 July 2021).
Urząd Miasta Krakowa (2015) *Raport o stanie miasta 2014, II. Zagospodarowanie przestrzenne*. Available at: https://www.bip.krakow.pl/zalaczniki/dokumenty/n/166299/karta (Accessed on: 21 July 2021).
Urząd Miasta Krakowa (2016) *Raport o stanie miasta 2015, II. Zagospodarowanie przestrzenne*. Available at: https://www.bip.krakow.pl/zalaczniki/dokumenty/n/193058/karta (Accessed on: 21 July 2021).
Urząd Miasta Krakowa (2017) *Raport o stanie miasta 2016, II. Zagospodarowanie przestrzenne*. Available at: https://www.bip.krakow.pl/zalaczniki/dokumenty/n/219509/karta (Accessed on: 21 July 2021).
Urząd Miasta Krakowa (2018) *Raport o stanie miasta 2017*. Available at: https://www.bip.krakow.pl/zalaczniki/dokumenty/n/253681/karta (Accessed on: 21 July 2021).
Urząd Miasta Krakowa (2019) *Raport o stanie miasta 2018*. Available at: https://www.bip.krakow.pl/zalaczniki/dokumenty/n/253681/karta (Accessed on: 21 July 2021).
Urząd Miasta Krakowa (2020) *Raport o stanie miasta 2019*. Available at: https://www.bip.krakow.pl/zalaczniki/dokumenty/n/287199/karta (Accessed on: 21 July 2021).
Urząd Miasta Krakowa (2021) *Raport o stanie miasta 2020*. Available at: https://www.bip.krakow.pl/zalaczniki/dokumenty/n/318038/karta (Accessed on: 21 July 2021).
Wollmann, H., and Lankina, T. (2003) "Local Government in Poland and Hungary: From Post-Communist Reform towards EU Accession", [in:] Baldersheim, H., Iliner, M., and Wollmann, H. (eds.) *Local Democracy in Post-Communist Europe*. Wiesbaden: Springer, p. 91–122.

Notes

1 The amount accounts for the denomination of the Polish currency in 1995 and has been recalculated to provide comparable data throughout the analysed period.
2 The amount accounts for the denomination of the Polish currency in 1995 and has been recalculated to provide comparable data throughout the analysed period.

4 Kraków in the face of the transformation

The economic life of the city

Krzysztof Broński

The purpose of this chapter is to provide an outline of the issues related to the development of economy in Kraków during the systemic transition, i.e., after 1989. Due to the complexity of the subject and the varied state of research, it discusses selected elements from the portfolio of business activities in the city. The investigation concerns both traditional and modern sectors of the economy, specifically industry, construction, commerce, modern business services, and start-ups as catalysts of city development. Moreover, it features the institutions that support the development of entrepreneurship in Kraków. The research uses legacy data and is based on the new institutional economy approach.

Economic transformation in Poland

The functioning of the real socialism economy in Poland and many other countries of the world proved the utopian nature of that theoretical concept and its inconsistency with everyday life. After the communists lost the parliamentary elections in June 1989, Poland's first non-Communist government was formed in September 1989 and was led by Tadeusz Mazowiecki. His deputy prime minister and the minister of finance was Leszek Balcerowicz.

The political changes made possible a systemic transformation that also included the realm of the economy. The transformation started in the 1990s and brought a profound change in the rules of engagement: a transition from a centrally managed to a market economy. It embraced a holistic change in the general purposes and conditions of operation of all businesses.

Constitutional reforms, the reactivation of territorial governments and provision of instruments for the creation and simulation of development of territorial units, privatisation, and deregulation, all fundamentally changed the structure of the economy and set in motion the market mechanisms that had been liquidated under the Communist reign. In fact, both the economic and social structures inherited from Communism proved highly resistant to the introduced changes (Siwek, 2002, p. 49). It must also be emphasised that the initiation of the process of development at the time of transformation of the economy required changes in social standards, informal institutions,

DOI: 10.4324/9781003252757-5

and the links and connections between various forces, values, and pressure groups (Tridico, 2007, p. 96).

It was hard for the Polish economy to move towards more efficient developmental processes in 1989 as it was overwhelmed by the low efficiency inherited from many years of working as a centrally controlled economy. However, decisions concerning economic reforms could not be postponed. Leszek Balcerowicz believed that fast action, or "shock therapy", was necessary. A similar opinion on fast-progressing reforms was expressed by Bronisław Geremek, one of the most important politicians during the period of transition.

Speed was necessary to overcome the macroeconomic crisis in a country engulfed by hyperinflation. In 1990, the annual inflation rate came close to 250% (Kaliński, 2009, p. 52). Relying on the assistance of American economists Jeffrey Sachs and David Lipton, and the funds from the International Monetary Fund and the World Bank, Balcerowicz drafted and implemented a programme of reforms in 1989–91 (Piątkowski, 2019, p. 205). The reforms included liquidation of the remnants of the central system used for managing the economy, reactivation of territorial authorities and municipal ownership, conducting privatisation, tax reform, converting state enterprises into independent ones, the introduction of convertible currency, liberalisation of foreign trade, demobilisation, development of a real estate market, commercialisation of the banking and insurance sector, facilitation of the operation of foreign investments in the Polish market, and the introduction of social benefits for the unemployed (Kaliński, 2009, p. 36). The programme of reforms was critically assessed by some economists including Grzegorz Kołodko, a future minister of finance, and Tadeusz Kowalik (Rolski, 2013).

In the last days of December 1989, the Polish parliament adopted a number of laws that introduced a new economic order from 1 January 1990. The Polish reforms had the support of international financial institutions (Morawski, 2017, pp. 50–51). Thanks to them, hyperinflation was quickly curbed, the Polish zloty reached a realistic exchange rate and became internally convertible, the banking system was transformed, and the internal retail market was balanced. The first stage of introduction of the reforms brought a short-lived recession related to the transformation which was nonetheless painful for society. The direst phenomena included unemployment and growing poverty.

There were no native capitalists or capital after the end of the command and distribution economy endeavoured to attract foreign investors and the capital necessary for financing the investments and the introduction of new technology (Paprocki, 2017, p. 95).

The transition period was dominated by the necessary reconstruction of the institutions and restructuring of the economy, and the investment in innovation was insufficient and would not grow. It was only Poland's accession to the European Union in 2004 that helped to reverse this trend (Woodward, 2019, p. 95). To a certain extent, joining the EU crowned the 15 years of transformation and was evidence of the maturity of the market economy and of the attainment of European Community standards.

Kraków during the systemic transformation

Cities, especially metropolitan centres, were the lenses that focused on the problems of systemic transformation in Poland.

Kraków, currently the second most populous city of Poland, is a very good laboratory for analysing the economic change during the post-1989 systemic transformation. The reinstitution of self-government at the municipal level and the first post-war democratic elections held on 27 May 1990 opened a new chapter in the contemporary history of Kraków. These were the local authorities that created a new vision of Kraków and assumed responsibility for its implementation.[1] The new authorities "inherited" a city with inefficient raw-material-intensive heavy industry, outdated infrastructure, and anachronistic systems of management. The region's largest employer was the Lenin Steelworks (from 1990 known as the Tadeusz Sendzimir Steelworks), which employed approx. 38,500 people in 1980 and around 30,000 by the late 1980s. (*Monografia*, 1994, p. 37).

From the start of the transformation, it seemed obvious that development should exploit the heritage potential of the city as its natural capital, provide favourable conditions for business, and make Kraków recognised as the cultural capital of Poland. Emphasis was also laid on the need to build the image of the city as a location that would attract people who are looking for attractive employment or education opportunities. During discussions on the course of development of the city, slogans could be heard about building a modern knowledge-based economy, and a city with efficient governance-guaranteeing comfort of life for its citizens.

In 1991, Kraków covered an area of 327 km^2 and was inhabited by 750,540 people. In the last 30 years, its population has not grown significantly, and as of 2019, it had 779,100 permanent residents. It is important to note that each year it offers temporary accommodation to tens of thousands of people, mostly students.

From the start of transformation, Kraków was a magnet attracting foreign capital. Companies with foreign capital blossomed, encouraged by the law on companies with foreign shares that was adopted on 14 May 1991 and which liberalised the transfer of profits. That law was used in 1992 to incorporate the State Agency of Foreign Investment (PAIZ), which issued permits for incorporating companies with the participation of foreign capital. The number of such companies in Kraków grew markedly from 1991 and they represented various fields of the economy: from industrial production to construction, research and development, to services for tourists.

A profound change in the property law also took place in the Polish economy during the transformation. It was visible in the dynamic development of private sector businesses, a process that was much weaker in the public sector (Harańczyk, 1998, pp. 59–60). The process was also very visible in Kraków.

In 1991, there were 12,600 state-owned enterprises registered in the REGON system operating in Kraków, and 45,570 enterprises run by natural persons who were registered for tax purposes (Urząd Miasta Krakowa,

Gospodarka, 1992, p. 1). As of the end of 2020, there were 152,850 registered enterprises, of which as many as 147,410 operated in the private sector (Urząd Miasta Krakowa, 2021, p. 103). In 2020, most Kraków enterprises (some 27,780) were active in the commerce and repairs section, with professional, academic, and technical activity coming second with a far smaller number of entities (23,000), followed by construction with 13,600 entities. The total number of economic entities grew by 23% in the first decade of the 21st century, and in 2010–19, the number of businesses in Kraków grew by 27% (Table 4.1).

State-owned companies, private legal persons, labour cooperatives, and private businesses were operating in Kraków early in the 1990s.

There was a significant increase in the number of businesses in Kraków in 2005–20, with the largest rise in the group of microenterprises (employing 9 or fewer persons), while the number of large enterprises (employing over 250 people) was falling. Microenterprises accounted for between 94.8% and 96.6% of the total number of businesses, while the share of large enterprises (employing over 250 people) ranged from 0.2% to 0.1% (Table 4.2).

In 2020, Kraków's economy was dominated by companies run by natural persons (95,820), which accounted for 62.7% of all businesses. The remaining 37.3% were legal persons and organisational units with no legal personality,

Table 4.1 Business entities in Kraków by ownership, 1991–2019

Sectors	*Year*							
	1991	*1994*	*1997*	*2000*	*2005*	*2010*	*2015*	*2019*
Total, including:	29,963	60,707	74,707	91,790	104,292	115,687	130,233[a]	146,919[a]
Public sector	951	1,161	1,115	1,225	1,967	1,472	1,434	1,374
Private sector	29,012	59,546	73,592	90,565	102,325	114,215	126,562	141,925

Source: Urząd Miasta Krakowa, 1992, 1994, 1997, 2000, 2006, 2011, 2016, 2020.

a Broken down into sectors by ownership, without entities that do not provide information about the form of their ownership in the REGON register.

Table 4.2 Legal status of entities running business in Kraków in 2005–20

Legal status of the entities	*Year*			
	2005	*2010*	*2015*	*2020*
Total, including:	104,292	115,687	130,233	152,837
State-owned enterprises	10	10	8	7
Cooperatives	411	404	418	236
Companies and commercial law partnerships, including:	10,047	14,447	23,859	31,325
Joint-stock companies	437	495	593	556
Natural persons	n.d.	79,368	82,027	95,822

Source: Urząd Miasta Krakowa, 2006, 2011, 2016, 2021.

which included 31,300 commercial companies that accounted for 20.5% of the total number of business entities. Of the total number of commercial companies, limited liability companies accounted for 81.1% of the total, joint-stock companies – for 1.8%, and companies with foreign capital – 16.3%. Changes in employment in the enterprise sector also took place at the time of transformation. In 1996, employment was highest in the production sector, followed by construction, and then trade and repairs. Two decades later, in 2019, employment was highest in businesses operating in trade and repair of motor vehicles, followed by industrial processing.

In 1993, the act on National Investment Funds was adopted, and was followed three years later by the act on the commercialisation and privatisation of state enterprises. Those acts provided the foundation for embarking on the path of privatisation. Capital privatisation meant the transformation of the largest and best functioning state enterprises into companies owned solely by the Treasury of the State, and the shares in these independent companies later became the subject of public tenders and bids. Moreover, companies owned solely by the Treasury of the State were also included in the process of mass privatisation through the National Investment Funds. Small- and medium-sized enterprises, as well as those in difficult economic situations, could take advantage of the liquidation path, which allowed the sale of state property, its apport into companies, and leasing for profit (Kaliński, 2017, pp. 92–93). The privatisation of businesses as well as the insolvency of many businesses resulted in a fall in employment in Kraków, but since 2005, a continuous rise in the number of jobs has been observed. Compared with 2005, by 2018, the number of employed had grown by approximately 43% (Figure 4.1).

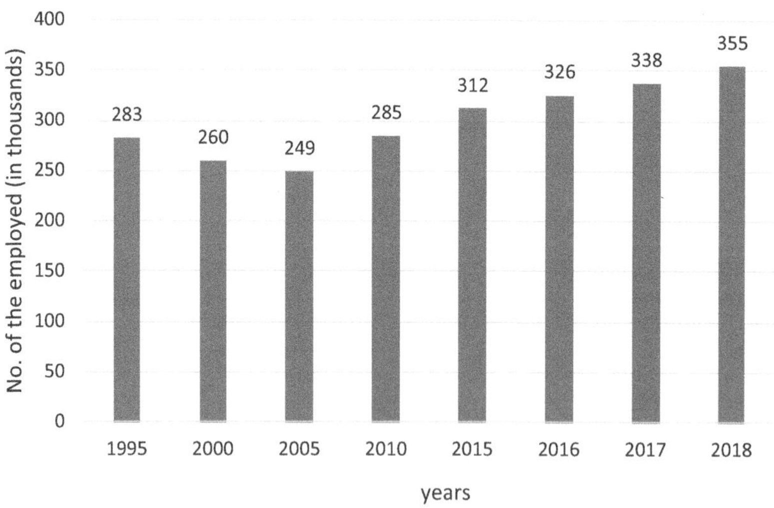

Figure 4.1 Employment in Kraków in 1995–2018.
Source: Urząd Statystyczny w Krakowie, 2005, 2013, 2017, 2019.

Early in the 1990s, Kraków's environment was highly polluted. While reducing production in businesses heavily dependent on raw materials, it was only the installation of infrastructure helping to save the environment that resulted in a significant reduction of particulate matter and gaseous pollutions. Emissions of particulate pollution over the last 30 years were reduced by a factor of over 60, and of gaseous emissions – by a factor of over 20.

The economic transformation was accompanied by unemployment, a phenomenon caused by overemployment by businesses during the time of a centrally controlled economy. The introduction of a free-market economy required the optimisation of employment. In 1991, the unemployment rate in Kraków was around 6%, then, in 1992, it rose to 9%, and followed a falling trend in 1992–2019, although the COVID-19 pandemic in 2020 caused the unemployment rate to grow (Figure 4.2).

Kraków's trade sector played an important role in the employment in the past decade of the 20th century. In the 1990s, its ownership structure saw profound changes that resulted in almost complete privatisation. There were 33,800 entities – both natural persons and civil partnerships – running trading business in Kraków in 1999, which accounted for approximately 39.5% of all the entities listed in the business activity register (Urząd Miasta Krakowa, 2000).

The effects of the globalisation of trade were experienced on top of the transformation process. After 1990, Kraków was subjected to major development pressure from the expansion of large-format shops (Hołuj, 2015, p. 73). The HIT Hipermarket opened in Kraków in 1996, and the Park Handlowy Zakopianka shopping centre replaced the demolished Solvay industrial plant in 1998. In 2010, the total supply of modern commercial spaces with gross leasing area of over 5,000 m^2 in Kraków amounted to 461,670 m^2. In

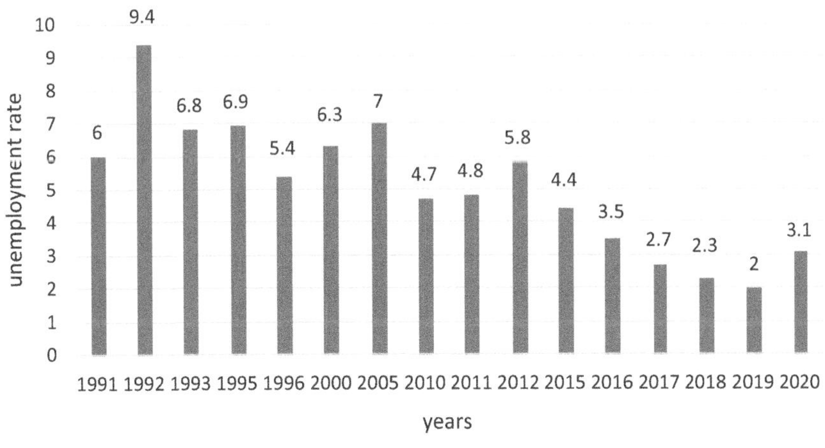

Figure 4.2 Unemployment rate in Kraków in 1991–2020.

Source: Urząd Miasta Krakowa 1992, 1996, 2000, 2006, 2011–13, 2016–19, 2021.

2018, modern shopping premises in Kraków and its vicinity already covered 615,000 m² (*Krakowski Rynek Nieruchomości*, 2019, p. 17).

Traditional branches of industry were also subjected to restructuring and modernisation.

Late in 1990, the management of the Sendzimir Steelworks (HTS) presented the concept for reorganising it into a holding company (*Monografia*, 1994, p. 61). The modernisation and restructuring of Kraków's largest industrial facility resulted in major reductions in employment. While there were still around 30,000 people working in the steelworks in the late 1980s, the number had dropped to 17,400 in 1996, and in 2002, it stood at just 8,700. Production, and consequently employment, continued to decrease in the following years, and its ownership changed. In 2002, HTS became part of the Polskie Huty Stali SA (PHS) holding. In 2000, the shares of PHS were purchased by a foreign investor, LNM Holdings NV, and the Sendzimir Steelworks started operation as part of Ispat Polska Stal company. In the following year, the company transformed into Mittal Steel Poland SA. Thanks to the privatisation conducted in 1997–2004, the steelworks emerged from the slump and avoided the threat of bankruptcy. In 2018, it employed around 3,500 people. However, in 2020, the last blast furnace and the steel plant part of the works was closed down.

The tobacco producer Zakłady Przemysłu Tytoniowego (ZPT) was transformed into a joint-stock company of the State Treasury in 1994, and two years later, Philip Morris signed a contract with the Polish Ministry of Ownership Transformations regarding its privatisation. Philip Morris assumed 33% of the company's shares for a payment of $227 million, undertaking to make further investments into upgrading of the factory. The modernisation of the company, which at the time was Poland's largest cigarette producer (accounting for 31% of the market), began in the same year. In 1998, the enterprise changed its name to Philip Morris Polska SA, and in 2003, it opened a modern production centre in Czyżyny. The value of the whole investment, comprising the purchase of ZPT shares and modernisation of the plant, had exceeded $500 million by 2005. It was the largest foreign capital investment in Kraków in the 1990s.

The Polfa pharmaceutical production plant was transformed into a company owned solely by the State Treasury in 1994, and then underwent privatisation in 1997. Its strategic partner was Pliva, a Croatian company that invested over $200 million into Polfa. At the time, the plant manufactured more than 60 types of pharmaceuticals and employed over 1,200 people. In 1996–98, a modern production division was built and since 2008, the company has been owned by the Israeli Teva Group.

Krakowska Fabryka Kabli, a manufacturer of cables, was transformed into a company with shares held by the State Treasury in 1994, and a year later – into a joint-stock company. In 1997, KGHM Polska Miedź SA became a strategic investor, and in 1999, a majority share was purchased by Zakłady Kablowe Tele-Fonika s.c., which was based in nearby Myślenice. In 2000,

Zakład Maszyn Kablowych spółka z o.o. was spun off, while the assumption of the majority of the shares in Elektrim Kable SA by Tele-Fonika KFK SA in 2003 resulted in the creation of a new entity. The TELE-FONIKA Kable SA group, which is fully owned by Polish capital, is spearheading the global cable sector as it is a leading European manufacturer of cables and wires with great potential for development.

Kraków is home to the central offices of a number of major industrial companies. The largest includes CANPACK SA, one of the world's leading producers of packaging that has operations in 19 countries of Europe and South America, southern Asia, the Middle East, and Africa.

The shift from a centrally managed to a market economy resulted in the return of the ground rent mechanism, which led in turn to the deglomeration of numerous industrial plants situated in or near the central districts of towns and cities and their transfer to the outskirts or outside the city limits. The economic transformation contributed to the reduction or discontinuation of operations for some industrial facilities in Kraków, as well as to the privatisation and restructuring of businesses. Employment was reduced and production moved from central locations to the peripheries of Kraków or outside the city. This freed up land in favourable locations that was subsequently taken over by developers for the construction of residential, office, and service spaces.

Zakłady Cukiernicze Wawel was an established Kraków confectionery company. In 1992, its management decided to transform the enterprise into an employee-owned company and its shares have been publicly traded since 1998. In 2006, the production facilities of Wawel SA, previously operating in four locations in the city, were moved to a single modern production plant that was built in nearby Dobczyce, while the headquarters of the company remained in Kraków. The land was sold to a developer who built residential estates there.

Another large Kraków industrial plant was the Zakłady Budowy Maszyn i Aparatury im. Ludwika Zieleniewskiego (Zieleniewski), a machine manufacturer with origins that reach back to the 19th century. In 1996, the Kraków-based Wolfram company purchased the foundry from Zieleniewski and in 2000, NFI PIAST SA sold a strategic package of Zieleniewski's shares to Wolfram. In 2008, Zieleniewski SA transferred production from Kraków to nearby Niepołomice, while the seat of the company's board remained in Kraków. The former premises of "Zieleniewski" were taken over by residential developments.

In 1996, units of territorial governments were granted the right to conduct business activity as companies under commercial law and to entrust tasks to legal and natural persons (Kaliński, 2017, p. 101). In 1996, the utilities owned by the Municipality of Kraków set up a tax capital group. The agreement between them remained in force until the end of 1999 and was later extended twice to 2020. The dominant company of the tax group is Krakowski Holding Komunalny SA, and its subsidiaries are the Miejskie Przedsiębiorstwo

Energetyki Cieplnej SA (providing heat), Miejskie Przedsiębiorstwo Komunikacyjne SA (ensuring public transport), and Miejskie Przedsiębiorstwo Wodociągów i Kanalizacji SA (water and wastewater).

One of Kraków's advantages for the development of business is its favourable position on the crossroads of major transport routes, close to the conurbation of Silesia and the southern border of Poland. The accessibility of the city is reinforced by the currently ongoing infrastructure investments. With the accession of Poland to the European Union, the whole country was included into the common aviation area and Kraków, as the capital of the Małopolska Region gained a variety of new air connections. In 2019, Kraków–Balice Airport had a network that consisted of over 140 regular connections to four continents (Europe, Asia, North America, and Africa) offered by 24 carriers. The volume of passenger traffic in Balice has grown each year: in the first year, after Poland's accession to the EU and the launch of operations by the low-cost airlines, over 1.5 million passengers were served, and this number had grown to 8 million by 2019.

Easy access, the developing office and telecommunications infrastructure, highly qualified staff, and competitive labour costs are factors decisive for the attractiveness of the city to business. Moreover, Kraków boasts a "particular humanist climate that favours not only hard work but also personal development, a fact appreciated by foreign and also national decision-makers" (Romanowski and Walkowiak-Markiewicz, 2015, p. 84).

Liberalisation of the banking law in post-1989 Poland resulted in a rapid increase in the number of new banks. Twelve were incorporated in 1989, with as many as 40 more following in 1990 (Morawski, 2017, p. 165). Three banks opened in Kraków in 1990–91: Krakowski Bank Mieszkaniowy, Bank Współpracy Regionalnej, and Bank Staropolski. They used state and private capital, as well as the funds of the commune. The largest bank was Bank Przemysłowo-Handlowy (BPH), which was incorporated as a joint-stock company when it was spun off from the structures of the National Polish Bank (NBP) in 1989. In 1995, BPH was privatised.[2] Midway through the 1990s, seven banks operating in Kraków had their headquarters here – including Bank Spółdzielczy Rzemiosła, Krakowski Bank Spółdzielczy, Bank Przemysłowo-Handlowy SA, Bank Współpracy Regionalnej SA – and a further 24 Polish and foreign banks had branches and regional offices here. Bank Współpracy Regionalnej was taken over by Deutsche Bank 24 SA (Komański, 1998, pp. 76–77). Over the following decades, the banking sector changed, and with the progression of Warsaw-centrism, Kraków lost its position as the place where banks had their headquarters. Currently (2020) there are only two minor banks that have their central offices in the city – Bank Spółdzielczy Rzemiosła w Krakowie and Krakowski Bank Spółdzielczy – although there are also branches, partner offices, and numerous financial clearing centres of Polish and foreign banks operating here.

The cities of the early 1990s suffered from a severe deficit of housing, so the emergence of the developer as an institution was recognised as being as important as private enterprise was in other segments of economics. In Kraków, the first residential units for sale were built in the mid-1990s, yet it took until 1998 for developer-led construction to stabilise. In 2013–18, developers delivered a total of 47,400 dwellings in Kraków, which accounted for 93% of the total built in the city (Strzeszyński, Krochmal, and Wójciak, 2019, p. 1). From 2008, aside from the small number of dwellings built for individual needs, developer construction was the only source of supply to the city's residential housing stock. Developer activity also had an increasing impact on the city's economy. The operation of developer companies not only thoroughly changed the picture of the residential market in Kraków, but was also material for the development of the city's residential resources. In the mid-1990s, these amounted to approximately 243,400 dwellings, a number that had grown to 389,200 by 2018.

Kraków after Poland's accession to the European Union

A breakthrough in the development of the city came with Poland's accession to the European Union. EU membership must be treated as a civilisational and developmental leap and reinforcement of the institutional foundations of the economy, state, and civil society, whose construction began with the systemic transformation in the late 1980s and early 1990s. The fundamental benefit that all Polish cities – Kraków included – have drawn from the EU are the EU funds that are used for investment projects in road building, public transport, municipal economy, as well as projects in education, welfare, culture, tourism, and social integration. The 15 years that have passed since accession have seen Kraków receive grants of nearly PLN 4.8 billion, with its own contribution totalling over PLN 3.9 billion.

The modern economy sector in Kraków

From the start of the transformation, Kraków has held a high position in the IT services sector in Poland. The first IT companies developed here as early as the mid-1980s. In 1993, a private IT company was incorporated under the name of Comarch. Its dynamic development resulted in the development of the Comarch Capital Group that by 2019 boasted 56 companies operating globally, and employing several thousand highly qualified professionals (programmers, IT engineers, and economists) in 90 offices situated in 34 countries, and with projects in over 60 countries on 6 continents. The strategic direction of the Comarch Group's development include advanced IT solutions.

In 1998, Motorola set up its R&D Software centre in Kraków. As one of Motorola Solutions' main technology centres, it is responsible for software development for a broad range of products and services that Motorola delivers to customers around the world. The Central European location makes it possible for Polish experts to provide technical support to clients from Europe, the Middle East, and Africa.

The IBM Software Lab launched in Kraków in 2005, joining the network of 40 research and development centres that the American corporation operates all around the world. The Kraków centre is IBM's only such facility in Central and Eastern Europe.

The city is a vibrant academic centre, delivering highly educated employees to many sectors of the modern economy. The number of institutions of higher education and students, as well as the variety of the courses taught, are important gauges of academic potential. In Kraków, this consists of 10 public and 13 non-public institutions of higher education, as well as the faculty and students. In 2019, there were nearly 130,000 students enrolled in bachelors, masters, postgraduate, doctoral, and extra-mural studies, which included Poland's largest group of science and IT students.

Numerous research and development centres catering to the modern industries, the completed investments, and the highly skilled workforce are all advantages that lead to Kraków being perceived as an appropriate place for investment and business activity. The city's development strategy favours the orchestration of cooperation of a broad spectrum of businesses, institutions, and groups around local initiatives in support of investment.

These strengths have made Kraków an attractive place for investors who have opened their business service centres in the city (Kopyciński, 2021). Businesses from this sector began to operate in Kraków back in the 1990s, initially as research and development centres. The R&D centres operating here belong both to commercial businesses and academia. Their purpose is to provide technological and scientific support for specific sectors and specialisations, and to develop new products and services that make use of the research. The various R&D centres operating in Kraków in 2019 included the Aptiv Technical Centre, IBM Software Solutions Laboratory, Google Research & Development Centre, Sabre Global Capability Center, the research and development centre of Deltavista Group, FQS Poland – the research and development centre of Fujitsu Kyushu Systems Limited (FJQS), and the Selvita Research Centre that focused on drug research (Urząd Miasta Krakowa, 2020, pp. 149–150).

One of most important institutions of this type operating in Kraków is the Aptiv Technical Centre, which has been a leading hub of research and development for the automotive sector since 2000.[3] Its engineers' creations include the first motion control system for the automotive sector, and active safety technologies for vehicular traffic that are changing the face of the global motoring sector.

The intensification of competition has become a significant feature of the contemporary economy. The relationships between businesses, countries, and regions are significantly influenced by two phenomena: outsourcing and offshoring. Kraków is not only Poland's largest outsourcing services centre but is also a Central and Eastern European leader and a significant international player. The operations of businesses in this sector concentrate on finance and accounting, HR and payroll, customer care, and supply chain management services, as well as IT support and software development (Jamry, 2019, p. 67). In 1996, Capgemini opened one of the first outsourcing centres in the city that employs over 3,000 people. In 2012, there were more than 25,000 people working in the business services sector in Kraków, both in business process outsourcing (BPO) and shared services centres (SSC), which accounted for 23% of the total employment in the BPO/SSC sector in Poland. Since 2013, Kraków has appeared in the top 10 of the prestigious Tholons Top 100 Outsourcing Destinations ranking,[4] which assesses regions' attractiveness for investment into business services. In 2018, Kraków ranked 6th among the world's 100 best outsourcing destinations.

In 2016, employment in the modern business services sector in Kraków amounted to 50,300 people (ABSL, 2016, p. 12). At the time, the corresponding numbers for Warsaw and Wrocław were 36,700 and 34,200 people, respectively. This means that nearly every fourth person employed in the modern business services centres in Poland was employed in the capital of the Małopolska Region. There were 234 business services centres in Kraków in the first quarter of 2020, which, in Poland, put the city into second place behind Warsaw, which had 279 such centres. Other Polish cities with between 100 and 200 centres included Wrocław (188), the Tri-city of Gdańsk, Gdynia, and Sopot (158), Poznań (113), and Katowice and its metropolitan area (110) (ABSL, 2020, p. 22). In the same quarter, Kraków was Poland's leader in the volume of employment in the business services sector, boasting total employment of 77,700 people (23% share in the total employment in the sector), compared with 64,000 in Warsaw, and 52,000 in Wrocław (ABSL, 2020, p. 56). Most of those people employed in Kraków worked in SSC/GBS centres (Figure 4.3).

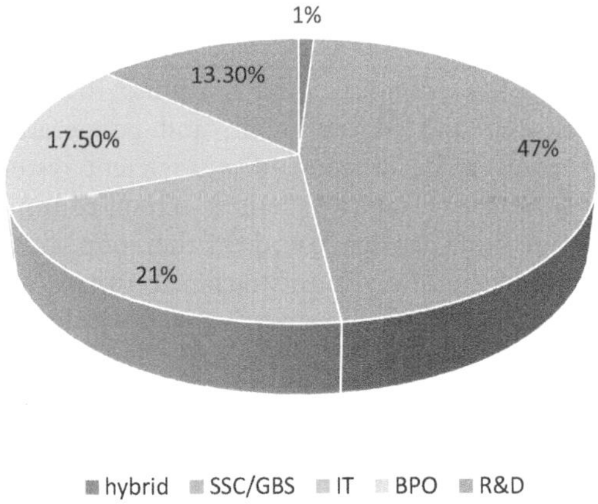

Figure 4.3 The structure of employment in business service centres in Kraków in 2020.

Source: ABSL, (2020) *Sektor nowoczesnych usług biznesowych w Polsce*. Warszawa: ABSL, p. 43.

When appropriate multipliers are taken into account, the modern business services sector generates at least 100,000 jobs in Kraków. The city is Poland's first in terms of the numbers of highly skilled staff. In the first quarter of 2020, there were 41 centres employing 500 or more people, with the workforce in 22 centres exceeding 1,000 people. In Kraków, 47% of the people employed in the business services sector were operating in the SSC/GBS sector, 21% worked in IT, 17.5% in the BPO, 13.3% in R&D, and only 1% operated in the hybrid model (ABSL, 2020, p. 43). It is worth emphasising that the graduates of Kraków's higher education institutions account for a significant share of the employees of the modern business services sector, notably modern technologies and the R&D subsector. The level of advancement of the services provided by these people is often on a par with that in their parent companies in Western Europe and the United States. The city is increasingly frequently considered a mature labour market where the skills and quality (and not the cost) of services provide the main competitive advantages (Grycuk, 2017, p. 149).

Other than generating new jobs, the development of the business services sector increases the dynamism of other services sectors, as both cater to the corporations and their personnel (Borkowska, 2018, p. 56) . The development of the business and IT services outsourcing sector also has a significant positive impact on the economy of Kraków in terms of ecology, as it reduces the negative pressure on the natural environment that, as a rule, accompanies economic development. The IT/BTO services are predominantly related to the use of modern IT and communication technologies, which has a relatively low negative impact on the environment. The IT services sector owes its development to both external impulses and local entrepreneurship (Micek et al., 2017, p. 18).

Business environment institutions

Building the innovative quality of the economy calls for more than just supporting entrepreneurship, research and development, and cooperation between sectors – it primarily requires the creation of an efficient system covering all the entities that contribute, even to the smallest extent, to innovation development. The system of innovation is based on the cooperation of entities representing three partners: public administration, business, and academia (Mazur, 2015, p. 3). Kraków has become a perfect platform for the cooperation of science, business, and territorial government. The support delivered to entrepreneurs by local authorities is increasing, and is offered in the form of funding or promotion, the promotion of the city's scientific and academic potential, the building of a platform for cooperation, calls for grant proposals, real estate tax relief, etc.

Next to Warsaw, Kraków is Poland's most important office market and a good European location for investment by the modern business services sector. Late in 2013, the total availability of modern office space in Kraków was estimated to exceed 547,500 m^2, which made the city the second largest office market (after Warsaw) in Poland. In 2017, the total supply of office space in Kraków exceeded 1,000,000 m^2, and grew to approximately 1,420,000 m^2 by 2019. In 2020, the cumulated business volume of business space for rent exceeded 1,550,000 m^2. Such growth results from a strong demand for office space, represented mostly by the modern business services sector.

Kraków's advantage is its high potential stemming from the graduates of numerous courses related to the creative sectors. In the future, the city could achieve a high ranking in this area, both in Poland and internationally. All it needs to do is to build and retain efficient channels for transferring human capital between knowledge centres and innovation hubs (primarily business, which translates competences into specific implementations). The process is supported by technology transfer centres, an organisationally varied group of not-for-profit consulting, training, and information units that run programmes that support technology transfer and commercialisation. In 2019, the list of such centres operating in Kraków included the Centre for Integrated Systems Development of the Jagiellonian University, the Technology Transfer Centre of the Kraków University of Technology, the Technology Transfer Centre of the AGH University of Science and Technology in Kraków, the Technology Transfer Centre of the University of Agriculture in Kraków, the Medical Technology Transfer Centre Technology Park, and the Małopolska Technology Transfer Centre – the Progress and Business Foundation (Urząd Miasta Krakowa, 2020, p. 150).

Entrepreneurship incubators are a particular form of support for the process of incorporating and developing businesses. There are different institutions of the type operating in Kraków. Their number includes the Nowa Huta Entrepreneurship Incubator, the Academic Entrepreneurship Incubator, the Academic Entrepreneurship Incubator of the John Paul II Pontifical University in Kraków, and the Jagiellonian Centre of Innovation – Academic Entrepreneurship Incubator. Moreover, Kraków Technology Park (KPT) also operates a technology incubator.

In turn, the technology parks offer support related to commercial workspace that is designed to attract investors (Rutkowska-Gurak, 2011). The Kraków Technology Park is an institution that has been operating in the business environment since 1997, when it was incorporated by the initiators of the Kraków Special Economic Zone, namely the Municipality of Kraków, the Jagiellonian University, the Kraków University of Technology, the AGH University of Science and Technology, the Tadeusz Sendzimir Steelworks and the State Treasury. As long as the special economic zones operate in Poland, that is until 2026, KPT will be the managing company for the special economic zone that has been known as the Polish Investment Zone since 2018. The KPT supports the establishment and development of innovative businesses from the high tech sector and the optimisation of the conditions for technology transfer and commercialisation. The services offered by KPT include access to basic infrastructure (offices, conference rooms, technology incubator services) as well as to specialist infrastructure, organisation of events, financial services, consultancy, training, market research, and the promotion and popularisation of new technologies. Its current and former clients comprise both enterprises operating in the sector of traditional industry and businesses connected to technology innovations in various sectors. The activity of KPT is a very good example of how cooperation between the public administration, academia, and business, that is channelled towards the support of innovation, builds favourable conditions for the economic development of the city. Another institution supporting the business environment is the Centre for Supporting Investors and Innovative Economy which operates as part of the Municipal Department for Entrepreneurship and Innovation. Set up in 2006 as the Centre for Investor Services and Economic Promotion, it changed its name to the Investor Care Centre in 2011, and has operated under the current name since 2018. It offers substantive support for Polish and foreign investors, for example, by organising meetings with investors that include presentations of the city's business environment, as well as organising meetings with HR companies, real estate agencies, and institutions of higher education.

Worth including in the list of institutions supporting the development of entrepreneurship in Kraków is the Chamber of Commerce and Industry, which was reactivated in 1989 on the power of the Act of 30 May 1989 on economic self-government.

A variety of clusters also operate in Kraków. A cluster is a geographic concentration of interrelated entities (entities operating in related sectors, business environment institutions, public institutions, non-governmental organisations, and research and academic units) that at the same time cooperate and compete with one another.[5] They are organised to encourage member companies and institutions to develop their potential through synergy effects. Cluster initiatives are financed partly from public funds, through cluster development support programmes. Kraków is currently home to a dozen clusters operating in new technologies, the creative industries, and life science (Urząd Miasta Krakowa, 2021, p. 133).

The meetings industry in Kraków

Kraków is an important hub for the meetings industry in Poland, and thousands of congresses and conferences are held here every year. The number of events in 2008 amounted to 2,700, in 2016 to 3,500, and in 2019 to as many as 8,400. In 2017, the meetings industry generated 3.38% of the city's GDP and provided nearly 19,000 jobs (Borodako et al., 2018, pp. 5–6).

For Kraków, tourism also has an important economic function. The tourist sector is estimated to provide 29,000 permanent jobs in the city, a number that exceeds 40,000 when the appropriate multipliers are applied. It should be emphasised that tourism is more than just an important source of revenue as it is also a social phenomenon that builds the city's identity. The number

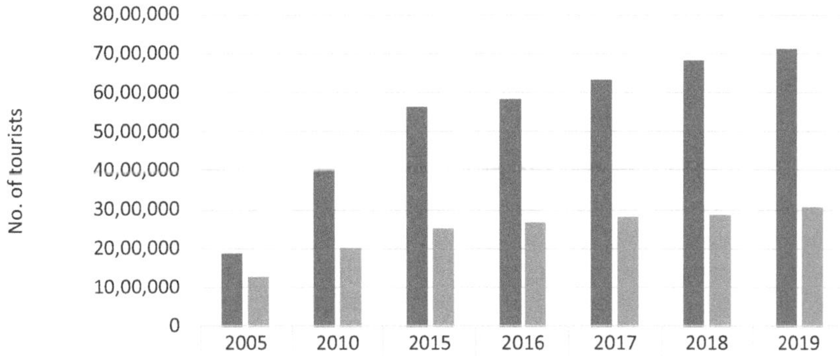

	2005	2010	2015	2016	2017	2018	2019
domestic tourists	1,850,000	4,050,000	5,630,000	5,850,000	6,300,000	6,800,000	7,100,000
foreign tourists	1,250,000	2,000,000	2,520,000	2,650,000	2,800,000	2,850,000	3,050,000

■ domestic tourists ■ foreign tourists

Figure 4.4 Tourists in Kraków in 2005–19.

Source: Based on: Urząd Miasta Krakowa, 2006, 2011, 2016–20.

of tourists in Kraków increased dynamically in 2005–19. Inbound tourism is dominated by domestic arrivals. In 2019, tourists spent PLN 7.5 billion in Kraków (Figure 4.4).

The creative and biotech sectors, and start-ups

The creative industries play an increasingly large role in Kraków's economy. They are not directly connected to traditionally understood cultural activity, yet they exploit the potential developed by the culture sector (Klasik, 2010, p. 50). They include areas such as architecture and interior design, fashion and design, film and TV production, radio and music production, software development, advertising and related activities, artistic crafts, and the visual arts (Sanetra-Szeliga, 2018, p. 244). Dominant in this sector are micro-businesses that employ fewer than nine people.

Kraków is also a significant centre of the biotech sector in Poland. The establishment of the Centre for Technology Transfer (CITTRU) by the Jagiellonian University in 2000 can be considered the event that initiated the development of the sector. CITTRU provided services for the processes of technology commercialisation, with life sciences being the centre's particular field of support from the earliest days of its activity. With time, the university also incorporated the Jagiellonian Innovation Centre, a company managing the Life Science Park (2008), Poland's first science and technology park fully dedicated to the life sciences.

In 2014, the Małopolska Biotechnology Centre was developed as a shared initiative of the Jagiellonian University and the University of Agriculture in Kraków. Although it did not contribute directly to the development of new biotechnological companies in the city, it reinforced the external connections of Kraków's biotechnology sector through cooperation with recognised scientific institutions (notably the Max Planck Gesellschaft, Centre National De la Recherche Scientifique and Kyoto University) and the employment of foreign experts (Strzałka, 2015).

Seed companies (start-ups), whose founders focus on the implementation of their proprietary concepts, have also assumed an important place in Kraków's economy.[6] These enterprises employ thousands of people and produce solutions used around the world. The emergence of start-ups became another stage in the technological development in the city's economy. Kraków boasts an increasing number of technology-based start-ups that have become successful in the global world of advanced technologies. Of the total of 2,700 start-ups in Poland in 2016, 11% came from Kraków (Skala and Kruczkowska, 2016, p. 18). One of the factors favouring their development in Kraków is the high level of education of the local population (Kumięga, 2017, p. 96).

Kraków in business rankings

Towards the end of the second decade of the 21st century, Kraków no longer resembles the drab and dreary, environmentally polluted, post-communist city that faced entirely new economic and social challenges as it stood on the threshold of systemic transformation. In the past decade, the city has achieved high positions in various business rankings.

In the fDi Tier 2 Cities of the Future 2020/21 ranking, a listing of non-capital cities that attract investors, Kraków ranked 10th for business friendliness. In turn, in the ranking of fDi's European Cities and Regions of the Future 2020/21, compiled by the prestigious fDi Magazine, Kraków won accolades in the following categories: Top 10 East European Cities of the Future 2020/2021 (10th place), Top 10 Large European Cities of the Future 2020/2021 (8th place), the economic potential category of the Top 10 Large European Cities of the Future 2020/2021 (7th place), and the business friendliness category of the Top 10 Large European Cities of the Future 2020/2021 (7th place).

In CEE Investment Report 2019: Thriving Metropolitan Cities, a ranking of the most dynamically developing cities of the European Union, Kraków ranked 8th in Europe and 2nd in Poland. In turn, in the Tholons Services Globalization City Index 2019, Kraków made it to 11th place in its Top 100 Super Cities ranking. In 2019, Forbes ranked Kraków second in the Business Friendly City category for cities with populations of 300,000 ÷ 999,000. The city has also made it to the top of the fDi Polish Cities of the Future 2019/2020 (Krakowski, 2020, p. 4) where Kraków was listed as the best destination among the regional capitals (the first position being taken by Warsaw), and held a high second place in three categories: economic potential, human capital and lifestyle, and business friendliness. This means that the city that offers high quality of life and municipal infrastructure competes on quality and not low price, while at the same time offering the best location in Europe for businesses from the SSC sector.

In conclusion, it must be noted that Kraków's economy underwent a fundamental ownership and qualitative change at the time of systemic transformation (i.e. after 1989). The city moved away from the environmentally harmful industries that consumed large amounts of raw materials. The Lenin Steelworks (known as the Sendzimir Steelworks since 1990) was privatised and modernised, and reduced its employment levels until the major parts of it that used raw materials were closed in 2020. The fundamental changes in the economic structure of the city took place in a peaceful manner, without the social conflicts that were characteristic of the time of economic change and were seen in many other cities. The external capital that arrived acquired the existing industrial facilities and started new businesses. Over the past two decades, the sector of modern business services has developed intensively. The degraded post-industrial brownfield sites were revitalised and new functions were introduced on them. Various utilities operating as part of the municipal holding companies developed their activity. Cultural heritage, whose variety and quality makes Kraków notable in Europe and the world, is an important asset that favours development. To meet the challenges of the 21st century, notably competition from other Polish and European cities, Kraków must persistently follow the strategy of developing as a modern metropolis, not only as a capital of high culture, an academic centre, and a tourist destination, but also as a place where a smart and diversified economy is developing.

Bibliography

ABSL (2016) *Sektor nowoczesnych usług biznesowych w Polsce*. Warszawa: ABSL.

ABSL (2020) *Sektor nowoczesnych usług biznesowych w Polsce*. Warszawa: ABSL.

Borkowska, A. (2018) "Wpływ outsourcingu na wybrane aspekty rozwoju ekonomicznego na przykładzie miasta Krakowa", *Przedsiębiorczość Międzynarodowa*, 4(1). Available at: DOI:10.15678/PM.2018.0401.04 (Accessed on 25 July 2021).

Borodako, K. et al. (2018) *Wpływ ekonomiczny branży spotkań na gospodarkę Krakowa*. A study by Małopolska Tourism Organisation (MOT) for the Municipality of Kraków. Kraków: Małopolska Organizacja Turystyczna.

Grycuk, A. (2017) "Klastry a rozwój regionalny. Klaster usług biznesowych w Krakowie", *Studia BAS*, 1(49), pp. 133–167.

Gurba, K. (2006) "Klaster przyszłością gospodarki? Krótka analiza teorii klastrów", [in:] Gurba, K., and Maziarka, K. (eds.) *Nauka i biznes: strategie współpracy*. Kraków: Centrum Innowacji, Transferu Technologii i Rozwoju Uniwersytetu (CITTRU), Uniwersytet Jagielloński, pp. 12–18.

Harańczyk, A. (1998) *Miasta Polski w procesie globalizacji gospodarki*. Warszawa: Wydawnictwo Naukowe PWN.

Hołuj, D. (2015) *Samorząd Krakowa wobec wyzwań metropolitalności*. Kraków: Wydawnictwo Uniwersytetu Ekonomicznego.

Jamry, T. (2019) "Geograficzne i ekonomiczne aspekty rozwoju sektora usług biznesowych", *Prace Geograficzne*, 158, pp. 65–85.

Kaliński, J. (2009) *Transformacja gospodarki polskiej w latach 1989–2004*. Warszawa: Oficyna Wydawnicza SGH.

Kaliński, J. (2017) "Przekształcenia własnościowe", [in:] Jarosz-Nojszewska, A. (ed.) *Problemy gospodarcze Trzeciej Rzeczypospolitej*. Warszawa: Oficyna Wydawnicza SGH, pp. 91–104.

Klasik, A. (2010) "Od sektora kultury do przemysłów kreatywnych", [in:] Gwóźdź, A. (ed.) *Od przemysłów kultury do kreatywnej gospodarki*. Warszawa: Narodowe Centrum Kultury, pp. 47–63.

Komański, A. (1998) "Kraków – siedziba ważnych instytucji życia gospodarczego regionu", [in:] Purchla, J. (ed.) *Metropolitalne funkcje Krakowa*, vol. 2, Kraków: Międzynarodowe Centrum Kultury, pp. 75–79.

Kopyciński, P. (2021) "The embeddedness of firms and employees in Central Europe: Krakow as an offshoring and outsourcing centre", [in:] Mamica, Ł. (ed.) *Outsourcing in European Emerging Economies: Territorial Embeddedness and Global Business Services*. London and New York: Routledge.

Krakowski Rynek Nieruchomości 2018 (2019) Kraków. Knight Frank; Instytut Analiz Monitor Rynku Nieruchomości, mrn.pl.

Kumięga, P. (2017) "A Kraków to... miasto innowacji. Gospodarka kreatywna jako czynnik rozwoju miast na przykładzie Krakowa – adaptacja koncepcji 3T Richarda Floridy", *Zarządzanie Publiczne*, 1(37), pp. 91–102.

Mazur, D. (2015) "Współpraca sektora nauki, biznesu i administracji publicznej jako główne wyzwania współczesnej polityki rozwoju miasta na przykładzie Krakowa", *Zarządzanie Publiczne*, 1(29), pp. 1–10.

Micek, G. et al. (2017) "Nowe branże gospodarki w Krakowie: Czynniki i mechanizmy rozwoju", *Studia Ekonomiczne, Zeszyty Naukowe Uniwersytetu Ekonomicznego w Katowicach*, 320, pp. 18–45.

Monografia Huty im. Tadeusza Sendzimira w Krakowie 1954–1994 (1994) Multi-author publication, Kraków: Wydawnictwo Huty im. T. Sendzimira.

Morawski, W. (2017) "Modernizacja systemu bankowego", [in:] Jarosz-Nojszewska, A. (ed.) *Problemy gospodarcze Trzeciej Rzeczypospolitej*. Warszawa: Oficyna Wydawnicza SGH, pp. 163–174.

Nieć, M. (2019) *Startupy w Polsce. Raport 2019*. Available at: https://www.parp.gov.pl/storage/publications/pdf/Startupy-w-Polsce---raport-2019_200117.pdf (Accessed on 24 July 2021).

Paprocki, W. (2017) "Transformacja ku gospodarce cyfrowej", *Open Eyes Book 2*. Kraków: Fundacja Gospodarki i Administracji Publicznej.

Przeszłość ma przyszłość. Rozmowy z Jackiem Purchlą. (2020) Kraków: Księgarnia Akademicka.

Piątkowski, M. (2019) *Europejski lider wzrostu. Polska droga od ekonomicznych peryferii do gospodarki sukcesu*. Warszawa: Wydawnictwo Poltex.

Rolski, M. (2013) "Krytyka planu Balcerowicza w ujęciu Grzegorza Kołodki oraz Tadeusza Kowalika", *Studia Ekonomiczne. Uniwersytet Ekonomiczny w Katowicach*, pp. 88–100.

Romanowski, R., and Walkowiak-Markiewicz, K. (2015) "Znaczenie centrów nowoczesnych usług biznesowych dla rozwoju metropolii w Polsce", *Studia Oeconomica Posnaniensia*, 3(8), pp. 67–88.

Rutkowska-Gurak, A. (2011) "Parki technologiczne jako element otoczenie innowacyjnego miasta", *Kwartalnik Nauk o Przedsiębiorstwie*, 20(3), pp. 79–86.

Sanetra-Szeliga, J. (2018) "Kultura – zasób strategiczny?", *Open Eyes Book*, No. 3, Kraków: Fundacja Gospodarki i Administracji Publicznej, pp. 237–253.
Siwek, T. (2002) "Czeskie miasta po roku 1989", [in:] Słodczyk, J. (ed.) *Przemiany bazy ekonomicznej i struktury przestrzennej miast*. Opole: Wydawnictwo Uniwersytetu Opolskiego, pp. 45–52.
Skala, A., and Kruczkowska, E. (2016) *Raport: polskie startupy 2016*. Fundacja Startup Poland. Available at: https://startuppoland.org/wp-content/uploads/2021/11/Raport-Polskie-Startupy-2016-official-3.pdf (Accessed on 25 October 2021).
Strzałka, K. (2015) "Małopolskie Centrum Biotechnologii Uniwersytetu Jagiellońskiego. Geneza powstania, sposób funkcjonowania i znaczenie dla koncepcji uniwersytetu badawczego", *Zagadnienia Naukoznawstwa*, 3(205), pp. 377–385.
Strzeszyński, J., Krochmal, P., and Wójciak, E. (2019) *Znaczenie deweloperów mieszkaniowych dla gospodarki Krakowa. Wpływ deweloperskich inwestycji mieszkaniowych na rozwój Krakowa i wpływy do budżetu miasta w latach 2013–2018*. Instytut Analiz Monitor Rynku Nieruchomości. mrn.pl.
Tridico, P. (2007) "Rozwój społeczny i wzrost gospodarczy w gospodarkach w okresie transformacji: rola instytucji", *Zarządzanie Publiczne/Public Governance*, 1(1), pp. 95–124.
Urząd Miasta Krakowa (1992) *Raport o stanie miasta 1991. Gospodarka*, Available at: https://www.bip.krakow.pl/zalaczniki/dokumenty/n/287199/karta (Accessed on 12 July 2021).
Urząd Miasta Krakowa (1994) *Raport o stanie miasta 1993*. Available at: https://www.bip.krakow.pl/zalaczniki/dokumenty/n/287199/karta (Accessed on 12 July 2021).
Urząd Miasta Krakowa (1997) *Raport o stanie miasta 1996*. Available at: https://www.bip.krakow.pl/zalaczniki/dokumenty/n/287199/karta (Accessed on 12 July 2021).
Urząd Miasta Krakowa (2000) *Raport o stanie miasta 1999*. Available at: https://www.bip.krakow.pl/zalaczniki/dokumenty/n/287199/karta (Accessed on 12 July 2021).
Urząd Miasta Krakowa (2001) *Raport o stanie miasta 2000*. Available at: https://www.bip.krakow.pl/zalaczniki/dokumenty/n/287199/karta (Accessed on 12 July 2021).
Urząd Miasta Krakowa (2006) *Raport o stanie miasta 2005*. Available at: https://www.bip.krakow.pl/zalaczniki/dokumenty/n/287199/karta (Accessed on 12 July 2021).
Urząd Miasta Krakowa (2011) *Raport o stanie miasta 2010*. Available at: https://www.bip.krakow.pl/zalaczniki/dokumenty/n/287199/karta (Accessed on 12 July 2021).
Urząd Miasta Krakowa (2012) *Raport o stanie miasta 2011*. Available at: https://www.bip.krakow.pl/zalaczniki/dokumenty/n/287199/karta (Accessed on 12 July 2021).
Urząd Miasta Krakowa (2016) *Raport o stanie miasta 2015*. Available at: https://www.bip.krakow.pl/zalaczniki/dokumenty/n/287199/karta (Accessed on 12 July 2021).
Urząd Miasta Krakowa (2017) *Raport o stanie miasta 2016*. Available at: https://www.bip.krakow.pl/zalaczniki/dokumenty/n/287199/karta (Accessed on 12 July 2021).
Urząd Miasta Krakowa (2018) *Raport o stanie miasta 2017*. Available at: https://www.bip.krakow.pl/zalaczniki/dokumenty/n/287199/karta (Accessed on 12 July 2021).
Urząd Miasta Krakowa (2019) *Raport o stanie miasta 2018* Available at: https://www.bip.krakow.pl/zalaczniki/dokumenty/n/287199/karta (Accessed on 12 July 2021).
Urząd Miasta Krakowa (2020) *Raport o stanie miasta 2019*. Available at: https://www.bip.krakow.pl/zalaczniki/dokumenty/n/287199/karta (Accessed on 12 July 2021).
Urząd Miasta Krakowa (2021) *Raport o stanie miasta 2020*. Available at: https://www.bip.krakow.pl/zalaczniki/dokumenty/n/318038/karta (Accessed on 12 July 2021).

Urząd Statystyczny w Krakowie (2005) *Rocznik Statystyczny Krakowa*, Kraków: Urząd Statystyczny w Krakowie.
Urząd Statystyczny w Krakowie (2013) *Rocznik Statystyczny Krakowa*, Kraków: Urząd Statystyczny w Krakowie.
Urząd Statystyczny w Krakowie (2017) *Rocznik Statystyczny Krakowa*, Kraków: Urząd Statystyczny w Krakowie.
Urząd Statystyczny w Krakowie (2019) *Rocznik Statystyczny Krakowa*, Kraków: Urząd Statystyczny w Krakowie.
Woodward, R. (2019) "Innowacje", [in:] *Nasza Europa: 15 lat Polski w Unii Europejskiej. Wartości, instytucje, swobody, polityki sektorowe, problemy i kluczowe wyzwania*. Warszawa: CASE – Centrum Analiz Społeczno-Ekonomicznych, pp. 95–101.

Notes

1 See: *Przeszłość ma przyszłość. Rozmowy z Jackiem Purchlą*, Kraków, 2020, p. 87.
2 In 2001 BPH merged with Powszechny Bank Kredytowy. The merged company was headquartered in Warsaw.
3 The global division of Delphi in 2017 resulted in the incorporation of two independent companies: Aptiv, dealing with electronic appliances for the automotive sector, advanced safety technologies, and powertrains.
4 *Tholons Top 100 Outsourcing Destinations: Rankings*, Tholons, December 2013 – the world's leading ranking of this type is compiled by Tholons, an international corporation providing strategic consultancy in outsourcing and investments.
5 It must, however, be noted that even though experts believe that development of clusters brings a range of benefits, there is no such certainty about their establishment being a proper approach or the degree to which state institutions should be involved establishing them. See: Gurba (2006, p. 14).
6 Start-ups were defined as follows in *Raport Startupy w Polsce 2019*:

> A start-up is an entity represented in this study by a person who is either at the stage of setting up the company, or having run it for a period of up to 3.5 years, and using technology/methods of work that have been available in the market for no more than 5 years for the production of their services/products.
>
> (Nieź, 2019, p. 4)

5 Kraków

An eventful city

Joanna Sanetra-Szeliga

This chapter discusses the part of Kraków's cultural policy that treats events as resources for the development of the city. Using the theoretical approach proposed by Greg Richards and Robert Palmer (2010), it presents the path that Kraków has taken from being a mere city of events, to being an eventful city of the 21st century. Starting with the European mega-events of the European Cultural Month 1992 and the European City of Culture 2000, Kraków developed a vision of a "city of festivals" that has been consistently implemented using instruments such as the Kraków Festival Office, which coordinates the event ecosystem of the city. Today, Kraków is a city where almost 80 festivals, over 8,400 MICE events, and 240 mass events take place every year, and one that has a determined approach to benefit from them on many socio-economic levels.

The experience economy, events, and the city

Throughout the history of the economy, various elements have played an important role in urban development. The contemporary world sees yet another approach emerge, one in which experiences can be seen as key drivers. According to B. Joseph Pine and James H. Gilmore (1998a), besides raw materials, goods, and services, there is another development resource – experiences. Obviously, experiences have always been included in market transactions. Now, however, they move to a separate plane as another source of value creation. "An experience occurs when a company intentionally uses services as the stage, and goods as props, to engage individual customers in a way that creates a memorable event" (Pine and Gilmore, 1998b). Experiences do not arise in isolation from other types of economic goods. To create an experience, both material products and services are usually necessary, and, above all, the presence of a given customer along with their knowledge and sensitivity to determine the level of consumption. There are two ways to think about experiences – customer participation (passive and active) and connection or an "environmental relationship, that unites customers with the event or performance (absorption or immersion)" (*ibid.*). Experiences can be related to entertainment, educational events, and even escapism or aesthetics.

DOI: 10.4324/9781003252757-6

Barbara Marciszewska (2010, p. 16) claims that the list could be even longer; for example, in the case of tourism, it could include integration, culture-forming, creating experiences, or research. The experience economy represents to a large extent the demand side of the economy, focusing on the consumer. As Katarzyna Dziewanowska (2015, p. 30) emphasises, the role of the producer of an experience good in this concept is special, because in their striving to create unforgettable experiences, they can provide the presence of appropriate stimuli that can create the customer experience only under certain conditions and consumer readiness. The researcher calls the concepts presented by Pine and Gilmore "the experience economy of the first generation". A second-generation economy would be characterised by the progressive personalisation of the experience-creation process, thanks to which the experience would be co-created with the consumer by guide companies. In effect, the provider of the experience would be the customer himself or herself.

In experience economy, cities deal with designing memorable experiences by giving them themes, harmonising impressions with positive cues, and eliminating the negative ones. Often that includes offering certain types of memorabilia and engaging all the senses of the consumer (Pine and Gilmore, 1998b). The growing demand for experience goods provides cities with an opportunity to use these new resources for development. This brings events into the picture – events that can be seen as the emanation of experiences. Events are those happenings (such as festivals, congresses, etc.) that are characterised by their complexity (usually they consist of a series of different actions), a limited duration and place, an element of celebration, the audience, and a group of stakeholders (Richards and Palmer, 2010, pp. 2–3). Events for a wide audience, often open-air events, have always been organised in cities – from ancient times, through the pre-industrial period (religious rituals, tournaments, carnivals, coronations, etc.), the industrial revolution (part of the free time and recreation culture with one of the first events being the Great Exhibition in London in 1851) and the post-industrial approach to festivals that treats them as a part of a broader concept of the city's cultural capital (Gold and Gold, 2005). Soon, events became factors stimulating the process of revitalising the city (especially post-industrial, post-military and degraded areas). The strategies at the beginning of the 21st century became even more sophisticated, the focus slowly shifting from physical transformation, image improvement, and even economic development towards the "soft" impacts – e.g., social revitalisation or improving the quality of life of residents and not only supporting business and attracting investors. The second major change in the approach to events is thinking of their long-term legacies (Smith, 2012, pp. 44–45).

Creating an eventful city is an element of a proactive strategy of creating new resources that make the city attractive and are an element of building a city's competitive advantage. Richards (2017, p. 534) adds that the concept derives from an idea that events are "temporal and spatial tools to utilise urban resources in order to achieve a range of policy outcomes for the city as a whole".

In explaining why events have become a popular tool in urban policy, thereby challenging the "previous dominance of the importance of built heritage in cultural and economic development strategies", Richards and Palmer (2010) draw our attention to the fact that events can be more flexible, they can offer experience, atmosphere, and fulfil the need "of being there". They can also help differentiate physical environments and "cost less and achieve greater impact in the short term" (p. 19).

However, it should be remembered that not every event, regardless of its cost, will be contributing to a city's pro-development policy. Richards and Palmer point out that the mere fact of organising events does not make a city "a city of events". There is a difference between a "city with events" and a "city of events", a title that many cities involved in organising events strive for – see Table 5.1 for the distinction between the two. Donald Getz (2007, p. 141) suggests that cities that want to base their strategy or part of it on events should create a whole portfolio of events, small and large, aimed at different target groups, organised in various fields, with different goals and expected results. This allows cities to maximise the value (financial as well as social and cultural) of a set of events in a given period. It should also be remembered that events must be well placed in the local context – copy-paste events from another city have little chance of success in stimulating local development. Although cities, of course, compete with each other for the title of hosts of touring and travelling events (such as the EXPO World Exhibitions, the Olympic Games, or the European Capital of Culture), they are often driven more by their prestige and marketing potential than by strategic development programming.

Table 5.1 Relation between a city and events – two approaches

A city with events	*The eventful city*
Approach: sectoral, tactical, reactive	Approach: holistic, strategic, proactive
City as a container for events	City as a generator of events
Acting ad hoc	Coordinated actions
Competition between different events	Cooperation between different events
Pandering to audiences	Provoking the public
Left brain thinking (analytical thinking)	Right brain thinking (abstract thinking)
Event policy	Events as a policy tool
Market-led	Market leader
City marketing	City making
Spectacle	Involvement

Source: Richards and Palmer, 2010, p. 43 (modified).

On the way to the eventful city

Looking back at the 30 years of Kraków in the democratic system and market economy presents us with two milestones on its path to become an eventful city: the European Cultural Month of 1992 and the European City of Culture 2000 with the creation of the Kraków 2000 Festival Office.

European Cultural Month 1992

Already at the beginning of the transformation period from a centrally planned economy to a market economy, and from the communist system to a democracy, the new and first democratically elected local authorities wanted to open Kraków to the world and capitalise on its rich culture and heritage. This was reflected in their efforts to host the first ever European Capital Month (ECM) in June 1992. The ECM was an extension of the celebration of European Cities of Culture[1] to the new democracies of Central Europe, and their incorporation into the European and global life of cultural diversity, intercultural dialogue, and mutual understanding. It was the first cultural mega-event, i.e., a large-scale cultural activity of a dramatic character, mass popular appeal, and international significance (Roche, 2000) in Central Europe, and it was a bold move given the state of both the country and the city. As Jacobs recalls, Kraków was one of the cities that suffered the most as a result of economic degradation after the Second World War. Therefore, the level at which the city's reanimation began was relatively low (1984, p. 200). The main goal of the ECM was

> to use Kraków as a forum for presenting European cultural phenomena and for displaying Poland's most interesting artistic achievements. For the Cracow audience and for Poland as a whole it was to be the first presentation of its kind on such a scale.
>
> (Purchla, 1993, p. 13)

Being, in a way, a continuation of the 1991 experience of organising the Cracow Symposium on the Cultural Heritage of the Conference on Security and Cooperation in Europe, the ECM was a part of the new development policy of the city, i.e., an attempt to create a festival industry in Kraków (one of the new opportunities for a historic city). The goal of the ECM was, then, to become "a laboratory enabling Cracow's present-day possibilities to be tested, as well as various organisational and financial solutions" (p. 14).

The organisers faced a number of difficulties in preparing the event. Having only eight months to prepare made it impossible to invite all the artists they wanted to invite and to promote the event properly (the lack of experience in the tourism sector was another issue). June 1992 also turned out to be the peak of the political crisis in Poland (the country had three prime ministers in a short time!). Moreover, the country as a whole faced great difficulties with a political crisis, an economic recession, and the collapse of the state budget. This translated into financial problems for the ECM organisers who, due to the lack of developed commercial sponsorship, were solely dependent on public funds. While the municipal self-government was still at the stage of development and was not able to contribute more than 3.2% of the ECM budget, the Ministry of Culture and Art transferred only half of the initially promised budget. This forced changes in the programme of the event.

Bearing in mind that the budget of the ECM almost equalled the municipal budget for culture, the organisers had to face the discussion on the legitimacy of spending public funds on a cultural festival (while there were so many other serious problems to be solved in the city), and not only the challenges of difficult political and financial situation, economic problems and, above all, the impoverishment of the society and the problem of attendance at the event (pp. 16–18). However, as it turned out, Kraków residents had a rather positive view of the whole event (only 8% declared that too much public money had been spent on the ECM) (Karwińska and Marszycka, 1992, p. 48).

The whole endeavour proved to be a success. The audience reached 300,000 people who attended 242 events (including 40 free open-air events, 30 exhibitions, 60 music and theatre events), where about 8,000 artists performed (2,500 of them representing 25 different foreign countries, including Western Europe, United States, Japan, Brazil, and Israel) (pp. 41–43). The direct cost of the events was calculated at PLZ 36 billion, and the direct revenue was PLZ 3 billion.[2] Estimates say that during their stay in Kraków in June 1992, tourists spent around PLZ 6 billion in the city (indirect income related to the festival). There was also a positive impact on the city's brand – before coming to Kraków, only 18% of tourists coming to the city for the first time thought it was a "living, modern city". This number rose to 53% of tourists leaving the city after their first visit. Some 80% of those who had visited Kraków sometime before noticed an improvement in the city since their last visit (Comedia, 1992). More than half of the tourists (60%) declared their willingness to return to the city within the next five years, and 87.2% of the participants stated that, in their opinion, the ECM made the city a pleasant place. Almost the same number said that the festival programme must have had a positive effect on the image and perception of the city (Karwińska and Marszycka, 1992, p. 48). During the ECM, 250 people were employed, and despite the fact that it was only temporary work, it offered a unique opportunity for that time to cooperate in the production of international events and gain experience (which can be described as the educational impact of the ECM).

The success of the first mega-event in Kraków led the municipal authorities to believe that the idea of "festival city" and "festival industry" may indeed be a path to follow as far as the cultural policy of the city was concerned. It has to be noted that at that time, the awareness of the socio-economic potential of culture and cultural heritage was rather low, both among the decision-makers and the general public. Moreover, the cultural policy of the city was still in a development stage (see below).

European City of Culture 2000

With the success of the ECM, the municipality was seriously considering hosting the European City of Culture (ECC). Since 1985, the ECC, now the European Capital of Culture (ECoC), has been the most recognised cultural initiative of the European Communities (now the European Union). It is a year-long celebration of art and culture designed to "highlight the richness and diversity of cultures in Europe, celebrate the cultural features Europeans share, increase European citizens' sense of belonging to a common cultural area, foster the contribution of culture to the development of cities" (European Commission, 2016). With the experience of more than 60 cities, now it proved also to be a trigger for regeneration, internationalisation, cultural branding, and tourism.

At the beginning, Kraków planned to apply jointly for the title with a partner city – Nuremberg. However, when it lost to Weimar in an internal German competition for the ECC 1999 title, Kraków decided to submit an application on its own, despite the initial lack of commitment and clear support from the Ministry of Culture (Glondys, 2010, pp. 35–45). At the end of 1995, the European Communities decided to award the title of ECC in the millennium year of 2000 to Kraków and eight other cities – Avignon, Bergen, Bologna, Brussels, Helsinki, Prague, Reykjavik, and Santiago de Compostela. Preparing an application for the title of European City of Culture 2000 was handled by the Culture Department of the City of Kraków, and its implementation was carried out by the Festival Office, initially run by the Culture Foundation from Warsaw and then (1997) transformed into a municipal cultural institution, the Kraków 2000 Festival Office. A Programme Council was also established that included world-famous artists, and experienced managers and animators of culture.

Kraków was the first city to offer a five-year programme of cultural events as an European City of Culture. Each year preceding the end of the millennium was to be devoted to a different field of art, and the artistic patronage of the events was to be assumed by well-known Polish artists. The whole programme was given the following goals:

- promotion of cultural heritage and contemporary creativity,
- presentation of Kraków as a meeting place for Eastern and Western cultures,
- establishment of new institutions, cultural activities, events of international quality and importance, and activation of existing cultural institutions,
- promotion of participation in culture,
- reflection on the spirituality of contemporary Europe and its rich roots, including Judeo-Christian ones,
- promotion of an active way of spiritual and intellectual development, especially among young people,
- promotion of cultural achievements and presentation to tourists of the attractiveness of Kraków and Poland (Biuro Kraków 2000, 2000/2001).

Despite the experience of Glasgow 1990 (Booth and Boyle 1993), which proved that such a mega event can have a significant contribution to the socio-economic development of a city, the goals related to this domain were not considered (except for the reference to tourism in the last point of the above-mentioned goals), and no infrastructure development was planned. The approach to the ECC was best evidenced by the title of the event – the Kraków 2000 Festival ("festival", i.e., primarily emphasising the visual and performative arts).

The motto of the celebration of Kraków 2000 was "Thought – Spirituality – Creativity". The first element of the slogan, "Thought", was primarily reflected in the programme of the 600th Anniversary of the Revival of the Kraków Academy (now the Jagiellonian University). "Spirituality" referred mainly to the celebrations of the 1000th anniversary of the Kraków diocese and the three religions of this region of Europe: Orthodoxy, Judaism, and Catholicism. The "Creativity" component illustrated the achievements of the greatest Polish artists of the 20th century, including Konrad Swinarski, Mikołaj Górecki, and Sławomir Mrożek (Interview 1).

The projects implemented in 2000 included those organised directly by the Festival Office, those proposed by the members of the Programme Council, events resulting from cooperation with other European Cities of Culture 2000, projects selected as part of a nationwide competition, and projects submitted from outside the competition. In total, 121 cultural projects were implemented, including 574 events. Most of them represented the visual arts (exhibitions) – 32, including Wyspiański and Kantor exhibitions, as well as exhibitions of applied arts (e.g., Find – Finnish Design 2000) or the presentation of the latest communication technologies in an exhibition entitled Communication. Performing arts were represented in 33 projects (not counting interdisciplinary projects) – for example, the Great Performances Series, Orthodox Church Music Festival, Kraków Ballet Spring, and the Court Dance Festival. A number of projects in the field of popular culture and addressed to a wide audience were also implemented, such as the open-air show Kraków Legends – Floating of the Wreaths 2000, the International Street Theatre Festival, an exhibition of Venetian nativity scenes in the Small Market Square, or the Millennium Night closing in 2000: New Year's Eve 2000/2001.

As it has already been mentioned, no economic goals were set for the Kraków 2000 Festival. However, like any particularly large event, Kraków 2000 had an impact on the city's social and economic environment. Due to the lack of impact research, one can only relay the available data. The number of tourists visiting Kraków grew through the 1990s and reached 4.4 million visitors in the millennium year. Upward trends were also visible in other Polish cities, but at the turn of the century, they began to reverse in most large Polish cities. However, this was not the case in Kraków, so it can be concluded that the increased number of cultural events and promotion of the city delayed the negative trend as the municipal office informed (Urząd Miasta Krakowa, 2001). This thesis seems to be confirmed also by the fact that in 2001, when the cultural offer of Kraków was limited, a decrease in the number of visitors was also observed in this city. However, cultural and tourist operators expressed their doubts about the role of the Kraków 2000 Festival as a factor increasing the number of visits to Kraków (lack of sufficient promotion) (Hughes et al., 2003). As for the expenses incurred by tourists, the Kraków branch of the Institute of Tourism estimated that the average cost of visiting Kraków for both foreign and Polish tourists was around PLN 3,000. The funds spent in the city depended on the length of stay and the wealth of individuals. Almost a third of tourists spent from PLN 701 to PLN 1,500 in Kraków. The expenditure of 23% of them was in the range of PLN 301–700 (Urząd Miasta Krakowa, 2001).

Organisation of mega-events often encompasses or triggers special investments in the city infrastructure (transport/communication, cultural, or sports). Although it was not included in the Kraków 2000 programme, there were intensive conservation and construction works carried out in Kraków in the years preceding the millennium (including the courtyard of the Wawel Royal Castle, the porches and gates of St Mary's Basilica). Also, in the years 1999–2000, several investments were made in the field of transport (new roads, renovation of old roads, new tram lines) and renovation of the sewage and gas infrastructure. It should, therefore, be emphasised that certain investments in the city were made and, in a sense, they prepared the city for the Kraków 2000 celebrations (Urząd Miasta Krakowa, 2001). However, they were all planned separately by individual departments of the city authority and there was no coherent plan combining all forces to prepare the city to be the ECC 2000.

Events and event infrastructure in Kraków

For years, one of the challenges faced by anyone wishing to organise any big event in Kraków was the lack of a large auditorium that would accommodate more people than the Philharmonic Hall (817 seats) or the Juliusz Słowacki Theatre (530 seats). A mega-event such as the European City of Culture could have been an incentive to deal with the problem, as had been the case in other cities that had held the title. However, it was not included in the Kraków 2000 plans. Nevertheless, it must be admitted that regardless of the official programme of the ECC, there were initial plans to build a 2,000-seat concert hall that was to be part of the long-planned Musical Theatre. Due to political changes, this project was not funded. For a similar reason, another idea could not be implemented – a lightweight, multifunctional hall that could be built in six months and then used for cultural and sports events, exhibitions, and fairs. In both cases, the main problem was the constantly changing political situation, financial difficulties and, I would argue, the lack of thinking about culture and events in terms of urban development. According to some experts (Interview 2), it was a mistake to organise a five-year festival before the ECC year instead of trying to upgrade the cultural infrastructure that would have served Kraków's cultural life for many years to come.

Kraków had to wait 14 more years to benefit from a proper event infrastructure. The opening of the ICE Kraków Congress Centre provided the city with a prestigious venue overlooking the Vistula river and Wawel castle. It can seat 1,915 participants in the Penderecki Auditorium, 594 in the Theatre Hall, and 400 both in the Chamber Hall and in Conference Hall complex (Krakowskie Biuro Festiwalowe, 2018). The International Exhibition and Convention Centre EXPO Kraków offers 14,000 sqm of space, including seminar rooms and two halls that not only can host presentations of large and heavy objects, but can also be transformed into a 5,000-guest auditorium (EXPO Kraków, 2021). Finally, the TAURON Arena Kraków is a multifunctional facility that provides a place for different types of meetings, including cultural and sports events ranging from concerts, festivals, film screenings, musicals, circus shows, and ice-skating shows, to the organisation of competitions in 18 world championship disciplines. It is the biggest venue in Kraków (61,000 sqm) and can host up to 20,400 participants with 15,030 seats in the grandstands and further 3,500 (or 9,300 standing places) in the court (Tauron Arena, 2021).

The opening of these facilities allowed a steady increase in the number of MICE (Meetings, Incentives, Conferences, and Exhibitions) events over the next few years, thus improving Kraków's competitive position (see Figure 5.1). The events included mostly conferences and congresses (about 68%), corporate and team-building events (about 29%), and trade fairs (about 3%) in various fields (medical, technical, IT and communication, economic and political, humanities, commercial, and services) (Berbeka et al., 2015, pp. 3, 13). Just in 2013, the MICE sector contributed 2.37% of the GDP of Kraków (PLN 1.689 billion) to the city's economy, creating more than 12,000 full-time equivalent jobs, providing 2.4% of the city's income via

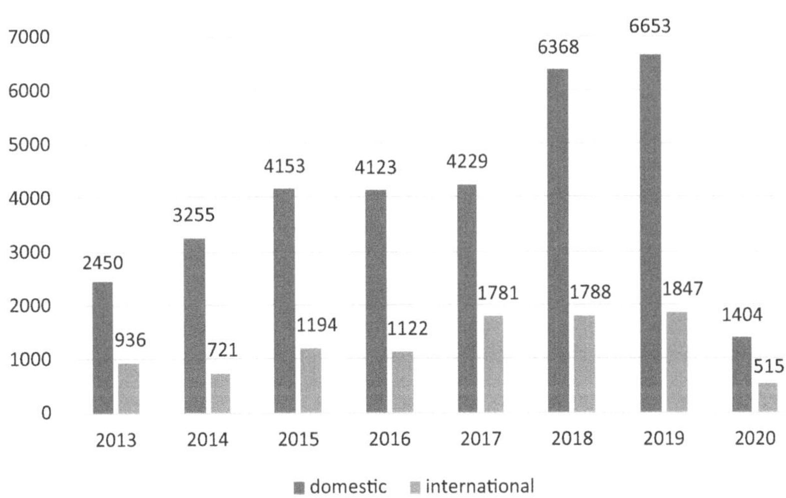

Figure 5.1 Number of MICE events in 2013–20 in Kraków.
Source: Berbeka et al., 2015–20.

taxes (PLN 89 million), and generating just over 1 million hotel nights in Kraków's hotels (Borodako et al., 2014, pp. 9–15). Given the increase of the events in the following years, it seems safe to assume that these numbers could have even doubled by 2020 but unfortunately the COVID-19 pandemic put a halt to this booming industry.

Cultural and development policies

The first official document that presented priorities for cultural policy in Kraków was the Strategy for Culture Development in 2010–14 (Rada Miasta Krakowa, 2010). It does not mean, of course, that the cultural sector was not supported by the municipality before 2010. However, the actions undertaken were rather random and occasional without a clear vision for the municipal cultural policy (Szulborska-Łukaszewicz, 2003, p. 74). One explanation for the lack of a cultural policy could lie in the negative connotations with the term "policy" (a legacy of the communist period); another was the neoliberal withdrawal by the authorities from public patronage and the state's protective function towards culture that was seen in the 1990s. Similarly, the administrative reforms and consequent changes in the local government obligations towards culture may have also had an impact here. Anyhow, the municipality was supporting a number of its own local cultural institutions as well as NGOs and individual artists. The City of Kraków Patronage for Culture Programme. Grants and Purchasing of Services (2000) gave some insight into Kraków's vision – it was to be a place of European culture, with a diverse and rich cultural offer that meets the needs of the local community, supports young artists, and safeguards local heritage. The only problem here, as Szulborska-Łukaszewicz underlines, is that it is an implicit vision without any explicit obligations on the policy level (2003, p.75). It needs to be mentioned here that the Kraków Development Strategy (Zarząd Miasta Krakowa, 1999) in force at the beginning of the millennium actually mentioned a proposed programme for supporting large cultural events, especially festivals, and it saw the need to build proper venues for such events (p. 11) and to promote select permanent cyclical cultural events, especially of a festival nature, including international ones (p. 35). Interestingly, the document does not mention the ECC 2000 title nor sees it as a development opportunity. Senior officials both in the municipality and the Kraków 2000 Festival Office stated that there had been no strategic plan linking all areas of the city's functioning with the organisation of the festival, and it often seemed as if the municipality lost interest in the mega-event once it had been handed over to the Festival Office (Interview 1 and 3).

The Cultural Strategy of 2010 (Rada Miasta, 2010) was one of the first municipal strategies for culture in Poland. It was based on the concept of the sustainable development that guaranteed equal opportunities for development to cultural institutions, individual artists, NGOs, and entrepreneurs in the field of culture. With its 150 festivals of both renown and tradition, and a touch of novelty, Kraków was mentioned as "Kraków – the City of Festivals" as one of the city's strengths in the SWOT analysis. The threats included a lack of auditorium, which hindered access to cultural events. The idea of Kraków – a City of Congresses was included as an opportunity (after a proper venue was completed). Goal III.2 of the strategy was entirely devoted to Kraków as a city of large events and festivals. The following actions were planned in this field: further development of the city of festivals brand, promotion of the city through festivals, financial support for festivals, supporting new forms and trends in art (e.g., design, fashion). The greatest weakness of the document was the underestimation of the city's social fabric. "The Strategy was written as if there were no residents in Kraków" (Gierat-Bieroń, 2012).

The main achievements of the strategy regarding events was the development of literary festivals that strengthened the Kraków – the City of Literature brand and supported the successful application of Kraków to become the UNESCO Creative City of Literature (2013), as well the building of the ICE and Tauron Arena that contributed to the Kraków – a City of Congresses brand. There was a general increase in the budget for grants offered to the cultural sector, including three-year grants for high-budget festivals. Kraków's festivals had been gaining recognition not only in Kraków but in other cities as well, with Kraków Nights, the Jewish Culture Festival, the Dragons' Parade, the Kraków Film Music Festival, the Boska Komedia / Divine Comedy International Theatre Festival, the Unsound Festival, and the Kraków Theatre Reminiscences (Rada Miasta Krakowa, 2017, p. 41). The priorities in the new Culture Development Programme to 2030 included the coordination and management of festivals (III.3) that was subdivided into two subcategories of actions: strengthening common cultural and economic capital of festivals through joining the power of the top festival brands of Kraków and defining joint priorities for festival development in the city (p. 95).

Moreover, Kraków's Development Strategy 2030 refers to the role of events. Acquiring more scientific, economic, political, and cultural events for Kraków is part of the actions that aim at making Kraków a node in the network of the metropolises of Poland, Europe, and the world. There is also a need to intensify cooperation in the organisation of prestigious events on an international scale between actors from different fields. The city wants to "maintain the richness, diversity and high quality of the cultural portfolio, providing the residents of Kraków with equal and universal access to cultural events, meeting places and creative discussions" (Municipality of Kraków, 2018, p. 72). The latter meant finally turning more attention towards residents and their cultural needs. There is also the goal of being a European Capital City of Culture, whose aims include strengthening the image of Kraków as a festival and congress city by expanding the rage of events, supporting existing brands and creating new ones and facilitating residents' access to the events.

Kraków Festival Office

The Kraków 2000 Festival Office was the only new municipal cultural institution established (in 1997) for the Kraków 2000 celebrations and, as it has continued its activity to this day (since 2005 as the Kraków Festival Office – KBF), it is seen as one of the most important legacies of the ECC 2000 in Kraków.[3] It is also perceived as an important milestone in implementing the idea of a festival city in Kraków.[4] In 2008, the KBF created the 6 Senses brand that supported the promotion strategy of the city through organising cultural events. A number of renowned flagship events was meant to be used to communicate the image of Kraków as city "of great events, most of all valuable events of different cultural circuits, festivals related to the strongest parts of the city's cultural potential" (Rudolf et al., 2015, p. 35).

Today the KBF is rather presented as a Polish acronym that "stands for culture, business and festivals", which aligns well with the way the institution defines itself:

> It means people behind hundreds of events held in the city every year. It means meetings with representatives of culture and business. It means emotions evoked by performances at huge outdoor stages. It means unforgettable memories of concert halls. It means countless events at venues throughout Kraków: the well-known ones which have long been bringing culture to the city, and the small, hidden ones that illuminate alternative themes and directions.
>
> (Krakowskie Biuro Festiwalowe, 2021)

It is responsible for organising prestigious and critically acclaimed Kraków festivals: Misteria Paschalia, Opera Rara, Sacrum Profanum (music), the Kraków Film Music Festival, Conrad (prose) and Miłosz (poetry) festivals (literature) as well outdoor mass events such as the Wianki – Celebration of Music. Also, it operates the UNESCO City of Literature programme, supports film production, organises the Kraków Book Fair, and supports a number of external initiatives and events (e.g., Divine Comedy Theatre Festival).

Is Kraków an eventful city?

Looking back at Table 5.1 that lists the conditions that make up an eventful city, I would argue that Kraków seems to be fulfilling most of them. Every year, there are over 250 events[5] organised in the city that are defined by Statistics Poland as "mass events" (Figure 5.2), as well as over 8,400 MICE events (Figure 5.1). The city hosts almost 80 festivals every year – many of these are generated by the city itself, while others are proposed by cultural institutions and NGOs. The festival ecosystem of the city is supported and coordinated by the KBF. Some of the festivals have a long history, such as the Kraków Film Festival, which dates back to 1961 making it one of the

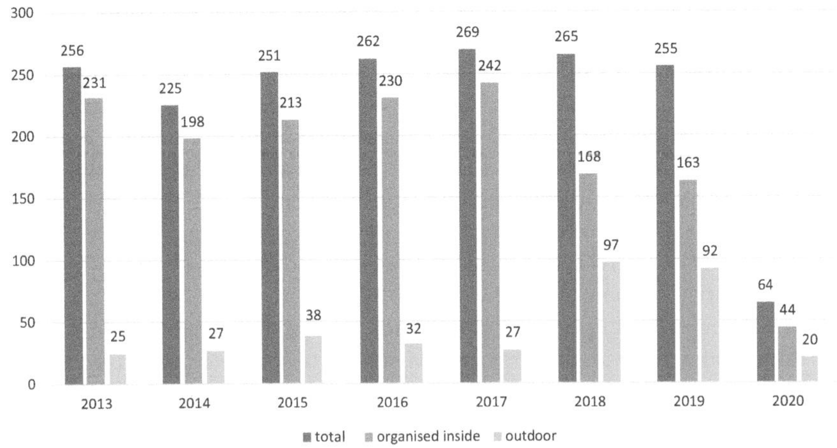

Figure 5.2 Organisation of art, entertainment, and sports mass events in Kraków.
Source: BDL, Statistics Poland (9 November 2021).

oldest events in the world dedicated to documentary, animated, and short feature films. The first Jewish Culture Festival was created in 1988. The ECC provided the impetus for a couple of new initiatives, including the now well-known Sacrum Profanum Festival. Other festivals are newer but still developed brands and a faithful audience (e.g., Unsound, Divine Comedy, Film Music Festival). The Conrad Festival won the prestigious EFFE Award 2019–2020 for outstanding art festivals. After two milestones in making Kraków an eventful city (or rather festival city, terminology more frequently used in Kraków) – the ECM 1992 and ECC 2000 – the city continued to apply to host touring events. The municipality wanted Kraków to host the 24th Olympic Winter Games in 2022 but the inhabitants rejected this idea with a majority of votes in a referendum in 2014. Despite some controversy (e.g., opposition from the Common City Association), Kraków is to host the European Games in 2023.

Piaskowski (2021) emphasises that there were two stages to the development of events in Kraków. One was right after the fall of communism (1989), when events became platforms for dialogue and windows for integration with the rest of the world. And the second was after 2007, when events became "a major element of the city's cultural policies as tools supporting the development of the creative economy, making the most of new cultural venues and driving cultural tourism." Although Rudolf et al. claim that, at that time, the idea of a festival city was perceived rather in terms of city marketing than a tool to increase quality of life or benefits derived directly from the socio-economic potential of culture (2015, p. 35), the approach has gradually been changing with new strategic documents coming into force.

Kraków has lately become an important actor in the field of events, including international ones with an audience of almost two million participants.

These audiences are not only tourists, as close to 80% of Kraków residents declare that they take part in the city events (Piaskowski, 2021). In 2016, Kraków received a prestigious IFEA (International Festivals and Events Association) World Festival & Event City Award that honoured cities that provide an environment conducive to successful festival and events. Kraków was awarded the title in recognition of its perseverance in building the city's position as a leader among the festival cities in Central and Eastern Europe. But not only that. One of the reasons given for distinguishing the city was its orientation of the festivals to engage the local community and strengthen the cultural identity of the city.

Festivals make an important contribution to the city economy.[6] Research into four major festivals in Kraków (Misteria Paschalia, Film Music Festival, Wianki – Celebration of Music, and Sacrum Profanum) provides interesting evidence of this as their total economic impact for Kraków amounts to PLN 19 million (with the Film Music Festival accounting for about half the amount) and for Poland – PLN 28 million. One can calculate a so-called "grant effectiveness indicator" that illustrates how much money was generated by investing PLN 1 in festivals. In case of Misteria Paschalia, its value was PLN 1.10, and in the case of the Film Music Festival – PLN 3.60 (Chrzanowski, 2017, pp. 84–85). As one of the senior officials at the municipality emphases (Interview 4), events can be also seen as drivers for entire cultural sectors. One cannot forget that an event is a place to present oneself and one's achievements, make new contacts, look for cooperation opportunities (e.g., the Film Music Festival helped some musicians sign contracts with Netflix).

Kraków seems also to be aware of the importance of exchanging knowledge and best practices with other cities, both in Poland and beyond. It takes an active part in the discussions held by the Coalition of Cities, which is an informal gathering of ECoC 2016 candidate cities and Wrocław (the ECoC 2016 winner), which could be called a network or a think tank for the exchange of knowledge and experience of Polish local governments and cultural institutions. It is also one of the founding members of the Festival Cities Network. Established in 2015, the network brings together representatives of six festival cities: Adelaide, Barcelona, Berlin, Edinburgh, Montreal, and Kraków, to share their experience and appreciation of festivals, their socio-economic impact, and their role in sustainable development.

The strategy used by Kraków to become an eventful city seems to be a combination of what Greg Richards (2017, pp. 537–540) calls "event-centric eventfulness" (concentration on developing the number, range, and type of events to stage, all coordinated by the KBF) and "sector-centric eventfulness", which sees events as important platforms for particular economic, social, and cultural activities in the city (i.e., what is indicated in the Kraków strategic documents). One may also find emerging elements of the network-centric eventfulness approach with Kraków's determination to link the city with global networks and establish the city as an events hub.

Bibliography

Berbeka, J. et al. (2015) *The Meetings Industry in Kraków 2015*. Kraków: Cracow University of Economics Foundation, Municipality of Kraków.

Berbeka, J. et al. (2016) *The Meetings Industry in Kraków 2016*. Kraków: Cracow University of Economics Foundation, Municipality of Kraków.

Berbeka, J. et al. (2017) *The Meetings Industry in Kraków 2017*. Kraków: Cracow University of Economics Foundation, Municipality of Kraków.

Berbeka, J. et al. (2018) *The Meetings Industry in Kraków 2018*. Kraków: Cracow University of Economics Foundation, Municipality of Kraków.

Berbeka, J. et al. (2019) *The Meetings Industry in Kraków 2019*. Kraków: Cracow University of Economics Foundation, Municipality of Kraków.

Berbeka, J. et al. (2020) *The Meetings Industry in Kraków 2020*. Kraków: Cracow University of Economics Foundation, Municipality of Kraków.

Biuro Kraków 2000 (2000/2001) *Program Kraków 2000 Europejskie Miasto Kultury. Raport*. Kraków: Biuro Kraków 2000 (typescript).

Booth, P. and Boyle, R. (1993) "See Glasgow, See Culture", in: Bianchini, F. and Parkinson, M. (eds.) *Cultural Policy and Urban Regeneration: The West European Experience*. Manchester and New York: Manchester University Press, 21–47.

Borodako, et al. (2014) *Influence of the Meetings Industry on the Economy of Kraków*. Kraków: Fundacja Uniwersytetu Ekonomicznego w Krakowie.

Chrzanowski, M. (2017) *Krakowskie festiwale muzyczne a potencjał kreatywny i gospodarczy miasta. Raport z badań*. Kraków: Krakowskie Biuro Festiwalowe.

Comedia (1992) *Monitoring the European Cultural Month in Cracow in June 1992: A Summary*. London: Comedia (typescript).

Drzał-Sierocka, A. et al. (2017) *Festiwale filmowe w Polsce. Raport*. Warszawa: Fundacja Obserwatorium, SWPS.

Dziewanowska, K. (2015) "Gospodarka doświadczeń – podstawowe zagadnienia", in: Kacprzak, A. et al. (eds.) *Gospodarka doświadczeń. Perspektywa polskiego konsumenta*. Warszawa: Wydawnictwo PWN, 30–62.

European Commission (2016) *Culture and Creativity. European Capitals of Culture*. Available at: https://ec.europa.eu/culture/policies/culture-in-cities-and-regions/european-capitals-of-culture (Accessed on: 10 September 2021).

EXPO Kraków (2021) *EXPO Kraków*. Available at: https://expokrakow.com/gb/-about-expo-krakow.html (Accessed on: 10 September 2021).

Getz, D. (2007) *Event Studies: Theory, Research and Policy for Planned Events*. London: Butterworth-Heinemann.

Gierat-Bieroń, B. (2012) "Kraków: kultura przez duże "K"", *Salon 24*, 21 March. Available at: https://www.salon24.pl/u/iobywatelski/401280,krakow-kultura-przez-duze-k (Accessed on: 15 September 2021).

Glondys, D. (2010) *Kraków. Europejskie Miasto Kultury. Summa Factorum*. Kraków: Wydawnictwo Attyka.

Gold, J.R. and Gold, M.M. (2005) *Cities of Culture: Staging International Festivals and the Urban Agenda, 1951–2000*. Farnham-Burlington, VT: Ashgate.

Hughes, H. et al. (2003) "The Significance of European 'Capital of Culture' for Tourism and Culture: The Case of Kraków 2000", *International Journal of Arts Management*, 5(3), 12–23.

Jacobs, J. (1984) *Cities and the Wealth of Nations: Principles of Economic Life*. New York: Vintage Books.

Karwińska, A. and Marszycka, M. (1992) *Europejski Miesiąc Kultury – Kraków "92. Raport z badań* (typesript), Kraków.
Krakowskie Biuro Festiwalowe (2018) *About ICE Kraków*. Available at: http://icekrakow.com/en/about-ice-krakow (Accessed on: 14 October 2021).
Krakowskie Biuro Festiwalowe (2021) *About KBF*. Available at: https://kbf.krakow.pl/en/about-kbf/ (Accessed on: 14 October 2021).
Marciszewska, B. (2010) *Produkt turystyczny a ekonomia doświadczeń*. Warszawa: Wydawnictwo C.H. Beck.
Municipality of Kraków (2018) *Kraków Development Strategy: This Is Where I Want to Live. Kraków 2030*. Available at: https://www.bip.krakow.pl/plik.php?zid=212318&wer=0&new=t&mode=shw (Accessed on: 17 August 2021).
Piaskowski, R. (2021) *A City of Festivals*. Available at: https://krakowculture.pl/en/dziedziny/festivals/ (Accessed on: 18 September 2021).
Pine, J. II B. and Gilmore, J.H. (1998a) "Welcome to the Experience Economy", *Harvard Business Review. Economic Cycles and Trends*, July–August. https://hbr.org/1998/07/welcome-to-the-experience-economy
Pine, J. II B. and Gilmore, J.H. (1998b) *The Experience Economy: Work Is Theatre and Every Business a Stage: Goods and Services Are No Longer Enough*. Boston, MA: Harvard Business School Press.
Purchla, J. (1993) *Europejski Miesiąc Kultury w Krakowie. Czerwiec 1992*. Kraków: Międzynarodowe Centrum Kultury.
Rada Miasta (2017) *Program Rozwoju Kultury w Krakowie do roku 2030*. Załącznik do uchwały Nr LXXIX/1933/17.
Rada Miasta Krakowa (2010) *Strategia rozwoju kultury w Krakowie na lata 2010–2014*. Załącznik do uchwały Nr CXIV/1524/10.
Richards, G. (2017) "Emerging Models of the Eventful City", *Event Management*, 21, 533–543.
Richards, G. and Palmer, R. (2010) *Eventful Cities: Cultural Management and Urban Revitalisation*. Oxford and Burlington, MA: Elsevier.
Roche, M. (2000) *Mega-events and Modernity: The Olympics, Internationalism and Supernationalism: International Sports Events and Movements in the Inter-war Period*. New York: Routledge.
Rudolf, A. et al. (2015) *Raport końcowy z badania sektora kultury. Krakowska kultura – stan obecny i perspektywy rozwoju*. Warszawa: Agrotec Polska Sp. z o.o.
Smith, A. (2012) *Events and Urban Regeneration: The Strategic Use of Events to Revitalise Cities*. Oxon and New York: Routledge.
Szulborska-Łukaszewicz, J. (2003) "Polityka kulturalna Miasta Krakowa – przemyślana strategia czy przypadek?", *Zarządzanie w kulturze*, 4, 73–85
Tauron Arena Kraków (2021) *About Us*. Available at: https://www.tauronarena-krakow.pl/en/about-us/ (Accessed on: 19 October 2021).
Urząd Miasta Krakowa (2001) *Raport o stanie miasta 2000, rozdz. XI*. Available at: http://www.bip.krakow.pl/zalaczniki/dokumenty/n/71682/0/karta (Accessed on: 22 October 2021).
Zarząd Miasta Krakowa (1999) *Strategia Rozwoju Krakowa. Misja i cele główne. Załącznik Nr 1 do uchwały nr XXXIII/235/99*. Available: https://www.bip.krakow.pl/_inc/rada/uchwaly/show_pdf.php?id=3290 (Accessed on: 23 October 2021).

Interviews:

1 Interview with a senior level official from Kraków 2000 Festival Office at the time of the ECC (13 September 2007).
2 Interview with a renowned Kraków expert in culture, heritage, and their policies on Kraków 2000 and its legacy (28 September 2007).
3 Interview with a senior level official in the municipality in the 1990s (5 September 2007).
4 Interview with a senior level official in the municipality currently dealing with cultural policy (21 October 2021).

Notes

1 What is now known as the European Capital of Culture initiative was initially called the European City of Culture. The change of name was introduced by Decision 1819/1999/EC in 2005.
2 The budget of the ECM was roughly equal to the budget of the city of Kraków for culture at the time. The ECM budget *sensu largo* amounted to PLZ 35,298,749,000, while the city budget for culture was PLZ 38,188,000,000 (Purchla, 1993, p. 53). The above amounts are in PLZ that is the "old" Polish złotys, a currency that was denominated to PLN (i.e., the "new" Polish złotys) in 1995 at a conversion rate of 1PLN = PLZ 10,000.
3 Another important legacy of Kraków 2000 are two festivals that have continued their activities until today: the Rozstaje / Crossroads Festival of Traditional Music (now EtnoKraków//Rozstaje/Crossroads) and the Court Dance Festival (now Cracovia Danza Court Dance Festival).
4 Drzał-Sierocka et al. even say that the fact that Kraków has an institution dedicated to coordinating festival activities in the city makes Kraków the Polish leader of municipal cultural policy for supporting festivals (2017, p. 18).
5 The number rapidly diminished in 2020 due to the COVID-19 pandemic.
6 Just as the MICE events – see above.

6 Kraków spatial development after 1989

Michał Wiśniewski

The new general spatial development plan for Kraków prepared by the team of Zygmunt Ziobrowski (Urząd Miasta Krakowa, 1988) was approved in 1988 on the eve of the political and economic transformation in Poland. Due to the rapid demographic and spatial development of the city in the preceding decades, it was already the fourth such document since 1945 (Firlet, 2007, pp. 663–714). It started off by recognising the system that produced the previous versions, especially the general spatial development plan of 1977 developed by the team of Krystian Seibert (Urząd Miasta Krakowa, 1977) that remained in force, as discredited. The new plan was the first to cover Kraków and the neighbouring communes and envisaged the development of the city as a metropolis (Seibert, 1983).

The new design from 1988 also encompassed the city and its environs and was based on the assumptions made earlier, as well as those already partially implemented as far as the development of the road system and the deployment of the residential districts was concerned (Purchla, 2007b, pp. 17–24). Until the end of the 1940s, Kraków, with its current population of around 300,000, developed as a concentric system with the hub in the historic centre. The construction of the Lenin Steelworks, one of Poland's largest industrial facilities, and the accompanying district of Nowa Huta situated approximately 8 km to the east of the centre did away with that principle. The further development of the steelworks complex resulted in the development of a 10-kilometre-long belt of residential districts on the northern side of the city, which eventually changed the distribution dynamics of the city's population (Urząd Miasta Krakowa, 1967). Development of a similar belt began on the southern side a decade later.

The starting point

In 1988, there were already 750,000 people living in Kraków and the city covered 327 km^2, nearly twice its area immediately after the Second World War (168.3 km^2) and more than 50 times as much as early in the 20th century (5.77 km^2). At the time, the rapid inflow of new residents continued while the idea of two belts of development was sufficiently advanced to make it

DOI: 10.4324/9781003252757-7

impossible to stop. Emphasis was laid not on the further development of the city, but on the connection of the already extant fragments and districts. Crossing the Vistula River was a great challenge for Cracovians in the late 1980s, as the number of bridges was insufficient and travelling from the relatively close districts of Prokocim and Nowa Huta required going via the historical centre. Zygmunt Ziobrowski's plan adjusted the current state to the actual needs and parameters that defined the further development of Kraków, and was decisive for the start of numerous strategic investments, e.g., dual carriageways and bridges, which were carried out over the following three decades (Wiśniewski, 2018, pp. 235–286).

A year after the document was approved, Poland became the stage of deep political change as parliamentary democracy and a free-market economy were reinstated. Initially, the new political situation and the economic changes primarily meant a successive phase of the crisis that had lasted for over a decade and a further weakening of the construction market. At the same time, the changes initiated in 1989 resulted in the emergence of two factors of key importance for a change in thinking about the development of the city, spatial planning included. The first was the reinstitution of the territorial authorities in 1990 and the rejection of the hierarchic vertical structure in public administration that made the city authorities an extension of the central state government (*Dziennik Ustaw* 1990, 1990). In 1990, the city authorities regained their autonomy, and the prerogatives of the community-level authorities now included spatial planning (Purchla, 2016, pp. 109–116).

The second key phenomenon were ownership changes that included returning control over land and many buildings to the pre-war owners and their inheritors. After the Second World War, property was nationalised in Poland and ownership was limited in various ways. In Kraków, the phenomenon of nationalisation was most extreme in the case of land taken over by the state for the development of the Lenin Steelworks and other industrial facilities, and for the construction of new residential estates. Most of that land was agricultural with a low level of urban development (Gołaszewski, 1955). The areas allocated for future transformation were retained in their current state, and a provision preventing any change of land use was employed for agricultural land.

After 1945, compulsory administration by the state was extended to the areas developed before the Second World War that had been private before 1939. This meant they remained in the hands of their pre-war owners who had no influence on the actual use of the buildings, the level of rent, or the scale and means of letting their property to tenants (Purchla, 1996, pp. 269–284). The new principles of real estate management had a fundamental bearing on their condition and accelerated degradation (Beiersdorf, 1996, pp. 98–100).

After 1990, the ownership title became a key parameter decisive for the use of land and real estate. Soon after the local authorities were reinstated in Kraków, the compulsory administration of pre-war property was abolished and, wherever possible, control over the buildings was handed over to their former owners or their heirs (Purchla, 2007a, pp. 87–93). Many residential buildings and numerous townhouses and villas survived in the districts that were urbanised before 1989. The Register of Immovable Heritage of the Małopolska Region (Rejestr zabytków nieruchomych województwa małopolskiego) extends legal protection over approximately 1,250 sites, of which over 1,000 are residential buildings (Wojewódzki Urząd Ochrony Zabytków, 2021). The register of built heritage held by the Kraków Municipality, which provides a weaker form of protection, extends to approximately 6,500 sites of which around 5,000 are residential buildings from the Middle Ages to the period between the two world wars (Urząd Miasta Krakowa, 2021a). The research into the real estate market in Kraków estimated that the entire stock of such buildings in the city is twice as large (Bartuś, 2019). A decided majority of historical residential buildings are private property, many of them with undetermined ownership.

It quickly became obvious in light of the changes that the provisions of the binding general spatial development plan, which divided the city into sections in line with their functions, failed to account for property rights and infringed the so-called "Little Constitution" of 1992 (*Dziennik Ustaw* 1992, 1992). In 1994, the Kraków Municipal Council adopted the new general spatial development plan for the city. Prepared again by the team of Zygmunt Ziobrowski, it was an update of the previous one. The main courses of city development were upheld, as were the key provisions of the previous planning document. The changes included the boundaries of the study, which were now narrowed down to the city limits, and some detailed arrangements, categories, and divisions of plots (Urząd Miasta Krakowa, 1994).

It was only a year later that the Polish Parliament adopted a new regulation, fundamental for cities, which struck at the numerous provisions of such acts of local law. The new Act on the protection of land, adopted in 1995, excluded the territory lying within the city limits (*Dziennik Ustaw* 1995, 1995). From then on, a huge part of Kraków ceased to be protected by the earlier laws. Owners of plots not recognised as agricultural in the general spatial development plan could start taking steps to develop their land. The changes that came into force in 1995 were the first step in a direction that was very dangerous for the city and was related to the development of the poorly connected suburban areas.

Another important phenomenon that made a powerful impact on the real estate market ensued from the transformation of the status of co-operative housing. Post-war Poland created a model for the development of residential housing that entailed state-supported housing cooperatives operating as its main actors (Skotarczak, 2015). Kraków's largest co-operative gathered tens of thousands of members who gained the right to rent a flat on joining. Due to the very high rate of migration of the rural population to the cities, the model was never sufficient and the waiting period for a co-operative flat ranged from several to nearly 20 years. The quality of the buildings and their fixtures and finishes were generally criticised. The Polish construction industry of the 1960s began to use prefabrication on a large scale and *wielka płyta*, or prefabricated concrete slabs, quickly became the hallmark of the Polish post-war residential estates (Cymer, 2019). After 1989, the former tenants were offered an opportunity to buy their flats at relatively low rates. The new regulation turned the tenants of the buildings owned by the cooperatives into owners and members of tenant-owned communities. Some 100,000–200,000 dwellings were privatised, and for some residents, they became a means to play the property market.

New investments

The first symptoms of an upward trend in the Kraków construction market of the 1990s stemmed from public investments, e.g., the building of the Polish Radio building (1999), the construction of the headquarters for the Regional Court (2001), as well as new buildings for institutions of higher education such as the new wing of the Jagiellonian Library (2002). Other new phenomena were the developments initiated by the territorial authorities. In 1997, the continuous thoroughfare of Karmelicka, Królewska, and Podchorążych streets was, a year later ul. Zwierzyniecka followed suit, and in 1999, it was the turn of Aleja Róż or Nowa Huta's key public space.

Late in the 1990s, work on the construction of three new bridges over the Vistula began. The Kotlarski Bridge connected the districts of Grzegórzki and Zabłocie, providing a road and tram (light rail) connection to the undeveloped areas in the south-eastern part of the city. The Zwierzyniecki Bridge did not have such an impact on the further development of the city, but it made possible a new connection between the districts of Salwator and Dębniki, and for ul. Generała Bohdana Zielińskiego to be built, which made the access to the city from the west easier by eliminating the need to travel through the centre (Motak, 2002, pp. 51–58). The third, the Wanda Bridge, connected Nowa Huta to Bieżanów and Prokocim. Besides these investments, in the period in question, two collision-free intersections were built on Opolska and Stelli-Sawickiego streets. The key road investments were developed in a short time and completed in 2001 and 2002, representing a real breakthrough in the development of the transport network.

The changes in road development initiated by the city coincided with the investments made by the state. The development of the motorway ring road around Kraków started in the 1980s. In 2003, the southern section of the road, part of the A4 motorway running from Zgorzelec on the German border to Korczowa by the Ukrainian border, was opened, and in 2017, the motorway bridge over the Vistula was commissioned (Generalna Dyrekcja Dróg Krajowych i Autostrad, 2021a), while the closing of the city's external ring road is planned for 2023 (Generalna Dyrekcja Dróg Krajowych i Autostrad, 2021b). The city's main airport operates near the ring road on the western side of the city. In 1994, John Paul II Airport got a modern terminal that has been extended several times since then (W biuro architektoniczne Wizja, 2021). The

Figure 6.1 Galeria Krakowska shopping centre, 2006.
Photo by P. Mazur.

airport handled around 200,000 passengers annually in the mid-1990s and served around 8.5 million passengers in 2020 (Kraków Airport im. Jana Pawła II, 2021). From the outset of the political and economic changes in Poland, Kraków Airport was one of the fastest developing airports in Central Europe.

Kraków Główny, a new railway station in the underground section of the new complex of railway tracks and platforms built since the 1980s, was commissioned in 2013 (Agencja Architektoniczna Centrum Sp. z o.o., 2021). Even earlier, in 2006, the new coach station opened on the eastern side of the railway station, and ul. Wita Stwosza was built, closing the city's second ring road: a line of streets intended for fast traffic, running along the line of the early 20th-century borders of Kraków. In 2008, a rapid tram line running in a tunnel of nearly 1.5 km under the station was opened to connect the northern and southern peripheries of the city. The outcome of these investments was the development of one of Poland's largest transport hubs to the north of the historical centre. Since 2006, it has been accompanied by the Galeria Krakowska, one of the city's largest shopping centres (IMB ASYMETRIA, 2021) (Figure 6.1).

The opening of a new space in the Dworzec Główny (literally "the main station") coincided with the acceleration of the work on the modernisation of the Kraków railway hub, which includes increasing the number of tracks crossing the city to four, construction of a railway flyover to the south of the station and a new railway bridge over the Vistula, and transformations of the Kraków Płaszów station and a handful of smaller stops (*Budujemy nową kolej w Krakowie*, 2021). Another important element of modernising the railway tracks in Kraków was the construction of the railway link in Podgórze in 2017: a complex of flyovers allowing a direct connection from Kraków Główny station to Skawina, Oświęcim, and Zakopane without the need to stop and change direction at Kraków Płaszów Station. The refurbishment of the Kraków railway hub is necessary for the development of the SKA fast commuter railway system, which has been operating since 2014 and whose purpose is to set up a real alternative for road traffic and public transport in the city (Urząd Miasta Krakowa, 2020a).

After 1989, the tram network long remained out of scope for new investments. In 2000, after a two-decade break, the first new track was constructed in the city and trams began to run along ul. Wincentego Witosa to the terminal in the Kurdwanów district. In 2008, the aforementioned tunnel under the railway station opened. The construction of a new tram line to Mały Płaszów terminal on the south-eastern side of the city, completed in 2010, was of special importance for the urban development of the city. Thanks to the construction of the Kotlarski Bridge and the development of the road grid around it, it was possible to design public transport lines to a poorly urbanised section of the city, where new residential estates immediately began to develop. Two years later, another line was built to the Czerwone Maki terminal and the nearby residential estates of the Nowy Ruczaj area and the new campus of the Jagiellonian University. In 2020, after an eight year break, the construction of yet another line was begun, this time running to the new estates developed on the northern side of the city in the area of Górka Narodowa (Miejskie Przedsiębiorstwo Komunikacyjne S.A. w Krakowie, 2013).

A document titled "Feasibility study for the construction of fast, collision-free railway transport in Kraków" concerning a system of fast railway serving the functions of the metro was produced on the commission of the municipal authorities in 2021 (Szybki Transport Miejski, 2021). Should it be developed, the system of tracks running partly underground will shorten travel times between the western and eastern sections of the city and will shift the future centre of city development towards the site of the former steelworks in its eastern part.

In parallel with the development of the railway transport, Kraków has invested in the development of dual carriageways. In 2004, the newly built ul. Jerzego Turowicza connected the southern settlements of the city and the motorway ring road (third) to the second ring road. Ul. Pułkownika Ryszarda Kuklińskiego was built in 2010 to connect the two ring roads on the eastern side of the city and, together with the new tram line, made possible the development of the Mały Płaszów area. The construction of the Trasa Łagiewnicka Route was commenced in 2018. It was intended to connect residential estates in Kurdwanów to those in Ruczaj, provide the main transport route within the southern belt of development in Kraków, and become an element of what is known as the "third ring-road", which is currently operating in a skeleton function only on the northern side of the city (Trasa Łagiewnicka S.A. w Krakowie, 2021).

Many other roads were also rebuilt and key intersections were also transformed, the most spectacular being the Rondo Ofiar Katynia roundabout where a three-level, collision-free system of fast roads was constructed and now provides access to the city from the north-west (Urząd Miasta Krakowa, 2012). In 2020, there were already over 530,000 cars registered in Kraków, or approx. 690 vehicles per 1,000 residents (Urząd Miasta Krakowa, 2021c, p. 202). On top of that, an average of about 250,000 cars enter the Kraków city limits each day. Like many other large Central European cities, Kraków has more cars than the cities of Western Europe. While there are approximately 830 cars per 1,000 inhabitants in Warsaw, the ratio in Berlin is only around 330. The EU average is 569, and Poland's is 642, which is Europe's fourth highest and below Luxembourg, Italy, and Cyprus (Eurostat, 2021). The drastic increase in the number of cars in Kraków after 1989 resulted from the breakdown of the system of public transport in Poland, making individual motorisation the only viable alternative (Trammer, 2019). The other factor that drove that rise was the rapid growth in new build developments, mostly residential, including suburbanisation of the city's outskirts (Figure 6.2).

New rules of engagement

Towards the end of the 1990s, the Polish Parliament started work on a new act on spatial planning. At the time, concern was expressed that the general spatial development plans in force may violate the right of ownership. Fearing a wave of lawsuits against the state and the potential for damages, the Parliament included a provision in the act that changed the previous manner

Figure 6.2 Rondo Ofiar Katynia roundabout, 2011.
Photo by P. Mazur.

of managing space in the city. As a result, on 1 January 2003, all the general spatial development plans adopted by Polish local governments before 1995 were invalidated (*Dziennik Ustaw* 2003, 2003). New planning tools were to be created in their place.

The act introduced the obligation to design a study of conditions and directions of spatial development for the commune (Ziobrowski et al., 1996). It was to be a strategic document defining the long-term objectives and parameters of city development. However, the act did not define the document as an act of local law, which, over time, proved to severely limit its causative power. The second and most important type of planning document envisaged in the new act were the local zoning plans (literally "local spatial management plans", Polish: *miejscowe plany zagospodarowania przestrzennego*). Every commune was expected to define the number of plans that were to be drawn up and the area they would cover. Moreover, the act did not define a deadline for their adoption.

In the areas where no local zoning plans had been adopted, the act made it possible to carry out developments on the grounds of a decision on site-development conditions (*warunki zabudowy*, being a planning permission), a set of guidelines drawn up by the local administration that defined the basic parameters of the development that could take place on a given plot. The new law made no decisions concerning the dependency between the decision on site-development conditions and the provisions of the study of conditions and directions of spatial development. The act on spatial planning meant that many Polish cities, Kraków included, lost the binding general spatial development plans. And at the same time, no obligation was laid on the local authorities to prepare new planning mechanisms while the act was being elaborated.

The work on the study of conditions and directions of spatial development for the Kraków Municipality had already commenced late in the 1990s, and the document was finally approved in 2003 (Urząd Miasta Krakowa, 2003). It was coordinated by Robert Kuzianik and supervised by deputy mayor and urban planner Zbigniew Zuziak. This did not help much, as the document that should have remained in force for a number of decades quickly became outdated. The work on the new study began in 2010, and it was eventually approved in 2014 (Urząd Miasta Krakowa, 2014). Jan M. Chmielewski was nominated the plenipotentiary of the mayor to coordinate work on the document (Brzosko-Sermak et al., 2014). In 2018, the city authorities announced that the new document also required updating and that a new one should be prepared (Urząd Miasta Krakowa, 2021b). Just in 2014–18, around 430 permits for construction were issued that violated the provisions of the binding study (Serafin, 2018). The scale of the phenomenon revealed the inefficiency of the mechanism.

At a time when the city most needed a thoughtful and far-sighted planning law, it was bereft of one. In 2003, the plans only covered around 1% of the city, which resulted in an avalanche of applications to issue a decision on site-development conditions. In 2005 alone, 3,510 such documents were issued

(Urząd Miasta Krakowa, 2006, p. 30). The number did not decrease in the following years, and 2,970 such decisions were issued in 2015 (Urząd Miasta Krakowa, 2016, p. 32). It quickly turned out that the legal mechanism expected to be used *ad hoc* became the most widespread and popular. Decisions on site-development conditions were used in Kraków for the construction of single-family houses, residential estates, and large-scale commercial premises.

Moreover, the process of drawing up local zoning plans proved to be far more time-consuming and costly than originally thought. One of the obstacles on the path to their adoption were the protests by owners of the plots covered by the planning procedure, who fought against any limitations on the potential developments that could decrease the commercial value of their land. As a result, the process of drafting local zoning plans dragged on for years. There were 226 such plans covering 70.8% of the city in force in Kraków in the autumn of 2021. Local zoning plans only fully covered the area listed as UNESCO World Heritage, Kraków's most valuable historical area, in 2017 (Urząd Miasta Krakowa, 2021e).

Rapid growth

The principles of shaping urban planning adopted by the Parliament efficiently limited the capacity of the local authorities to manage space. Consequently, in the wake of Poland's accession to the European Union and the rapid inflow of capital, Kraków saw highly dynamic development of residential housing. In 1991, the total housing stock in the city comprised 234,000 dwellings. The activity of housing cooperatives was still dominant, while about 20% of the newbuilt dwellings were single-family houses (Urząd Miasta Krakowa, 1992). In 2004, there were already 289,000 dwellings in Kraków. The local real estate market was dominated by private entities; individual enterprises were responsible for 19.3% of developments, and as many as 53.3% of dwellings for sale or rent were built by newly incorporated development companies. At the time, dwellings owned by cooperatives only accounted for 5.6% of new build dwellings, while dwellings of the Towarzystwa Budownictwa Mieszkaniowego housing associations, a mechanism set up by the state to stimulate the development of residential construction in Poland, accounted for 20.4% of the total (Urząd Miasta Krakowa 2005, p. 234). In 2010, there were 326,200 dwellings in Kraków. Individual developments covered 15.7% of all new real estate, while developments for sale and rent accounted for 84.1% (Urząd Miasta Krakowa, 2011, pp. 159–161). In 2020, there were already 412,600 dwellings in Kraków (Urząd Miasta Krakowa, 2021c, pp. 167–168). In just a decade, the entire stock increased by approximately 30%. The record year in the development of dwellings was 2019 when 13,039 units were added, of which 95% were earmarked for sales or rent (Urząd Miasta Krakowa, 2020b, pp. 199–200).

Żabiniec, a housing estate completed in the 1990s in District IV Prądnik Biały, on the northern side of the city was the only fairly large residential complex developed in Kraków at the time (Michalczak, 2010). The change in the quantity and size of new residential investments only came after 2000. Initially new estates were, as a rule, built on the outskirts of the existing complexes, for example, on the northern side of the estates in Mistrzejowice and on the southern part of the estate in Kurdwanów. The zone of most intense development of residential estate at the time, and, consequently, a new district of Kraków, was Nowy Ruczaj, situated in the vicinity of the Jagiellonian University Campus in Pychowice. While the population of District VIII Dębniki, where this complex is situated, was 51,500 in 2004, 15 years later, it exceeded 63,000, which is one of the highest growth dynamics in Kraków in the period in question (Urząd Miasta Krakowa, 2005, Figure I.1, 2021c, p. 26).

The quality and form of the new residential estates made them stand out against the complexes built before 1989. The positive change resulted from the standard of finishes in the new buildings. Unfortunately, the new complexes built on small, formerly agricultural plots had major functional drawbacks, were only provided with little shared space, including greenery, that as a rule lost out to the residents' needs for car parking. Another problem was the dominance of road systems around the new estates, which were very often built as self-contained systems. Fenced off from the city and from one another, they left their residents unable to move within the district. As the new residential estates developed on the power of a decision on site-development conditions, they formed a patchwork of unrelated spatial arrangements with residential monofunctionality (Gądecki, 2009). Up until the initiation of the planning procedures, there had been no reason to discuss the needs of the residents, and the community was not obliged to provide the new estates with access to public services, such as schools and walk-in healthcare centres. A particular paradox can be seen in the fact that having an adjacent residential estate that was built before 1989 and was furnished with these public services and recreational spaces was often decisive for the success of a new development.

The dominance of private property and the lack of planning tools resulted in only one new park being developed in Kraków after 1989. Park Dębnicki, covering less than 5 ha, opened in 2003 (Pawłowska, 2009, pp. 49–70). The hurdle for creating the subsequent parks was the need for the municipal authorities to buy back land. No major purchases had taken place before 2016. The purchase of a large area by the nature reserve near the former stone quarry in Zakrzówek by a private developer, and the announcement of the intention to build another residential estate in its direct vicinity resulted in a grassroots protest in 2011 that led to the stalling of the development and the eventual takeover of the area by the local authorities (Akcja Ratunkowa dla Krakowa, 2021). The development was of more than just symbolic significance as it blazed the trail to new investments in managing green areas.

In 2016, the Kraków authorities set up the Kraków Municipal Greenspace Authority (ZZM, Zarząd Zieleni Miejskiej), a special institution responsible for the condition of the city's greenery (Zarząd Zieleni Miejskiej, 2021). Despite numerous investments into the existing parks and the setting up of the miniature pocket parks, there was no success in carving out a large new park comparable with the green areas that Kraków developed between the two world wars or just after the Second World War.

The new residential estates springing in Kraków after 2000 quickly became a serious challenge for the city as they generated spatial, transport, and visual chaos. These problems became most pronounced in the locations that had not been urbanised earlier, for example, in the aforementioned new residential estates in Nowy Ruczaj, Górka Narodowa, and Nowy Płaszów.

Some new estates were also built in the areas formerly used by industry. The economic changes that followed in the wake of the transformation of 1989 spelled bankruptcy for many industrial facilities in Kraków. The trend of transforming the brownfield sites left by such factories, demolishing former production buildings and replacing them with new residential buildings was especially visible just after Poland's accession to the European Union in the wake of the inflow of capital.

One of the first such complexes in Kraków was Wiślane Tarasy, an estate built on the site of the production buildings of the Zieleniewski Machine Building Facilities. The historical buildings of the factory survived in a relatively good condition until the early 21st-century when, after being purchased by a private developer, they were demolished. The buildings constructed soon afterwards made no reference to the historical context of the district (IB Inter-Bud Developer, 2021). Likewise, most of the buildings of the former factories on the land previously occupied by the vodka factory in nearby Grzegórzki, and the area of the post-industrial district of Zabłocie on the other side of the river, were demolished and transformed (ATAL, 2021). They were all replaced by new dense residential and service developments. Another telling example of similar changes was the transformation of the former Kraków Factory of Measuring Equipment in Bronowice into the Salwator City residential estate (SALWATOR. Gwarancja Bezpieczeństwa, 2021).

In most cases, the new developments have cannibalised the existing city resources and made use of the previously built road infrastructure and public services. Intensification of development in the city became widespread in the second decade of the 21st century. One of the most iconic cases is the Avia estate, a greenfield development in the vicinity of two other residential estates in Czyżyny district, halfway between Kraków and Nowa Huta (B2 STUDIO, 2021). An area originally intended for a large park that accompanied the existing developments was turned into a new estate of 3,500 dwellings, and the city's first 16-floor residential buildings. The entire complex is one of the most densely developed in the city (Figure 6.3).

In parallel with the new residential estates, districts of single-family houses and terraced developments were built on the city outskirts and beyond its borders. One characteristic feature of suburbanisation that sprawled into the suburbs of Kraków after 2000 is the very poor network of road connections

Figure 6.3 Osiedle Avia residential estate, 2017.
Photo by P. Mazur.

(Ziobro, 2019). The houses and whole complexes of terraced houses developed in many areas can only be accessed along roads built to the standards of a one-way street. As all communes are equal before Polish law, major cities have no special tools that would let them influence the neighbouring communes (*Dziennik Ustaw* 1990, 1990). Suburbanisation has already resulted in detrimental changes on the outskirts of the metropolises, i.e., the locations to which city centre residents began to move especially after 2000 (Kajdanek, 2013), for people working in the city and using its infrastructure pay their taxes in other communes. Moreover, very dense development and poor public transport have reinforced the problem of the rapid increase in the number of cars.

A new way of life

Late in the 1990s, Kraków first came face to face with the phenomenon of major investments in shopping centres. The Géant mall was developed on ul. Generała Tadeusza Bora-Komorowskiego in 1997, and a year later, Carrefour opened on ul. Zakopiańska and IKEA on ul. Josepha Conrada. Tesco opened on ul. Kapelanka in 2001, and the M1 shopping mall and Plaza, the city's first shopping centre, opened on Aleja Pokoju street. By 2018, there were already 15 major commercial centres in Kraków, with three more in the adjacent communes. In 2020, such spaces covered around 615,000 m^2 of gross leasable area (GLA) just in Kraków (Urząd Miasta Krakowa, 2018). The great majority of such developments were based on typical designs adjusted to local conditions, hardly different from similar premises built for the major chain stores in Western Europe. Yet in Poland, such complexes have most frequently been built not on the outskirts of the city but in the vicinity of historical districts and large residential centres.

The Géant, M1, and Plaza malls were built in the very heart of the metropolis, on undeveloped sites located by the main roads connecting the centre of Kraków to Nowa Huta. Each had a far-reaching impact on its environment, as further developments arose nearby. Soon after the construction of Géant, Kraków's first multiscreen cinema and one of Poland's largest aquaparks/waterparks opened in its vicinity. A decade later, two large office building complexes and the Serenada shopping centre joined the cluster (W biuro architektoniczne Wizja, 2021). The site intended in the 1970s as the location of a large academic district that was supposed to connect the centre of Kraków to Nowa Huta and lay by the arterial road providing the connection to the northern districts and estates of Kraków, grew into one of the largest commercial hubs catering both for the city and nearby locations. The significance of the site lies in its competitive character for the traditionally understood centre. The possibility of reaching it mostly by means of individual transport makes it an exterritorial island in the city space.

More such sites were built in Kraków and the case of the Carrefour shopping complex on ul. Zakopiańska (IMB ASYMETRIA, 2021) is worth noting. It was constructed on the premises of the former Solvay factory (Krzak, 2005, pp. 9–11). Once production in the soda factory on the southern side of the city ceased, the remaining brownfield site was reclaimed. A decision was made to retain some buildings of the complex and adapt them for commercial purposes. A new road system was designed in the vicinity, and premises for the construction of large-space shops were delimited. With time, the area was built over by Multiplex Cinema City, the Zakopianka shopping centre, and a handful of other commercial facilities (IMB ASYMETRIA, 2021). In 2002, the construction of the Sanctuary of Divine Mercy in Łagiewniki was completed to the east of the shopping precinct. A decade later, the former settling ponds of the soda works were developed into the John Paul II Centre. These two monumental religious complexes attract masses of tourists. Together with the nearby shopping area, they generate the largest inflow of people and vehicular traffic in the city.

The transformation of the former Solvay premises was the first far-going intervention into a post-industrial area in the city. In the following years, several other commercial complexes, mostly retail, followed a similar model. In 2005, the premises of the former municipal slaughterhouse in Grzegórzki, which is relatively close to the historic city centre, was developed with the Galeria Kazimierz shopping mall (IMB ASYMETRIA, 2021). Again, a large part of a valuable industrial site was demolished to provide the space for a new development. A year later, the largest intervention of this type came with the opening of Galeria Krakowska, at the time the city's largest retail complex, built on the premises formerly used by the railway in the direct vicinity of the city centre.

The development of that complex was an old offshoot of the urban development competition from 1966 for the new centre of Kraków in the direct vicinity of the historic centre, which prejudged retaining the railway station on its original site. In 1995, that idea became the lodestar for the urban planning competition won by the team of Romuald Loegler (Fabiański, Purchla, 2012, p. 154), whose design was used for drafting the Coordination Plan. The multifunctional complex was expected to provide a new space for life in the city and a bridge between the historical centre and the railway station. Late in the 1990s, the US developer Tishman Speyer Properties delivered the winning bid in the tender for the development of the Kraków Transport Centre (KCK), but the development never took place (Fijałek, 2004). A few years later, the area was developed with the Galeria Krakowska, one of the largest retail sites in the city as it covers around 60,000 m^2 GLA, a development that disrupted the services market in the historic centre. In the following years, Nowa Pawia street was built alongside the mall and over time, residential buildings, hotels, and office blocks were also built, which completed the process of transforming the area in the direct vicinity of the train station, one that had taken nearly five decades.

In 2009, another investment of this type was carried out in the south of Kraków, on the premises of the former Bonarka industrial site (IMB ASYMETRIA, 2021). Like Solvay, the ground polluted by industry had to be reclaimed prior to development. Historical industrial buildings were also demolished in this area to be replaced by one of Poland's largest commercial sites, covering approximately 90,000 m^2 GLA, which soon prompted the construction of office buildings in its vicinity (Figure 6.4).

Figure 6.4 Galeria Bonarka shopping centre with the surrounding office blocks, 2009. Photo by P. Mazur.

The large-format retail centres played a particular role in the spatial development of the city. Their locations, and often also their scale, did not result from the authorities' conscious spatial planning policy but were a derivative of ownership changes and the investment capacity of foreign businesses. From the point of view of Western investors, each of the developments mentioned above stood out thanks to its advantageous location, which was helpful in obtaining a quick return on the investment as they were all developed in the vicinity of thoroughfares and large residential estates built before 1989. From the point of view of the spatial planning policy of the local authorities, these investments were islands standing out from the space of the city that furthermore intensified vehicular traffic between peripheral districts, the city centre, and the suburbs, bringing no city-forming functions or infrastructure into the space of the metropolitan area that could have had a positive influence on the further development of the city.

New jobs

Another type of development proliferating in Kraków, especially after 2000, are office buildings. With Poland's accession to the European Union, large Polish cities became the investment target for Western and global companies that opened their business services centres here. In 2021, the number of jobs in such centres and IT hubs in Kraków was estimated to have exceeded 82,000. The indirect impact of that market is estimated at 66,000 additional jobs. Kraków is the largest centre of this type of services in Poland and had 247 service centres operating there ("Sektor nowoczesnych usług biznesowych w Polsce 2021", 2021). This dynamic new labour market forced the development of numerous investments in developing office space.

The phenomenon intensified after 2010. No major office district arose in Kraków as most developments of the type were carried out as a single building or a cluster of a few buildings. New office buildings have usually been raised alongside the major roads leading to the city and the main arteries connecting individual districts. Many office blocks were constructed in former industrial areas, for example, along Wadowicka and Zakopiańska streets and in the vicinity of the shopping centres discussed above. The former industrial district of Zabłocie, the area around Galeria Bonarka, and the environs of the campus of the Kraków University of Technology in Czyżyny became very important locations for the development of office space.

The year 2020 marked the completion of the construction of the Unity Tower office complex that replaced the unfinished skyscraper of the Polish Central Engineering Associations (NOT) (Dunikowski, Kliche, 2020, pp. 84–91). Rising to a height of 102.5 m and offering around 50,000 m^2 GLA, it is the highest building in the city and one of only a few high rise office buildings in Kraków, as such functions are usually located in low- and medium-rise buildings. The Unity Tower office block was built close to the city centre by the Rondo Mogilskie roundabout on the eastern side of the railway station, within the buffer zone of the area listed as World Heritage by UNESCO in 1978. Juxtaposition with the single-family houses surrounding its base gives an impression of chaos and provokes questions about the future of this type of development.

Breaking the impasse

In 2013, the first debate on the new labour district took place in Kraków, accompanied by the announcement of a competition for the development of the premises of the former steelworks complex (Stangel, 2014, pp. 259–275). In 2004, the Kraków steelworks had become the property of the international conglomerate Arcelor Mittal Poland, which was responsible for the management of the site (Arcelor Mittal, 2021). The gradual phasing out of production resulted in many production buildings falling out of use and the demolition of others. Nowe Centrum Administracyjne, literally "new administrative centre", a company owned by the state, was incorporated in 2014 (Nowe Centrum Administracyjne, 2021), and endeavours to extend public institutional control over the area where the steelworks began. The move did not result in full success, and the future of the steelworks still remains unknown.

The competition organised in 2013 made it possible to design an advanced concept for the development of a large expanse of the city, covering both the factory and its vicinity, with the highest accolade awarded to the work of Michał Stangel and the ARCA Biuro Projektów Urbanistyki i Architektury team. Its authors emphasised the opportunities opened up by the network of railway links to the eastern part of Kraków. The design suggested the development of a number of minor centres of settlement along the railway lines, and the earmarking of the post-industrial land for the development of labour-related functions. In 2019, the last blast furnace of the Kraków steelworks complex was extinguished (Wantuch, 2019). This symbolic event opens a new chapter in the discussion about the future of the former steelworks.

After 2003, due to the lack of local zoning plans and in the wake of the influx of EU funds, management of space through major investments – in most cases serving culture, education, and sports – became a surrogate for spatial planning in Kraków. Since the early 1990s, Kraków has developed as a major centre of tourist services. The mass inflow of visitors after 2004 was the reason why the local authorities eagerly invested public funds into new investments supporting tourist services. In 2010, the space below the surface of the Main Market Square of Kraków was opened to visitors and an exhibition devoted to the history of the city in the Middle Ages was organised there by the Museum of Kraków. At the same time, the former Oskar Schindler's Enamel Factory in Zabłocie, made famous by Steven Spielberg's Oscar-winning production, became home to a branch of the same museum devoted to the time of occupation during the Second World War, and to the MOCAK Museum of Contemporary Art in Kraków. At the same time, the

National Museum in Kraków, Poland's largest and oldest museum, carried out numerous renovation works and refurbishments. The Gallery of Polish Art in the Cloth Hall (Sukiennice) reopened in 2010. Yet, the most important moment ensuing from the modernisation of that museum was the relaunch of the Czartoryski Princes Museum in 2019 after many years of closure. In 2010, the Polish Aviation Museum expanded its facilities, and in 2014, the Cricoteka Centre for Documentation of the Art of Tadeusz Kantor was completed. The work on the transformation of the headquarters of the Museum of Municipal Engineering in the former tram depot (discussed in the chapter on Kraków architecture and globalisation) continued in parallel.

The new buildings of the museums and cultural institutions represented the other, lighter side of the transformations taking place in the space of the city. The construction of the ICE Kraków Congress Centre and the Tauron Arena for sports and events, the refurbishment of two football stadiums, and the construction of several other sports facilities can be perceived in a similar light. Those powerful gestures in the city space filled in a functional gap and allowed the development of new types of cultural and entertainment functions. Most of the structures are iconic and provide new dominants in the city's skyline.

To a certain extent, the investments of institutions of higher education, and primarily of the Jagiellonian University, complement the activities of the city in the creation of new architecture and new public space. The concept of building a new campus of Poland's largest and oldest university on the south-western side of the city, on the site of the former Pychowice village and in the vicinity of the extant Ruczaj-Zaborze housing estate, originated as far back as the early 1990s. Midway through the decade, the urban development plans for a spacious campus were developed and received state guarantee expressed in a special act (Uniwersytet Jagielloński w Krakowie. Powstanie kampusu. Krok po kroku, 2021). The first section of the new campus was completed in 2000. Its development continued without interruption for the next two decades in parallel with the dynamic development of the Nowy Ruczaj housing estate. The development of the campus was the largest state investment into city development in Kraków. Having no similar options, other higher education institutions usually built individual buildings in the vicinity of their headquarters. The exception is the privately owned Andrzej Frycz Modrzewski Kraków University, which built a spacious campus in the post-industrial district of Zabłocie in 2000–07 (EKSPO, 2021) (Figure 6.5).

A new hope

The Jagiellonian University also gained support in the form of the new University Hospital built in 2019 in Prokocim, in the vicinity of the Children's Hospital and the campus of the Medical College. Its construction sealed the development of a major medical district in the south-eastern part of the city (Szpital Uniwersytecki w Krakowie, 2021). Moreover, the completion of

Figure 6.5 Campus of the Jagiellonian University in Pychowice, since 2000. Photo by P. Mazur.

that prestigious development stripped the historical hospital buildings situated in Wesoła district in the city centre of their prior healthcare functions. It is precisely Wesoła, together with the former premises of the steelworks, that represents the key challenges that Kraków currently faces. In 2019, the Kraków authorities purchased the buildings and land in Wesoła from the Jagiellonian University and entrusted them to the management of the Kraków Development Agency (Agencja Rozwoju Miasta Krakowa, 2021). A cluster of historical buildings of major historical and symbolic value standing on a site of nearly 50 ha are situated in the direct vicinity of the very centre of the city and the historical district of Kazimierz: Kraków's two main tourists attractions. The purchase of such a large area by the municipality is unprecedented both in the history of the city and in the recent history of Poland. The work on the local zoning plans for the area started in 2021 (Urząd Miasta Krakowa, 2021d). The results of the activities conducted in Wesoła could be decisive for the future of the historical city centre: its further degradation and depopulation, or revival.

The history of urban development in Kraków after 1989 illustrates the challenges that numerous cities in Central Europe have faced in this period. The breakdown of industry-driven growth, the inflow of foreign capital invested in commercial facilities, office and logistics centres, and residential housing, the weakness of planning mechanisms, and the attempt to counter the negative trends with major public investments are only some of the fundamental phenomena that have been decisive for the changes taking place in such cities as Kraków in recent years. To a great degree, their future will depend on the skilful management of the problems discussed above and the development of new proprietary tools allowing a more harmonious model of city development consistent with the principles of sustainability.

Bibliography

Agencja Architektoniczna Centrum Sp. z o.o. (2021) Available at: http://www.aac.krakow.pl/ (Accessed on: 31 October 2021).

Agencja Rozwoju Miasta Krakowa (2021) *Zagospodarowanie terenów dzielnicy Wesoła.* Available at: http://armk.pl/wesola (Accessed on: 31 October 2021).

Akcja Ratunkowa dla Krakowa (2021) *Kalendarium.* Available at: https://akcjaratunkowadlakrakowa.pl/kalendarium/ (Accessed on: 31 October 2021).

Arcelor Mittal (2021) Available at: https://poland.arcelormittal.com/ (Accessed on: 31 October 2021).

ATAL (2021) Available at: https://atal.pl/ (Accessed on: 31 October 2021).

B2 STUDIO (2021). Available at: http://b2studio.com.pl/ (Accessed on: 31 October 2021).

Bartuś, K. (2019) *Rynek zabytkowych kamienic w Krakowie w 2019 roku. Rok rekordowych cen.* Available at: https://www.mrn.pl/analizy/analizy,178,3,Rynek-zabytkowych-kamienic-w-Krakowie-w-2019-roku.html (Accessed on: 31 October 2021).

Beiersdorf, Z. (1996) "Ochrona i konserwacja dóbr kultury w Krakowie w latach 1944–1989. Próba oceny", [in:] Małecki, J.M. (ed.) *Kraków w Polsce Ludowej. Materiały sesji naukowej Towarzystwa Miłośników Historii i Zabytków Krakowa, 27 maja 1995 r.* Kraków: Towarzystwo Miłośników Historii i Zabytków Krakowa, pp. 98–100.

Brzosko-Sermak, A. et al. (2014) *Kraków. Wyzwania rozwojowe polityki przestrzennej*, Warszawa: Oficyna Wydawnicza Politechniki Warszawskiej.

Budujemy nową kolej w Krakowie (2021) Available at: http://krakow-rudzice.pl/ (Accessed on: 31 October 2021).

Cymer, A. (2019) *Architektura w Polsce 1945–1989.* Warszawa: Centrum Architektury, Narodowy Instytut Architektury i Urbanistyki.

Dunikowski, M., and Kliche, K. (2020) "Przebudowa Szkieletora/Kraków", *Architektura-Murator*, 9.

Dziennik Ustaw (1990) "Ustawa z dnia 8 marca 1990 r. o samorządzie gminnym", *Dziennik Ustaw 1990*, 16, 95. Available at: https://isap.sejm.gov.pl/isap.nsf/DocDetails.xsp?id=WDU19900160095 (Accessed on: 31 October 2021).

Dziennik Ustaw (1992) "Ustawa Konstytucyjna z dnia 17 października 1992 r. o wzajemnych stosunkach między władzą ustawodawczą i wykonawczą Rzeczypospolitej Polskiej oraz o samorządzie terytorialnym", *Dziennik Ustaw 1992*, 84, 426. Available at: https://isap.sejm.gov.pl/isap.nsf/DocDetails.xsp?id=wdu19920840426 (Accessed on: 31 October 2021).

Dziennik Ustaw (1995) "Ustawa z dnia 3 lutego 1995 r. o ochronie gruntów rolnych i leśnych", *Dziennik Ustaw 1995*, 16, 78. Available at: http://isap.sejm.gov.pl/isap.nsf/DocDetails.xsp?id=wdu19950160078 (Accessed on: 31 October 2021).

Dziennik Ustaw (2003) "Ustawa z dnia 27 marca 2003 r. o planowaniu i zagospodarowaniu przestrzennym", *Dziennik Ustaw 2003*, 80, 717. Available at: https://isap.sejm.gov.pl/isap.nsf/DocDetails.xsp?id=WDU20030800717 (Accessed on: 31 October 2021).

EKSPO (2021) Available at: http://ekspo.com.pl/ (Accessed on: 31 October 2021).

Eurostat (2021) *Passenger Cars in the EU*. Available at: https://ec.europa.eu/eurostat/-statistics-explained/index.php?title=Passenger_cars_in_the_EU (Accessed on: 31 October 2021).

Fabiański, M., and Purchla, J. (2012) *Architektura Krakowa Przewodnik*, Kraków: Wydawnictwo Literackie.

Fijałek, K. (2004) *Tishman odchodzi z Krakowa. I z Polski*. Available at: http://wyborcza.pl/1,75248,1937442.html (Accessed on: 31 October 2021).

Firlet, E. (2007) "Zmiany przestrzenno-urbanistyczne Krakowa w latach 1939–2006", [in:] Wyrozumski J. (ed.) *Kraków. Nowe studia nad rozwojem miasta*, Biblioteka Krakowska, 150. Kraków: Towarzystwo Miłośników Historii i Zabytków Krakowa.

Gądecki, J. (2009) *Za murami: osiedla grodzone w Polsce – analiza dyskursu*, Toruń: Wydawnictwo Naukowe Uniwersytetu Mikołaja Kopernika.

Generalna Dyrekcja Dróg Krajowych i Autostrad (2021a) Available at: https://www.gov.pl/web/gddkia (Accessed on: 31 October 2021).

Generalna Dyrekcja Dróg Krajowych i Autostrad (2021b) *Zaprojektowanie i budowa drogi S 52*. Available at: https://s52-polnocnaobwodnicakrakowa.pl/ (Accessed on: 31 October 2021).

Gołaszewski, T. (1955) *Kronika Nowej Huty*. Kraków: Wydawnictwo Literackie.

IB Inter-Bud Developer (2021) Available at: https://www.mieszkania.inter-bud.pl/ (Accessed on: 31 October 2021).

IMB ASYMETRIA (2021). Available at: http://imbasymetria.pl/ (Accessed on: 31 October 2021).

Kajdanek, K. (2013) *Suburbanizacja po polsku*. Kraków: Wydawnictwo Nomos.

Kraków Airport im. Jana Pawła II (2021) Available at: www.krakowairport.pl/pl/firma/biznes/uslugi-lotnicze/statystyki (Accessed on: 31 October 2021).

Krzak, I. (2005) "Zagospodarowanie terenu po Krakowskich Zakładach Sodowych "Solvay", *Aura*, 12, pp. 9–11.

Michalczak, J. (ed.) (2010) *Architekci Małopolski 2010*. Available at: https://www.mpoia.pl/index.php/dzialalnosc/publikacje# (Accessed on: 31 October 2021).

Miejskie Przedsiębiorstwo Komunikacyjne S.A. w Krakowie (2013) Available at: www.mpk.krakow.pl (Accessed on: 31 October 2021).

Motak, M. (2002) "Nowe mosty w Krakowie", *Architektura & Biznes*, 6, pp. 51–58.

Nowe Centrum Administracyjne (2021) Available at: http://nca.malopolska.pl/ (Accessed on: 31 October 2021).

Pawłowska, K. (2009) "Partycypacja społeczna w podejmowaniu decyzji dotyczących przyrody w mieście", *Zrównoważony rozwój–zastosowania*, 3, pp. 49–70.

Purchla, J. (1996) "Miasto niepokorne. Znaczenie okresu 1945–1956 dla rozwoju Krakowa po drugiej wojnie światowej", [in:] Broński, K., Purchla, J., Szpak, J. (eds.) *Kraków–Małopolska w Europie środka. Studia ku czci profesora Jana M. Małeckiego w 70 rocznicę urodzin*. Kraków: Towarzystwo Miłośników Historii i Zabytków Krakowa, pp. 269–184.

Purchla, J. (2007a) "Kryzys planowania czy kryzys miasta?", [in:] Małecki, J.M. (ed.) *Krajobraz Krakowa wobec zagrożeń*. Kraków: Towarzystwo Miłośników Historii i Zabytków Krakowa, pp. 87–93.

Purchla, J. (2007b) "Rozwój przestrzenny i problemy urbanistyczne miasta w XIX–XX wieku", [in:] Noga, Z. (ed.) *Atlas historyczny miast polskich. Vol. 5 Małopolska*, part 1 Kraków. Kraków: Towarzystwo Miłośników Historii i Zabytków Krakowa, Wydawnictwo Antykwa, pp. 17–24.

Purchla, J. (2016) "Powrót do miasta – trudne narodziny samorządu w Krakowie w roku 1990", [in:] Purchla, J. (ed.) *Kraków – Metropolia. W 25. Rocznicę samorządu terytorialnego w III Rzeczpospolitej*, Kraków: Księgarnia Akademicka, pp. 109–116.
Purchla, J. and Sepioł, J. (eds.) (2015) *Form Follows Freedom. Architektura dla kultury w Polsce 2000+*. Kraków: Międzynarodowe Centrum Kultury.
SALWATOR. Gwarancja Bezpieczeństwa (2021) Available at: http://www.salwator.com.pl/ (Accessed on: 31 October 2021).
Seibert, K. (1983) *Plan Wielkiego Krakowa*, Kraków-Wrocław: Wydawnictwo Literackie.
"Sektor nowoczesnych usług biznesowych w Polsce 2021" (2021) Available at: https://shop-absl.pl/Sektor-Nowoczesnych-Uslug-Biznesowych-w-Polsce-2021-p112 (Accessed on: 31 October 2021).
Serafin, D. (2018) "Kraków wydał 431 pozwoleń na budowę niezgodnych ze stadium". Available at: wiadomosci.onet.pl/krakow/krakow-setki-kontrowersyjnych-pozwolen-na-budowe/c8rjks5 (Accessed on: 31 October 2021).
Skotarczak, T. (ed.) (2015) *Spółdzielnie mieszkaniowe. Dylematy funkcjonowania i rozwoju*. Warszawa: C.H. Beck.
Stangel, M. (2014) "Konkurs urbanistyczny w procesie budowania miasta. "Nowa Huta przyszłości"", *Biuletyn Komitetu Przestrzennego Zagospodarowania Kraju PAN*, 253, pp. 259–275.
Szpital Uniwersytecki w Krakowie (2021) Available at: https://www.su.krakow.pl/ (Accessed on: 31 October 2021).
Szybki Transport Miejski (2021) Available at: https://stm.krakow.pl/ (Accessed on: 31 October 2021)
Trammer, K. (2019) *Ostre cięcie. Jak niszczono polską kolej*, Warszawa: Wydawnictwo Krytyki Politycznej.
Trasa Łagiewnicka S.A. w Krakowie (2021) Available at: https://3obwodnica.krakow.pl/ (Accessed on: 31 October 2021).
Uniwersytet Jagielloński w Krakowie. Powstanie kampusu. Krok po kroku (2021) Available at: https://www.uj.edu.pl/kampus/historia-budowy (Accessed on: 31 October 2021).
Urząd Miasta Krakowa (1967) *Plan ogólny Miasta Krakowa 1967 – nieobowiązujący*. Available at: https://www.bip.krakow.pl/?sub_dok_id=49205 (Accessed on: 31 October 2021).
Urząd Miasta Krakowa (1977) *Plan ogólny Miasta Krakowa 1977 – nieobowiązujący*. Available at: https://www.bip.krakow.pl/?sub_dok_id=49206 (Accessed on: 31 October 2021).
Urząd Miasta Krakowa (1988) *Plan ogólny Miasta Krakowa 1988 – nieobowiązujący*. Available at: https://www.bip.krakow.pl/?sub_dok_id=49207 (Accessed on: 31 October 2021).
Urząd Miasta Krakowa (1992) *Raport o stanie miasta 1991*. Available at: https://www.bip.krakow.pl/zalaczniki/dokumenty/n/72118/0/karta (Accessed on: 31 October 2021).
Urząd Miasta Krakowa (1994) *Plan ogólny Miasta Krakowa 1994 – nieobowiązujący*. Available at: https://www.bip.krakow.pl/?sub_dok_id=49209 (Accessed on: 31 October 2021).
Urząd Miasta Krakowa (2003) *Studium uwarunkowań i kierunków zagospodarowania przestrzennego Miasta Krakowa (z dnia 16 kwietnia 2003 r.)* Available at: https://www.bip.krakow.pl/?dok_id=2414 (Accessed on: 31 October 2021).

Urząd Miasta Krakowa (2005) *Raport o stanie miasta 2004*. Available at: https://www.bip.krakow.pl/?dok_id=2032 (Accessed on: 31 October 2021).

Urząd Miasta Krakowa (2006) *Raport o stanie miasta 2005*. Available at: www.bip.krakow.pl/?dok_id=14849 (Accessed on: 31 October 2021).

Urząd Miasta Krakowa (2011) *Raport o stanie miasta 2010*. Available at: www.bip.krakow.pl/?dok_id=52967 (Accessed on: 31 October 2021).

Urząd Miasta Krakowa (2012) *Dokument archiwalny. Projekt: Budowa tunelu pod Rondem Ofiar Katynia*. Available at: www.bip.krakow.pl/?dok_id=50044 (Accessed on: 31 October 2021).

Urząd Miasta Krakowa (2014) *Studium uwarunkowań i kierunków zagospodarowania przestrzennego Miasta Krakowa - Dokument ujednolicony 2014*. Available at: https://www.bip.krakow.pl/?bip_id=1&mmi=48 (Accessed on: 31 October 2021).

Urząd Miasta Krakowa (2016) *Raport o stanie miasta 2015*. Available at: https://www.bip.krakow.pl/?dok_id=79963 (Accessed on: 31 October 2021).

Urząd Miasta Krakowa (2018) *Krakowski Rynek Nieruchomości*. Available at: https://www.bip.krakow.pl/?sub_dok_id=21093 (Accessed on: 31 October 2021).

Urząd Miasta Krakowa (2020a) *Studium wykonalności dla Szybkiej Kolei Aglomeracyjnej na terenie Krakowa*. Available at: https://www.bip.krakow.pl/?dok_id=120873 (Accessed on: 31 October 2021).

Urząd Miasta Krakowa (2020b) *Raport o stanie miasta 2019*. Available at: www.bip.krakow.pl/?dok_id=133270 (Accessed on: 31 October 2021).

Urząd Miasta Krakowa (2021a) *Gminna ewidencja zabytków*. Available at: https://www.bip.krakow.pl/?dok_id=57315 (Accessed on: 31 October 2021).

Urząd Miasta Krakowa (2021b) *Sporządzane studium uwarunkowań i kierunków zagospodarowania przestrzennego Miasta Krakowa*. Available at: https://www.bip.krakow.pl/?dok_id=94336 (Accessed on: 31 October 2021).

Urząd Miasta Krakowa (2021c) *Raport o stanie miasta 2020*. Available at: https://www.bip.krakow.pl/?dok_id=146665 (Accessed on: 31 October 2021).

Urząd Miasta Krakowa (2021d) *Wesoła – rejon ulicy Kopernika – Projekt planu, projekt ustaleń*. Available at: https://www.bip.krakow.pl/?dok_id=129536 (Accessed on: 31 October 2021).

Urząd Miasta Krakowa (2021e) *Wydział Planowania Przestrzennego*. Available at: https://www.bip.krakow.pl/planowanieprzestrzenne (Accessed on: 31 October 2021).

W biuro architektoniczne Wizja (2021). Available at: https://www.wizja.krakow.pl/ (Accessed on: 31 October 2021).

Wantuch, D. (2019) "Wygaszają wielki piec w krakowskim kombinacie". Available at: https://krakow.wyborcza.pl/krakow/7,44425,25438003,wygaszaja-wielki-piec-w-krakowskim-kombinacie.html (Accessed on: 31 October 2021).

Wiśniewski, M. (2018) "Architektura jako miernik rozwoju metropolitalnego Krakowa na przełomie XX i XXI wieku", [in:] Purchla, J. (ed.) *Krakow. Metropolia. T. III. Dziedzictwo*. Kraków: Księgarnia Akademicka, pp. 235–286.

Wojewódzki Urząd Ochrony Zabytków (2021) *Wykaz obiektów wpisanych do rejestru zabytków nieruchomych województwa małopolskiego z uwzględnieniem podziału na powiaty i gminy. Stan na lipiec 2021*. Available at: https://www.wuoz.malopolska.pl/wp-content/uploads/2021/07/Rejestr-powiaty-lipiec-2021.pdf (Accessed on: 31 October 2021).

Zarząd Zieleni Miejskiej (2021) Available at: https://zzm.krakow.pl/ (Accessed on: 31 October 2021).

Ziobro, A. (2019) "Urban Sprawl in the Context of Cracow City Limit", *IOP Conference Series: Materials Science and Engineering*, 471, 112036. Available at: https://iopscience.iop.org/article/10.1088/1757-899X/471/11/112036/pdf (Accessed on: 31 October 2021).

Ziobrowski, Z. et al. (1996) *Studium uwarunkowań i kierunków zagospodarowania przestrzennego gminy: poradnik metodyczny*. Kraków: Instytut Gospodarki Przestrzennej i Komunalnej.

7 Kraków and its region

Mutual relations after 1989

Piotr Miodunka

The starting point: Kraków and the region in around 1989

For most of the time since the Second World War, Kraków was Poland's third largest city, yet, thanks to its cultural functions and specific historical and geographic circumstances, it was considered the country's second most important city. Traditional strong bonds connected it to Western Galicia (a province of the former Austria–Hungary) that remained in Poland after 1945. Good transport connections to the north led Kielce, a city 120 km distant, to gravitate towards Kraków together with the entire Kieleckie Region (today: the Świętokrzyskie Region). In turn, the contacts with the western part of the historical Małopolska region weakened, as it remained under the influence of the dynamically developing Upper Silesian urban area.[1]

The current administrative divide was not immaterial for the scope and power of the city's impact. Until 1975, Kraków, as independent city (*miasto wydzielone*), was the capital of the large Kraków Region. In 1975, in the wake of a thorough reform of the administrative divisions that increased the number of regions (or voivodeships, Polish *województwa*) from 17 to 49, it became the centre of a small metropolitan region (*województwo miejskie*, 3,254 km^2 in area, 1.23 million inhabitants in 1990, of which 61% lived in Kraków). Apart from Kraków being its capital city, the region consisted of 38 communes, 10 of which had headquarters in towns (Figure 7.1). It was one of the country's three metropolitan regions where the main representative of the state authorities was not the voivode, but the mayor of the voivodeship city. Its area and shape generally matched what later became the Kraków Metropolitan Area in 2003–18.

Kraków of the late 1980s attracted people from the whole of Poland, as it had done earlier, and was an important cultural and scientific hub. It was even known as the spiritual capital of the country (thanks to its ties to Pope John Paul II). Every child in Poland was expected to visit the city on a school trip, and Wawel Hill, with its castle and cathedral made a great impression on people from the countryside to the south who arrived in the city. However, for the inhabitants and people working in the city, the situation looked different.

DOI: 10.4324/9781003252757-8

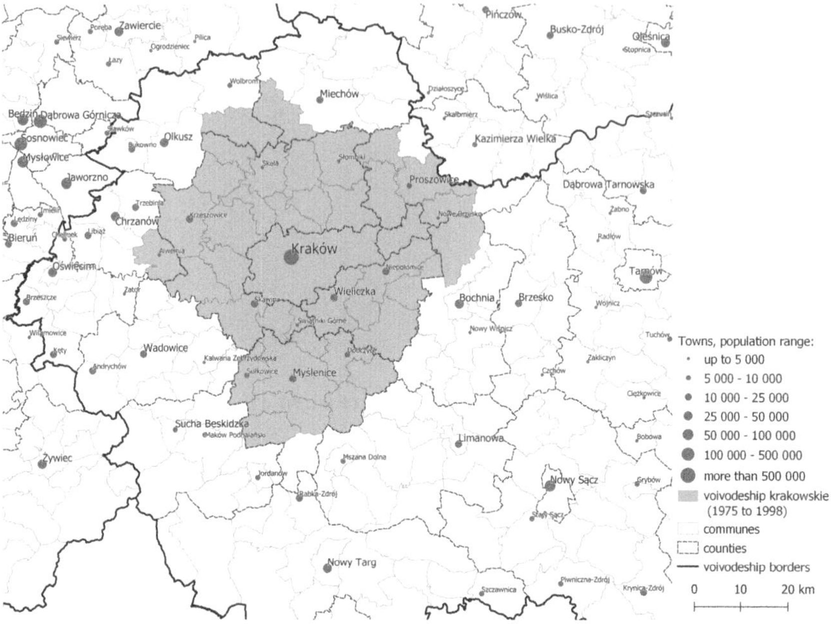

Figure 7.1 Changes of administrative divisions around Kraków after 1989. By M. Ilba.

The crisis in the collective construction sector nearly completely stalled the inflow of new residents. The city had land at its disposal, yet much of it, such as the former villages to the east of the steelworks complex, was degraded and unattractive. At the same time, the phenomenon of suburbanisation, in the Western sense, was absent from Kraków as well as other communist cities: "Earlier, the spatial expansion of the cities and the development of the suburban zones meant that the social groups that had no chance of finding a place to live in the city itself were pushed into those areas. That was especially true for the populations migrating from the countryside to the city. For those migrants, settling in the suburban zone was a stage on the path to a home in the city. (…) Generally, in the 1960s and the 1970s, most suburban areas were inhabited by people of low social status" (Węcławowicz et al., 2006, p. 145).

In the 1980s, the crisis of residential construction and shortages in the food supply resulted in the expansion of the zone of intensive commuting to Kraków for work (over 30 people per 1,000 residents). In 1988, it covered (according to the present administrative division), the Bocheński, Myślenicki, and Wielicki counties as well as almost the entire Krakowski county (save for a single commune), part of the Proszowicki county, some communes from the Wadowicki county, and one (Alwernia) from Chrzanowski county. Kraków's catchment area was especially developed towards the south and east. The small local farms could not support the farmer but they did ensure there was enough to eat, which reinforced the model of daily travel to the city to work (Zborowski, 2005, pp. 128–132) aided by the extended public transport network composed of trains and buses.

The model for managing Kraków-sized cities, which subjects the region to the administrative power of the city, favoured investments supporting the metropolitan centre. A good example is the supply of Kraków with drinking water. In 1974, a makeshift water intake from the Raba River was set up around Dobczyce, with a 23-kilometre-long pipeline, but the artificial reservoir (Dobczyce Lake) and the final water intake were only completed in 1987. Currently, the Dobczyce water intake covers 50% of Kraków's demand for water, and, at the same time, it supplies neighbouring locations (Biedrzycka, 2014, pp. 42–44).

Did the small town and rural areas of the Kraków Metropolitan Region benefit from being close to a metropolis in the days of the People's Republic of Poland? That cannot be ascertained by comparing multiple parameters portraying the social and economic development with the neighbouring Tarnowskie Region (Table 7.1), whose capital is in a city with a population of around 120,000, i.e., much smaller than Kraków. The area around Kraków was better supplied with water from collective intakes and telephones than its neighbours, while its access to healthcare and pharmacies was somewhat poorer, and access to libraries was far worse. It is also hard to assume that the health and readership needs could have been satisfied in Kraków, as, statistically, the situation in Tarnów was much better in this respect.

The administrative and metropolitan frameworks

In 1990, after communes were established as units of territorial self-government, regional offices were set up as ancillary bodies of the central administration. The Kraków Region was divided between three such offices, with the largest one, headquartered in Kraków, also catering for 25 other communes. A fundamental reform of the territorial administration and division came into effect on 1 January 1999, when the three-tier division into communes (*gminy*), counties (*powiaty*), and regions (also voivodeships, *województwa*) was introduced. The new regions were far larger, and Kraków became the capital of the Małopolska Region (15,182 km^2, population of 3.22 million) and the seat of both the central and local administrations. However, local delegations of the regional institutions were set up around the region for the convenience of the inhabitants, so Kraków usually provides direct services to the neighbouring counties as well as the western and sometimes the southern section of the region. Kraków is both a separate county and the capital of the "land county" (*powiat ziemski*), which comprises the neighbouring communes. Krakowski county covers an area of 1,230 km^2, counts a population of 280,000 (2020), and consists of 17 communes that form an incomplete ring around the city (Figure 7.1). The missing elements in the ring are Wielicki county to the south-east, and a short section of the border with Proszowicki county.

Table 7.1 Access to selected elements of infrastructure in Kraków and Tarnów regions in 1990

	Kraków Region		*Tarnów Region*	
	Kraków	*Other communes*	*Tarnów*	*Other communes*
Landlines per 1000 inhabitants	158.4	53.7	137.7	47.9
Consumption of water from the public water supply in households per capita (in m^3)	64.2	18.6	71.0	18.2
Book collections: volumes per 1,000 inhabitants	2,333.3	2,962.4	3,681.0	3,968.2
Physicians per 10,000 inhabitants	35.2	8.2	36.1	10.0
Number of inhabitants (in 1000s) per pharmacy	10.9	12.6	8.7	11.4

Source: WUS, 1991.

Attempts to define the impact of Kraków in its metropolitan role, i.e., to delineate the Kraków Metropolitan Area (KMA), were made from the beginning of the transformation. In the end, the KMA was formally set up in the regional zoning plan in 2003, but the final decision to join the KMA belonged to the individual communes (Więcław-Michniewska, 2011, p. 240). Besides Kraków, the metropolitan area included as many as 50 communes, all but two (Alwernia and Radziemice) from the former Kraków Metropolitan Region, and most of the remaining 14 situated to the south-west and south-east. Altogether, they cover 4068 km^2 and are inhabited by 1.4 million people, including the metropolis. At the same time, a far smaller suburban zone composed of just 12 municipalities, the Kraków Functional Area (KFA), was delineated. The foundations of the KMA were fundamentally changed in the next zoning plan for the Małopolska Region that was approved in 2018. This time, the KMA was defined almost identically to the suburban zone. It covered 16 communes besides the metropolis and reached the borders of the Kraków county to the west and, to a lesser degree, in the east, as well as comprising three communes from Wielicki county. With 1,483 km^2 and 1.1 million inhabitants (2018), it is a far smaller territory than the previous "big" KMA, which had 300,000 fewer people.

For a long time, the borders of the metropolitan area defined in the official documents were not translated into actual activities or concrete initiatives. It was only in June 2014 that Kraków and the 14 neighbouring communes established the Metropolia Krakowska Association (Stowarzyszenie Metropolia Krakowska). The association is the body implementing the new instrument for territorial development under the EU cohesion policy known as Integrated Territorial Investments (ITI). In 2019, work on the plan for the development of the Kraków Metropolis started, and the association has already launched joint actions concerning areas such as public transport and environmental

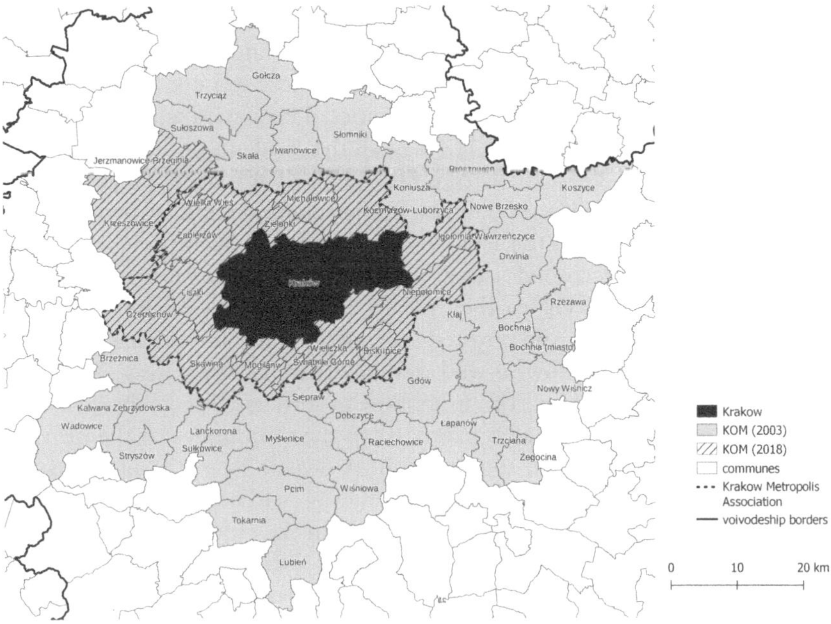

Figure 7.2 Changes of the concept of the Kraków Metropolitan Area in the 21st century. By M. Ilba. (KOM is the Polish acronym for the KMA.)

protection. In addition, the association is the only organisation that carries out real activity on the metropolitan scale, even though the area of its operation only comprises 1,275 km^2 and 1.06 million inhabitants (Figure 7.2). The above are not all the versions of the KMA that have been developed in recent years (Noworól, 2014, p. 84; Gołąb-Korzeniowska, Węcławowicz-Bilska and Wójtowicz-Wróbel, 2019, pp. 20–30, 80–84).

The cooperation of the territorial authorities and the "small" Kraków Municipal Area is only gathering momentum. A model for it could be the joint work in Metropolia Poznań, an analogous association set up in 2007 that brings together the city of Poznań, 21 nearby communes, and Poznański county, to surround the metropolitan city with a full ring (Metropolia Poznań, 2021).

Suburbanisation and migrations

Suburbanisation is the phenomenon of people moving from a city to the surrounding rural areas while maintaining strong connections to the city (work, education). In Poland, the process began after 1989 and marked a major change from communist times, when most people moving to the area around the city were migrants from the country who did not have the opportunity to find housing in the city. The generally low social status of the people living in the suburbs began to change due to the increasing numbers of migrants from Kraków who began arriving here in the 1990s and had higher economic and social status. By 2002, the areas around Kraków did not attract as many migrants as did those around other major cities. Those who settled there from 1989 to 2000 only accounted for 11.6% of all the residents of the metropolitan area (compared with 19.1% in Warsaw and 13.1% in Wrocław) (Węcławowicz et al., 2006, pp. 145–146). Nevertheless, the phenomenon of demographic suburbanisation started in the late 1980s/early 1990s, even though only the Zielonki commune recorded a clearly positive balance of migration out of all the communes adjacent to the city. In the first years of the 1990s, this phenomenon accelerated and covered successive communes to the north and many to the south of Kraków, as well as some situated further away (Table 7.2).

Early in the 21st century, the migration of settlers to the suburban areas of Kraków only developed as it extended to the communes to the north of the city as well as to several to the south. A decade later, the phenomenon spread not only to communes lying further away, while the inflowing population included a greater share of people living in the cities, predominantly in Kraków. Save for the cases of Niepołomice and Wieliczka (the latter being a slightly larger city) adjacent to Kraków, the rural areas were more attractive than even the small towns. This suggests that the expectation of finding peace and quiet, and the desire to live in a "bucolic" rural environment provides a powerful motivation to move out of Kraków (Raźniak, 2014, pp. 26–29).

In 2006–16, 66,000 people moved out from Kraków, and nearly 66% of them (24,000) moved to the 67 communes lying within a 35-kilometre radius of the city. The rest moved to communes lying farther away and to other major cities. The intensity of suburbanisation is at a medium level in the case of Kraków, as more people living in Poznań and Warsaw migrate to the vicinity of those cities. On the other hand, the target area of migration from Kraków is spread fairly widely, almost comparable to the situation in Warsaw (Pytel, 2017, pp. 127–145). Nevertheless, there are locations (Fig. 8.3) where the areas of dense development have sprawled beyond the limits of what was designed as Kraków Urban Area (*Krakowski Zespół Miejski*, KZM) in the 1970s.

The phenomenon of suburbanisation around Kraków is not evenly distributed (Figure 7.4). As a rule, the communes of Proszowicki county are the destinations of Cracovians' migrations, even if their general demographic balance is

Table 7.2 Cities and communes of the KMA (excluding Kraków, in the administrative borders from 2003 to 2018 with positive migration balances in 1988–2020[a])

	1988	*1995*	*2002*	*2011*	*2020*
Number	8	34	35	48	44
%	13	53	55	75	69

a The Kraków Metropolitan Area comprised 50 communes, but if the cities are excluded from the municipal–rural communes, it consisted of 65 spatial units in total.

Source: Kurek, Wójtowicz, and Gałka, 2013, pp. 66–70; GUS, 2021.

Figure 7.3 Kraków Metropolitan Area in 2021. By M. Ilba.

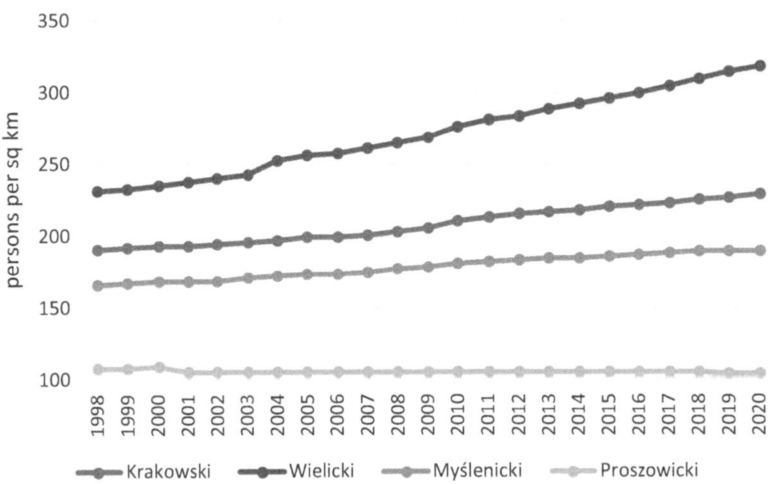

Figure 7.4 Population density in the counties surrounding Kraków in 1998–2020. Source: own work based on GUS, 2021.

stagnant. Low population density (104–106 people/km^2) suggests that the area is still typically farmland that retains its rural character. The other extremity is Wielicki county, with a population density exceeding 300 people/km^2 and the highest increase in population in 1998–2020. The most dynamically developing communes (with population increases above 10%) in the earlier wave of suburbanisation (2005–10) in the area of where the impact of the city was strong, i.e., the KFA (referring to the members of the Metropolia Krakowska Association), were the communes situated to the north of Kraków: Michałowice (20.1%), Zielonki (17.6%), and Wielka Wieś (10.9%). The phenomenon was somewhat less evident in the south, i.e., Mogilany (12.7%) and Wieliczka (10.1%). The suburbs grew at a slower pace in the following six years, with only Zielonki (14.3%) and Niepołomice (10.4%) retaining the pace from the previous period (Brańka and Musiał-Malago, 2018, p. 64). These communes are obviously where the number of new homes is increasing, but also where their development is becoming increasingly professional. Individual investors are still the majority, yet an increasing proportion of the new homes are built for sale or rent by professional developers. The phenomenon was most active to the north of Kraków, initially mostly in the Zielonki commune, but in recent years, developers have become most particularly interested in the communes of Wielka Wieś and Zabierzów and in the rural areas of Wieliczka commune (and offered 484 homes of the total of 1,063 in 2018–20), where the zoning plans have assigned a large area of land for residential construction.

Zielonki commune is the first that comes to mind in the context of the process of suburbanisation of Kraków (Figure 7.5), its location being a decisive factor (Figure 7.6). The centre of Zielonki is only around 7.5 km from central Kraków, and moreover, the village lies in the vicinity of attractive landscapes and its educational establishments are rated highly (Ciryt, 2021). With 488 people/km^2 in 2020, Zielonki is the most densely populated rural commune in the vicinity of Kraków. Not only is a large influx of new residents recorded here, similar to the other communes to the north, but it is

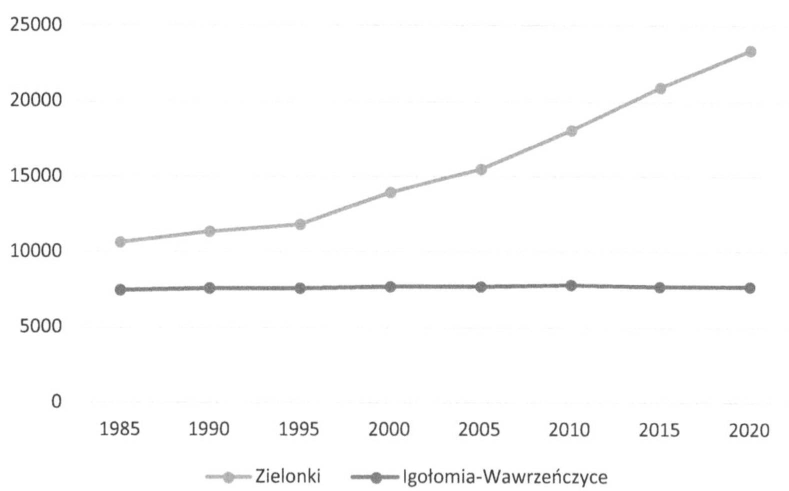

Figure 7.5 Population of Igołomia-Wawrzeńczyce and Zielonki communes in 1985–2020.

Source: own work based on WUS 1991, GUS, 2021.

Figure 7.6 Suburbanisation of areas to the north of Kraków, the example of Zielonki commune: in the mid-1990s (above) and currently (below).

Source: https://mapy.geoportal.gov.pl/imap/Imgp_2.html

primarily the most desirable rural area for development. In 2008–16, as many as 991 out of 2,232 homes handed over to residents were the result of such investments (Sarzyński and Stec, 2018, p. 36). The share of professional developers in recent years has continued to grow, and the corresponding number for 2017–20 is 515 out of 911 (GUS, 2021).

At the other end of the scale is Igołomia-Wawrzeńczyce, a neighbouring commune to the east (Figure 7.5). Although it lies fairly far from the city centre (approx. 24 km from Igołomia and 27 km from Wawrzeńczyce), it has quite good transport connections with the nearest tram (light railway) terminals being 9 km and 12 km away, respectively. The economic focus of the commune is still agriculture, primarily the production of vegetables. The commune recorded the highest positive migration balance (+87) in 1995–99. It was followed by five-year periods with neutral or negative balances. In 1990–2020, the population rose by less than 200 people, i.e., 2.4% (GUS, 2021).

The acceleration of suburbanisation in the current century resulted in a dynamic increase in the price of land for residential construction. In 2004–12 alone, they increased by a factor of two in the communes surrounding the city, with the highest, a five-fold increase, observed in the Niepołomice commune (Musiał-Malago, 2014, pp. 74–75).

Suburbanisation favours the phenomenon known as "urban sprawl", or the uncontrolled and chaotic spreading of residential developments. This phenomenon is visible in the belt of villages bordering Kraków to the north and south, and is most intense in the Wielka Wieś and Zielonki communes (Hołuj, 2018, pp. 80–82). Moreover, even in these communes, the new developments and increase in population is concentrated in the most favourably situated locations (Raźniak, 2015, pp. 31–37). This phenomenon is ordered only to a small extent by the approval of local zoning plans. Estimates that take the allocation of land for residential construction in the area of Metropolia Krakowska as their starting point mention future populations ranging from 670,000 to 1,000,000 inhabitants in the suburban areas (compared with the current 285,000) (Noworól, 2014, p. 88).

Suburbanisation of the area around Kraków is connected with many problems, both typical and related to the specific circumstances. Besides the difficulty in commuting to work resulting from the insufficient transport infrastructure and vulnerabilities of public transport, they include environmental conflicts resulting from the anthropogenic pressure on areas of high natural value (Ojcowski Park Narodowy and the whole area to the north-west of Kraków), and residential developments in areas threatened by flooding and landslides. Awareness of the latter is growing, although very slowly. The waning interest in migrating to Czernichów commune in the second decade of the 21st century may be the result of the flooding of the Vistula River (2010) that reached the village (Raźniak and Nowotnik, 2015, p. 59). Landslides are a problem that primarily involves the hilly area south of Kraków, including Wieliczka commune, where even areas in controversial locations are designated for residential development (Dybała, 2021).

Migration from Kraków does not always entail an increase in revenue from (income) tax in the target commune, as maintaining formal links to the city is beneficial for the migrants for a variety of reasons.[2] This explains why official data on the number of residents in the communes adjacent to the city is lower than the actual number.[3]

The economic suburbanisation generates commuting in the reverse direction: from the city to the countryside. It results from the pushing out of many forms of activity that are either burdensome for the environment or uneconomical from the centre of the city. One of the aspects of economic suburbanisation is the development of large-format shopping centres on the city outskirts and in the adjacent communes, due to the easier availability of land and more convenient access, an example being Modlniczka near Kraków with the Futura Park shopping mall (Figure 7.7) (Guzik, 2015, p. 7).

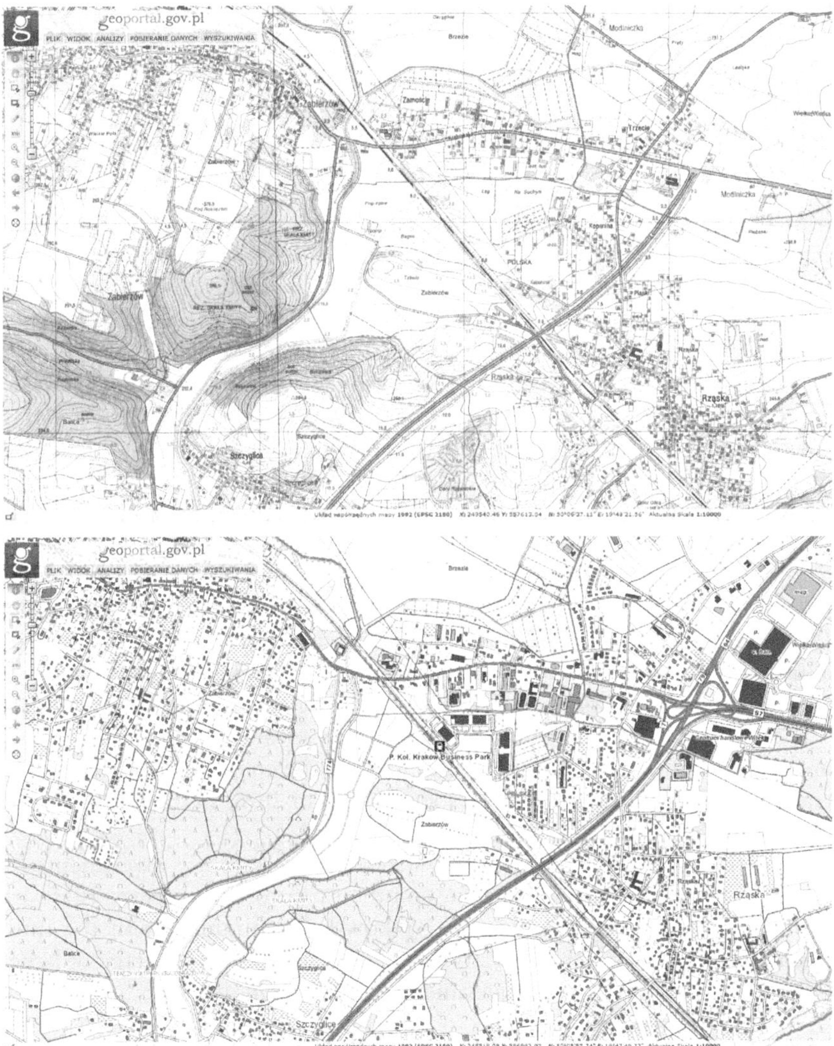

Figure 7.7 Suburbanisation of areas to the north-west of Kraków, the example of Zabierzów and Wielka Wieś communes: in the mid-1990s (above) and currently (below).

Source: https://mapy.geoportal.gov.pl/imap/Imgp_2.html

A spectacular case of economic suburbanisation is Niepołomice and, to a lesser extent, the Zabierzów and Dobczyce communes. In 1990, the small town of Niepołomice, situated 24 km to the east of the centre of Kraków, boasted 7,000 inhabitants, and the entire commune, rural areas included – 19,200. After 1989, Niepołomice bet on industry, offering the flat land to the south and west of the city, in the vicinity of the main railway line from Kraków to Rzeszów and Przemyśl, to investors. The scale of that investment, beginning with the Coca-Cola production plant in 1993, followed by the MAN plant producing HGVs (2007), and the mills of the Polskie Zakłady Zbożowe from Kraków (2018), as well as many other facilities, has attracted human resources from the metropolis to the commune. The proximity of the ancient forest of the Puszcza Niepołomicka also encourages people to settle there for good. At the time of writing (2020), the city has a population of 14,000, and the entire commune – 29,600 people. Many developments in the field of recreation in the commune exceed the usual standards, and they include covered riding arenas and tennis courts, and even a golf course in Ochmanów that is capable of attracting people from the entire metropolitan area.

Lying slightly further away (28 km) and not as well connected (due to the lack of a railway), Dobczyce did not experience such spectacular success, even though an old Kraków chocolate brand moved there in 2006. Another major local production plant specialising in dedicated rubber products, which was earlier connected to Kraków, discontinued production in 2008. Nevertheless, both the town and the commune have recorded a positive inflow of people, with the population of Dobczyce growing from 12,000 in 1990 to 15,300 in 2020.

Zabierzów is a rural commune lying on the western border of Kraków, surrounded by attractive countryside and very well connected (with a railway, motorway, and an international airport). In 1990, it had a population of 19,700, and recently (in 2020), of 25,800. Besides small and medium-sized industry, it also has one of the first office complexes in the metropolitan area and one of the largest in Poland, built in 2002–09. Known for years as "Kraków Business Park", thousands of employees work here, and it has therefore made a significant contribution to making the commune second only to Kraków in terms of the number of jobs (13,800 in 2016) in the KFA (Brańka and Musiał-Malago, 2018, p. 67).

The other communes also try to attract new economic investments by developing Economic Activity Zones on their territory. Currently, these are situated in eight of the Metropolia Krakowska communes, with the most recent addition being in Liszki (2018). There is, however, a shortage of larger spaces (over 50 ha) for major investments around Kraków.

As far as permanent migration to Kraków is concerned, there is a strong tendency for migration from the cities and towns of the Podkarpackie Region, which can be explained by historical developments. In 2016–18, nine of the 20 cities with the largest number of people migrating to Kraków were in that region (637 people altogether), five in the Silesian Region (317 people) and only two in another neighbouring region, Świętokrzyskie (203 people).

Commuting to work

In communist Poland, regular – as a rule, daily – commuting to work was the fundamental determinant of the scope of impact of a city on its surrounding area. Low labour efficiency generated a vast demand for a workforce that, with the inadequacy of residential construction in the city, could only be satisfied by workers from the rural areas. Low-capacity family farming forced people to have two jobs, and the emergence of a large group of rural workers (*chłoporobotnicy*) was observed, especially in areas with small farms and less favourable natural conditions for agriculture. The latter was of special significance in southern Poland, that is in the former Austrian Partition. After the systemic transformation of 1989, both the directions and scale of commuting changed, as did the social and demographic characteristics of the commuters. The uneducated peasant-workers were the first to bear the brunt of group redundancies and reduction of employment in large state enterprises, which were most sorely affected by the systemic transformation (Guzik, 2015, pp. 5–6).

As a result, the number of people commuting to work in Kraków in 1996 was 62,000, which was 5,000 fewer than in 1988 (Zborowski, 2004, p. 33). Interestingly, even with the processes of suburbanisation having started, the number of migrants shuttling back and forth in 2006 remained at the same level. According to the more credible data from 2011, there were 96,500 people arriving in the central city for work, of whom 73,600 came from 180 communes of the Małopolska Region, of which 33,400 came from the neighbouring Krakowski and Wielicki counties alone. Compared with 2006, far more people left from and arrived in the northern communes of Krakowski county and from Proszowicki county. Beside Kraków, the largest numbers of people travelling to work were recorded in Skawina (5,300), Zabierzów (4,700), and Wieliczka (4000) (Stowarzyszenie Metropolia Krakowska, 2015, p. 35). In 2016, this group was believed to be somewhat smaller: 84,000 (of whom 67,500 were from the region). Most of the arrivals in Kraków comprised the 4,800 people living in the Wieliczka commune–, 2,600 from the Skawina commune –, and 2,000 each from the rural communes of Zabierzów and Zielonki. The area of intensive commuting to Kraków (more than 20% of all people leaving the commune) covered nearly the entire "large" KMA (without the Bocheński county but including the Miechowski county). The area of less intensive commuting (from 5% to 20%) extended to nearly the whole of the Małopolska Region (save for the eastern and southern edges, which were barely accessible by public transport), and even reached the Świętokrzyskie Region (Kazimierza Wielka county). A significant increase in the number of people commuting to work in other centres of the suburban zone became visible in 2011–16. In the case of Zabierzów, it represented a number (8,500) that was barely lower than for Nowy Sącz, a city with a population of over 80,000 (with 12,800 commuters). In turn, Skawina attracted 7,100 workers from outside the territory of the town.

The question of leaving Kraków to work in the nearby communes is a less obvious phenomenon. In 2006, there were only 8,800 such people, a number that grew to as many as 30,800 in 2011 (the highest number on a national scale), before dropping again to 19,900 in 2016. Of the outbound flow, 18% was directed to Zabierzów, 8.1% to Skawina, and 7.8% to the Niepołomice commune (Guzik, 2015, pp. 28–30; US Kraków, 2019a, pp. 9–11).

The estimation of the costs of commuting to work in the KMA communes (in 2003–18), which cover both the direct costs (consumption of fuel and depreciation of vehicles) and lost time came to PLN 557 million a year for the entire KMA, of which commuters to Kraków accounted for PLN 400 million. It must also be noted that the costs of travelling to the two neighbouring communes with well-developed economies were also very high – Zabierzów (PLN 33.3 million) and Skawina (PLN 22.4 million) (Lityński, 2018, pp. 91–92).

The phenomenon of children commuting to school reflects both the processes of suburbanisation and of wider connections to the city, corresponding more closely to commuting to work. The detailed data from 2018 demonstrate that Kraków is Poland's second city after Warsaw as far as the number of children commuting to school is concerned, with 14,000 children in this group. Interestingly, in the case of the youngest children attending primary schools it ranks third, overtaken by Poznań, which is evidence of a more intensive migration to suburban areas there. Generally, the phenomenon of children commuting to primary school, often connected with their parents' commute to work, takes place from the whole ring of locations around Kraków, yet is most intensive in the suburban communes to the north, where it also reaches the second ring of suburban communes. Worth noting are the large number of children from Wieliczka, which validates its function as a dormitory town. In the case of lower secondary schools, the zone covered by commuting is far smaller and does not extend to the communes situated to the east. In this case, it is curious to note the largest inflow comes from Wieliczka, and the highest intensity of commuting comes from the rural commune of Liszki (which has not yet been subjected to intensive suburbanisation) with nearly one in three children of lower secondary school age commuting to Kraków. Commuting to upper secondary schools generally corresponds to commuting to Kraków for work, but with one difference: the intensity of such commuting, expressed as the proportion of these children out of all those aged 16–18 living in an area, is far greater to the north of Kraków. Evidently, the smaller cities situated south of the metropolis satisfy the demand for education in local secondary schools (GUS, 2018, pp. 21, 58–61).

Transport accessibility

In 1989, there were 29 city bus lines extending beyond the administrative borders of the city, yet only two of them reached the communes in the second ring (Czernichów and Iwanowice). Municipal transport did not reach

Wieliczka and its vicinity. Many lines were liquidated after 1990, yet suburban transport developed on the southern side. By 1994, there were already 38 such lines, and in 2012, there were 64. Fast lines to Wieliczka and Niepołomice were launched in 2008 and 2010, and in 2021, to Michałowice. The ITI strategy envisages further development of the fast lines (called "metropolitan") to all the communes of the Metropolia Krakowska that have no access to the railway (Stowarzyszenie Metropolia Krakowska, 2020, p. 6). As of 2013, the Municipality of Kraków signed agreements concerning the organisation of public bus transport with 15 communes (nearly all the adjacent ones, with the exception of Koniusza and Igołomia, as well as Czernichów, Skała, Iwanowice, and Słomniki).[4] At the time, there were 65 bus lines (2 of them express) extending beyond the borders of the city and covering routes with a total length of some 1,100 km (of which around 400 km was within the city limits). Around 1,200 of the 2,700 bus stops were situated in the communes reached by municipal transport (Miasto Kraków, 2013, p. 81). Currently, there are already 73 suburban bus lines. Although the bus network is being developed, its efficiency depends on the throughput of the roads leading to the city, which is a major problem.

The development of private transport was a novelty in the 1990s. For around 20 years, a large number of small, usually overcrowded buses in poor technical condition and arriving late, accounted for the characteristic image of roads in the city and the suburbs. Now, this branch of transport, still of great significance, has been subjected to control and somewhat ordered. The network of private bus connections densely covers the area to the north of the Vistula River and Kraków within a radius of approx. 35 km, reaching even as far as 55 km to the south-east.

The fate of railway connections, which provided the core of public transport prior to 1990, was characteristic of the new reality. The technical condition of the main railway lines crossing Kraków gradually deteriorated until the beginning of the 21st century. Poland's accession to the EU marked the start of an overhaul that seemed never ending. Minor branches were liquidated. In 2000, passenger railway traffic on a short, electrified line to Niepołomice was suspended and its demolition began in 2005, the embankment being used for the construction of the town's ring road. More ambitious plans to build new railway lines leading to Kraków have been designed recently, primarily to cater for the needs of the metropolitan area and provide connections to Myślenice and Niepołomice (!).[5]

The construction of the fast commuter railways (*szybka kolei aglomeracyjna*) is laborious and slow. The analysis was completed in 2007–11, and in 2013 the regional authorities incorporated Koleje Małopolskie, a new company responsible for transport. Plans included the commissioning of three lines by the end of 2014: Wieliczka–Balice Airport, Trzebinia–Tarnów, and Sędziszów–Podbory Skawińskie. However, only the first opened along the full track in 2015, while the others only opened certain sections (Kraków–Sędziszów in 2015, and Kraków–Tarnów in 2016). Due to renovation work continuing on railway lines, the sections to the west of Kraków, i.e., to Skawina and to Trzebinia, had not opened by 2021. The assessment of functioning of the oldest of the lines, which runs mainly across the city, is negative. Some accompanying infrastructure is missing, and renovations resulting in constant interruptions in the operation of the trains are rife (e.g., October and November 2021). Moreover, tickets for the municipal transport in the Wieliczka commune are not integrated into the Małopolska Karta Aglomeracyjna unified system (Najwyższa Izba Kontroli, 2020, pp. 7–16).

Commuter railways are far more advanced in other Polish cities of a similar size (Łódź, Poznań, Wrocław). The first were launched in Poznań in 2018, and now there are 5 leading to 8 terminals outside the metropolis. The system of metropolitan railway (S-Bahn) in Dresden in Germany is somewhat similar to that in Kraków, but the system of 3 lines operating there is complemented by other carriers offering transport in other directions, and the whole is coordinated (a single ticket) by the Transport Association of the Upper Elbe (Verkehrsverbund Oberelbe). The Dresden S-Bahn serves around 15 million passengers a year, of which 2.9 million are accounted for by the line leading to the airport. Kraków's line from Wieliczka to the airport provided transport for 3.6 million passengers annually, but the falling number of services brought that number down to a stable level of 2.5–2.6 million passengers in the next two years (Aerosieger.de, 2016; Najwyższa Izba Kontroli, 2020, pp. 38–39; S-Bahn Dresden, 2021; Verkehrsverbund Oberelbe, 2021).

Only 35–45% of people living in the counties around Kraków (Krakowski and Wielicki) used public transport for their obligatory travel needs (i.e., to work and school) in 2014 (Województwo Małopolskie, 2014, p. 40).

Problems with the organisation of public transport mean transport problems within the city. According to the data for 2015–16, some 130,000 vehicles entered Kraków during a 24-hour period, of which as many as 55,000 come from several neighbouring communes (KFA). Of those, 90% were passenger cars. The heaviest traffic was recorded between north-west and south-east and was generated by only four routes with the best conditions (dual carriageways). It was also estimated that an estimated 35,500 people travelled to Kraków during the morning rush hour, of which only 27% travelled by public transport – the share of rail was as low as 6% (Stowarzyszenie Metropolia Krakowska, 2017, pp. 45–50). However, the study conducted in the following year demonstrated that the number of vehicles crossing the borders of the city on a single day had increased to around 240,000, excluding transit. Little wonder, therefore, that the highest number of passenger cars per 1,000 inhabitants in the region (685 in 2018) was recorded where the public transport worked worst, that is in Proszowicki county (US Kraków, 2019a, p. 377).

Services for the Metropolitan Area

Kraków brings together 11 outlets of the leading DIY retail chains. These chains account for approximately 75% of the DIY market, and their retail outlets account for over 40% of the sales of construction materials in Poland. Only two of them (Modlniczka and Wieliczka) are situated outside the administrative limits of the city. The closest other outlets of these chains are situated around 60 km to the west of Kraków, while others are even further away. The IKEA store in Kraków, with its 11 stationary and mobile collection points, caters for the Małopolskie and Podkarpackie regions.

Some of Poland's most fertile soils lie to the north-east of Kraków, around the town of Proszowice; an area with powerful agricultural traditions. Despite that, Kraków has no appropriate facilities to enable wholesale trade in agricultural and horticultural produce (like the WGRO (Wielkopolska Agricultural & Horticultural Exchange) in Poznań). The Kompleks Handlowy Rybitwy wholesale market is the closest substitute, but its infrastructure is far from adequate. In fact, instead of trying to develop a well-equipped wholesale market with the potential of also catering for the Silesian Region and foreign markets (the current website of Rybitwy operates in Hungarian and Romanian), the Municipality intends the area for high-rise development. This has given rise to rumours about the liquidation of the complex and the possibility of organising the market in a different part of Kraków (Nowa Huta) or even outside the metropolis (e.g., Proszowice, Słomniki) that have circulated for years (Gąciarz, 2017; KH Rybitwy, 2021; Jeżak, 2021).

A change concerning the distribution of the cinemas and cinema going reflects, to a degree, more extensive changes in how free time is spent in shopping malls, where multi-screen cinemas are often located. In the 1980s, there were 33 cinemas operating in the former Kraków Metropolitan Region, of which two-thirds were situated in Kraków itself. Obviously, the metropolis offered a larger proportion of shows (75%) and generated a larger share of cinema visits (86%). The 1990s and the beginning of the 21st century marked a major crisis for this form of activity. In 2000, there were only 23 cinemas (and only four of them outside the city) in an area of a similar size to the former Kraków Region (covering Kraków and four counties). Here, the domination of the city as far as the number of shows and visits is concerned was clear (97% in each category). In turn, the number of cinema visits in 2018 in an area close to the KMA was far greater than in the 1980s, yet it was only concentrated in 14 venues, of which 11 were situated in Kraków. Compared with the number of shows and cinema visits, the cinemas in the KMA represent no competition whatsoever, at 2% and 1%, respectively. It can therefore be assumed that the residents of nearly the entire metropolitan area take advantage of the offering of Kraków cinemas (WUS Kraków, 1988, p. 108, 1991, p. 69; US Kraków, 2001, pp. 424–425, 2019b, p. 340).

Natural resources: tourism

Kraków was already perceived as a city with bad air pollution in the 1980s, even though the most noxious part of the aluminium plant in Skawina was closed in 1981. Production cutbacks and the modernisation of the former

Lenin Steelworks, the combined heat and power plant in Kraków, and the power plant in Skawina after 1989 did not improve the situation much. What came to the fore then was the phenomenon of smog, that is, fog combined with car exhaust fumes and the smoke from numerous coal boilers both in the centre and on the outskirts of the city. The situation was long believed to be limited only to the city, but in 2016, the widespread use of sensors testing particulate matter (e.g., PM 2.5 and 10) in smaller towns and villages disclosed a similarly catastrophic situation in the communes surrounding Kraków, mostly to the west of the city, i.e., the direction from which winds bring pollution into the city. The introduction of a ban on burning solid fuels in 2019, preceded by a campaign of removing coal boilers, caused an instant improvement in air quality in Kraków, in parallel with a stagnation in the neighbouring communes. The situation was reversed: the city that had for decades been considered a bad polluter now ever more often proves to be a "green" island in the smog, especially in winter (Airly, 2020, pp. 30–31).

A specific environmental impact of the metropolitan city is observed in the rural locations situated further away. The village of Bęczarka, lying 25 km away from the city in Myślenice commune, is an example. It is fairly easily accessible from Kraków, mostly, thanks to the nearby dual carriageway to Zakopane. Its population was 860 in 1988, 934 in 2002, 1,019 in 2011, and 1,120 in 2020. The smallholdings do not provide sufficient sustenance (the average amount of agricultural land per farm in 2010 was only 1 ha), which is why most inhabitants commute to work in Myślenice or Kraków. As a result, arable land lies fallow and is gradually overgrown with bushes and trees.[6]

Weekend tourism in communist Poland was mostly limited to Sundays, as free Saturdays were not standard in the 1980s. That was decisive for the short distances covered in day trips out of the city, e.g., to Ojcowski National Park and Myślenice-Zarabie or as breaks for rest (company Sundays in Zarabie). The development of private transport after 1989 and the increasing number of nonworking days extended short trips out of the city, especially towards the south – into the Gorce and Tatra mountains. So, in 1995, two out of every three people using the bathing spots in Zarabie were residents of Kraków; in 2002, they accounted for only approximately 50% of bathers (Faracik, 2006, pp. 10, 78–79).

The phenomenon of "second homes" around Kraków started in the 1960s/1970s.

> The first summer homes at the time developed mostly due to family ties. Some buildings in the 1980s/1990s were built in areas especially envisaged for summer developments in zoning plans. In the 1990s, brick houses were built in allotment gardens without legal and/or planning arrangements for the recreation purposes of their owners, often multi-storey with large usable spaces.
>
> (Faracik, 2006, p. 61)

Such houses concentrate in the suburban zone (similar to the former metropolitan region) to the south (Myślenice, Stróża, Wiśniowa, Raciechowice) and in the Alwernia commune in the west. Around 90% of their owners are residents of Kraków.

Currently, the areas around the metropolis try to exploit all their tourist advantages, for example, by attracting weekend tourists with a specialised offer. For example, the above-mentioned Zarabie in Myślenice has recently completed mountain bike routes. Operating in the vicinity of the city are two golf courses: in Ochmanów (Niepołomice commune, 1999) and Paczółtowice (Krzeszowice commune, 2002). Wiśniowa commune in Myślenicki county has invested in the reconstruction (2007) and equipment of the astronomical observatory on Mt Lubomir, 40 km to the west of Kraków. There are 14 horse-riding centres within just the suburban zone (Faracik, 2006, p. 67), and a number of ski stations have been opened for the use of the residents of the metropolis who want to avoid the tiring journey to the Tatra Mountains.[7] A growing number of agritourist farms prepare special day stay offerings (without accommodation) for city children to familiarise them with farm animals, taste regional produce, and have fun outdoors (Faracik, 2006, p. 93).

Summary

The links between Kraków and the region underwent organic changes after 1989. The city opened up to investment and migration, and land prices were liberated. The belt of communes lying to the north, west, and south of Kraków became an area of intensive demographic, economic, and landscape changes. With time, these processes led to the development of zones of different functionalities around the central city: typical dormitory towns to the north-west and south (including the town of Wieliczka), centres of business activity to the west (Skawina, Zabierzów), and the self-sufficient commune of Niepołomice. The areas to the north-east have retained their agricultural character and one can only hope that this will not change in future. Unfortunately, transport-wise, the whole suburban area is quite poorly integrated and the main axis connecting business centres outside the city of Kraków and the airport, i.e., the A4 motorway, has reached its maximum throughput at some sections, with average daily motor traffic exceeding 80,000 vehicles (Generalna Dyrekcja Dróg Krajowych i Autostrad, 2021). Even though suburbanisation is not progressing as vigorously as around Warsaw and Poznań, it impacts the community dimension of the suburban areas; this is visible in the electoral preferences and the readiness to vaccinate against COVID-19, which are at levels close to those in Kraków itself.

The future course of suburbanisation is, to a degree, unknown. Around the country, the coronavirus pandemic reinforced interest in single-family housing outside the city, but this is still hardly noticeable in the official data. In 2020, the balance of migration to Krakowski county was higher than in the previous years, yet the flow was in the other direction in the case of

Myślenicki and Wielicki counties. The preliminary data for the first half of 2021 suggests that the records for the positive migration balance could have been broken at least in the counties neighbouring the city.[8] By drawing from the data on the new permits for residential developments in 2020, we are likely to see a stabilisation at the level observed over the several previous years (GUS, 2021). This could eventually be evidence of a certain slowdown of suburbanisation, though it is also possible that due to the growing price of land, settlement will sprawl to communes situated farther away. That is the more probable scenario, as major road investments along the north–south axis should be completed in the next few years. The case with economic suburbanisation may be different as the completion of the external ring road with dual carriageways (in the north and east) could activate the area in their vicinity, both in the metropolis and outside it. Generally, however, in future, the functional ties between Kraków and the region will dominate the structural ones related to suburbanisation.

The challenge for the future lies in the coordination of activities ensuring the coherence and sustainable development of the metropolitan area. Here, difficulties already emerge at the stage of defining its extent. The currently binding form of the KMA and the agreements in force between the communes define it narrowly, more narrowly than in the case of the Poznań Metropolitan Area. The "small" KMA can successfully provide municipal transport services for suburban communes, yet the issue of the metropolitan railway already exceeds its domain.

Kraków still does not seem to make full use of its extensive potential and – focused on innovation, the R&D sector, and outsourcing services – shows no ambitions of organising a modern agricultural market. This could additionally trigger the restoration of horticultural traditions in the south of Małopolska. Such charming locations as Lanckorona and the open-air architecture museum in Wygiełzów are still insufficiently known by tourists, mostly due to their poor accessibility by public transport.

Bibliography

Aerosieger.de (2016) *Flughafen Dresden feiert 15 Jahre Anbindung durch S-Bahn S2*. Available at: https://www.aerosieger.de/news/7136/flughafen-dresden-feiert-15-jahre-anbindung-durch-s-bahn-s2.html (Accessed on 30 October 2021).

Airly (2020) *Oddychaj Polsko. Raport o stanie powietrza, Kraków*. Available at: https://airly.org/en/static/AIRLY_RAPORT_onet_2020-ec24a5b3f0c49784a24001a3965f7d2a.pdfec24a5b3f0c49784a24001a3965f7d2a.pdf (Accessed on 19 October 2021).

Biedrzycka, A. (2014) "40-lecie Zakładu Uzdatniania Wody Raba", *Nowoczesne Budownictwo Inżynieryjne*, 6(57), pp. 42–44.

Brańka, P. and Musiał-Malago", M. (2018) "Współpraca międzysamorządowa a funkcjonalność obszarów miejskich na przykładzie zintegrowanych inwestycji terytorialnych Krakowa' [in:] Kudłacz, T. and Musiał-Malago", M. (eds.), *Funkcjonalne miasto w teorii i praktyce na przykładzie Krakowa i Krakowskiego Obszaru Metropolitalnego*. Kraków: Uniwersytet Ekonomiczny w Krakowie, pp. 58–73.

Ciryt, B. (2021) "Ludzie na potęgę sprowadzają się do gminy Zielonki. Jest uznana za najlepsze miejsce do zamieszkania", *Dziennik Polski*. Available at: https://dziennikpolski24.pl/ludzie-na-potege-sprowadzaja-sie-do-gminy-zielonki-jest-uznana-za-najlepsze-miejsce-do-zamieszkania zdjecia/ar/c9 15535103 (Accessed on 2 November 2021).

Dybała, B. (2021) "Mieszkańcy drżą o przyszłość swoich domów i Wzgórza Kaim. Zostało zabudowane, osuwa się ziemia", *Gazeta Krakowska*. Available at: https://gazetakrakowska.pl/mieszkancy-drza-o-przyszlosc-swoich-domow-i-wzgorza-kaim-zostalo-zabudowane-osuwa-sie-ziemia/ar/c1-15826433 (Accessed on 1 November 2021).

Faracik, R. (2006) *Turystyka w strefie podmiejskiej Krakowa*. Kraków: Instytut Geografii i Gospodarki Przestrzennej Uniwersytetu Jagiellońskiego.

Gąciarz, A. (2017) "Proszowice to najlepsze miejsce dla giełdy rolnej", *Dziennik Polski*. Available at: https://dziennikpolski24.pl/proszowice-to-najlepsze-miejsce-dla-gieldy-rolnej/ar/12618879 (Accessed on 31 October 2021).

Generalna Dyrekcja Dróg Krajowych i Autostrad (2021) *Generalny Pomiar Ruchu 2020/2021*. Available at: https://www.gov.pl/web/gddkia/generalny-pomiar-ruchu-20202021 (Accessed on 9 December 2021).

Gołąb-Korzeniowska, M., Węcławowicz-Bilska, E. and Wójtowicz-Wróbel, A. (2019) *Małe miasta w obszarach oddziaływania metropolii. Przykład Krakowa*, Kraków: Wydawnictwo Politechniki Krakowskiej.

GUS (2018) *Dojazdy uczniów do szkół zlokalizowanych w miastach wojewódzkich*. Warszawa: Główny Urząd Statystyczny.

GUS (2021) *Bank Danych Lokalnych*. Available at: https://bdl.stat.gov.pl/BDL/start (Accessed on 31 October 2021).

Guzik, R. (2015) *Dojazdy do pracy w województwie małopolskim 2006–2011*. Kraków: Wojewódzki Urząd Pracy.

Hołuj, A. (2018) "Urban sprawl czy ekspansja rdzenia metropolitalnego? Analiza Krakowskiego Obszaru Metropolitalnego", [in:] Kudłacz T., Musiał-Malago' M. (eds), *Funkcjonalne miasto w teorii i praktyce na przykładzie Krakowa i Krakowskiego Obszaru Metropolitalnego*, Kraków: Wydawnictwo Uniwersytetu Ekonomicznego w Krakowie, pp. 74–83.

Jeżak, Ł. (2021) *Czy giełda spożywcza Rybitwy utrzyma się pośród wieżowców?* Available at: https://biznes.lovekrakow.pl/aktualnosci/czy-gielda-spozywcza-rybitwy-utrzyma-sie-posrod-wiezowcow_41411.html (Accessed on 31 October 2021).

KH Rybitwy (2021) *O nas*. Available at: https://khrybitwy.pl/o-nas.html (Accessed on 31 October 2021).

Kurek, S., Wójtowicz, M. and Gałka, J. (2013) "Przestrzenne zróżnicowanie zmian zaludnienia w krakowskim obszarze metropolitalnym w okresie 1988–2011", *Studia Miejskie*, 12, pp. 59–77.

Lityński, P. (2018) "Dysfunkcjonalność przestrzenna obszarów metropolitalnych i jej koszty", [in:] Kudłacz, T. and Musiał, M. (eds.), *Funkcjonalne miasto w teorii i praktyce na przykładzie Krakowa i Krakowskiego Obszaru Metropolitalnego*, Kraków: Wydawnictwo UEK Uniwersytetu Ekonomicznego w Krakowie, pp. 84–93.

Metropolia Poznań (2021) *Rada metropolii*. Available at: http://metropoliapoznan.pl/strona, 17,rada_metropolii.html (Accessed on 30 October 2021).

Miasto Kraków (2013) *Plan zrównoważonego rozwoju publicznego transportu zbiorowego dla gminy Kraków i gmin sąsiadujących, z którymi gmina Kraków zawarła porozumienie w zakresie organizacji publicznego transportu zbiorowego*. Available at: https://www.bip.krakow.pl/?sub_dok_id=57922 (Accessed on 2 November 2021).

Musiał-Malago", M. (2014) "Procesy suburbanizacji obszarów podmiejskich Krakowa", *Zeszyty Naukowe Uniwersytetu Ekonomicznego w Krakowie*, 12(936), pp. 63–77.

Najwyższa Izba Kontroli (2020) *Informacja o wynikach kontroli NIK, delegatura w Krakowie, Szybka kolej aglomeracyjna w aglomeracji krakowskiej, linia commuter1: Kraków lotnisko–Wieliczka Rynek-kopalnia*, Warszawa. Available at: https://www.nik.gov.pl/plik/id, 23516,vp, 26250.pdf (Accessed on 15 October 2021).

Noworól, A. (2014) "Problemy i wyzwania dotyczące rozwoju obszarów metropolitalnych na przykładzie Krakowskiego Obszaru Metropolitalnego", *Zeszyty Naukowe Uniwersytetu Ekonomicznego w Krakowie*, 12(936), pp. 79–93.

Pytel, S. (2017) "The influence of migrations on the suburbs of large cities in Poland", *Studia Miejskie*, 28, pp. 121–147.

Raźniak, P. (2014) "Zróżnicowanie migracji ludności w Gminie Wielka Wieś, jako wyraz procesów suburbanizacji strefy podmiejskiej Krakowa", [in:] Kaczmarska, E. and Raźniak, P. (eds) *Społeczno-ekonomiczne i przestrzenne przemiany struktur regionalnych*, vol. 1. Kraków: Oficyna Wydawnicza AFM, pp. 25–45.

Raźniak, P. and Nowotnik, D. (2015) "Zróżnicowanie procesów migracyjnych w wybranych gminach Krakowskiego Obszaru Metropolitalnego", *Stare i Nowe problemy badawcze w geografii społeczno-ekonomicznej*, 6, pp. 49–66.

S-Bahn Dresden (2021) *S-Bahn Dresden*. Available at: https://regional.bahn.de/regionen/sachsen/wir/ueb_s-bahn_dresden (Accessed on 30 October 2021).

Sarzyński, K. and Stec, A. (2018) "Suburbanizacja w Krakowskim Obszarze Metropolitalnym na przykładzie struktury przestrzennej wybranej gminy", *Biuletyn Stowarzyszenia Rzeczoznawców Majątkowych Województwa Wielkopolskiego*, 2(50), pp. 33–42.

Stowarzyszenie Metropolia Krakowska (2015) *Strategia ZIT dla Krakowskiego Obszaru Funkcjonalnego*. Available at: https://metropoliakrakowska.pl/wp-content/uploads/2018/11/Strategia-ZIT-KrOF_-4.0.pdf (Accessed on 27 October 2021).

Stowarzyszenie Metropolia Krakowska (2017) *Koncepcja integracji systemów transportowych na terenie Krakowskiego Obszaru Funkcjonalnego*. Kraków. Available at: https://metropoliakrakowska.pl/wp-content/uploads/2019/01/Koncepcja-integracji-system%C3%B3w-transportowych-KrOF.pdf (Accessed on 18 October 2021).

Stowarzyszenie Metropolia Krakowska (2020) *Koncepcja systemu transportu Krakowskiego Obszaru Funkcjonalnego, Załącznik nr 5 do Strategii Zintegrowanych Inwestycji Terytorialnych dla Krakowskiego Obszaru Funkcjonalnego*. Available at: https://metropoliakrakowska.pl/sektory/zit/strategia-zit (Accessed on 27 October 2021).

Urząd Statystyczny w Krakowie (2001) *Rocznik statystyczny województwa małopolskiego*. Kraków.

Urząd Statystyczny w Krakowie (2019a) *Dojazdy do pracy w województwie małopolskim w 2016 r.* Kraków.

Urząd Statystyczny w Krakowie (2019b) *Województwo Małopolskie*. Podregiony, powiaty, gminy, Kraków.

Verkehrsverbund Oberelbe (2021) *The VVO*. Available at: https://www.vvo-online.de/en/vvo/portrait/index.cshtml (Accessed on 30 October 2021).

Węcławowicz, G. et al. (2006) *Przestrzenne zagospodarowanie polski na początku XXI wieku*. Warszawa: Instytut Geografii i Przestrzennego Zagospodarowania im. Stanisława Leszczyckiego PAN.

Więcław-Michniewska, J. (2011) "Zróżnicowanie społeczno-gospodarcze gmin krakowskiego obszaru metropolitalnego", *Studia Miejskie*, 4, pp. 239–252.

Wojewódzki Urząd Statystyczny w Krakowie (1988) *Rocznik statystyczny województwa krakowskiego,* Kraków.

Wojewódzki Urząd Statystyczny w Krakowie (1991) *Rocznik statystyczny województwa krakowskiego,* Kraków.

Województwo Małopolskie (2014) *Plan zrównoważonego rozwoju publicznego transportu zbiorowego w województwie małopolskim, Kraków*. Available at: https://bip.malopolska.pl/umwm, a, 984919,uchwala-nr-lvi90814-sejmiku-wojewodztwa-malopolskiego-z-dnia-27-pazdziernika-2014-r-w-sprawie-uchwal.html (Accessed on 27 October 2021).

Zborowski, A. (2004) "Podejście funkcjonalno-strukturalne w badaniach delimitacji obszarów metropolitalnych w Polsce (przykład Krakowa)", [in:] Słodczyk, J. (ed*) Przemiany struktury przestrzennej miast w sferze funkcjonalnej i społecznej*. Opole: Wydawnictwo Uniwersytetu Opolskiego, pp. 25–39.

Zborowski, A. (2005) *Przemiany struktury społeczno-przestrzennej regionu miejskiego w okresie realnego socjalizmu i transformacji ustrojowej (na przykładzie Krakowa)*. Kraków: Instytut Geografii i Gospodarki Przestrzennej Uniwersytetu Jagiellońskiego.

Notes

1 Certain special administrations with headquarters in Kraków exercised their authority over the entire former Western Galicia (Polish National Railways) as well as the area around Kielce (the macro-region for spatial and economic planning, water management authority) until the 1990s, and in some cases even longer.

2 These for example include preferences in admitting children to kindergartens and schools.

3 This, however, becomes evident e.g., when making declarations on the collection of waste from private homesteads, when you also need to declare the number of inhabitants (Raźniak and Nowotnik, 2015, pp. 51–52).

4 On top of those, the communes of Brzeźnica and Krzeszowice were also covered on the grounds of a contract with another commune (Skawina and Zabierzów, respectively)

5 Consultations concerning the restitution of the railway link to Niepołomice, and building a new one along a different route started in the autumn of 2021, https://www.niepolomice.eu/ogloszenia/spotkanie-konsultacyjne-nt-polaczenia-kolejowego-do-niepolomic (Accessed on 14 October 2021).

6 A lack of data for the village itself, while the acreage of arable land being in agricultural use in the entire Myślenice commune shrank from 4,400 ha in 1996 to 1,800 ha in 2010 (GUS, 2021).

7 There were three in 2006: Myślenice, Siepraw, and Wierzbanowa in Wiśniowa commune, the next are Harbutowice (Sułkowice commune, 2013), and somewhat further away – Kasina Wlk and Skomielna Czarna.

8 Whether the "legalisation" of permanent address perhaps results from an increase in the number of such formal registrations by people who lived in specific places already earlier was caused by the lockdowns remains an open question.

8 Kraków architecture and globalisation

Michał Wiśniewski

Throughout the entire 20th century, Kraków was one of the key centres of Polish modern architecture. The robust environment, ambitious universities, dynamic development of the city, and openness to new ideas, all laid the foundation for exclusive aesthetic concepts (Włodarczyk, Włodarczyk, 2017). Another determinant came in 1989 with the opening of the borders and globalisation. An analysis of changes occurring after that date provokes the question of whether the collision of Kraków's architecture with the influx of new technologies and standards managed to create its own model of action and develop the local *genius loci* in a creative manner?

The phenomenon of the Kraków postmodernism

Kraków's architects have had the opportunity to take a close look at the changes taking place in world architecture since at least the late 1950s. That was when Miastoprojekt Kraków planning and design company started a close cooperation with the countries of the global South and began to develop urban designs for the cities in Syria, Libya, and Iraq, including Baghdad and Damascus. It is no coincidence that local architects had already begun to experiment with postmodernist ideas in the late 1970s. The changes in the approach to aesthetics became visible in the following decade when Poland was plunged into a profound political and economic crisis that killed off the construction market.

In 1985, the local branch of the Union of Polish Architects (SARP) organised the International Biennale of Architecture (MBA) in Kraków (Sepioł, 1985). Romuald Loegler, who stood at the helm of the organisation at the time, initiated an international architectonic confrontation that included a competition for the reclamation and revitalisation of former industrial districts, a new phenomenon in Poland at the time. The subject returned during the subsequent editions of the biennale and became one of the main threads of postmodernism in Kraków architecture. Going boldly beyond the Iron Curtain, over time it became one of the key voices in Polish architecture and an important factor in determining the activity of the local environment.

DOI: 10.4324/9781003252757-9

At the same time, the Faculty of Architecture of the Kraków University of Technology started a close cooperation with its counterpart in Venice. The peak of the exchange was in 1989 and was related to the workshops on the design of the Children's Village, a complex for an orphanage in Rajsko near Oświęcim, organised by Tomasz Mańkowski. The joint project was developed by a group that included Aleksander Noworól, Maria Mańkowska, Dariusz Kozłowski, Gianugo Polesello, Mario Botta, and Fumihiko Maki. The minor architectural composition, which never went beyond the design phase, could have become one of the most interesting examples of postmodernism that was developing in Poland at the time ("The Children's Village in Oświęcim. International Collaboration Project", 1994). More initiatives of that type followed, and in a city that had grappled with crises for years, they propelled local architecture towards previously unknown formal solutions.

Late in the 1980s, an increasing number of postmodernist infills were built in Kraków: designs that respected their context and complemented the degraded spaces in the historical districts (Włodarczyk, 2014). The most thought-provoking example of residential architecture of the time of transition is the Centrum E residential estate built on the southern side of the Socialist Realist complex in Nowa Huta (Jędruch, 2018, pp. 96–103). The design by Romuald Loegler emerged as the winner of the competition and included buildings of varied height, a division into quarters, and bright colours. The postmodernist estate was a reflection on the activity of its own environment over the previous decades and a creative extension of the key achievements in the spatial development of post-war Kraków.

The new complexes of religious architecture were important spaces for the development of postmodernist architecture in Kraków. The election of the Bishop of Kraków, Cardinal Karol Wojtyła, as Pope John Paul II redefined the place of religion in the life of communist-governed Poland and made possible the construction of many new churches. In just over a decade, over 2,000 new churches were built in Poland, 30 of them in Kraków alone. The new churches, many of them very large and situated in prominent locations, were spaces of formal experimentation (Cichońska, Popera, Snopek, 2016). Deserving special attention is the complex of the Resurrectionist Seminary in Zakrzówek in Kraków that was designed by Dariusz Kozłowski, Maria Misiągiewicz, and Wacław Stefański. The spacious compound of reinforced concrete was built in 1984–96 and the design referred to the main dominants in the space of the city and the nearby nature reserve. The arrangement of the sightlines, the lines of development, and the position of the towers and forms are decisive for the dramatic quality of the system and a reference to the historical centre of Kraków (Wroński, 2010, pp. 452–454) (Figure 8.1).

The intensive development of sacred architecture lasted until the early 21st century. The symbolic end of the phenomenon came in 2002 with the consecration of the Sanctuary of the Divine Mercy in Łagiewniki: the monumental, elliptical shape of Kraków's most important pilgrimage destination was designed by Witold Cęckiewicz (Karpińska, Leśniak-Rychlak, Wiśniewski,

Figure 8.1 Resurrectionist Seminary, designed by Dariusz Kozłowski, Maria Misiągiewicz, and Wacław Stefański, 1984–96.
Photo by P. Mazur.

2015, pp. 160–165). A decade later, this large arranged landscape was extended by the historicising Sanctuary of St John Paul II "Be not Afraid!" designed by Andrzej Mikulski and completed in 2012 (Sołjan, Liro, 2015, pp. 135–151).

Architecture of the time of transition

The post-1989 development of architecture in Kraków can be divided into two separate chapters. The first lasted until around 2004 and was linked to a fascination with postmodernism (Obtułowicz, Włodarczyk, Gajczyk, 1998). While the crisis continued to stifle the local construction market, many designers participated in the theoretical debate on new formal solutions. The latter period was related to Poland's increasing openness to the world, its accession to the European Union, and the inflow of foreign capital that paved the way for numerous private and public investments.

In the wake of the fall of the communist regime, the early 1990s were a time of hope and the birth of democracy in Poland. However, at the same time, the economy was strangled by inflation, production in the state-owned industrial plants fell, and unemployment grew at an increasing pace (Kaliński, 2009). It was then that the state-organised, collectivised model of development of residential construction finally collapsed and the state grants for the huge housing cooperatives came to an end, which caused them to stop building new estates (Foryś, 2017, pp. 31–41).

The bankruptcy of the system reinforced the general negative attitude to the earlier development of cities and criticism of the post-war modernist residential estates (Skotarczak, 2015). In parallel, an increasing amount of attention was paid to the problem of neglected public spaces, the transport infrastructure, and unmanaged green spaces. The changes taking place in Kraków's architecture in the first 15 years after the transformation focused on several crucial phenomena: state investments into new public buildings, investments of the territorial authorities into infrastructure and common spaces, private investments into residential construction, and the first private investments into commercial buildings, such as large shopping centres and offices (Fabiański, Purchla, 2012) (Figure 8.2).

A paradigm shift in the approach to design, and an increasing openness of Polish architecture to the world, came in the wake of the new projects. A particular illustration of the phenomenon is the building of the Manggha Museum of Japanese Art and Technology (Purchla, 2019, pp. 432–437). It is a new gallery that presents the collection of Japanese art brought to Kraków by Feliks Jasieński early in the 20th century and was built by the Vistula River nearly opposite to the Wawel Castle. Although the work of Arata Isozaki, it is the brainchild of Andrzej Wajda, the Oscar-winning Polish film director, who decided to allocate the funds from the Kyoto Prize he received in Japan for that purpose. Later, Krzysztof Ingarden, a Kraków architect, who interned at Isozaki's studio in the 1980s, supervised the construction of

Figure 8.2 Manggha Museum of Japanese Art and Technology, designed by Arata Isozaki, 1994.
Photo by P. Mazur.

this most important place that presents the culture of the Far East in Poland (Dziechciaruk-Maj, Nowak, Urbańska, 2009). The building shows the symbolic opening of Kraków to the world: the distinctive wavy roof brings to mind a river, a popular motif from Japanese woodcuts. In 2015, the Europe – Far East Gallery was added on its northern side, a minimalist design developed by the studio of Krzysztof Ingarden and Jacek Ewý (Domicz, 2015, pp. 56–63).

State institutions became active developers in the second half of the 1990s. Buildings for academia, the judiciary, and healthcare were built in Kraków. A major leap in the number of students in Poland after 1989 meant that the extant infrastructure of higher education institutions, which, as a rule, was worn out, was quite insufficient. Significant initiatives in the area were developed in Kraków, one of Poland's largest academic centres, by the Jagiellonian University – the country's oldest and largest university. In the mid-1990s, the team of Aleksander Böhm designed its new campus on the southern side of the city, in Pychowice. Covering a large area, it was to provide a part of a new district and be complemented with service and residential developments (Rygiel, 1998, pp. 30–31).

In 2000, the first section of the campus was delivered in time for the celebration of the 600th Anniversary of the Refounding of the Kraków Academy. It was a complex of low, minimalist pavilions designed by Marian Fikus (Mycielski, 2002a, pp. 13–17), and it initiated the development of an extensive compound arranged along the wide alley connecting the individual faculties. During the course of over two decades, several spacious buildings of the university were built on the campus, making it one of the largest such complexes in the country. Developed at different times, the buildings are highly varied in terms of both design solutions and the quality of the construction and finish. The whole makes a decent impression, even if the buildings of the Campus brought no quality into Kraków's architecture.

In parallel, the Jagiellonian University decided to build its Auditorium Maximum (2008) on ul. Krupnicza, in the city centre, to the design of Stanisław Deńko (Malkowski, 2008b, pp. 68–73), having earlier built the new wing of the Jagiellonian Library, the university's main book collection and the second-largest institution of this type in Poland, in the centre. Completed in 2002, the new building referred to the main building of the library from the 1930s. The architect of the new wing was Romuald Loegler, whose design proposed a postmodernist variation on the idea of a historical library (Stiasny, 2002, pp. 28–35). Even earlier, in 1998, the same architect completed the first stage of extension of the campus for the Cracow University of Economics (at the time known as the Academy of Economics) providing the city's first architectural composition that made a clear reference to the ideas of deconstructivism (Purchla, 2006).

Another of Romuald Loegler's designs of special importance was the Gate to the City of the Dead (1998), the central building and chapel of the Municipal Cemetery in Batowice, situated on the northern side of the city. The design broke away from the references to historical forms typical of such structures, as it proposed a form of an elongated reinforced concrete arc that he slit with a glass surface (Stiasny, 1999a, pp. 14–19). All three aforementioned designs generated much interest and had a bearing on the perception of Kraków architecture in Poland and in the world, as each was nominated for the Mies van der Rohe Award ("New Building for the Jagiellonian Library", 2021; "Teaching and Sports Pavilion of the Academy of Economics", 2021; "Blue end of the road", 2021), and Romuald Loegler became one of the first Polish architects to win international renown (Styrna-Bartkowicz, 2015) (Figure 8.3).

The development of postmodernism in Poland and Kraków followed different paths than in Western Europe and the United States, as it was not the new voice of private initiatives and did not develop in opposition to the public sector. In the new political and economic circumstances that lasted until the end of the 1990s, it paradoxically provided a tool used by the state and territorial authorities for the construction of their image. That phenomenon is very well illustrated by yet another of Romuald Loegler's designs: the Kraków Opera building (Tosza, 2008). Despite many attempts, Kraków had not managed to produce an opera building in the 20th century and success only came with the new political reality. The architect suggested turning the surviving building of the former horse-riding arena, which stood on a small plot near the city centre occupied by military buildings, into the lobby of an

Figure 8.3 The Gate to the City of the Dead, Batowice Cemetery, designed by Romuald Loegler, 1998.
Photo by P. Mazur.

opera theatre and added a spacious stage and audience hall at the back of the existing building. Completed in 2009, the Kraków Opera is one of the largest examples of the combining of a new spatial form with a historical building in the city, and at the same time evidence of the creative capacities of the regional government.

A new district of simple, elegant court buildings of a new modernist guise developed in the vicinity of the opera (Mycielski, 2002b, pp. 17–23). The new building of the Regional Court was commissioned in 2001. This modern stone-clad and highly glazed public building that opens onto the new square was an extension of the complex built for the law courts and prosecutors office in the 1970s. Designed by Wojciech Obtułowicz, the building introduces a new quality to the office and public architecture of Kraków, and its nomination for the Mies van der Rohe Award is no coincidence ("Cracow District Court", 2021). A decade later, the minimalist form of the Court of Appeals was built on its northern side (Czapnik, 2011, pp. 66–73).

Another investment by a state institution that had a strong impact on the space of the city is the building of Radio Kraków, Polish Radio's regional broadcaster, which was designed by Tomasz Mańkowski and Piotr Wróbel and completed in 1999 (Mańkowski, Wróbel, 1999, pp. 22–23). The five-storey building situated in a very visible location by the Aleje Trzech Wieszczów ring road – the most important urban development in Kraków between the two world wars – stands out thanks to its form: a section of an inverted cone (Stiasny, 1999b, pp. 4–19). The original shape led to it being another Kraków design honoured with a nomination for the Mies van der Rohe Award ("Radio Center – Kraków – Window to the World", 2021).

New quality of space

Late in the 1990s, academia, radio, and the courts produced a new space for the discussion about architecture in Kraków. The projects provided a break in the previous manner of shaping the space of the city, as they introduced new, postmodern aesthetics into the mainstream and heralded the course of changes that were to take place in the following years. In parallel, the Kraków local authorities began to make an ever-stronger impact on the shape of public space through their investments. In 1997, ul. Karmelicka, an important street situated to the west of the historical city centre, was redesigned, and a year later a similar change was introduced in ul. Zwierzyniecka. In both streets, vehicular traffic was limited and sections were transformed into *woonerfs* (Zamorska-Przyłuska, 1998, pp. 46–47). Soon, more investments into the revitalisation of public spaces followed.

The most important project of this type was the reconstruction of the plac Bohaterów Getta (literally "Ghetto Heroes Square") in Podgórze, which was completed in 2005, on a site in what was the Jewish ghetto during the Nazi occupation. The concept by Kazimierz Łatak and Piotr Lewicki was based on the transformation of the abandoned and neglected space of the former bus depot into a living monument and memorial space for Kraków's Jews who were murdered in the Holocaust. That was achieved by paving the square with uniform granite cobblestones and installing slightly oversized chairs cast in bronze on a regular grid pattern. Photographs of the ghetto from the time show furniture, notably chairs, that were taken from homes and then abandoned, which become a telling sign of memory. Nominated for the Mies van der Rohe Award ("New Zgody Square – Remodelling of the Bohaterów Getta Square", 2021) the design received a special mention by the European Prize for Urban Public Space in 2006 ("Ghetto Heroes Square", 2005) (Figure 8.4).

In parallel with the investments and redesign of selected streets and squares, the municipal authorities decided to build three new bridges over the Vistula, the design of two of them resulting from architecture competitions (Motak, 2002, pp. 51–58). Competitions, usually organised by the Kraków branch of the SARP, played an important role in the development of the debate on local architecture and provided a space for the confrontation and exchange of ideas within that local group. In Kraków, as in many other Central European cities, public institutions, whether state or local authority, continued to

Figure 8.4 Plac Bohaterów Getta/Ghetto Heroes Square, designed by Piotr Lewicki and Kazimierz Łatak, 2005.
Photo by P. Mazur.

define the course of development of architecture after the changes of 1989 by generating qualitative solutions, promoting a dialogue with the changes taking place in the world's architecture, and reaching for solutions that were appreciated in competitions. This model of artistic patronage became reinforced after 2004 with the accession of the region's countries to the European Union and the inflow of post-accession funds earmarked for the development of infrastructure (Purchla, Sepioł, 2015).

The free market

Late in the 1990s, this top-down model of building relations with global architecture clashed with another model resulting from the increasingly frequent and mass inflow of private capital to Poland and Kraków. As the economic conditions in the country continued to be poor during this period, every major investment was still positively received and its form – even if it failed to contribute any value to the cultural landscape of the city – did not become the subject of critical discussion.

The first commercial investments in Kraków comprised primarily of three types of structures: office buildings, large commercial sites, and other commercial buildings related to the development of the leisure industry. The office building designs were the most valuable for the further development of the city. In 2020, the Kraków office market offered over 1,500,000 m^2 of space, with more than half of all new space having been developed after 2015 (Czerski, 2019). That type of architecture began to develop in Kraków in the late 1990s. In 1990, the transformation of the former high-rise office block of the RUCH media conglomerate into the seat of the BPH Bank was completed. It was the city's first modern high-rise building with air-conditioning. Its distinctive features in the city space were the walls of characteristic blue glass and the slanted roof. The building dominated the eastern part of the city centre and was a harbinger of successive similar towers (Wiśniewski, 2021).

At the same time, the Kraków branch of the Bank Handlowy w Warszawie, designed by Kraków-based DDJM Studio and winning many accolades including a nomination for the Mies van der Rohe Award (Handlowy Bank Branch Office Building in Kraków, 2021), was completed. Its architects, Marek Dunikowski and Wojciech Miecznikowski, had experienced working abroad, as in the 1970s they worked on the design of the Al-Assad Library in Damascus (Stanek, 2012, p. 19). In the 1990s, they founded the DDJM Studio that delivered the city's key office projects, most of which combined global trends with local references. The Centrum Biurowe Lubicz (2001) is a spacious modern complex designed in a modernist style and with extensive glazing in the entrance zone (Majewski, 2000b, pp. 27–33). Not much later, in 2003–09, the Globe Trade Centre complex was built on ul. Armii Krajowej: three identical multistorey office towers with majestic vertical divisions. As similar form was given to the O3 Business Campus (Opolska Business Park) on ul. Opolska which was built in 2014–18. In both cases, the designs developed by DDJM Studio became the model for other, similar buildings in Kraków (BE DDJM. Projekty, 2021).

The most attractive projects in office architecture were the joint endeavours of two Kraków studios, nsMoonStudio and Wizja (Domicz, 2014, pp. 64–69). In 2014 they completed the design of Alma Tower on ul. Pilotów: a 13-storey, sculpture-like form with green façades. The distinctive hallmarks of the building are the unique openings in the cuboid form, with the divisions between the windows tapering towards the top and creating a particular impression. Stanisław Deńko, who stands at the helm of Wizja Studio, had much experience of working abroad as, in the 1970s, he designed the Polish Embassy in New Delhi in India with Witold Cęckiewicz (Deńko, Karpińska, Wiśniewski, 2017, pp. 79–83).

The largest project in the portfolio of nsMoonStudio under Piotr Nawara's leadership is the High Five office complex on ul. Pawia on the northern side of the railway station. The five buildings of different heights, with 5–9 floors, was completed in 2016–21. Their distinctive features are the slanting arrangement of the forms and partially also of the façades, and a dynamic pattern of the windows (moonstudio, 2021). Office space in Kraków was not developed in a single location, so there was no pressure to build high-rise towers. The city's office buildings are, as a rule, low, with around ten floors and arranged in small clusters.

Leisure areas

At the threshold of the 21st century, the private sector entered the space of Kraków not only with office buildings but also with investments into service buildings for the leisure industry. In 2001, DDJM Studio designed Multikino, a modern multiplex cinema on ul. Dobrego Pasterza in the northern part of the city. Featuring around a dozen cinema screens, including one that was then Poland's largest, was designed to resemble a corner of a city quarter. The decoration of the façades alluded to simple modernist solutions and neoplasticist painting. The whole was an interesting endeavour to seek its own model for commercial architecture in Kraków (Majewski, 2000a, pp. 52–56).

However, there were not many similarly successful endeavours, and in later years, commercial buildings became a major aesthetic and functional challenge for the city. In 2000, the aquapark was built close to the Multikino: once Poland's largest multifunctional water amusement park, today it still remains Kraków's largest (Studio A. Pracownia architektoniczna S.C. Marek Pakuła. Marzena Pakuła, 2021). The huge construction on an almost semicircular footprint features low-quality details that combine extensive glazing with reflective glass and references to historical architecture.

Kraków Aquapark was one of the first buildings that were so large and important for the cityscape yet so blatantly ignored the context and imposed a new aesthetic model on the city. That phenomenon was even more strongly represented by the city's first shopping centre complexes. Large-scale developments of this type were built on ul. Generała Tadeusza Bora-Komorowskiego (1997), Aleja Pokoju street (2001), and ul. Zakopiańska (1999) in 1997–2001 (Motak, 2007, pp. 104–108). They were all created for international chains and made use of a ready-made design that had worked elsewhere, which Kraków's architectural studios just adapted to local needs and regulations. Their aesthetic and city-forming effect cannot be considered successful.

This specific kind of adaptation of globally functioning designs made a powerful impact on the space of Kraków and played a negative role in the development of the local architecture (Stec, Sarzyński, 2017). Fifteen shopping centres offering nearly 615,000 m^2 of lettable space were developed in the city over the following two decades (Urząd Miasta Krakowa, 2018). In 2001, Galeria Plaza was completed; the city's first commercial project that combined commercial space of a high standard with a modern multiplex cinema. It was designed by the Kraków-based IMB Asymetria studio, which was also responsible for several similar projects built in the following years. In 2005, the space of the partially demolished cluster of historical public slaughterhouses in Grzegórzki was developed into Galeria Kazimierz, and a year later, Galeria Krakowska – the city's largest shopping space at the time – was delivered in the direct vicinity of the main railway station, followed by Galeria Bonarka in 2009, which opened on the premises of the former chemical works and is the largest shopping and commercial site in Kraków to date (IMB Asymetria, 2021).

None of the buildings described above can be considered consistent with the cityscape, or even aesthetically neutral. They point to the moment when the architecture of Kraków's public use buildings became largely subjected to mindlessly adopted global models. Their designs ignore the context, reaching for banal and repeatable solutions and redefining the cityscape around them by virtue of their scale. The only example of a remarkable shopping facility is Galleria Serenada, which was completed in 2018 and is located near the Multikino and aquapark. It is the work of Stanisław Deńko and the team of Wizja Studio. The original form of the building is not aggressive with respect to its environment, and its positive reception results from the original red concrete patterns covering the entire walls (W biuro architektoniczne Wizja, 2021).

In a tourist destination like Kraków, hotels play an important role. It is a paradox, but there have been no particularly ambitious projects of this type in Kraków since 1989. To a certain degree, the construction of the hotel of the Sheraton chain in the place of a historical brewery near Wawel in 2004 was symbolic. Despite an exceptional location and a prestigious investor, the construction is banal, superficially adapting typical solutions for hotel buildings from the United States or Western Europe. The most remarkable of the new Kraków hotels is the Park Inn Hotel built on ul. Monte Cassino in 2009. Its futuristic design consists of two superimposing forms that form an entire enclosed quarter. The design is the work of the well-known German studio of Jürgen Mayer and the local Ovotz design lab (Orlewicz, 2009, pp. 68–79).

A place to live

The development of the first commercial complexes coincided with a visible acceleration in residential development. The first years of the 21st century marked the beginning of very intensive suburbanisation of Kraków. Single-family houses and terraced complexes were built within an approximately 20-kilometre radius from the city centre, many of them in distant and poorly connected locations. This new phenomenon resulted from the gradual increase in Poles' wealth and the demographic peak of the 1970s and 1980s entering the labour market (Leśniak-Rychlak, 2019). Just after 1989, the housing shortage in Poland was estimated at around two million units, and currently, despite the many years of intensive production, it still stands at approximately 300,000 (Twardoch, 2019, pp. 41–47). This huge demand for housing had the strongest impact on the space of metropolitan centres like Kraków, where it resulted in the parallel development of several different types of buildings, notably the large-scale buildings of single-family houses.

The new architecture of Kraków's suburbs, in many cases with no access to public transport, which forced their inhabitants towards individual solutions, redefined the culturescape of the areas lying around the city. Most of the developments here have been typical, very incoherently related to the broadly construed traditional architecture, with the actual links expressed through the shape of the roofs or arrangement of the windows. Most such buildings in Kraków were developed in the vicinity of valuable natural locations, for example, in the Wola Justowska district on the western side of the city. Even more developments of this kind were constructed in the neighbouring communes, where the buffer zone separating the city from the historical villages and towns situated outside its boundaries was eroded in the 21st century. In parallel, the characteristic ancient field divisions in Kraków and its vicinity – long and narrow – was decisive for the emergence of a specific phenomenon, namely the construction of the densely set, long lines of terraced houses.

Standing out against this background are the luxurious villas and the small apartment complexes. Dom z gontu (literally: "house of wooden shingle"), a 2003 project by nsMoonStudio, was one of the first cases providing new models for residential construction (Wiśniewski, 2004, pp. 40–49). The modern building with three separate apartments was designed in a manner that refers to the region's traditional architecture, with shingle-clad walls. Three years after its completion, Dom z gontu won the accolade of being presented at the Poland – Icons of Architecture exhibition organised by *Architektura-Murator* magazine and promoted by the Polish diplomatic services in various parts of the world ("Polska. Ikony architektury", 2021). The Edge House, a spacious single-family house in Pychowice, was designed in a similar spirit: its futuristic form is integrated into a limestone crag. Przemysław Olczyk's concept won a nomination to the Mies van der Rohe Award ('Edge House', 2021).

The huge need for development of residential housing translated primarily into the development of multifamily developments. Kraków's residential resources nearly doubled in the three decades from 1989: in 1991, they comprised a total of 234,000 dwellings, in 2004, 289,000 dwellings, and in 2020, as many as 412,000 dwellings (Urząd Miasta Krakowa, 1992, 2005, 2021). A quantum leap in the number of such developments followed Poland's accession to the European Union, and most dwellings were delivered towards the end of the second decade of the 21st century.

However, new large residential compounds were already being developed in the 1990s. One such development lying on the northern side of the historic city centre, Żabiniec, features gabled roofs and an arrangement of apartment blocks based on historic quarters (Michalczak, 2010, p. 74). The complex was one of the few completed early after the systemic transformation. This type of construction clearly accelerated after 2000, with most developments choosing the southern side of the city, i.e., the vicinity of Kurdwanów, a residential district built in the previous decades, and in the poorly developed districts of Ruczaj and Kliny Borkowskie.

The Osiedle Europejskie estate, designed by the Kraków-based B2 Studio in this area of the city, was a breakthrough for Kraków residential construction (B2 STUDIO, 2021). The quality of the finishes and the density of development distinguish it from the estates built in the city in the 1970s and 1980s. Its buildings are clustered into quarters arranged close one to another, most having seven or eight floors. This design illustrates a new feature of residential construction in Poland: the tendency to pack the developments more closely together and build as much usable space as possible.

In the following years, B2 Studio became the leading designer of multifamily developments in Kraków, and it completed several large residential estates in various parts of the city. Particularly important for the studio's output is the Avia residential complex: situated by the defunct runway of the former Czyżyny airfield, it was the first to introduce multifamily developments with 17 storeys into the space of the city. Moreover, the urban planning aspect of the complex raised huge controversies from the outset and the estate itself has become an illustration and symbol of dangerous changes in Kraków's landscape (Radłowska, 2018).

A breakthrough came with the developments of the Mieszkaj w Mieście – Osiedle Wizjonerów (literally: "Live in a city – the visionaries' estate") in Bronowice district. This large and coherent urban arrangement designed by the Bytom-based Medusa Group studio is prominent for its original detail drawn from modernism, the differentiation of types of development, and care for access to green areas (Brataniec, 2017, pp. 68–74). The high standard of design applied here can be construed as an attempt to answer the intensifying criticism of the residential complexes delivered earlier.

In the context of large-scale production, smaller buildings look best, primarily the infills built among historical developments. Especially important is the work of the Piotr Lewicki and Kazimierz Łatak studio that based its original style on local heritage, drawing especially from interwar modernism. Prominent among the other works of the studio are their designs of minor residential and hotel buildings, e.g., the Hotel Pod Wawelem (Malkowski, 2008a, pp. 60–63) from 2008 on Plac na Groblach square, and the Aparthotel Lwowska in Podgórze (Majewski, 2017, pp. 60–65).

In search of the new order

The dynamically developing private sector played a key role in the process of change that has taken place in the city's culturescape. The territorial authorities have faced a particular paradox with respect to these phenomena. The rapid economic growth and inflow of accession funds after 2004 opened new options to the commune and the region and making up for the shortages and gaps in infrastructure and the quality of public space became a realistic proposition. The municipal authorities tried to compensate for the unfavourable changes related to the chaotic development of residential construction with new large-scale investments.

In 2002–06, the floor of the Main Market Square was changed and a new underground museum space was developed below it (Malkowski, 2010, pp. 46–61). Investments into new spaces for culture became especially important for further development of Kraków's architecture. The ICE Kraków Congress Centre, a modern, multifunctional complex for congresses and concerts designed by the studio of Krzysztof Ingarden and Jacek Ewý, was delivered in 2014 (Bojanowski, Domicz, Mycielski, 2015, pp. 52–72). Situated close to the Vistula, the wavy form of the building makes a reference to the nearby Manggha Museum of Japanese Culture and Technology mentioned earlier. With time, ICE Kraków has become one of the most important new symbols of the city.

The architects of that building are well known for many other projects completed in the city. The Wyspiański Pavilion (2007) is a small and narrow exhibition and office building built very close to the headquarters of the Kraków Municipal Office, on the site of the former All Saints' Church (Ogiński, 2007, pp. 62–67). The ceramic raster placed over the glazed façade generates a particular impression of a modern building that, nonetheless, remains in a dialogue with the historical surroundings (Figure 8.5).

A similar way of thinking was decisive for the design of the Małopolska Garden of Arts, a slightly larger building combining the functions of an art gallery, library, and theatre, which replaced a military horse-riding arena (Mycielski, Stiasny, 2013, pp. 34–53). Again, the designers made highly original use of ceramic elements, fashioning them into thin pilaster strips that protrude from the glass façade. The openwork loggia over the entrance to the theatre section, with a steel construction also making use of ceramic decorative elements, is particularly impressive. The building of the Małopolska Garden of Arts won many prizes, including the UIA Friendly and Inclusive Spaces Award of the International Union of Architects (UIA), and in 2015, it was yet another Kraków project nominated for the Mies van der Rohe Award ("Małopolska Garden of Arts", 2021).

Figure 8.5 Małopolska Garden of Arts, designed by Krzysztof Ingarden and Jacek Ewý, 2013.
Photo by P. Mazur.

It is worth noting that a new cultural function for post-industrial buildings became a frequent phenomenon in Kraków's architecture. Completed in 2010, the building of the MOCAK Museum of Contemporary Art Kraków based on the design of Florence-based architect Claudio Nardi used the space of the former Oskar Schindler's Enamel Factory in the Zabłocie district (Stiasny, 2011, pp. 30–41). The modernist building from the 1930s belongs to an industrial compound that was managed by Oskar Schindler at the time of the Nazi occupation. Alongside the ascetic museum that houses contemporary art organised in a former factory, its nearby office building was arranged into a branch of the Museum of Kraków with an exhibition devoted to the history of the city under German occupation (Figure 8.6).

Most attractive from the point of view of architecture, however, was the transformation of the former Podgórze municipal powerplant into the headquarters of the Cricoteka Centre for the Documentation of the Art of Tadeusz Kantor (Tomczak, 2015, pp. 64–73). The design of the building by Stanisław Deńko and nsMoonStudio was the winning entry in the architectural competition organised in 2006. The Cricoteka building includes a gallery space suspended over the historical powerplant. Thanks to the openwork façade made of weathered steel (COR-TEN), and the location in a very sunny spot by the river, the whole building changes depending on the time of day and season. It alludes to the oeuvre of Tadeusz Kantor, a key figure in post-war art and theatre in Kraków and Poland. Both MOCAK and Cricoteka won numerous prizes and many accolades, including nominations to the Mies van

Figure 8.6 Centre for the Documentation of the Art of Tadeusz Kantor, Cricoteka, designed by Piotr Nawara, Agnieszka Szultk, Stanisław Deńko, 2014.
Photo by P. Mazur.

der Rohe Award ("MOCAK, Museum of Contemporary Art in Krakow, former O. Schindler Factory", 2021; "Centre for the Documentation of the Art of Tadeusz Kantor Cricoteka", 2021).

Both buildings are part of the programme to revitalise the former industrial estates of the Zabłocie and Podgórze districts. The design to redevelop the former warehouse of the Kraków Fortress into the Home Army Museum on ul. Wita Stwosza near the main railway station followed similar assumptions and served similar purposes. The design was completed in 2011 and is the work of the Ryszard Jurkowski studio. It is another one of Kraków's buildings to be nominated to the Mies van der Rohe Award ("The Home Army Museum in Cracow", 2021).

Nomination to that prestigious award was also extended to the pavilion of the Polish Aviation Museum, which was delivered in 2010 ("Museum of Polish Aviation", 2021). Having no adequate facilities, the museum that operated on the city's outskirts in the Czyżyny district since 1964 had long grappled with the problem of low attendance. It was only the construction of a modern building designed by Pysall Ruge Architekten and Bartłomiej Kisielewski's Kraków-based Horizon studio that changed the situation. The new building of the Polish Aviation Museum, a raw, reinforced concrete block that reminds one of a moving propeller, is beyond doubt one of the most thought-provoking architectural projects in contemporary Kraków (Porębska, 2011, pp. 58–69) (Figure 8.7).

Figure 8.7 Polish Aviation Museum, designed by Bartłomiej Kisielewski and Pysall Ruge Architekten, 2010.
Photo by P. Mazur.

The new spaces assigned to culture have played a special role in the process of restoration and conservation of many historical buildings in the city centre. Especially fascinating examples of such projects are the transformation of the Pod Kruki mansion (The Ravens House) in the Main Market Square, home to the International Cultural Centre, designed by Romuald Loegler (Wiśniewski, 2019, pp. 180–207), and the adaptation of the 19th-century mansion housing the Czartoryski Princes Museum, which received a glazed roof over the internal courtyard thanks to Piotr Lewicki and Kazimierz Łatak (Kuryłowicz, Majewski, 2020, pp. 22–38).

Against the background of structures catering for the needs of cultural institutions, those delivered for the purposes of sports look less successful. Most attractive are the smaller projects, e.g., the ComCom Zone sports hall and swimming pool in Nowa Huta whose ascetic reinforced concrete form was sculpted by Wojciech Obtułowicz (Stiasny, 2008, pp. 48– 55). Similarly, the Cracovia football stadium designed by the Spanish Estudia Lamela studio and completed in 2010 gives a very good impression (Malkowski, 2011, pp. 48–55). High praise is also due to the diminutive sports hall of the Sports Championship Schools on ul. Grochowska, which was completed in 2017. This work of Marcin Brataniec and Urszula Forczek-Brataniec's Pracownia Architektury eM4 is a simple and ascetic form notable thanks to its façade of elongated panels of milky glass (Bujas, 2018, pp. 60–66).

However, the most important structure recently developed for sports purposes in Kraków is the KÄRCHER Cracovia Centennial Hall with the Sports Centre for the Handicapped (2018) (Haduch, Kuryłowicz, 2018, pp. 36–54), another Kraków building to be nominated for the Mies van der Rohe Award ("Cracovia 1906 Centennial Hall with the Sports Center for the Handicapped", 2021). Its sculpture-like form designed by the studio of Piotr Lewicki and Kazimierz Łatak features the characteristic fronts finished in weathered steel (COR-TEN) and a huge glass wall that opens the main hall to a panorama of the Błonia common and Kościuszko Mound, some of the most valuable green spaces in the city (Figure 8.8).

The turning point

Most of the buildings serving culture and sports arose in studios that opened in the 1990s or early in the 21st century. A new generation of younger designers and architects came to prominence in Kraków especially after 2000. The activity of the studios of Piotr Lewicki and Kazimierz Łatak (Biuro Projektów Lewicki i Łatak), Piotr Nawara and Agnieszka Szultk (nsMoonStudio), Bartłomiej Kisielewski (Horizon Studio), Bartosz and Michał Haduch (NArchitekTURA), Przemysław Olczyk (Mobius Studio), and Marcin Brataniec and Urszula Forczek-Brataniec (Pracownia Architektury eM4) represents a generational change in Kraków's architecture of the period. The fact

Figure 8.8 KÄRCHER Cracovia Centennial Hall with the Sports Centre for the Handicapped, designed by Piotr Lewicki and Kazimierz Łatak, 2018.
Photo by P. Mazur.

that these studios have carried out a large proportion of their projects outside the city is also telling. The work of these design teams allows one to state that Kraków has retained an important place on the architectural map of Poland and has managed to retain a high degree of sensitivity to the local context and genius loci that was formed in the early 20th century.

The rapid development of the city in the last three decades has paved the way to the opening of many new architecture studios. They are responsible for modelling the city's current image and introducing new architectural ideas and concepts into the space. Much of the shoddy post-1989 architecture developed in Kraków has failed to keep up with the ambitions and goals that local architects used to set themselves, and the mass production of buildings and inadequate spatial planning and zoning laws allowed a visible deterioration of its standards. The Unity Tower, the city's tallest office building built in the direct vicinity of Kraków's historic centre, is a particular symbol of this phenomenon.

Standing at over 100 m high, the structure of the building dates back to the 1970s. The crisis in the Polish economy stalled the construction for nearly four decades, leaving the unfinished skeleton as part of Kraków's skyline. The new design is the work of BE DDJM Architekci (formerly DDJM) and is designed around the existing core (Dunikowski, Kliche, 2020, pp. 84–91). The form produced is a dangerous precedent for a historical city: rather than belonging to a more extensive complex of office buildings, this new type of office block is surrounded by a district of single-family houses. Moreover, its final form is far more spacious than that assumed by the original design of half a century ago.

Another reason for the negative assessment is the low quality of architectural solutions and material choices. The completion of the work coincided with the outbreak of the COVID-19 pandemic, and the ensuing growth in working from home and the associated reduced demand for new office spaces may slow down the production of similar designs.

The Unity Tower is a symbol of the rapid flow of external investment capital to the cities like Kraków: capital that has been pumped into similar investments of standard design. Issues such as the quality and context of architecture are of no concern for most investors managing such capital. What matters far more is the budget, the pace of construction, and the final return on investment. Similar concerns prejudged the quality of many commercial, office, and retail projects, and the final guise of numerous residential compounds. Currently, this is the most important impact of globalisation – construed both as economic integration combined with the free flow of capital, and unification and standardisation of models and standards – on the architecture of Kraków.

That vast power of globalisation raises ambivalent feelings, as on the one hand it helped the city open to the world and become one of Europe's metropolitan centres, but on the other, it brought shifts of the paradigms concerning the development of space and disturbed what was strongest in Kraków's architecture, namely the skill of expressing the city's identity.

At the same time, the picture of the influence of globalisation and the development of the city remains extremely complex. The projects carried out here in this period have been unique on the national and Central European scale, with no fewer than 20 being distinguished with nominations to the Mies van der Rohe Award (compared with a total of 141 projects for Poland since the mid-1990s, of which 31 were from Warsaw, EUMiesAward, 2021). The daring forms, and architecture sensitive to the city's identity and cultural heritage represented by these buildings could not have come about without drawing courageously from what is the best and most inspiring in contemporary architecture. The truth about Kraków's architecture is somewhere between these two extremes. And even though the contemporary picture of the city may seem chaotic and under pressure from large-scale commercial and residential projects, Kraków is still one of the places where the pulse of Polish architecture beats the strongest.

Bibliography

B2 STUDIO (2021). Available at: http://b2studio.com.pl (Accessed on 31 October 2021).

BE DDJM. Projekty (2021). Available at: http://be-ddjm.com (Accessed on 31 October 2021).

"Blue End of the Road" (2021). Available at: https://www.miesarch.com/work/1229 (Accessed on 31 October 2021).

Bojanowski, K., Domicz, A., Mycielski, K. (2015) "Centrum Kongresowe w Krakowie", *Architektura-Murator*, 3, pp. 52–72.

Brataniec, M. (2017) "Zespół Mieszkaj w Mieście w Krakowie", *Architektura-Murator*, 11, pp. 68–74.

Bujas, P. (2018) "Hala Sportowa w Krakowie", *Architektura-Murator*, 4, pp. 60–66.

"Centre for the Documentation of the Art of Tadeusz Kantor Cricoteka" (2021) Available at: https://www.miesarch.com/work/574 (Accessed on 31 October 2021).

Cichońska, I., Popera, K., Snopek, K. (2016) *Architektura VII dnia*. 1st ed. Warszawa: Fundacja Nowej Kultury Bęc Zmiana.

"Cracovia 1906 Centennial Hall with the Sports Center for the Handicapped" (2021). Available at: https://www.miesarch.com/work/3824 (Accessed on 31 October 2021)

"Cracow District Court" (2021). Available at: https://www.miesarch.com/work/1911 (Accessed on 31 October 2021).

Czapnik, W. (2011) "Sąd Apelacyjny w Krakowie", *Architektura-Murator*, 5, pp. 66–73.

Czerski, J. (2019) *Rynek powierzchni biurowych w Krakowie. I kwartał 2019 r.* Available at: http://www.mrn.pl/analizy/Analizy, 3,3.html (Accessed on 31 October 2021).

Deńko, S., Karpińska, M., Wiśniewski, M. (2017) "Ambasada", *Autoportret*, 2, pp. 79–83.

Domicz, A. (2014) "Biurowiec Alma Tower w Krakowie", *Architektura-Murator*, 12, pp. 64–69.

Domicz, A. (2015) "Galeria Europa Daleki Wschód", *Architektura-Murator*, 15, pp. 56–63.

Dunikowski, M., Kliche, K. (2020) "Przebudowa Szkieletora / Kraków", *Architektura-Murator*, 9, pp. 84–91.

Dziechciaruk-Maj, B., Nowak, K., Urbańska, M. (eds.) (2009) *Manggha. Historia projektu*, Kraków: Centrum Sztuki Techniki Japońskiej Manggha.

"Edge House" (2021). Available at: https://www.miesarch.com/work/2448 (Accessed on 31 October 2021).

EUMiesAward (2021). Available at: https://www.miesarch.com/ (Accessed on 31 October 2021).

Fabiański, M., Purchla, J. (2012) *Architektura Krakowa Przewodnik*. Kraków: Wydawnictwo Literackie.

Foryś, I. (2017) "Spółdzielczość mieszkaniowa w Polsce po transformacji gospodarczej", *Studia i Prace Wydziału Nauk Ekonomicznych i Zarządzania*, 50/1.

"Ghetto Heroes Square" (2005). Available at: https://www.publicspace.org/works/-/project/d019-plac-bohaterow-getta (Accessed on 31 October 2021).

Haduch, B., Kuryłowicz, E. (2018) "Hala Cracovii", *Architektura-Murator*, 7, pp. 36–54.

"Handlowy Bank Branch Office Building in Krakow" (2021). Available at: https://www.miesarch.com/work/1805 (Accessed on 31 October 2021).

IMB Asymetria (2021). Available at: http://imbasymetria.pl/ (Accessed on 31 October 2021).

Jędruch, D. (2018) "Osiedle Centrum E – czyli piknik nad wiszącą skarpą", in Klaś, J. (ed.) *Nowa Huta. Architektoniczny portret miasta drugiej połowy XX wieku*. Kraków: Ośrodek Kultury im. C. K. Norwida, pp. 96–103.

Kaliński, J. (2009) *Transformacja gospodarki polskiej w latach 1980–2004*. Warszawa: Szkoła Główna Handlowa.

Karpińska, M., Leśniak-Rychlak, D., Wiśniewski, M. (eds.) (2015) *Witold Cęckiewicz*. vol. 1, *Rozmowy o architekturze. Projekty*, Kraków: Fundacja Instytut Architektury.

Kuryłowicz, E., Majewski, J.S. (2020) "Muzeum Czartoryskich", *Architektura-Murator*, 4, pp. 22–38.

Leśniak-Rychlak, D. (2019) *Jesteśmy wreszcie we własnym domu*. Kraków: Fundacja Instytut Architektury.

Majewski, J.S. (2000a) "Stal, popcorn i srebrne ekrany", *Architektura-Murator*, 9, pp. 52–56.

Majewski, J.S. (2000b) "Centrum Lubicz", *Architektura-Murator*, 12, pp. 27–33.

Majewski, J.S. (2017) "Aparthotel Lwowska w Krakowie", *Architektura-Murator*, 4, pp. 60–65.

Malkowski, T. (2008a) "Hotel pod Wawelem", *Architektura-Murator*, 1, pp. 60–63.

Malkowski, T. (2008b) "Audytorium Maximum Uniwersytetu Jagiellońskiego", *Architektura-Murator*, 7, pp. 68–73.

Malkowski, T. (2010) "Modernizacja Sukiennic i podziemne muzeum pod krakowskim rynkiem", *Architektura-Murator*, 12, pp. 46–61.

Malkowski, T. (2011) "Stadion Cracovii", *Architektura-Murator*, 2, pp. 48–55.

"Malopolska Garden of Arts" (2021). Available at: https://www.miesarch.com/work/573 (Accessed on 31 October 2021).

Mańkowski, T., Wróbel, P. (1999) "Radio Kraków u siebie", *Architektura & Biznes*, 5, pp. 22–23.

Michalczak, J. (ed.) (2010) *Architekci Małopolski 2010*. Available at: https://www.mpoia.pl/index.php/dzialalnosc/publikacje# (Accessed on 31 October 2021).

"MOCAK, Museum of Contemporary Art in Krakow, former O. Schindler Factory" (2021). Available at: https://www.miesarch.com/work/574 (Accessed on 31 October 2021).
MoonStudio (2021). Available at: https://www.moonstudio.com.pl/ (Accessed on 31 October 2021).
Motak, M. (2002) "Nowe mosty w Krakowie", *Architektura & Biznes*, 6, pp. 51–58.
Motak, M. (2007) *Architektura Krakowa 1989–2004. Nowe realizacje w kontekście miasta historycznego*. Kraków: Wydawnictwo PK.
"Museum of Polish Aviation" (2021). Available at: https://www.miesarch.com/work/459 (Accessed on 31 October 2021).
Mycielski, K. (2002a) "Instytut", *Architektura-Murator*, 1, pp. 13–17.
Mycielski, K. (2002b) "Sąd", *Architektura-Murator*, 5, pp. 17–23.
Mycielski, K., Stiasny, G. (2013) "Małopolski Ogród Sztuki", *Architektura-Murator*, 1, pp. 34–53.
"New Building for the Jagiellonian Library" (2021). Available at: https://www.miesarch.com/work/933 (Accessed on 31 October 2021).
"New Zgody Square – Remodelling of the Bohaterow Getta Square" (2021). Available at: https://www.miesarch.com/work/2745 (Accessed on 31 October 2021).
Obtułowicz, W., Włodarczyk, M., Gajczyk, M. (eds.) (1998) *Moderniści krakowscy. Projekty i realizacje*. Kraków: Stowarzyszenie Architektów Polskich SARP Oddział Kraków.
Ogiński, T. (2007) "Pawilon Wyspiański w Krakowie", *Architektura-Murator*, 10, pp. 62–67.
Orlewicz, A. (2009) "Hotel Park Inn w Krakowie", *Architektura-Murator*, 6, pp. 68–79.
"Polska. Ikony architektury" (2021). Available at: https://culture.pl/pl/wydarzenie/-polska-ikona-architektury (Accessed on 31 October 2021).
Porębska, E.P. (2011) "Muzeum Lotnictwa Polskiego w Krakowie – znak architektonicznej jakości", *Architektura-Murator*, 1, pp. 58–69.
Purchla, J. (2006) *Kampus Akademii Ekonomicznej w Krakowie / The Campus of the Cracow University of Economics*. Kraków: Centrum Rozwoju i Promocji Akademii Ekonomicznej w Krakowie.
Purchla, J. (2019) "Epilogue", in J. Purchla, (ed.) *Kraków: History & Art*. Kraków: Międzynarodowe Centrum Kultury.
Purchla, J., Sepioł, J. (eds.) (2015) *Form Follows Freedom: Architektura dla kultury w Polsce 2000+*. Kraków: Międzynarodowe Centrum Kultury.
"Radio Center – Kraków – Window to the World" (2021). Available at: https://www.miesarch.com/work/1803 (Accessed on 31 October 2021).
Radłowska, R. (2018) "Czyżyńska walka o przestrzeń. Starzy i nowi mieszkańcy, deweloperzy". Available at: https://krakow.wyborcza.pl/krakow/7,44425,23070812,czyzynska-walka-o-przestrzen-starzy-i-nowi-mieszkancy-deweloperzy.html (Accessed on 31 October 2021).
Rygiel, P. (1998) "Kampus Uniwersytetu Jagiellońskiego", *Architektura & Biznes*, 7, pp. 30–31.
Sepioł, J. (ed.) (1985) *I Biennale Architektury. Kraków, grudzień 1985 – styczeń 1986, Pałac Sztuki*. Kraków: Politechnika Krakowska im. T. Kościuszki, Stowarzyszenie Architektów Polskich SARP.
Skotarczak, T. (ed.) (2015) *Spółdzielnie mieszkaniowe. Dylematy funkcjonowania i rozwoju*. Warszawa: C.H. Beck.

Sołjan, I., Liro, J. (2015) "Nowe centrum pielgrzymkowe w krakowskiej dzielnicy Łagiewniki-Borek Fałęcki", *Peregrinus Cracoviensis*, 25(4), pp. 135–151.

Stanek, Ł. (2012) *Postmodernizm jest prawie w porządku. Polska architektura po socjalistycznej globalizacji*. Warszawa: Fundacja Nowej Kultury Bęc Zmiana.

Stec, A., Sarzyński, K. (2017) "Centra handlowe a gospodarka miasta na przykładzie Krakowa", *Optimum. Studia Ekonomiczne*, 6(90), pp. 214–229. Available at: GLAhttp://optimum.uwb.edu.pl/index.php/osj/article/view/134 (Accessed on 31 October 2021).

Stiasny, G. (1999a) "Brama do Miasta Zmarłych", *Architektura-Murator*, 4, pp. 14–19.

Stiasny, G. (1999b) "Radio Kraków", *Architektura-Murator*, 9, pp. 4–19.

Stiasny, G. (2002) "Dialog", *Architektura-Murator*, 1, pp. 28–35.

Stiasny, G. (2008) "Centrum sportu i edukacji w Nowej Hucie", *Architektura-Murator*, 12, pp. 48–55.

Stiasny, G. (2011) "Muzeum Sztuki Współczesnej MOCAK w Krakowie", *Architektura-Murator*, 8, 30–41.

Studio A. Pracownia architektoniczna S.C. Marek Pakuła. Marzena Pakuła (2021). Available at: http://studio-a.com.pl (Accessed on 31 October 2021).

Styrna-Bartkowicz, K. (2015) *Loegler Synopsis*. Kraków: RAM, Krakowska Akademia im. Andrzeja Frycza Modrzewskiego.

"Teaching and Sports Pavilion of the Academy of Economics" (2021). Available at: https://www.miesarch.com/work/949 (Accessed on 31 October 2021).

"The Children Village in Oświęcim. International Collaboration Project" (1994) *Space Design*, 363.

"The Home Army Museum in Cracow" (2021). Available at: https://www.miesarch.com/work/508 (Accessed on 31 October 2021).

Tomczak, M. (2015) "Niemożliwy most", *Architektura & Biznes*, 10, pp. 64–73.

Tosza, E. (ed.) (2008) *...a w Krakowie jest Opera / ... And There is Opera in Kraków*. Kraków: Opera Krakowska.

Twardoch, A. (2019) *System do mieszkania. Perspektywy rozwoju dostępnego budownictwa mieszkaniowego*. Warszawa: Fundacja Nowej Kultury Bęc Zmiana.

Urząd Miasta Krakowa (1992) *Raport o stanie miasta 1991*. Available at: https://www.bip.krakow.pl/zalaczniki/dokumenty/n/72118/0/karta (Accessed on 31 October 2021).

Urząd Miasta Krakowa (2005) *Raport o stanie miasta 2004*. Available at: https://www.bip.krakow.pl/?dok_id=2032 (Accessed on 31 October 2021).

Urząd Miasta Krakowa (2018) Krakowski Rynek Nieruchomości. Available at: https://www.bip.krakow.pl/?sub_dok_id=21093 (Accessed on: 31 October 2021).

Urząd Miasta Krakowa (2021) *Raport o stanie miasta 2020*. Available at: https://www.bip.krakow.pl/?dok_id=146665 (Accessed on 31 October 2021).

W biuro architektoniczne Wizja (2021). Available at: https://www.wizja.krakow.pl/ (Accessed on 31 October 2021).

Wiśniewski, M. (2004) "Dom w Krakowie", *Architektura-Murator*, 8, pp. 40–49.

Wiśniewski, M. (2019) "Eksperyment", in Purchla, J. (ed.) *Rynek Główny 25. Dzieje jednego adresu*. Kraków: Międzynarodowe Centrum Kultury.

Wiśniewski, M. (2021) "Kombinat Prasowo-Poligraficzny RSW 'Prasa' (współcześnie K1)". Available at: https://szlakmodernizmu.pl/baza-obiektow/kombinat-prasowo-poligraficzny-rsw-prasa-wspolczesnie-k1/ (Accessed on 31 October 2021).

Włodarczyk, M. (2014) *Dwa miasta Krakowa. Modernizm lat 1945–1990 w dzielnicach Kazimierz i Podgórze. Wybrane przykłady, lista obiektów architektonicznych*. Kraków: Stowarzyszenie Architektów Polskich SARP Oddział Kraków.

Włodarczyk, M., Włodarczyk, M. (2017) *Szlakami dziedzictwa. Przegląd architektury Krakowa lat 1945–1990 / Paths of legacy. Overview of Cracow architecture in the years 1945 1990*. Kraków: Stowarzyszenie Architektów Polskich SARP Oddział Kraków.

Wroński, J. Sz. (2010) *Kościoły Krakowa zbudowane w latach 1945–1989 jako wyraz przemian architektury sakralnej w Polsce na tle rozwoju architektury na świecie. Studium historyczno-architektoniczne*. Kraków: Akademia Wychowania Fizycznego im. Bronisława Czecha w Krakowie.

Zamorska-Przyłuska, E. (1998) "Na krakowskim bruku", *Architektura & Biznes*, 9, pp. 46–47.

9 Kraków culture heritage

On the way to globalising the national potential

Andrzej Laskowski

Introduction

Kraków has long been an exceptional place for Poles (Purchla, 2005, pp. 35–43; Dziedzic, 2009; Ziejka, 2010): its exceptional nature is instilled into people throughout their education. Children learn the Kraków legends, and young adults are taught the historical significance of the city for the history of the nation. In general, in the Polish consciousness, Kraków is the lay centre (from the 11th century), and the spiritual centre of power (from 10th/11th century). Over several centuries, it has been the capital of the country and the metropolis of the Roman Catholic Church, with the monarch's residence and the bishop's cathedral coexisting atop Wawel Hill, as well as Poland's oldest academic centre with the Jagiellonian University (UJ) being the oldest and leading academic institution. It was also the place of royal coronations and burials (the Cathedral), the pantheon of the greatest creators of national culture, a witness to grand political events and memorable insurgencies furthering independence, and finally, the city of the Pope and an important pilgrimage centre.

Simultaneously, Kraków is a city of metropolitan traditions and ambitions reaching far beyond the Polish border. Its Europeanness stems from the age-old relationships with its neighbours, validated through the Central European concepts related to the Hanseatic League, the Jagiellonian dynasty, and the Habsburg monarchy, as well as its architecture and culture (both tangible and intangible), which bears the brand of ideas known and applied in Europe, and was introduced by artists from various European centres as well as developed locally. Taken together, all that contributes to the wealth of its heritage, a unique combination that makes Kraków, albeit long demoted from the rank of a national capital, a visible point on the map, set between Warsaw, Berlin, Prague, Bratislava, Vienna, and Budapest (Purchla, 2000; Dziedzic, 2009).

The period discussed here is the time when Kraków reopened to the world after a spell of communism, marked by living behind the Iron Curtain, in isolation, with an unrelentingly imposed worldview channelled towards the Soviet east (Małecki, 1996; Chwalba, 2004). It is important to remember that Kraków, unlike Warsaw, did not lose most of its heritage resources during

DOI: 10.4324/9781003252757-10

the Second World War, and – following on the rich traditions of heritage conservation in Galicia and Poland between the two world wars – during the time of communism it remained an important centre of heritage preservation thinking for both the city and the region (Beiersdorf, 1996; Gaczoł, 2009, pp. 40–104; Krasnowolski, 2011). At the threshold of modern times, it was also capable of drawing historical reflection and building a vision of further actions concerning its heritage resources (Małecki, 1994) that consisted of nearly 1,200 structures within the city limits that were entered into the national register of built heritage, and over 6,300 listed in the municipal heritage register (Róziewicz, 2007). Many are examples of outstanding architecture, not only on the scale of the city and region, but also for Poland and even Europe (Purchla, 2007). Decisive for the supralocal dimension of this resource are primarily the variety, integrity, continuity, authenticity, grandeur, artistic merit, and multi-aspect programmes (Purchla, 2020, p. 32).

The inclusion of Kraków on the UNESCO World Heritage List and its consequences

Kraków's inclusion on the UNESCO World Heritage List was noticed on the international stage and had a significant impact on the developments in the city. Even though after the Second World War, Poland was itself in the zone of Soviet influence, Kraków found itself in the distinguished group of 12 sites from all over the world to be on the UNESCO World Heritage List (WHL), which was inaugurated in Washington in 1978. It was one of three European locations and one of only two listed cities – the other was Quito in Ecuador (for more information on the circumstances of Kraków bid and listing, see: Pawłowski, 2009) (Figure 9.1).

The entry covered Wawel, the city centre (Stare Miasto), the surrounding Planty Garden Ring, and the districts of Kazimierz and Stradom. It was made on the basis of Criterion IV, which requires that the site is "an outstanding example of a type of building, architectural or technological ensemble or landscape which illustrates (a) significant stage(s) in human history". In the case of Kraków, it was explained that "Kraków is an urban architectural ensemble of outstanding quality, in terms of both its townscape and its individual monuments. The historic centre of the town admirably illustrates the process of continuous urban growth from the Middle Ages to the present day". Great emphasis was laid on qualities such as the "high level of integrity", "a pervading authenticity", "city's panorama with its distinctive historic landmarks", "components from various periods", "the multiple styles and cultures", "diversity of influences", "different nations", "the culture of East and West", and "a cultural centre of European significance". The city was recognised as "one of the most outstanding examples of European urban planning", in which "the extraordinary density of monuments from various periods" are "preserved in their original forms and with their authentic fittings", many of

Figure 9.1 Centre of Kraków with the area entered on the original UNESCO World Heritage List in 1978 and its buffer zone established in 2011.

By M. Ilba.

them "designed and built by prominent architects and craftspersons", while the "three built-up areas create a cohesive urban complex in which significant tangible and intangible heritage have survived and are cultivated to this day" (Historic Centre of Kraków, 2021).

As much as that recognition was momentous, the current authorities found it troublesome. Despite its indisputable cultural merits, Kraków, like the whole country, plunged into a profound decline. Enduring in the shadow of the formidable steel-producing conglomerate propagandised by the communists, and surrounded by factories that had a significant negative impact on the environment, it felt the brunt of its neighbourhood (Purchla, 2005, pp. 46–49). The attention of the international community and the hazards resulting from the poor quality of the natural environment forced the authorities into action. In 1978, they incorporated the Civic Committee for the Restoration of Kraków Heritage (SKOZK): a civil society organisation that inspired and financed the work on Kraków's material heritage, understood as the common good belonging to all Poles. Subsequently, in 1985, the Kraków National Fund (NFRZK) was set up and the management of its assets was entrusted to SKOZK. A significant breakthrough came in 1990, when SKOZK gained an actual civic trait and the President of the Republic of Poland extended his patronage over the Committee, most of its funds now being donated from the budget of the Chancellery of the President of the Republic. Such treatment of Kraków is unique, as no other Polish city, even those recognised by inclusion on the WHL (Warsaw, Zamość, Toruń) can boast such preferences. Thanks to this, and regardless of grants from other sources, Kraków receives significant funding for the protection of its heritage (in the 21st century, the annual value never dropped below PLN 30 million, and even reached PLN 45.5 million in the record-breaking year of 2007). This makes it possible for SKOZK to provide non-returnable grants of as much as 50% of the eligible costs to finance each year's work on about 100 buildings, irrespective of their property status, which also includes those that are privately owned. Furthermore, the organisation of supervision and control guarantees high quality (Ziejka, 2009; Krasnowolski, 2020; SKOZK, 2021) (Figures 9.2 and 9.3).

The entry on the WHL led to the international community realising the value of Kraków. With the collapse of communism in Poland in 1989, and the rebirth of local self-government a year later, Kraków was finally free to create its own cultural and promotional policy. It did this by organising events of international ranking, many dedicated to cultural heritage. One of the first was the Symposium of the Conference on Security and Cooperation in Europe (CSCE) organised in the spring of 1991, where the representatives of Eastern and Western states discussed culture and heritage for the first time since the fall of the Iron Curtain. One outcome was the incorporation of the International Cultural Centre (ICC) in Kraków, with its seat at the Main Market Square 25. Innovative for its times, the institution became the role model and promoter of a new institutional approach to the issues of culture

Figure 9.2 The degraded historical developments in ul. Kanonicza in 1978. From the documentation of former PP PKZ (currently in the WUOZ Kraków Archive), Negative No. 21900/A.

Figure 9.3 The same historical developments in ul. Kanonicza after restoration. Current state.

Photo by the author, 2022.

in Poland, its ambitious programme bringing Poland and Kraków into global circulation in the discussions about cultural heritage and the role of culture in civil and economic life (Konferencje MCK, 2021). One of the ICC's early achievements was the organisation of the first ever European Culture Month in June 1992, as the city was awarded that honour by the European Communities (Purchla, 1993). Later, Kraków celebrated the title of the European City of Culture (Hughes, Allen, and Wasik, 2003) by organising the International Conference on Conservation Kraków 2000 (Kadłuczka, 2011). However, the highest quality event was the 41st Session of the World Heritage Committee organised in Kraków in July 2017 and presided over by a Cracovian, Professor Jacek Purchla, the founder and long-term director of the ICC. The session, which approved over 250 decisions with a global impact, was memorable for its emphasis on the role of civil society and inclusion of its representatives in the discussions (Bulletin 2017–2018, 2021).

These and other developments accompanied by the development of the necessary infrastructure have built the international position of the city. Kraków's metier in vying for global attention (e.g., against Warsaw) were the successive sites entered on the WHL that are situated in its vicinity: the Auschwitz–Birkenau Camp, the Wieliczka and Bochnia salt mines, the pilgrimage complex in Kalwaria Zebrzydowska, and the wooden Roman Catholic, Uniate, and Orthodox churches. As a result, in the first decades of the 21st century, Kraków began to be considered one of the most attractive tourist destinations in Europe and the world (Polityka, 2021).

A historical city in the face of profound economic changes

The fall of communism in Poland resulted in wide-ranging changes in all realms of life. The command-and-quota economy was replaced with a free market economy, and the ensuing rapid development of various forms of entrepreneurship resulted in the accrual of wealth by some citizens, as well as the growth in significance of ownership rights, which boosted investment possibilities. Furthermore, the opening of the domestic market to external investors brought an influx of foreign capital, especially after Poland's accession to the European Union in 2004 (for comparative data for the period 1998–2017, see: Sepioł, 2020, p. 12, Figures 1 and 2). In Kraków, this meant enhanced investment pressure on areas dense with heritage sites, as investment in real estate became the safest and most profitable form of saving (Sepioł, 2020, p. 18), while investment in heritage turned into an element of playing the market to multiply the capital invested (Purchla, 2020, p. 34). The negative traits of the process involved a disregard for the specific nature of urban complexes, maximum development of the plots, a tendency to oversize new buildings, radical vertical and horizontal extension of existing buildings, and the introduction of solutions alien to the local culture and architectural tradition.

The questions of ownership concerning not only the victims of the Holocaust and their heirs had an overwhelming impact on the condition of the historical built environment of the entire city after 1945, while the revival of the right to ownership after 1989 proved to be a process that was neither easy nor automatic. Moreover, the lack of a legal owner or – a condition common in Kraków – the existence of multiple owners of a single property, actually means the lack of an owner or the existence of multiple owners who are not always wealthy and frequently have conflicting interests. These situations have resulted in the degradation of townhouses that now, 30 years after the transformation, are easily distinguished from those that have already been renovated. In turn, the takeover of whole or parts of properties by the new owners, who are often not connected to the location or the city itself, results in the demolition or extensive transformation of the historical substance of the buildings (which are often badly degraded).

Kraków and the new legal regulations

The fact that legislation could not catch up with the restitution of property and economic changes had fateful consequences. The Act on the protection of goods of culture from 1962 failed to account for the changing reality (Szpanowski, 2011, pp. 211–215). It was only in 2003 that it was replaced by the Act on the protection and care of monuments/heritage,[1] which divided the heritage realm with roles in protection (domain of the administration) and care (property of owners and users). It strongly emphasised ownership rights, assigned certain prerogatives to the President of the Republic and self-governments, and introduced new forms of protection – Monument of History (PoCH, 2019) and Culture Park (CP) (Myczkowski, 2007; Böhm, 2011, pp. 151–153) – as well as provisions in the local ordinances, including the local zoning (spatial planning) plans (Böhm, 2011, pp. 148–151). Nevertheless, in the face of the need to increase the scope of protection and deal with contemporary problems and threats, the Act is considered insufficiently effective in many areas (Purchla, 2011; Szmygin, 2011; Szpanowski, 2011).

The revival of municipal self-government in Poland in 1990 meant entrusting it with many tasks, including heritage protection. Kraków appointed a Municipal Heritage Preservation Officer as early as 1990. However, the competences of the office were limited until 2004, when it was entrusted with the issuing of certain decisions, e.g., permits for conservation and preservation works (Gaczoł, 2009, pp. 305–307, 313). In 2006, the city councillors voted the Zwierzyniecki Culture Park (one of Poland's first) into existence, yet their decision was revoked by the voivode (regional governor) and the concept was abandoned (Zachariasz, 2008). The Stare Miasto Culture Park was endorsed in 2010: it extended to the most important section of the area entered on the WHL, that is, the historical centre and Wawel Hill. That decision became a role model for other local governments setting up culture parks in the historical centres of Wrocław, Łódź, and Poznań. The "culture park" is a tool that allowed many aspects of operation in the historical core to be regulated, such as the organisation of traffic, mass events,

Figure 9.4 Large-size commercials on the façades in the north-western corner of the Main Market Square before the regulations of the Stare Miasto Culture Park came into force.

Photo by the author, 2010.

display of advertisements and signage, and the location and size of cafés and beer gardens, which significantly improved the aesthetic quality of the area (Figure 9.4).

In 2019, city councillors approved the Nowa Huta Culture Park and started working on setting up following ones: Kazimierz and Stradom (established in May 2022, it covers the rest of the area recognised as world heritage), and the oldest part of the Podgórze district with the Krzemionki limestone hills (Parki kulturowe, 2022). These developments prove that the city authorities recognise the culture park as a proper instrument for managing protected areas, even though there is criticism that they are being introduced too sluggishly and they cover too small an area (Sepioł, 2020, p. 18). It is, however, worth noting that culture parks are not very popular as a form of protection due to the high potential for generating conflict.

Spatial planning in the city was originally covered by the general zoning plan of 1988 (amended in 1994). It terminated in 2003 when the Polish Parliament passed the Spatial Planning Act. The land use study for the city of Kraków (*Studium Uwarunkowań I Kierunków Zagospodarowania Przestrzennego Miasta Krakowa*, literally the "study of the conditions and directions of the spatial development of the city of Kraków") that replaced it, was a strategic document that opened the door to individual local zoning (spatial management) plans, as it included guidelines for the development of space in a given area, as well as covering conservation and preservation. This long process is still underway, with the local zoning plan for the city centre only drafted in 2010. Currently, at the end of November 2021, there are 229 local zoning plans in force in Kraków, covering only 71.3% of its area (Planowanie przestrzenne, 2021). This means that where such plans are missing, construction can still follow the individual decision of a civil servant who does not need to follow the provisions of the plan issuing a decision about the conditions of building-up and managing an area (Böhm, 2011, p. 149). This realm of legislation can easily be recognised as the weakest and most irrational link in the system for managing space, and is responsible for many unfavourable developments in the historic areas.

Quite recently, the issue of outdoor advertising has also been regulated at the local level. In 2015, the Polish Parliament endorsed the Landscape Act, giving local authorities the power to make decisions in this area. Kraków approved its landscape resolution early in 2020. It defines the principles for deploying urban furniture, fencing, and advertising hoardings and devices in the city. It divides Kraków into zones, with the most restrictive regulations in the areas of greatest natural and cultural merit (Uchwała krajobrazowa, 2021).

The central and local regulations mentioned above provide the main legal framework to conduct heritage protection policy in Kraków. Imperfect and failing to keep up with the changing reality, they have left openings for various actions that have not always served the public. The sluggish decision-making of conservation offices, the large concentration of capital in the real estate business, the rapid pace of design and construction works, and the lack of proper supervision have all resulted in controversial developments, including numerous vertical and horizontal extensions, emerging in the city.

Restoring memory: The case of Kazimierz and Podgórze in Kraków

A significant problem that Kraków had to face immediately after 1989, which was also a challenge in other Central European countries (Murzyn-Kupisz and Purchla, 2009) was a "disinherited heritage, a heritage without inheritors", i.e., the inheritance of the Jewish community that made up 25% of the city's population before the Holocaust (Purchla and Skotnicki, 2007, p. 5). The problem was particularly pertinent in the district of Kazimierz, which had been almost exclusively Jewish before the Second World War, and Podgórze – the location of targeted Nazi oppression of the Jews. Embarking on that subject in Kraków was the result of the conviction that remembrance and identity are important constituents of heritage that must be nurtured (Purchla, 2015, p. 16), especially in the face of the multiculturalism that was associated with the city as articulated by UNESCO. The plethora of initiatives include the annual Jewish Culture Festival that has been going since

1988 (Festiwal, 2021), the long-term operation of institutions, some initiated by foreigners, such as the Galicia Jewish Museum founded by Chris Schwartz in 2004 (Muzeum Galicja, 2021), and temporary exhibitions (e.g., Małecki, 2007b). In this context, Kazimierz has attracted special attention as it has been an area of drastic change from the very early 1990s (Murzyn, 2006; Murzyn-Kupisz, 2009). First the Holocaust, and then the policy of the authorities of communist Poland wrecked its uniqueness and reduced it to impoverishment. In the wake of the changes of 1989, the subject of ownership, which had been frozen for decades, became the subject of animated interest, sometimes illicit deals, and was immediately followed by the processes of gentrification and largely uncontrolled development (Figures 9.5 and 9.6).

Yet the attention of the local authorities focused only on selected sites, whether places of prayer (Catholic churches and synagogues) or the Museum of Municipal Engineering developed in the former tram depot (Rojkowska-Tasak, 2009, pp. 87–88). Paired with the passive attitude of the local government to designing the transformations and setting up legal regulations, these factors quickly transformed Kazimierz into Kraków's bar-and-café centre, which is mostly a triumph of commodification that barely incorporated any cultural, social, and community aspects (Murzyn-Kupisz, 2009; Kopeć,

Figure 9.5 Centre of Kraków's Kazimierz district: the eastern face of ul. Szeroka in 1985.

Photo by K. Maciąg. From the collection of PP PKZ (currently in the NID OT Kraków Archive), negative No. 37922/A.

Figure 9.6 A current view of the same area in Kazimierz, with filled-in urban tissue, extension of the house at No. 17, and plentiful new architectural detail.
Photo by the author, 2022.

2020, pp. 65, 72). Many unlicensed enterprises, whose symbol became one of the townhouses in the centre of the district (ul. Szeroka 12) (Janczykowski, 2020, pp. 81–82, 90–91), reflect the negative phenomena resulting mostly from the passive attitude of public authorities and the faulty conviction that the free market will be able to regulate social and economic relations most accurately. The example of Kazimierz demonstrated that an urban regeneration should be a planned and appropriately managed process and not a spur-of-the-moment unstructured decision, while the failure of the public authorities to counterbalance the pressure of capital brought about caricatured effects that are harmful and undesirable from the point of view of the public interest, often labelled as "McDonaldization" or "Disneyfication".

An attempt to recall symbolically Kraków's multi-ethnic tradition that was lost to the Holocaust was made in neighbouring Podgórze, where a suggestive installation composed of chairs arranged in the empty square dedicated to "the heroes of the ghetto" (which obtained an honourable mention in the European Prize for Urban Public Space in 2005) alluded to the liquidation of the ghetto that operated there in 1941–43. Another area in Podgórze connected to the martyrdom of the Jews are the premises of the former KL Plaszow concentration camp, an area that has not been developed since the Second World War (Niezabitowski, 2016). Even though hopes for prompt commemoration accompanied the architectural competition announced by the municipality in 2006 (Murzyn-Kupisz, 2009, pp. 394–396), it is only now that the first concrete activities have been undertaken, resulting in the incorporation of the KL Plaszow Museum (KL Plaszow, 2021).

Post-industrial and military heritage

A burning problem that emerged in the wake of the transformation of 1989 was the minimisation of the loss of historic matter caused by the bankruptcy and restructuring of enterprises and institutions. Such transformations had different results and, as a rule, were connected with the modification of the functions of individual areas and buildings – shopping centres, museums, cultural hubs, and offices were developed in this way. With time, large residential complexes began to develop in post-industrial locations, some of them adapting the legacy structures and others replacing them with apartment blocks.

Military structures, notably the forts of the 19th-century Kraków Fortress that were considered a resource worthy of being listed as world heritage (Janczykowski, 2009, p. 79), have proved to be a challenge. Only a handful of the forts have been adapted for cultural, recreational, or storage functions and some of the remainder are still used by the military, while others have been taken over by cultural or educational institutions. The carefully renovated building of the military barracks on ul. Rajska, close to the city centre, serves as the regional library. In turn, the building of the former military headquarters at ul. Stradom 12–14, currently being transformed into an apartment block, is an example of a developer's profound interference in a historic property in a way that disrupts the traditional development in the area. Another reason for concern is developer pressure on the green areas surrounding the forts.

Restoration of public spaces

One need that Kraków's authorities quickly became aware of was the improvement of the condition and appearance of public space, the most spectacular example of which was the reconstruction of the surface of the Main Market Square. Damage necessitated an overhaul. The first concepts were ready in 1993, yet the design adopted was the one by Andrzej Kadłuczka from 2002. It was implemented over the following years together with the later design for using underground sections of the Market Square for exhibition purposes. Finally, despite controversies and severe opposition, the whole design was built and the exhibition below the surface of the square was opened to the public in 2010 (Beiersdorf, 2008; Janczykowski, 2020, pp. 82–83; Kadłuczka, 2010). More public spaces were refurbished in the city centre (e.g., the Small Market Square and the Mariacki and Szczepański squares) and in the districts of Kleparz, Kazimierz, and Podgórze. The works resulted in traffic calming and the replacement of surfaces and city furniture, whose history-inspired forms were intended to correspond to the character of the place and the developments in their vicinity (Rojkowska-Tasak, 2009, pp. 83–84). Although often criticised, these investments have increased the aesthetic value of the urban space.

After the difficult experiences with Kazimierz, the space of Kraków witnessed several, sometimes large, successive urban regeneration projects that spread their effects to the wider surrounding area. Coming first to mind are the Kraków Transport Centre (Polish acronym: KCK) to the north-east of the historical centre (Kopeć, 2020, pp. 50–56, 66–67), and the post-industrial area of Zabłocie, including the part of Podgórze lying by the Vistula (Kopeć, 2020, pp. 56–60). In both cases, the adaptation of former buildings to the needs of cultural institutions as well as other purposes (including residential) became an important element of the transformation. Various stakeholder groups and funds acquired from a variety of sources were used for these developments. The KCK generated a problem as the future of the historical railway station building that, stripped of its original function and remaining partly in use, is still awaiting a thoughtful adaptation for new purposes. Time will tell whether the plans concerning the revival of Nowa Huta, partially riding on its heritage of socialist realism, will be successful (Kopeć, 2020, pp. 67–71).

From the rise of monasticism to the new horizons of protection

The rescuing from long-term ruin of the southern wing of the Romanesque Benedictine Abbey in Tyniec, the oldest surviving monastery in Poland, was a particular regeneration effort of the past three decades. It was achieved in 2006–08, and the original spaces of the building, now used for hotel, retreat, and exhibition functions, were retained, their interiors combining modern forms with meticulously revealed remnants of the former structure (Kanik, 2010).

This noteworthy development of one of the oldest sites within today's city limits highlights how important chronology is for the perception of heritage, just like the conventional time-limit that defines it. Even though the value of 19th-century heritage was still only breaking through in the early 1990s (Purchla, 1994), the discussions continuing in Central Europe soon concerned the attitude to post-Second World War heritage from the time of communism. In Kraków, that controversy pertained to the historical centre of Nowa Huta – the city and steelworks from the Stalinist period, which became the largest polluter and one of the strongholds of Solidarity in the 1980s (Purchla, 2005, pp. 46–48, 2008, pp. 365–371). In the end, the area has become not only an attraction visited by foreign tourists (Murzyn, 2008, p. 63), but also an object of complex protection, first by being entered onto the heritage register and as the centre of the Nowa Huta Culture Park since

2019. It is only politics that stands in the way of it being given the title of a Monument of History and being submitted to the WHL, despite such suggestions having been made (Janczykowski, 2009, p. 79).

Once the need to protect works of socialist realism had been accepted, the question of protecting the key achievements of socialist modernism was raised. After 2000, the Cracovia Hotel and the Kijów Cinema complex, as well as the Forum Hotel – all threatened with demolition in line with the investment plans of their new owners – became the subjects of heated debate in Kraków. Local community protests stopped the demolition and the hotel-cum-cinema complex was entered into the heritage register in 2016 (Janczykowski, 2020, pp. 87–88), which made it the newest complex of Kraków's built heritage with such protection. Earlier it was listed, for purely informative purposes, among the "works of contemporary culture", that is post-war works worthy of special attention and protection (*Atlas*, 2009, pp. 68–70). This evidence of care and appraisal of recent projects provides a good idea of the social awareness of the important role of continuity as a significant feature of Kraków's heritage.

The vicissitudes of fate also granted the city with the phenomenon of "heritage of atrocity" (or "dissonant heritage"), and even though the bold visions of the German planners were never completed, Kraków retains many traces of Nazi interventions, some of them even on Wawel Hill. Only the systemic publication of the results of studies on the subject makes readers aware of that delicate phenomenon (Purchla, 2008, pp. 363–365; recently: Purchla, 2018, pp. 101–143; Purchla and Komar, 2021), but it can be seen that it raises interest and, properly presented, could provide an attractive element of the developmental potential of the city, like other elements of heritage.

The upward thrust of the Kraków panorama

Historical panoramas are one of the unique values of Kraków (Małecki, 2007a; Kołodziej, 2020). The pressure from high-rise blocks that threaten them had already emerged between the two world wars (Purchla, 2005, p. 43). The first such post-war site, Biprostal in the Krowodrza district, raised no controversies as it is distant from the historical centre. It was a different case with the 1970s NOT office building, which is located in the vicinity of the Mogilskie Roundabout. Almost 100-m high, the skeleton construction was completed just before Kraków was entered onto the WHL and later stood unfinished for decades (Janczykowski, 2009, pp. 77–78). That "heritage leftover of communism" found itself in the buffer zone established in 2010 around the part of the city listed as a world heritage site. After years of wrangling with the investors, the conservation authority allowed its completion according to a new design (Janczykowski, 2020, pp. 83–84). The development exposed the long-term lack of efficient planning provisions that were capable of protecting the panoramas, and the relativity of the so-called "principle of good neighbourhood" introduced in the Spatial Planning (Zoning) Act (Kołodziej, 2020, pp. 147–148) (Figure 9.7).

Figure 9.7 A panorama of Wawel from Krzemionki Zakrzowskie Hill, with the "extra" tower of the former NOT skyscraper (currently Unity Tower) in the background.

Photo by the author, 2021.

As a result, the structure built after 2015 and called the Unity Tower, devoid of any individual expression and notably oversized, now competes with the skyline of the spires of historical Kraków and introduces a strong dissonance to its panoramas. There are more such office blocks and high-rise buildings in the city, both the legacy of communism and recently designed, and the fervour to build more of them will quite likely intensify. A warning indicating that the phenomenon cannot be tolerated is the fact that a similar development has led to Vienna being threatened with removal from the WHL (Historic Centre of Vienna, 2021).

Movable and intangible heritage

Kraków's heritage resources also comprise movable heritage, mostly kept in churches, private collections, and museums. Museums are institutions that have experienced major qualitative and quantitative progress since 1989. They entered the new reality as fossilised organisations with a barely attractive image. The situation changed, thanks to the effort of many entities, notably the strong involvement of local authorities and private initiatives. Many museums and their branches have developed and been set up in historical structures adapted for them, or in dazzling new buildings built for them (Purchla and Sepioł, 2015). They serve to display spectacular projects designed for them (e.g., Thesaurus Cracoviensis), exhibitions demonstrating the European roots and connections of the city (the Underground Market), the trauma of the German occupation (the former Schindler's Factory) and the city's modern face (the building and the collections of the Museum of Contemporary Art in Kraków – MOCAK). In 2016, the National Museum in Kraków became the beneficiary of unprecedented interventionism when the Polish State bought the collection from the heirs of the Czartoryski family (including the famous paintings by da Vinci and Rembrandt) together with the seat of Poland's oldest museum, and then purchased the post-war Cracovia Hotel from a private investor with the intention of turning it into the Centre for Architecture and Design. These transactions put an end to a long-running ownership dispute and protected an attractive site from destruction (Janczykowski, 2020, pp. 85–88). Also worth mentioning is the gift of Karolina Lanckorońska, who, in 1994, donated a collection of outstanding works of Italian painting from the 13th to the 17th centuries (Kolekcja Lanckorońskich, 2021) to collections of Wawel Royal Castle. All this has made the offer of Kraków's museums more attractive, modern, varied, and adapted to providing services to a wider range of visitors, compensating for the deficit of museum objects of global significance. Intangible heritage is an important advantage for Kraków: it is the city-symbol of Poland and all things Polish, known to every Pole from numerous legends, associated with recurring festivities and observances, and with unique skills, dances, and melodies (Bilińska-Głód, 2013). Their significance evolves from national to international, which found its expression in 2018 when Kraków's tradition of nativity scenes was inscribed on UNESCO's Representative List of the Intangible Cultural Heritage of Humanity (*Krajowa lista*, 2019).

University heritage: Kraków as the centre of reflection on heritage

Human resources are another element of Kraków's capital. As Poland's most ancient academic centre whose traditions reach back to the 14th century, it not only remained the main centre of the conservation thought in post-1989 Poland but also became a significant centre of reflection on heritage of at least Central European significance. It owes this to the vigorous activity of some academic institutions and entities, as well as the International Culture Centre. From its earliest days, the latter has created international forums for discussion, with those dedicated to the heritage of the countries of the Visegrád Group, that is Czechia, Hungary, Poland, and Slovakia, having gained particular prominence (*Forum dziedzictwa*, 2021).

Kraków is also a leading forge of conservation and preservation experts. Manual conservators are educated at the Academy of Fine Arts, which has been actively involved in international cooperation since 1989 (Korpal, 2010), while future architects and urban planners are educated at the Kraków University of Technology, and public servants and museum experts hone their skills at the Jagiellonian University and the John Paul II Pontifical University. Each of these academic institutions also runs specialist postgraduate studies, while the Cracow University of Economics and the ICC run jointly the outstanding Academy of Heritage specialising in cultural heritage management. The work of the association of its graduates on the conservation of Polish culture heritage abroad is an extraordinary outcome (Szyper and Wiśniewski, 2013). Such a strong and vibrant expert community favours an expert publishing market. Alongside valuable works such as the materials from numerous conferences and books published in the Heritologia series by the ICC, expert periodicals, including the oldest *Ochrona Zabytków* (literally "heritage/monument protection") are published here. This is accompanied by numerous educational and promotional activities championed by institutions of higher education, museums, institutions of culture, and associations, with the most notable being the Society of Friends of Kraków History and Heritage (established in 1896 as Towarzystwo Miłośników Historii i Zabytków Krakowa, in which the word "friends" reads much closer to "lovers"). Other valuable actors are the local communities and organisations working on emphasising the identity and cultivating the traditions of a given district, for example, Podgórze or Nowa Huta.

Kraków and tourism: threats in the success's shadow

It is a paradox – though symptomatic for other cities as Venice and Amsterdam that are less iconic (Purchla, 1999; Lehtimäki, 2008) – that Kraków's cultural heritage resources have recently begun to fall victim to its marketing success. In 2005, the city was visited by over 7 million tourists, a number that rose to 13.5 million in 2018 (Murzyn, 2008, p. 63; Kowalczyk-Anioł, 2019, p. 15). Next to Brno, Debrecen, and Košice, Kraków recorded the largest growth in the number of tourists among Central European cities that are not capital cities, and could easily compete with the metropolises for that status (Tracz and Bajgier-Kowalska, 2020). In the case of Kraków, a significant share of this peak was accounted for by tourists and pilgrims arriving for religious reasons (Bogacz-Wojtanowska and Góral, 2018). Such rapid growth resulted in many negative phenomena, especially the escape of permanent residents from the city centre and its vicinity that was the outcome of the rigidly executed right to ownership, a general transition from residential to hotel, hospitality, and office functions, the reduction and change in the type of local services, as well as the oppressive and inappropriate behaviour of some visitors. The city centre has also been systematically abandoned by the Jagiellonian University, its centuries-old resident, which is now setting up a campus on the outskirts of the city. The statistics are merciless: since 1989, the centre of Kraków has lost over half of its permanent residents, while just in 2008–18 the number of hotels within the Planty Garden Ring increased from 57 to 179, with the number of hotel rooms doubling to 11,346, while other registered forms of accommodation having reached 4,392 beds, a number that, in recent years, has been augmented by unregistered short-term rentals whose number was estimated at 4,363 in May 2019 (Kowalczyk-Anioł, 2019, pp. 15–19). Although the Culture Park worked in combating assorted negative phenomena, its establishment did not stall this trend. As a result, the historical centre has recently become a kind of model, providing the background for assorted attractions and entertainment but often failing to assure security for their participants, both local and visitors. Interestingly, as far back as in 1980, Wacław Ostrowski, an eminent Polish historian of urban development, cautioned that restoration of historic cities (and their fragments) must not lead to their depopulation, also caused by excessive intensification of tourism (Ostrowski, 1980). The long months of the 2020 pandemic forced a reflection on whether his warning is not a prophecy for Kraków. For it turned out that, when severed from the inflow of visitors, the city that was nearly entirely delivered for their use became a model. One as beautiful as it is horrifying (Figures 9.8 and 9.9).

Conclusions

Kraków's varied cultural heritage, a problematic ballast for the communist authorities after the UNESCO decision, fairly quickly became a significant

Figure 9.8 The pressure from tourist and commercial signage in Kraków's Royal Route (ul. Floriańska) before the introduction of the Culture Park Stare Miasto.
Photo by J. Purchla, 2004.

Figure 9.9 The deserted Royal Route (ul. Floriańska) during lockdown, early April 2020.
Photo by the author, 2020.

advantage for the city after 1989 and began to be presented, and over time also perceived, as a factor supporting development (Purchla, 2020). A significant role in the change was played by the activity of the reborn municipal self-government (Rojkowska-Tasak, 2009), and later, Poland's accession to the EU, which resulted in a significant injection of European funds into culture and an increase in the number of tourists visiting the city. Importantly, the bankruptcy of many industrial sites caused by the political and economic transformation significantly helped to forestall an environmental catastrophe and reorientate the city away from being a major industrial hub to becoming a metropolitan service centre, with heritage potential favourable for the development of tourism. Paradoxically, the marginalisation of Kraków that continued in state policy after 1989 reinforced even further the fact that today, cultural heritage is the fundamental metropolitan function of Kraków, evidence of its role in the history of Poland in Europe, and important pro-development potential that has generated much social activism in recent decades.

As a major Central European metropolitan centre, Kraków shares the region's fate in terms of grappling with the problems typical for heritage (Purchla, 2011; Jagodzińska and Purchla, 2015). These include the need to redefine the object of protection and expand its current scope, the suitable adaptation of legislation and the administration, a full appreciation of intangible heritage, and the facing up to and provision of stewardship over the heritage of Holocaust victims, national minorities, the enemy and occupier, and the time of communism. The difficult history of the territory requires both our awareness and responsibility to make this impressive mosaic, composed of the rich cultural heritage of Kraków situated in the heart of Europe, not its burden but a lasting, generally understood, and wisely managed strength. For the saying that "the past has a future" is not an empty slogan (*Przeszłość*, 2020), yet much depends on our attitudes, civil sensitivity, and involvement.

The two decades from 1989 to 2019 were a good period for Kraków, as they featured dynamic economic growth, a lack of military conflicts, or the grave consequences of natural disasters. As far as heritage protection goes, it is beyond doubt that post-1989 Kraków is a great laboratory of change. Change that the city and its inhabitants desperately pined for after years of living in the communist reality, yet also change that no one had been ready for, and whose dynamics, if not vigour, surprised nearly everyone. Looking for formulas and means of reacting to the emerging problems and challenges that are entirely new required vigilance, keeping an open mind, and the ability to be accommodating. Despite the plentiful reservations and criticism, the balance for the period is positive and allows one to conclude that Kraków coped quite well with the new challenges. Perhaps the assessment of these developments will be fuller from a longer time perspective.

It is hard to disagree with the statement that "Post-1989 Central Europe is a Europe in search of identity – between national revival and globalisation" (Purchla, 2015, p. 12). An increasing demand for heritage stems precisely from globalisation and the growing economic significance of tourism: processes that threaten heritage yet simultaneously elevate its value and significance, bringing out the exceptional quality of what is local. The potential of Kraków's heritage – so rich and varied, and, in the decades of communism, fundamentally inaccessible to the Western consumer and therefore profoundly alien to them – has manifested itself with great force since 1989. Like no other Polish city, Kraków has always lived on its past yet at the same time eyeing up Western models. Existing behind the Iron Curtain it drew as much inspiration as it could from the culture of the West, yet transposed it in the spirit of its own tradition and current reality and created a new unique quality. The entry onto the WHL, and later the breakthrough of 1989, opened an opportunity for the city to show off the lavishness of its cultural achievements to the world. To show both the Polishness and the universal quality of its achievements. The proverbial Polish hospitality, openness, and craving for international contacts quickly met high culture but also clashed against consumerism, the desire for unification, and the expectation of experiencing mass culture. Examples of extreme reactions to these confrontations can be found in the post-1989 civil, economic, and cultural life of Kraków; from the activities and creations at the highest level, to the ruthless attempts at multiplying capital here and now and at any price. In both cases, the backdrop to these attitudes was the city that has plenty to offer the world, yet which – standing at a crossroads, with significant baggage of free market experience and an established brand – must now answer the question of what to grant from its "cornucopia", to whom, how, and at what price. Time will show whether this will be a road to the unification of its own culture and pandering to all preferences, or perhaps a well-thought-out gift, adjusted to the recipients' needs and intellectual capacity, of what is best of the local, most valuable and unique, and by that token, giving added value to everyone, whether visitor or local, and whether for a short stay or for a whole life. Gregory Ashworth, a recognised expert in heritage management, suggests that such a balance in development is a reasonable compromise: "The tourism industry needs heritage as a resource, but heritage does not necessarily need tourism" (Ashworth, 2008, p. 53).

Bibliography

Ashworth, G. (2008) "How do tourists consume heritage places?", [in:] Lehtimäki, M. (ed.) *Cultural heritage and tourism: potential, impact, partnership and governance*. Vilnius: Department of Cultural Heritage, Ministry of Culture of Lithuania, 52–58.

Atlas dóbr kultury współczesnej województwa małopolskiego (2009). Kraków: Urząd Marszałkowski Województwa Małopolskiego.

Beiersdorf, Z. (1996) "Ochrona i konserwacja dóbr kultury w Krakowie w latach 1944–1989. Próba oceny", [in:] Małecki, J.M. (ed.) *Kraków w Polsce Ludowej*. Kraków: Towarzystwo Miłośników Historii i Zabytków Krakowa, 91-–114.

Beiersdorf, Z. (2008) "Krakowski Rynek Główny dzisiaj", [in:] Małecki, J.M. (ed.) *Kraków – dziedzictwo lokacji*. Kraków: Towarzystwo Miłośników Historii i Zabytków Krakowa, 91–107.

Bilińska-Głód, K. (2013) "Niematerialne dziedzictwo kluczem do interpretacji dziedzictwa materialnego – studium Krakowa", [in:] Szyper, B. and Wiśniewski, M. (eds.) *Akademia Dziedzictwa 2002–2013. Przegląd problemów badawczych z zakresu zarządzania i ochrony dziedzictwa kulturowego w Polsce*. Kraków: Międzynarodowe Centrum Kultury, 221–242.

Bogacz-Wojtanowska, E. and Góral, A. (eds.) (2018) *Fenomen turystyki religijnej i pielgrzymek w Krakowie i Małopolsce*. Kraków: Stowarzyszenie Gmin i Powiatów Małopolski.

Böhm, A. (2011) "Protection of cultural landscape in Poland today", [in:] Purchla, J. (ed.) *Protecting and Safeguarding Cultural Heritage. Systems of Management of Cultural Heritage in the Visegrad Countries*. Krakow: International Cultural Centre, 143–153.

Bulletin 2017–2018 (2021) *Polish National Commission for UNESCO Review. Bulletin, 2017–2018*. Available at: http://www.unesco.pl/fileadmin/user_upload/Publikacje/UNESCO_Biuletyn_2017-2018_ENG.pdf (Accessed on 4 November 2021).

Chwalba, A. (2004) *Kraków w latach 1945–1989*. Dzieje Krakowa, Vol. 6. Kraków: Wydawnictwo Literackie.

Dziedzic, S. (2009) "Krakow: A cultural phenomenon", [in:] Dziedzic, S. and Rojkowska-Tasak, H. (eds.) *30 years on the UNESCO List. Krakow 1978–2008. Krakow: Municipality of Krakow. Culture and National Heritage Department. Office of Monument Protection*. Michałowice: Wydawnictwo Czuwajmy, 52–62.

Dziedzic, S. and Rojkowska-Tasak, H. (eds.) (2009) *30 years on the UNESCO List. Krakow 1978–2008*. Krakow: Municipality of Krakow. Culture and National Heritage Department. Office of Monument Protection; Michałowice: Wydawnictwo Czuwajmy.

Festiwal (2015) *Festiwal Kultury Żydowskiej.* Available at: jewishfestival.pl (Accessed on 20 November 2021).

Forum dziedzictwa (2021) *Forum Dziedzictwa Europy Środkowej.* Available at: https://mck.krakow.pl/forum-dziedzictwa-europy-srodkowej (Accessed on 4 November 2021).

Gaczoł, A. (2009) *Kraków. Ochrona zabytkowego miasta. Rzeczywistość czy fikcja?.* Kraków: Wydawnictwo WAM.

Historic Centre of Krakow (2021) *Historic Centre of Kraków.* Available at: http://whc.unesco.org/en/list/29 (Accessed on 15 November 2021).

Historic Centre of Vienna (2021) *Historic Centre of Vienna Inscribed on List of World Heritage in Danger.* Available at: https://whc.unesco.org/en/news/1684/ (Accessed on 22 November 2021).

Hughes, H., Allen, D. and Wasik, D. (2003) "Significance of European 'Capital of Culture' for tourism and culture: the case of Kraków 2000", *International Journal of Arts Management*, 5(3), 12–23.

Jagodzińska, K. and Purchla, J. (eds.) (2015) *The Limits of Heritage. The 2nd Heritage Forum of Central Europe.* Krakow: International Cultural Centre.

Janczykowski, J. (2009) "Protecting monuments in Krakow – factors and problems", [in:] Dziedzic, S. and Rojkowska-Tasak, H. (eds.) *30 years on the UNESCO List. Krakow 1978–2008. Krakow: Municipality of Krakow. Culture and National Heritage Department. Office of Monument Protection.* Michałowice: Wydawnictwo Czuwajmy, 75–79.

Janczykowski, J. (2020) "Realia ochrony krakowskich zabytków", [in:] Noga, Z. and Purchla, J. (eds.) *Dziedzictwo Krakowa w procesie transformacji.* Kraków: Towarzystwo Miłośników Historii i Zabytków Krakowa, 75–93.

Kadłuczka, A. (2010) "Rynek Główny w Krakowie: podziemne muzeum w aspekcie architektoniczno-konserwatorskim", [in:] Jasieńko, J., Kadłuczka, A. and Mandelli, E. (eds.) *Florencja i Kraków. Miasta partnerskie w Europie – wspólne dziedzictwo kultury.* Kraków: Towarzystwo Autorów i Wydawców Prac Naukowych UNIVERSITAS, 399–413.

Kadłuczka, A. (ed.) (2011) *Karta Krakowska 2000 dziesięć lat później.* Kraków: Wydawnictwo Politechniki Krakowskiej.

Kanik, J. (2010) "Wielka Ruina jednak nowa. Klasztor po remoncie z widokiem na przyszłość", [in:] Korpal, G. et al. (eds.) *Wspólnie dla ratowania piękna przeszłości. Materiały z konferencji.* Kraków: Wydawnictwo Artcards, 95–105.

KL Plaszow (2021) *Muzeum-Miejsce Pamięci KL Plaszow w Krakowie. Niemiecki nazistowski obóz pracy i obóz koncentracyjny (1942–1945).* Available at: www.plaszow.org (Accessed on 17 November 2021).

Kolekcja Lanckorońskich (2021) *Kolekcja Lanckorońskich.* Available at: http://3d.wawel.krakow.pl/ (Accessed on 19 November 2021).

Kołodziej, J. (2020) "Historyczne panoramy Krakowa i ich ochrona", [in:] Noga, Z. and Purchla, J. (eds.) *Dziedzictwo Krakowa w procesie transformacji.* Kraków: Towarzystwo Miłośników Historii i Zabytków Krakowa, 135–154.

Konferencje MCK (2021) *Archiwum konferencji.* Available at: https://mck.krakow.pl/konferencje/archiwum (Accessed on 19 November 2021).

Kopeć, M. (2020) "Procesy rewitalizacji a rozwój Krakowa", [in:] Noga, Z., Purchla, J. (eds.) *Dziedzictwo Krakowa w procesie transformacji.* Kraków: Towarzystwo Miłośników Historii i Zabytków Krakowa, 45–73.

Korpal, G. (2010) "60 lat działalności Wydziału Konserwacji i Restauracji Dzieł Sztuki ASP w Krakowie w aspekcie ochrony dziedzictwa kulturowego regionu", [in:] Korpal, G. et al. (eds.) *Wspólnie dla ratowania piękna przeszłości. Materiały z konferencji*. Kraków: Wydawnictwo Artcards, 23–32.

Korpal, G. et al. (eds.) (2010) *Wspólnie dla ratowania piękna przeszłości. Materiały z konferencji*. Kraków: Wydawnictwo Artcards.

Kowalczyk-Anioł, J. (2019) "Tourismification of the housing resources of historical inner cities. The case of Krakow", *Studia Miejskie*, 23, 9–25.

Krajowa lista niematerialnego dziedzictwa kulturowego (2019). Warszawa: Narodowy Instytut Dziedzictwa.

Krasnowolski, B. (2011) "Doktryny konserwatorskie a doświadczenie Społecznego Komitetu Odnowy Zabytków Krakowa", [in:] Krasnowolski, B. (ed.) *Doktryny i realizacje konserwatorskie w świetle doświadczeń krakowskich ostatnich 30 lat*. Kraków: Wydawnictwo WAM.

Krasnowolski, B. (ed.) (2011) *Doktryny i realizacje konserwatorskie w świetle doświadczeń krakowskich ostatnich 30 lat*. Kraków: Wydawnictwo WAM, 13–45.

Krasnowolski, B. (2020) "Fenomen Społecznego Komitetu Odnowy Zabytków Krakowa i jego sukcesy konserwatorskie", [in:] Noga, Z. and Purchla, J. (ed.) *Dziedzictwo Krakowa w procesie transformacji*. Kraków: Towarzystwo Miłośników Historii i Zabytków Krakowa, 95–133.

Lehtimäki, M. (ed.) (2008) *Cultural heritage and tourism: potential, impact, partnership and governance*. [Vilnius]: Department of Cultural Heritage, Ministry of Culture of Lithuania.

Małecki, J.M. (ed.) (1994) *Przeszłość i przyszłość zabytkowego Krakowa*. Kraków: Towarzystwo Miłośników Historii i Zabytków Krakowa.

Małecki, J.M. (ed.) (1996) *Kraków w Polsce Ludowej*. Kraków: Towarzystwo Miłośników Historii i Zabytków Krakowa.

Małecki, J.M. (ed.) (2007a) *Krajobraz Krakowa wobec zagrożeń*. Kraków: Towarzystwo Miłośników Historii i Zabytków Krakowa.

Małecki, J.M. (ed.) (2007b) *Świat przed katastrofą / A World before a Catastrophe*. Kraków: Międzynarodowe Centrum Kultury.

Małecki, J.M. (ed.) (2008) *Kraków – dziedzictwo lokacji*. Kraków: Towarzystwo Miłośników Historii i Zabytków Krakowa.

Murzyn, M.A. (2006) *Kazimierz. Środkowoeuropejskie doświadczenie rewitalizacji / The Central European Experience of Urban Regeneration*. Kraków: Międzynarodowe Centrum Kultury.

Murzyn, M.A. (2008) "Tourism: chances and treats to urban heritage. The case of Kraków", [in:] Lehtimäki, M. (ed.) *Cultural heritage and tourism: potential, impact, partnership and governance*. [Vilnius]: Department of Cultural Heritage, Ministry of Culture of Lithuania, 62–66.

Murzyn-Kupisz, M. (2009) "Reclaiming memory or mass consumption? Dilemmas in rediscovering the Jewish heritage of Krakow's Kazimierz", [in:] Murzyn-Kupisz, M. and Purchla, J. (eds.) *Reclaiming memory: urban regeneration in the historic Jewish quarters of Central European cities*. Krakow: International Cultural Centre, 363–396.

Murzyn-Kupisz, M. and Purchla, J. (eds.) (2009) *Reclaiming memory: urban regeneration in the historic Jewish quarters of Central European cities*. Krakow: International Cultural Centre.

Muzeum Galicja (2021) *Żydowskie Muzeum Galicja*. Available at: https://galiciajewishmuseum.org (Accessed on 15 November 2021).

Myczkowski, Z. (2007) "Park kulturowy jako forma obszarowej ochrony zabytków", *Ochrona Zabytków*, 2, 105–116.
Niezabitowski, M. (ed.) (2016) *Płaszów. Odkrywanie*. Kraków: Muzeum Historyczne Miasta Krakowa.
Noga, Z. and Purchla, J. (eds.) (2020) *Dziedzictwo Krakowa w procesie transformacji*. Kraków: Towarzystwo Miłośników Historii i Zabytków Krakowa.
Ostrowski, W. (1980) *Zespoły zabytkowe a urbanistyka*. Warszawa: Wydawnictwo Arkady.
Palmer, R. and Purchla, J. (2010) *Kultura a rozwój 20 lat po upadku komunizmu w Europie / Culture and development 20 years after the fall of communism in Europe*. Kraków: Międzynarodowe Centrum Kultury.
Parki kulturowe (2020) *Parki Kulturowe w Krakowie*. Available at: parkikulturowe.krakow.pl (Accessed on 16 November 2021).
Pawłowski, K.K. (2009) "Charter on the Rights and Obligations of World Heritage Cities", [in:] Dziedzic, S. and Rojkowska-Tasak, H. (eds.) *30 years on the UNESCO List. Krakow 1978–2008. Krakow: Municipality of Krakow. Culture and National Heritage Department. Office of Monument Protection*. Michałowice: Wydawnictwo Czuwajmy.
Planowanie przestrzenne (2021) *Wydział Planowania Przestrzennego*. Available at: https://www.bip.krakow.pl/planowanieprzestrzenne (Accessed on 19 December 2021).
PoCH (2019) *Protection of Cultural Heritage*, 7 [special issue: *Monuments of History – protection, management, promotion*]. Edited by PKN ICOMOS and Lublin University of Technology in Warsaw and Lublin
Polityka turystyki (2021) *Polityka zrównoważonej turystyki Krakowa na lata 2021–2028*. Available at: https://www.bip.krakow.pl/_inc/rada/posiedzenia/show_pdfdoc.php?id=117239&_ga=2.76442578.696821110.1639092612-1960694149.1639092612 (Accessed on 20 November 2021).
Przeszłość ma przyszłość. Rozmowy z Jackiem Purchlą (2020). Kraków: Wydawnictwo Znak.
Purchla, J. (1993) *Europejski Miesiąc Kultury w Krakowie czerwiec 1992 / European Cultural Month in Cracow June 1992*. Kraków: Międzynarodowe Centrum Kultury.
Purchla, J. (1994) "Dziewiętnastowieczny Kraków jako problem konserwatorski", [in:] Małecki, J.M. (ed.) *Przeszłość i przyszłość zabytkowego Krakowa*. Kraków: Towarzystwo Miłośników Historii i Zabytków Krakowa, 39–55.
Purchla, J. (1996) *Kraków – prowincja czy metropolia?*. Kraków: Towarzystwo Autorów i Wydawców Prac Naukowych UNIVERSITAS.
Purchla, J. (ed.) (1999) *Dziedzictwo a turystyka*. Kraków: Międzynarodowe Centrum Kultury.
Purchla, J. (2000) *Cracow in the European Core*. Cracow: International Cultural Centre.
Purchla, J. (2005) *Heritage and transformation*. Kraków: International Cultural Centre; Małopolska School of Public Administration at the Cracow University of Economics.
Purchla, J. (2007) "Dziedzictwo architektoniczne Krakowa", [in:] Róziewicz, M. (ed.) *Kraków. Zabytki architektury i budownictwa w Polsce*. Warszawa: Krajowy Ośrodek Badań i Dokumentacji Zabytków, 9–17.
Purchla, J. (2008) "Dilemma of Post Totalitarian Heritage (Polish Experiences)", [in:] Tomaszewski, A. (ed.) *Values and criteria in heritage conservation*. Firenze: Polistampa, 363–371.

Purchla, J. (ed.) (2009) *Raport o systemie ochrony dziedzictwa kulturowego w Polsce po roku 1989*. Warszawa: Narodowe Centrum Kultury.

Purchla, J. (2011) "Towards a system of heritage preservation in Poland", [in:] Purchla, J. (ed.) *Protecting and safeguarding cultural heritage: systems of management of cultural heritage in the Visegrad countries*. Krakow: International Cultural Centre.

Purchla, J. (ed.) (2011) *Protecting and safeguarding cultural heritage: systems of management of cultural heritage in the Visegrad countries*. Krakow: International Cultural Centre.

Purchla, J. (2015) "Central Europe and its heritage: The dilemmas of transformation", [in:] Jagodzińska, K. and Purchla, J. (eds.) *The limits of heritage: the 2nd heritage forum of Central Europe*. Krakow: International Cultural Centre, 11–22.

Purchla, J. (2018) *Miasto i polityka. Przypadki Krakowa*. Kraków: Towarzystwo Autorów i Wydawców Prac Naukowych UNIVERSITAS.

Purchla, J. (2020) "Dziedzictwo kulturowe jako zasób prorozwojowy Krakowa", [in:] Noga, Z. and Purchla, J. (eds.) *Dziedzictwo Krakowa w procesie transformacji*. Kraków: Towarzystwo Miłośników Historii i Zabytków Krakowa, 25–44.

Purchla, J. and Skotnicki, A.B. (2007) "Przywrócić pamięć' / "Restoring memory", [in:] Małecki, J.M. (ed.) (2007b) *Świat przed katastrofą / A World before a Catastrophe*. Kraków: Międzynarodowe Centrum Kultury, 5–7.

Purchla, J. and Komar, Ż (eds.) (2021) *Dissonant heritage? The architecture of the Third Reich in Poland*. Krakow: International Cultural Centre.

Purchla, J. and Sepioł, J. (eds.) (2015). *Form Follows Freedom: architecture for Culture in Poland 2000+*. Kraków: International Cultural Centre.

Reklewska, M. (2000) *Dziedzictwo a rozwój. Doświadczenie Krakowa*. Kraków: Międzynarodowe Centrum Kultury.

Rojkowska-Tasak, H. (2009) "Activities of Krakow's municipal government in the field of World Heritage", [in:] Dziedzic, S. and Rojkowska-Tasak, H. (eds.), *30 years on the UNESCO List. Krakow 1978–2008. Krakow: Municipality of Krakow. Culture and National Heritage Department. Office of Monument Protection*. Michałowice: Wydawnictwo Czuwajmy, 81–88.

Róziewicz, M. (ed.) (2007) *Kraków. Zabytki architektury i budownictwa w Polsce*. Warszawa: Krajowy Ośrodek Badań i Dokumentacji Zabytków.

Sepioł, J. (2020) "Kraków w procesie transformacji", [in:] Noga, Z. and Purchla, J. (eds.) *Dziedzictwo Krakowa w procesie transformacji*. Kraków: Towarzystwo Miłośników Historii i Zabytków Krakowa, 7–23.

SKOZK (2021) *Społeczny Komitet Odnowy Zabytków Krakowa*. Available at: www.skozk.pl (Accessed on 4 November 2021).

Szmygin, B. (2011) "Transformation of the Heritage Protection System in Poland after 1989", [in:] Purchla, J. (ed.) *Protecting and safeguarding cultural heritage: systems of management of cultural heritage in the Visegrad countries*. Krakow: International Cultural Centre.

Szpanowski, P. (2011) "Organisation of heritage protection in Poland", [in:] Purchla, J. (ed.) *Protecting and safeguarding cultural heritage: systems of management of cultural heritage in the Visegrad countries*. Krakow: International Cultural Centre, 211–222.

Szyper, B. and Wiśniewski, M. (eds.) (2013) *Akademia Dziedzictwa 2002–2013. Przegląd problemów badawczych z zakresu zarządzania i ochrony dziedzictwa kulturowego w Polsce*. Kraków: Międzynarodowe Centrum Kultury.

Tomaszewski, A. (ed.) (2008) *Values and criteria in heritage conservation*. Firenze: Polistampa.

Tracz, M. and Bajgier-Kowalska, M. (2020) "Zmiany w ruchu turystycznym w wybranych miastach dziedzictwa kulturowego państw Grupy Wyszehradzkiej (V4)", *Prace Komisji Geografii Przemysłu Polskiego Towarzystwa Geograficznego*, 34(3), 67–83.

Uchwała krajobrazowa (2021) *Uchwała krajobrazowa – Zasady i warunki sytuowania obiektów małej architektury, tablic reklamowych i urządzeń reklamowych oraz ogrodzeń.* Available at: https://www.bip.krakow.pl/?dok_id=128261 (Accessed on 22 November 2021).

Zachariasz, A. (2008) "Zwierzyniecki Park Kulturowy", *Czasopismo Techniczne*, 1–A, 77–99.

Ziejka, F. (2009) "Not at once Krakow was... restored", [in:] Dziedzic, S. and Rojkowska-Tasak, H. (eds.) *30 years on the UNESCO List. Krakow 1978–2008.* Krakow: Municipality of Krakow. Culture and National Heritage Department. Office of Monument Protection. Michałowice: Wydawnictwo Czuwajmy, 63–74.

Ziejka, F. (2010) *Serce Polski. Szkice krakowskie.* Kraków: Księgarnia Akademicka.

Note

1 More universal than "monument", the Polish word *zabytek* (plur. *zabytki*) translated by some into "a heritage object" suggests a tangible historical "piece" rather than a site or an abstract notion. Used in this sense in this particular law and elsewhere, the word caused a controversy among Polish specialists, as its use was believed to narrow down the scope of protection just to "individual objects" and to fail to include sites.

That reference aside, the term is translated into "heritage" throughout the article (e.g., when the Heritage Preservation Officer is mentioned in the following paragraph) and the book. [Editor's note]

10 Kraków

A creative city

Joanna Sanetra-Szeliga

The aim of the chapter is to examine Kraków using the concept of a creative city, as elaborated by a number of researchers, including Charles Landry (2000) and Richard Florida (2002). It emphasises the role of culture, the creative industries, cultural infrastructure, and the "creative class" in a discussion about the key resources of a city. We will look at Kraków from four different angles: creative capital, the cultural and creative industries, cultural and scientific infrastructure, as well as the urban quality of life. The analysis will be accompanied by a presentation of Kraków's positions in two creative city indices (the EU's Cultural and Creative Cities Monitor and Landry and Hyams's Creative Cities Index) and its activities as the UNESCO Creative City of Literature.

What is a creative city?

At the turn of the 20th and in the early 21st centuries, the discussion on the city's development was largely dominated by the concept of a creative city. The literature on the subject does not present a single definition of what a creative city is, but in principle, the concept emphasises the role of creative industries, cultural infrastructure, and the so-called creative class in planning city development and using its resources. To a large extent, the term "creative city" was popularised not only in academia but also among decision-makers, politicians, and the public, thanks to the wide readership of books such as Charles Landry's "Creative City" (2000) and Richard Florida's "The Rise of the Creative Class" (2002), as well as their authors' consulting activities to individual cities. The concept is part of a larger shift in understanding the role of arts, heritage, and culture in local development that has been observed since the late 1990s. Richard Smith and Katie Warfield (2007, p. 283) notice two approaches to value orientation and the definition of a creative city. On the one hand, there are culture-centric orientations, where the central value is placed on the arts, culture, community well-being, and inclusion (the creative city as a place of diverse and inclusive arts and culture). On the other hand, is the econ-centric approach, where the focus is on urban economic

DOI: 10.4324/9781003252757-11

sustainability and well-being through creative industries (the creative city as a place of economic innovation, creative talent, and creative industries) (Smith and Warfield 2007, p. 283).

By combining both approaches, a creative city can be described as one that can produce competitive cultural and creative goods and services, as well as a high-quality cultural offer, while being resilient to change, thanks to its creative, and thus innovation, capital. Moreover, thanks to its local, also cultural, resources, a creative city is able to attract investment into both the innovative economic sectors and creative people. According to Sharon Zukin, a creative city fosters its creativity by promoting "generous and inclusive culture" and having "an impatient desire for new things, while valuing the old" (2004).

To better understand the phenomenon of a creative city, numerous indices have been developed and can be categorised into two types: creative stocks and creative flows (Hartley et al., 2012). Creative stock indices are based mainly on Florida's creative class theory (2002) and measure diversity, openness, tolerance, and vibrancy of the creative sectors (output, employment, participation and talent), human and social capital, and the quality of life. Probably the best known here is the Creative Cities Index prepared by Richard Florida (2002) in which he claimed that talented people (a so-called "creative class") were attracted to cities characterised by a combination of factors he called 3T: technology – a function of innovation and concentration of hi-tech talent – the number of people with at least a bachelor degree, and tolerance – diversity, openness, a friendly attitude towards people of different religious or ethnic backgrounds, or sexual orientation.

The cultural life of a city is seen as an important part of many of other indices that fall into the same class – both on the supply side (cultural offer, employment in the creative sector, economic contribution of the creative industries) – e.g., European Creativity Index (KEA, 2009, p. 187) and Creative Vitality Index (Villa, 2018) – and demand side (inhabitants participation in cultural life) – e.g., Design Creativity and Innovation Scoreboard (Hollanders and van Cruysen, 2009). Further, the Silicon Valley Creative Communities Index (Kreidler and Trounstine, 2005) proposes the inclusion of cultural assets (tangible and intangible – talent and the general aesthetic quality of the city environment) and resources to develop them. Moreover, the importance of social capital as a factor in fostering creativity is mentioned in many indices, such as the European Creativity Index or the Creative Communities Index. Creative flow indices, exemplified by the Global Power Cities Index, include cultural indictors in one of their subsets but generally shift attention away from cultural issues towards a city's infrastructure, basic services, innovation and technology performance, networking and exchange, and its world status.

Charles Landry, a person largely associated with the roots of the creative city concept, presents a different approach. He emphasises that "a culture of creativity" (creativity understood as "applied imagination using qualities such as intelligence, inventiveness and learning along the way") needs to be

> embedded within how the urban stakeholders operate. (…) By encouraging creativity and legitimising the use of imagination within the public, private and community spheres, the ideas bank of possibilities and potential solutions to any urban problem or opportunity will be broadened.
> (Landry, 2000, pp. xxi–xxii)

Starting from the cultural and creative industries, the author broadens the scope of the necessary creativity and innovation to include the political, social, and economic spheres. He highlights the new role of hard infrastructure and its potential in creating spaces that stimulate interpersonal communication and creative thinking. He also emphasises the importance of "soft creative infrastructure", which is a term used to describe the mental infrastructure and the atmosphere in the city.

Most of the features mentioned above can be integrated using "the creative agglomeration of polycentric structure" (Klasik, 2011), adapted and developed here to verify the thesis of Kraków being a creative city (see Figure 10.1).

First, there is creative capital, which itself is a composite of different types of capital: cultural, human, institutional, and social. It is generated by people from the creative professions (such as Florida's creative class), as well as civic local communities and visionary self-government, local, and regional leadership. Second, there is the tangible (e.g., facilities and venues) and intangible (e.g., partnerships, networks) infrastructure of the culture and science sector that also includes information and communication technologies.

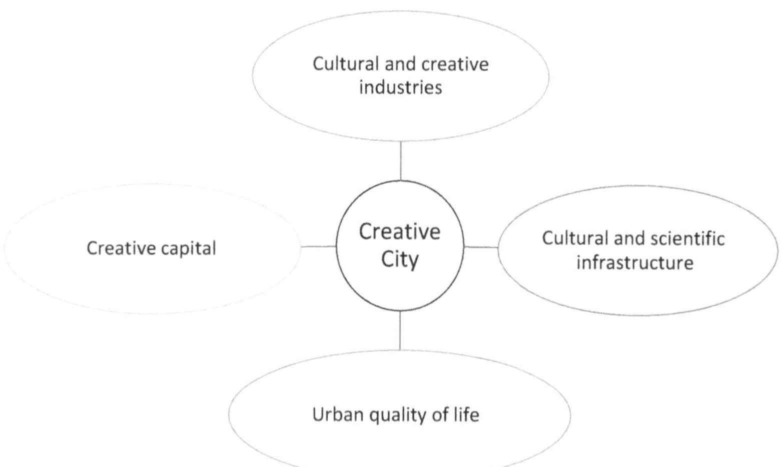

Figure 10.1 Creative city of polycentric structure.
Source: Klasik, 2011, p. 9. Adapted and expanded.

Here, I would include creative districts, cultural quarters, or technology parks. Third, there is quality of life, a factor responsible for attracting both creative people and organisations. And last but certainly not least, there are cultural and creative industries, the core of the creative economy.

Kraków's creative capital

A discussion on creative capital should start with the theory of creative capital (or the creative class) developed by Richard Florida (2002), who claims that the basis of local development are the creative people who choose where to live based on the innovation, diversity, and tolerance characteristics of a place. They make up a so-called "creative class", defined as an economic class composed of people "who add economic value through their creativity" by "doing work whose function is to create meaningful new forms". The core of this class are scientists and engineers, entertainers, actors, designers, architects, writers, publishers, public opinion makers, university professors, analysts who "produce new forms or designs that are easily marketable and widely applicable". They are called the super-creative core, in addition to which the creative class includes "creative professionals who work in a wide range of knowledge-intensive industries" (e.g., the high-tech sector, financial services, health care, business management) and who are required to think independently and engage in creative problem solving (pp. 68–69). The third group can be called "Bohemians" – meaning representatives of the artistic professions (musicians, photographers, designers etc.). Florida's theory received much acclaim and as much misunderstanding and criticism; the latter concerned mainly its cause–effect sequences, methodological inaccuracies, and neoliberal worldview (e.g., Dreher, 2002; Glaeser, 2004; Peck, 2005; Moretti, 2012).

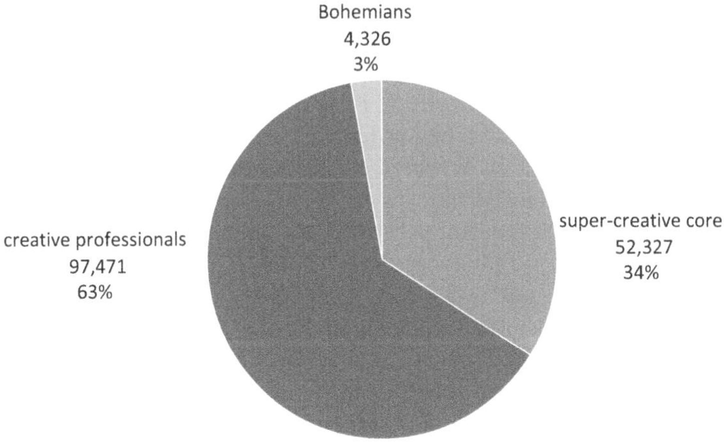

Figure 10.2 Composition of the creative class in Kraków (2010).
Source: Own, based on Wojnar, 2016, p. 100.

Adapting Florida's definition and using the International Standard Classification of Occupations ISCO–08, Katarzyna Wojnar calculated that in 2010, there were 154,034 professionals[1] in Kraków that fell into the category of the creative class (31.18% of all Kraków's residents of working age). The super-creative core professionals made up 34% (see Figure 10.2), which was typical of big cities with well-developed metropolitan functions. There also seemed to be quite a lot of potential to enlarge the group of creative professionals by increasing the number of specialists able to commercialise and provide technical and administrative support for ideas and innovations proposed by the super-creative core (Wojnar, 2016, pp. 85, 100–102).

Creative professionals can also be counted in other ways, using different definitions and sources. Monika Murzyn-Kupisz and Jarosław Działek tried to assess the number of professional artists active in Kraków. Based on the 2002 National Census 2002 (later censuses did not allow for the necessary data to be extracted), they calculated that the total number of architects, writers and journalists, visual artists, performing artists, and audio visual artists amounted to 5,118 people (compare with Bohemians in Figure 10.2). Given the relatively low mobility of Poles, one could suspect that this number would have stayed more or less the same, although it cannot be ignored that artists move into or out of Kraków due to different reasons. The lack of sufficient statistical data does not allow for any conclusions to be drawn here, but rather presents us with a snapshot of the situation in Kraków at the beginning of the 21st century (2017, p. 193). The REGON registry provides more data.[2] In 2021, there were 762 entities that dealt with broadly understood art – actors and theatre directors, scenography designers, dancers, sculptors, painters, journalists, writers, etc. that had registered their economic activity in the REGON database, chiefly as microenterprises (meaning, in most cases, self-employment – all but 11 fall into the category of 1–9 employees).

There would be no such creative capital in Kraków if the city were not an important academic centre. In 2020, there were 129,900 students (including 8,100 foreigners) studying in more than 20 higher education institutions, both public and private (Urząd Statystyczny w Krakowie, 2020). These included the Jagiellonian University, the second oldest in Central Europe (established in 1364), which has consistently occupied the top positions in various rankings of the best universities in Poland.[3]

Social capital can be an important part of the equation here. According to research (for detailed discussion see e.g., Kurowska and Theiss, 2018), Poland is a country of rather low civic social capital, strong familialistic bonds, satisfactory level of informal capital (friends, neighbours, family), and in-group solidarity. This places Poland at the tail end of rankings of social capital in Europe (Czapiński, 2015, pp. 351–353).

The low level of social capital should be considered one of the most serious development barriers that contributes to the low level of innovation in the country. It does not vary much between Polish regions, although it is relatively high in Małopolska (whose capital is Kraków) (Rada Ministrów, 2020, pp. 7–10). Given the proven correlations between the quality and standard of life and social capital, Kraków (being a relatively wealthy city with a high percentage of well-educated residents) does quite well in comparisons of the level of social capital in Poland (Czapiński, 2015, pp. 351–362). However, it is still not satisfactory, and the low level of social trust, engagement in local civic matters, and the quality of social dialogue in Kraków are seen as weaknesses and threats in the development strategy of the city (Municipality of Kraków, 2018, p. 35).

Creative capital is dependent on the quality of local government (Landry, 2000). In this aspect, Landry's research (2018) is not exactly perfect in the case of Kraków, especially regarding cooperation with civil society and social dialogue. One of the senior officials in the municipality (Interview 1) claims that the city is rather conservative, afraid of (necessary) radical changes, does not take risks, and does not like to question the status quo.

Kraków's cultural and scientific infrastructure

To describe this aspect of conditions for creativity, one can turn to Gunter Törnqvist (1983) and his concept of a creative milieu, which is characterised by four features: a large resource of mobile and exchangeable information, knowledge (and its accumulation), competence in certain areas, and the ability to use these three creative features in order to create something new and innovative. Creating such a place takes time, as it takes time to build libraries or archives and to develop traditional skills.[4]

Table 10.1 Cultural institutions in Kraków (including those run by the municipality)

	Total	*Municipal institutions*
Public libraries and their branches	61	59
Cultural centres and their branches	61	53
Philharmonic halls	1	
Orchestras	3	2
Galleries	40	1
Theatres	17	8
Operas	1	
Cinemas	12	
Museums and their branches	42	6

Source: BDL, Statistics Poland (9 November 2021); Miasto Kraków. BIP, 2021.

Kraków is home to over 230 cultural institutions run by various level of public administration and private entities (Table 10.1). The city is prominently represented in the Polish Map of Research Infrastructure (Ministerstwo Nauki i Szkolnictwa Wyższego, 2020), thanks to its numerous universities and research facilities. Moreover, there are 140 scientific and pedagogical libraries in Kraków.

If cultural and creative entities are located in close proximity to one another, they can create a cultural district (quarter) or a creative cluster.

Basically, these are areas with a concentrated production of goods based on broadly defined culture. They arise from the combination of an appropriate location and the idiosyncratic nature of culture (Santagata, 2002). The production of goods and services is deeply rooted in local traditions, heritage, and creativity related to a given place and time of creation, often also based on individual tacit knowledge.

Cultural quarters, such as the museum district in Vienna (MuseumsQuartier Vienna) or the theatre neighbourhood in New York (Broadway), in addition to their basic offer (exhibitions, performances) provide many goods and services related to the basic activities (e.g., workshops, meetings, lectures) as well as complementary goods and services (in the field of leisure and entertainment) – such as restaurants, cafés, shops, parks and green areas. The accumulation of a cultural offer in one place becomes a magnet attracting potential consumers. When a certain critical mass is achieved, a positive impact on the socio-economic development can be observed. An important element here is also the influence on the perception of the city and its reputation. This aspect is often the reason why city authorities decide to invest in such a district (Santagata, 2002, p. 18). In Kraków, Zabłocie, with Oskar Schindler's Enamel Factory and the MOCAK Museum of Contemporary Art in Kraków, tends to be described in terms of a cultural district. It is also where Kraków Artistic Schools, providing education in the field of fashion, creative photography, and interior design, and the Andrzej Frycz Modrzewski Kraków University, are located. And this is also where the municipality is creating the Socio-Economic Innovations Cluster Zabłocie 20.22.

A cluster is a geographic concentration of vertically and horizontally connected companies and institutions, including specialised suppliers, service providers, companies conducting related activities, institutions (e.g., universities, research and development entities, industry organisations, business environment institutions), which simultaneously compete and cooperate (Porter, 2009, pp. 213–214). Often the functioning of clusters is based on the so-called triple helix model, i.e., cooperation between representatives of business, science, and administration. Late in the 2010s and early in the 2020s, a rash of cluster initiatives appeared in Kraków. Some of them (e.g., the European Games Centre, Krakowska Strefa Dizajnu, Małopolski Cluster of Information Technologies) did not grow much beyond an embryonic phase. One that is worth mentioning here is the Kraków Film Cluster (2015) that gathers over 300 professional companies, organisations, and film artists. It defines itself as a platform for services, cooperation, and information, as well as promotional and educational activities.

Urban quality of life in Kraków

The quality of life appears in many contemporary concepts of socio-economic development as it becomes one of the important determinants of decisions about the location of business/investment and where individuals choose to live. We can find confirmation of this thesis in the work of Robert J. Rogerson (1999), who deals with the competitive struggle between cities and distinguishes the quality of life as one of the factors influencing the attractiveness of the city to potential investors and residents. Quality of life also appears in the previously mentioned work of Richard Florida and his theory of the creative class (3T factors). Verifying his thesis in the European context showed that creative workers in Europe were much more territorially rooted than in the United States. Central Europeans, for example, highly valued proximity to family and friends in their mobility decisions. Among other soft factors, the most frequently enumerated were a rich offer of recreation and entertainment in the region, cultural diversity, and an attractive natural environment (Stryjakiewicz, 2008; Martin-Brelot et al., 2010). Statistical analysis of factors that make a given city attractive for the Polish creative class led Wojnar (2016, p. 162) to claim that the quality of life and the quality of cultural and recreation offer of a city are crucial factors in attracting the creative class to a city. Individual analysis of various indicators adds another factor important for Polish creative class – openness and tolerance. Basically, a city needs to fulfil both people's day-to-day needs and higher-order needs – such as aesthetic and intellectual (Karwińska, 2009, s. 13).

Various studies present Kraków as a relatively good place to live. The Report on the Quality of Life in European Cities (Bolsi et al., 2020) paints a particularly positive picture, in which 90% of residents claim to be satisfied with living in Kraków (−6 pp. as compared with 2015). Moreover, the majority (61%) sees positive changes in the last years in this field. However, it is not easy to find good housing at reasonable prices. People are rather satisfied with the public transport and the city's cleanliness; 85% are satisfied with the public space (−4 pp). One of the few areas of dissatisfaction is air quality (only 18% satisfied) but to be fair, it has to be said that there have been a number of successful initiatives run by the municipality to make improvements in this area. Regarding the local public administration, over 60% respondents are satisfied with the time it takes to get a request resolved by the local public administration, but less than half see the procedures used by local administration as straightforward and easy to understand. In a quality of life ranking prepared by *Polityka* weekly and the AGH University of Science and Technology, Kraków was ranked third among 66 Polish cities with an index value of 95.88 (Gądecki, 2018). Particular high scores were received in the fields of health services, effective local authorities, free time, and active local community. In addition, research commissioned by the municipality presented many positive opinions. The overwhelming majority, 89%, of respondents, is satisfied with living in Kraków and over 60% would not consider moving away. The most negative responses concerned the quality of air (50% negative responses), cost of living (32%), and availability of parking (27%). Public services, culture and entertainment, and cleanliness received well over 60% positive responses (Chrzanowski, 2018).

As far as one of the Florida's 3T factors, tolerance, is concerned, respondents of the EU report (Bolsi et al., 2020) seem to find Kraków open and tolerant as 81% of respondents state that the city is a good place for LGBTQ people to live in. Unfortunately, it does not align with the results of the survey conducted directly within the LGBTQIA community in Kraków, where 63.4% of the respondents claim to have experienced discrimination (of which 61% was verbal violence and 20% reported physical attacks). These were not one-off incidents – the majority of acts of physical violence and vandalism were recurring. Moreover, half of the respondents thought of moving out of Kraków, with discrimination being one of the driving motives (Czerwiński et al., 2020, pp. 45–46).

Culture is an important part of urban quality of life (Sanetra-Szeliga, 2017) as it impacts the subjective evaluation of health or security and plays a crucial role in building a sense of belonging, one's identity, sense of accomplishment, learning and, of course, entertainment. Kraków's many cultural entities provide a broad and diverse cultural offer for a varied audience.

Kraków, home of cultural creative industries

The cultural and creative industries are the backbone of most of the creative city definitions. However, there is no single, commonly agreed, definition of this type of entity. An analysis of the use of the term allows four types of definitions to be distinguished (Bińczycka et al., 2018, p. 30):

- distinguishing and describing the characteristics of the goods and services produced
- based on the characteristics of the resources necessary for industry development
- focusing on the specificity of people working in these industries
- limited to listing the areas it comprises.

The first type focuses on the fact that the cultural and creative products and services (outputs of the creative industries) are covered by copyright, patents, and trademarks (Howkins, 2001; Throsby, 2001; WIPO, 2003), as well as the fact that they contain a symbolic value (Throsby, 2001; UNESCO, 2009) that exceeds their use value (Scott, 2004). The intellectual property is generated by human creativity, talent, and skill, and this is the basis for the second approach (DCMS, 1998; Throsby, 2001). The third type emphasises creative individuals, i.e., people with appropriate characteristics who, thanks to their creativity, produce products and services of significant economic value (Florida, 2010). The fourth type consists mainly of the listing of various types of activities that comprise cultural and creative industries.

The definition adopted in this chapter[5] is based on the distinction between various culture-related activities, as presented by Throsby (2001) and popularised by KEA European Affairs (2006), which draws on each of the presented types of definitions. The model of the cultural sector is centred on "the locus of origin of creative ideas and radiating outwards as those ideas become combined with more and more other inputs to produce a wider and wider range of products" (Throsby 2001, p. 113). The core of the model are the creative arts as traditionally defined: visual and performing arts, cultural heritage, literature. In the cultural sector in Poland, these activities are mainly undertaken by public cultural institutions (organised and supported by national, regional, and local authorities). Apart from the intellectual property and drawing on traditionally understood culture, what distinguishes cultural industries is their commercial, mass, and profit-oriented character. Publishing, phonography, radio, television, and the film and video game industries would fall into this category. Creative industries[6] produce no longer strictly cultural goods and services but rather creative goods and services[7] that include advertising, architecture, design, and fashion. One may say that culture is not the final product here but rather a tool used in the production process, very often acquiring typically functional features.

Kraków's considerable potential for growth in the field of cultural and creative industries stems from the complementarity of its resources: educational institutions, promotional and support activities from such institutions as Kraków Festival Office and Kraków Technology Park, cultural institutions and non-governmental organisations supporting the development of certain types of industries, as well as the diversity of already existing creative and cultural industries. In total, in 2021, there were close to 8,000 companies that could be classified as belonging to the cultural and creative industries. As elsewhere in Poland, the majority were organised in the form of microenterprises (97.69% of all entities classified as belonging to the cultural and creative industries).

The analysis of the entities registered in the REGON register[8] in Kraków sheds some light on the composition of the cultural and creative industries that are active in the city. The most numerous domains in 2021 were advertising and the visual arts (see Figures 10.3 and 10.4), which aligns with the trends observed for the whole of Poland. The latter also belongs to the fastest-growing domain, with a 26% increase in the past five years. A closer look reveals that it is, thanks to a large increase in the number of entities that deal with specialised design activities (such as designing fabrics, fashion, jewellery, furniture, industrial design, etc.) and photographic activities. Specialised design is in fact one of the fields with the highest number of enterprises (985), with only advertising agency activities (2,245 entities, including Agencja Reklamowa S4, Hand Made, Insignia, Opus B, Eskadra) and architectural activities (1,446) being more numerous. It should be emphasised that with Kraków being a historic city, many of the architectural design studios also have experience in the field of the comprehensive adaptation of buildings and urban space under conservation protection. The most famous include Ingarden & Ewý Architekci, Atelier Loegler i Partnerzy, Horizone Studio, DDJM Architectural Office, and Miastoprojekt.

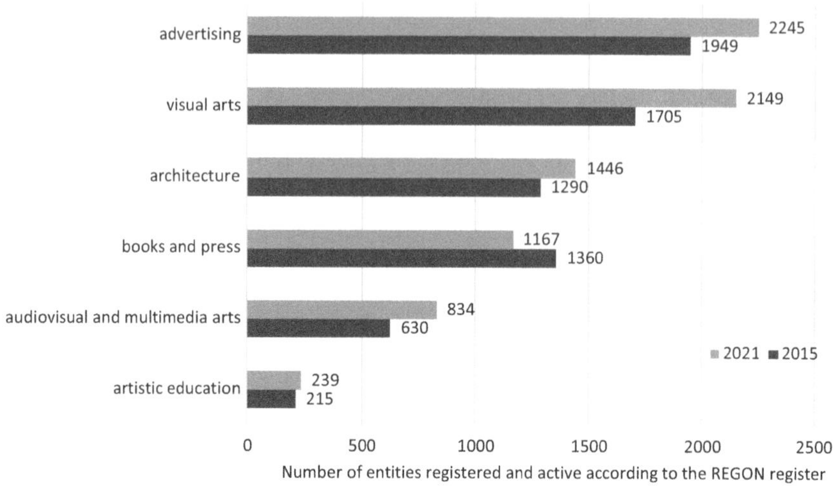

Figure 10.3 Culture and creative industries in Kraków, by domain.[9]
Source: Own elaboration based on REGON data for 31 December 2015 and 30 September 2021 received from Statistics Poland.

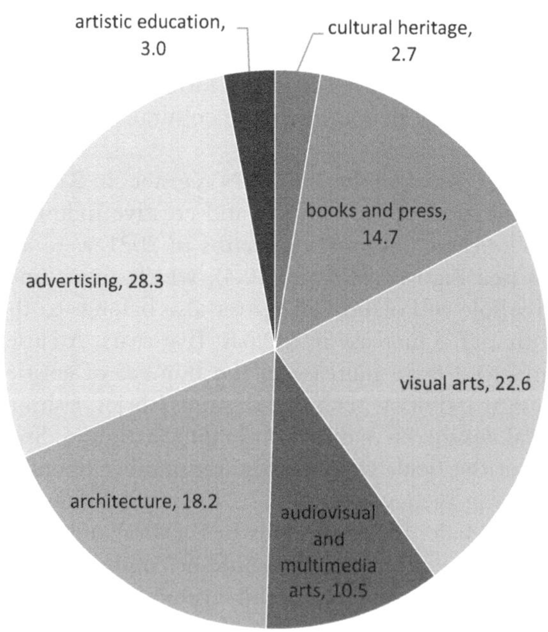

Figure 10.4 Culture and creative industries in Kraków (2021) (%).
Source: Own elaboration based on REGON data for 31 Decemeber 2015 and 30 September 2021 received from Statistics Poland.

In the sectors of graphic design, industrial design, and fashion, there are close to a thousand active entities. If we just take the fashion industry, there is the Vistula company that has been operating in Kraków since 1948 (currently specialising in the design and distribution of high-quality fashion for men), as well as numerous smaller companies. One such example would be KOKOWorld, famous for its fair-trade approach, that combines fashion with social projects, and brings together craftspeople, Polish ones included, from various corners of the world together. The most important fashion event is Cracow Fashion Week.

The fields of film, video, and television programme production activities, translation and interpretation activities, as well as photographic activities, number around 500 entities per field. The all-Poland trend of a sharp decrease in the number of entities categorised under "books and press" is also visible in Kraków, with a decrease of 14.8% in this domain (retail sale of newspapers and stationery in specialised stores and publishing of newspapers were particularly affected).

Bearing in mind that Kraków is a UNESCO Creative City of Literature, the field of books and the press deserves special attention here. Annually, there are over 4,500 titles (every third – scientific, every fifth – fiction) published by Kraków's publishing industry (Kraków. UNESCO City of Literature, 2013a). On the one hand, there are the old, large, and renowned publishing houses such as ZNAK and Wydawnictwo Literackie, which were established in the 1950s and publish mostly fictional literature, including titles by Polish Nobel Prize winners. On the other hand, there are also new entities, such as Korporacja Ha!art and Karakter (both founded in 2000), which are perceived as more open and experimental (Dzięgielewski, 2017, pp. 42–43). There are also publishing houses specialising in poetry (e.g., a5 publishing house), Catholic publications (with the oldest Polish Catholic publishing house WAM [1872]), scientific (e.g., Jagiellonian University Publishing House, Universitas Publishing House), and musical (e.g., Polskie Wydawnictwo Muzyczne).

Although the number of bookshops, a complementary activity to the publishing industry, has been falling over the years in Kraków, there are still over 90 entities registered in the field of retail sale of books in specialised stores. These include bookshops run by the publishing houses, such as Księgarnia pod Globusem (Wydawnictwo Literackie) and bookstores/literary cafés (e.g., Lokator, Massolit Books). The oldest bookstore in Poland (established in 1610), if not Europe (Krawczuk et al., 2010), operates in the Kromer tenement house on the Main Market Square.

Kraków is not only a UNESCO Creative City but also one of the first cities (1978) whose historic centre has been listed on the UNESCO World Heritage List. Maintaining this status requires not only adequate policy regulations but also a number of entities experienced in the protection and conservation of movable and immovable heritage: there were 214 such entities in Kraków in 2021.

As far as the mass-media is concerned, there is a public regional television station (TVP3 Kraków) broadcasting local news, weather forecasts, commentary on events in the region, etc. with the possibility of online viewing via the krakow.tvp.pl website. Kraków was also home to Wisła Television that in 1997, together with TVN, created one of the largest TV stations in Poland – TVN. TVN still has a branch in Kraków, (TVN24 Kraków) but these two large companies are not registered in the city. Instead, the REGON database presents nine small companies that deal with public and licence television programme broadcasting. In contrast, the regional public radio (Radio Kraków – broadcasting since 1991) and the first private and independent commercial radio station in Poland now broadcasting nationally (RMF radio, established in 1990) are registered in Kraków, along with eight other similar companies. It is worth mentioning that Radio Kraków and RMF are among the few large firms (with 50–249 employees) in the Kraków cultural and creative industries. In fact, there are only 19 companies employing more than 50 people that could be categorised as belonging to the cultural and creative industries.

Film, video, and television programme production, and post-production activities saw a significant increase in the number of entities that undertook them (an increase of 40.1% in the number of production and 111.8% in the number of post-production entities over the last five years!). This growth can be related in part to the support for the production of film production, provided by the Regional Film Fund in Kraków and the Kraków Film Commission (2021) (so far, 17 feature films and series, 18 documentaries, 6 animated films).

Kraków is an important computer video games centre in Poland (second only to Warsaw) (Bobrowski et al., 2017, p. 68) with gaming and software companies, such as Bloober Team, Gamesture, Nano Games, Reality Games, and the CD Projekt RED branch (based in Kraków since 2013). The industry is actively supported by the Kraków Technology Park, which organises initiatives such as the Digital Dragons Incubator (an incubation programme for start-up games studios) and the largest Digital Dragons industry conference in Central Europe.

Kraków in selected creativity rankings

Creative Cities Index

In 2018, Charles Landry conducted a broad analysis of Kraków's creative potential using his Creative Cities Index as a tool. This allowed him to pinpoint the fields where the city was developing well, and which domains required further attention and support (see Figure 10.5). The overall average score for Kraków across all domains was 55.76%, which put it in the "good, but with room for improvement" category and placed the city as the 10th among the 20 cities that had been analysed.

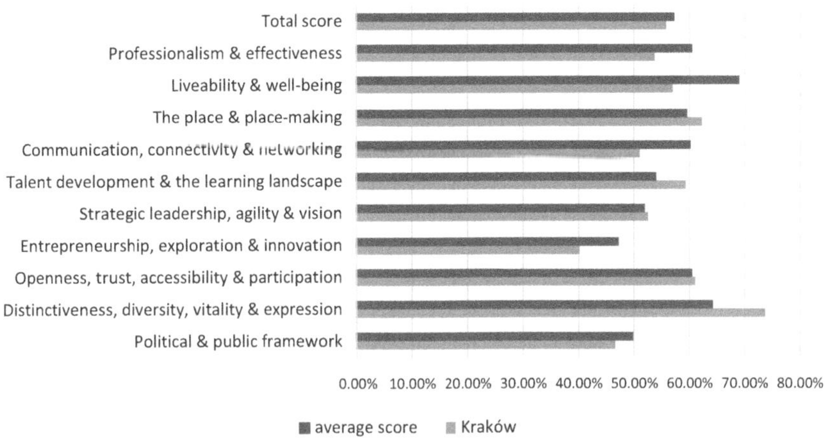

Figure 10.5 Creative Cities Index: Kraków in comparison with other cities.
Source: Own, based on Landry, 2018, p. 12.

The analysis showed that Kraków is perceived

> as a distinguished and interesting city with an excellent reputation, a dynamic art and culture scene, and a good academic system. It is easy to navigate, pedestrian-friendly, and has efficient city transport; it is relatively cosmopolitan and open. However, it is one of the lowest-scored cities for networking, cross-sector collaboration, business friendliness, bureaucracy, and the ability to implement and act.
>
> (Landry, 2018, pp. 2–3)

The results show Kraków as a city that "is good at reviving and expressing creativity in relation to its physical attributes and cultural vitality and is also good at identifying and developing it. However, it is less able to support, capture and use his creativity. Kraków seems to have a good atmosphere, mainly physical, for creativity, but it also shows potential for further development" (Landry, 2018, p. 12). To sum up, Landry argues that based on the definitions used in the Index and its methodology, Kraków is more an artistic than a creative city, but he sees a clear creative potential that could be unleashed.

Culture and Creative Cities Monitor

The Creative Cities Monitor was developed by the Joint Research Centre (JRC) of the European Commission, and it collects and processes data in three domains: cultural vibrancy, creative economy, and enabling environment (Montalto et al., 2019). Figure 10.6 shows Kraków's results as compared with other Polish cities covered by the analysis.

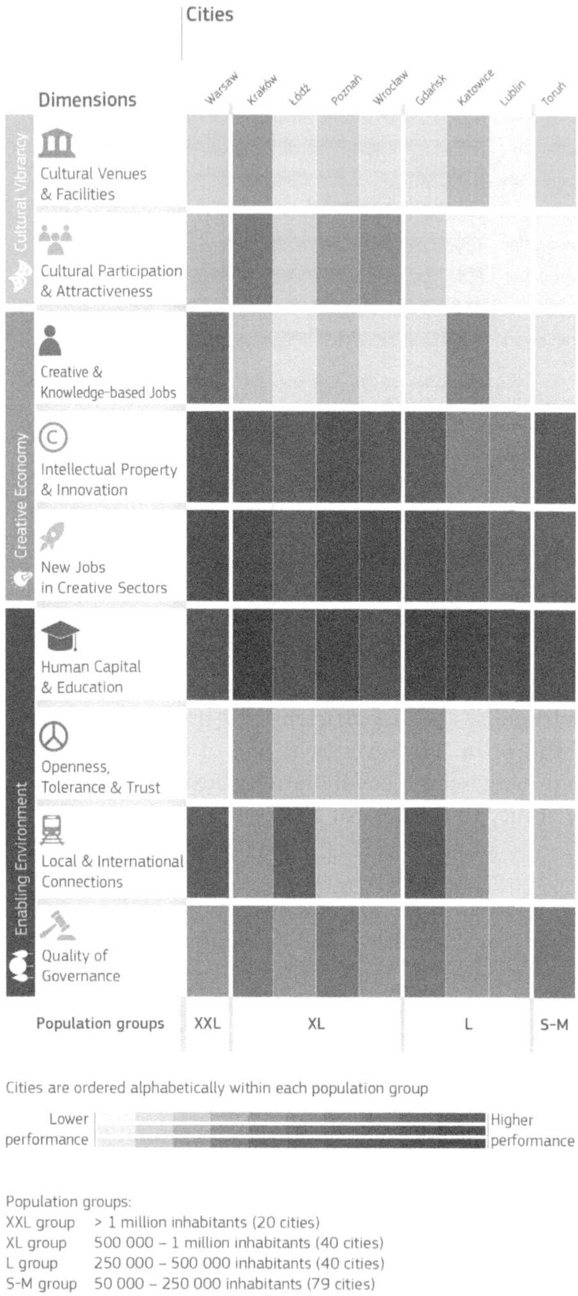

Figure 10.6 The Creative Cities Monitor: Kraków's scores.
Source: European Commission, Joint Research Centre 2019.

Kraków performs relatively well, given its less favourable socio-economic conditions (in comparison with other European cities). Compared with the results from 2017, in 2019, Kraków increased its score by about 22 points due to improvements on *Jobs in new media & communication enterprises* and *Jobs in new enterprises in other creative sectors* categories.

Kraków achieved 10th position in *Cultural Vibrancy* among 190 cities covered by the Monitor, mainly as a result of its good performance in *Cultural Participation & Attractiveness*, it ranked 8th among the 40 ranked European cities with 500,000 to 1 million inhabitants. It did even better regarding *Human Capital & Education* category where it held 4th position.

Kraków – UNESCO Creative City of Literature

UNESCO awards the Creative City title to those cities "that have recognised creativity as a strategic factor of sustainable development as regards economic, social, cultural and environmental aspects" and aim at making creativity an essential component of urban development, strengthening the creation, production, distribution and dissemination of cultural activities, goods, and developing hubs of creativity and innovation and broaden opportunities for creators and professionals in the cultural sector services, improving access to and participation in cultural life as well as the enjoyment of cultural goods and services, integrating culture and creativity into local development strategies and plans (UNESCO, 2004).[10]

The title of Creative City of Literature was awarded to Kraków in 2013. The city prides itself on being "the cradle of the Polish language and Polish literature" with many renowned authors associated with it, including the Nobel Prize winners Czesław Miłosz and Wisława Szymborska, as well as Joseph Conrad Korzeniowski and Stanisław Lem. It is where the first scriptorias in Poland were established (in the 11th century) and the first prints were published. It is still the seat of many prestigious publishing houses and the location of one of the largest book fairs in Poland. The city is a host to the most important literary festivals in Poland: the Miłosz Festival and Conrad Festival. Local writers and publishers receive the highest number of nominations for the leading Polish literary awards. A number of libraries operate in the city, public as well as scientific, academic, and university. That number includes Kraków's largest and most important library with a centuries-old tradition and international significance – the Jagiellonian Library, which houses the most important relics and masterpieces of the Polish language and world literature (Kraków. UNESCO City of Literature, 2013b).

Behind the title there is a strategic programme that included ten fields: integration of the diverse literary life, developing ties between literature, new media, and creative industries, promoting readership, organising literary events and festivals, supporting the development of the publishing industry, creating conditions for putting literature in the public space, supporting young and emerging artists and writers through grants and scholarship programmes, developing ties between literature and human rights, and widening and deepening international cooperation in the literary sector and literary education (Rada Miasta Krakowa, 2016). The actions undertaken to implement the programme include Conrad Festival being the largest literary festival in Poland and one of the largest in Europe, the Miłosz Festival that is the biggest international poetry event in Central Europe, a support programme for Kraków bookshops, a literature residency programme, and a number of educational activities.

Conclusions

Becoming a creative city is a never-ending process. Such a city must be flexible and react to changes in its socio-economic environment and adapt to global trends. In order to do this, it must have a solid creative base to build on. Kraków has been building such a base for years now – it is a city of vibrant cultural life, well-protected heritage, and important educational and scientific facilities. The quality of life is at a relatively good level. The city is rather well connected with the world via different transport routes. What could be improved are its networking and cooperation skills – both on the local and international levels (e.g., participation in the Eurocities network [Interview 1]). There is a myriad of cultural and creative industries. It is a UNESCO Creative City of Literature.

Kraków's scores in the above-mentioned rankings of creative cities are rather average when compared with other cities. Therefore, there is a need, and also the potential, for improvement. For example, creativity is a part of the Kraków's Development Strategy (Municipality of Kraków, 2018), starting with its vision of "a modern, creative metropolis using its cultural potential" (p. 11), its mission of creating a smart metropolis that builds a creative economy (p. 23) and becoming a leader in entrepreneurship based on creativity, which translates in planned activities, such as the stimulation of the development of creative industries by increasing the influence of culture on the economy, the active usage of the UNESCO creative network, and stimulating the transfer of knowledge and experience in the latest trends in culture creative and heritage sectors. In Landry's opinion (2018, p. 38), however, the document does not take full advantage of the potential of the cultural and creative industries and this is something that could be developed. There could also be more done in the field of dialogue with the residents, as well as building openness, tolerance, and trust.

As Landry said: "Kraków has the potential to become a creative city with a leading position in the world. It has a few of the right ingredients, will it, however, choose to put them together, strengthen his networking skills, start listening and learning?" (Landry, 2018, p. 3). It is a process.

Bibliography

Andersson, Å. (1985) "Creativity and regional development", *Papers in Regional Science January*, 56(1), 5–20.

Bína, V. et al. (2012) *European Statistical System Network on Culture. Final Report*. Luxembourg: ESSnet-Culture. Available at: http://ec.europa.eu/assets/eac/culture/library/reports/ess-net-report_en.pdf (Accessed on: 14 October 2021).

Bińczycka, E. et al. (2017) *Ekonomiczne aspekty kultury. Raport z pracy metodologicznej 3.074.* Kraków: Urząd Statystyczny w Krakowie (typescript).

Bińczycka, E. et al. (2018) "Cultural and creative industries in 2014–2016", *Research Studies.* Warszawa – Kraków: Statistics Poland – Statistical Office in Kraków.

Bobrowski, M. et al. (2017) "Kondycja polskiej branży gier '17" *Krakowski Park Technologiczny.* Available at: https://www.kpt.krakow.pl/wp-content/uploads/2018/03/kondycja-polskiej-branzy-gier17.pdf (Accessed on: 20 September 2021).

Bolsi, P., et al. (2020) *Report on the Quality of Life in European Cities, 2020,* Luxembourg: Publications Office of the European Union, 2020. Available at: https://ec.europa.eu/regional_policy/sources/docgener/work/qol2020/quality_life_european_cities_en.pdf (Accessed on: 25 September 2021).

Chrzanowski, M.A. (2018) *Podsumowanie wyników badania jakości życia i jakości usług publicznych w Krakowie. Raport Badawczy.* Kraków: Inquiso.

Czapiński, J. (2015) "Stan społeczeństwa obywatelskiego" [in:] Czapiński, J. and Panek, T. (eds.) *Social diagnosis 2015: objective and subjective quality of life in Poland.* Warszawa: Rada Monitoring Społecznego, 332–372.

Czerwiński, M. et al. (2020) *Dyskryminowani/e. Sytuacja osób LGBTQIA w Krakowie.* Kraków: Fundacja Równości.

Department of Culture, Media and Sport (DCMS) (1998) *Creative Industries Mapping Documents.* Available at: https://www.gov.uk/government/publications/creative-industries-mapping-documents-1998 (Accessed on: 19 October 2021).

Dreher, Ch. (2002) "Be Creative or Die", *Salon.* Available at: https://www.salon.com/2002/06/06/florida_22/ (Accessed on: 15 September 2021).

Dzięgielewski, M. (2017) "Komponenty segmentu instytucjonalnego w polu literackim i ich kondycja", [in:] Dzięgielewski, M. et al. (eds.) *Dramat i życie, czyli raport z badania krakowskiego pola literackiego.* Kraków: Krakowskie Biuro Festiwalowe, 38–52.

European Commission, Joint Research Centre (2019) *The Cultural and Creative Cities Monitor. 2019 Edition. Poland.* Publications Office. Available at: https://data.europa.eu/doi/10.2760/389681 (Accessed on: 14 September 2021).

Florida, R. (2002) *The Rise of the Creative Class: And How It's Transforming Work, Leisure, Community and Everyday Life.* New York: Basic Books.

Gądecki, J. (2018) "Wymiary szczęścia. Ranking jakości życia", *Polityka.* Accessed at: https://www.miasta.pl/uploads/attachment/file/2367/RANKING_MIAST-Polityka.pdf (Accessed on: 10 March 2021).

Glaeser, E.L. (2004) *Review of Richard Florida's The Rise of the Creative Class.* Available at: https://scholar.harvard.edu/glaeser/publications/book-review-richard-floridas-rise-creative-class (Accessed on: 10 September 2021).

Hartley, J. et al. (2012) *CCI-CCI Creative City Index 2012.* ARC Centre of Excellence for Creative Industries and Innovation Queensland University of Technology. Available at: http://www.cci.edu.au/sites/default/files/CCI%20Creative%20City%20Index%202012%20Final%20Report.pdf (Accessed on: 10 September 2021).

Hollanders, H. and van Cruysen, A. (2009) *Design, Creativity and Innovation: A Scoreboard Approach.* PRO INNO /INNO Metrics. Available at: https://citeseerx.ist.psu.edu/viewdoc/download?doi=10.1.1.924.793&rep=rep1&type=pdf (Accessed on: 10 September 2021).

Howkins, J. (2001) *The Creative Economy: How People Make Money from Ideas.* London: Penguin.

Karwińska, A. (2009) "Społeczno-kulturowe uwarunkowania cech miasta kreatywnego. Możliwość budowania lokalnego 'kapitału kreatywności'", [in:] Klasik, A. (ed.)

Kreatywne miasto – kreatywna aglomeracja. Katowice: Wydawnictwo Akademii Ekonomicznej w Katowicach

KEA European Affairs (2006) *The Economy of Culture in Europe: Study prepared for the European Commission*. Available at: http://ec.europa.eu/culture/library/studies/-cultural-economy_en.pdf (Accessed on: 18 October 2021).

KEA European Affairs. (2009, June). *The impact of culture on creativity: A study prepared for the European Commission (Directorate-General for Education and Culture)*. Available at: https://europa.eu/capacity4dev/file/18617/download?token=Fzta9pMB (Accessed on: 20 September 2021).

Klasik, A. (2011) "Kreatywne przemysły w kreatywnej aglomeracji", *Biuletyn KPZK*, 246.

Kraków Film Commission (2021) *Our films*. Available at: http://film-commission.pl/en/our-films/ (Accessed on: 20 September 2021).

Kraków Film Klaster (2015) *About*. Available at: http://film.krakow.pl/krakow-film-klaster/ (Accessed on: 20 September 2021).

Kraków. UNESCO City of Literature (2013a) *Krakow's Publishing Houses*. Available at: http://krakowcityofliterature.com/city-of-literature/creative-industries/krakows-publishing-houses/ (Accessed on: 20 September 2021).

Kraków. UNESCO City of Literature (2013b) *Why Kraków*. Available at: http://krakowcityofliterature.com/city-of-literature/why-krakow/ (Accessed on: 18 September 2021).

Krawczuk, A. et al. (2010) *Main Market Square 23: The Story of a Krakow Bookshop 1610–2010*. Kraków: Wydawnictwo MWK.

Kreidler, J. and Trounstine, Ph. J. (2005) "Creative Community Index. Measuring Progress toward a Vibrant Silicon Valley", *Inquiries into Culture Series*. Cultural Initiatives Silicon Valley. Available at: https://www.issuelab.org/resources/8886/8886.pdf (Accessed on: 18 October 2021).

Kurowska, A. and Theiss, M. (2018) "Solidarity practices in Poland their social capital foundation", [in:] Lahusen, C. and Grasso, M. (eds.) *Solidarity in Europe: Citizens' Responses in Times of Crisis*. Cham: Palgrave Macmillan. https://doi.org/10.1007/978-3-319-73335-7_5.

Landry, Ch. (2000) *The Creative City: A Toolkit for Urban Innovators*. London: Earthscan.

Landry, Ch. (2018) *Kraków uwolniony. Uwolnienie energii kreatywnego potencjału miasta. Raport dla Miasta Krakowa* (typescript), Kraków.

Martin-Brelot, H. et al. (2010) "The spatial mobility of the "Creative Class': A European perspective", *International Journal of Urban and Regional Research*, 34(4), 854–870.

Miasto Kraków. BIP (2021) *Instytucje Kultury*. Available at: https://www.bip.krakow.pl/?mmi=22 (Accessed on: 15 October).

Ministerstwo Nauki i Szkolnictwa Wyższego (2020) *Polska Mapa Infrastruktury Badawczej*. Available at: https://www.gov.pl/attachment/a5839d22-680b-44ed-9708-cbaefd9498d2 (Accessed on: 20 September 2021).

Montalto, V. et al. (2019) *The Cultural and Creative Cities Monitor. 2019 edition*. Luxembourg: Publications Office of the European Union.

Moretti, E. (2012) *The New Geography of Jobs*. Boston, MA and New York: Houghton Mifflin Harcourt.

Municipality of Kraków (2018) *Kraków Development Strategy: This is where I want to live. Kraków 2030*. Available at: https://www.bip.krakow.pl/plik.php?zid=212318&wer=0&new=t&mode=shw (Accessed on: 17 August 2021).

Murzyn-Kupisz, M. and Działek, J. (2017) *Artyści w przestrzeni miejskiej Krakowa*. Kraków: Universitas.

Peck, J. (2005) "Struggling with the creative class", *International Journal of Urban and Regional Research*, 29(4), 740–770.

Perspektywy (2021) *Ranking wg typów uczelni 2021. Ranking szkół wyższych – Perspektywy 2021*. Available at: https://2021.ranking.perspektywy.pl/ranking/ranking-uczelni-akademickich/rankingi-wg-typow (Accessed on: 15 October 2021).

Pine, II B.J. and Glimore, J.H. (1999) *The Experience Economy: Work Is Theatre and Every Business a Stage: Goods and Services Are No Longer Enough*. Boston, MA: Harvard Business School Press.

Porter, M.E. (2009) *On Competition*. Boston, MA: Harvard Business School.

Rada Miasta Krakowa (2016) *Uchwała nr XXXVII/632/16 z dnia 17 lutego 2016 r. w sprawie przyjęcia programu Kraków – Miasto Literatury UNESCO*. Available at: https://www.bip.krakow.pl/?dok_id=167&sub_dok_id=167&sub=uchwala&query=id%3D21281%26typ%3Du (Accessed on: 30 September 2021).

Rada Ministrów (2020). "Uchwała nr 155 w sprawie przyjęcia 'Strategii Rozwoju Kapitału Społecznego (współdziałania, kultury, kreatywność) 2030'. Załącznik nr 1", *Monitor Polski*. Warszawa.

Rogerson, R.J. (1999) "Quality of life and city competitiveness", *Urban Studies*, 36(-5–6), 969–985.

Sanetra-Szeliga, J. (2017) "Kultura jako element składowy jakości życia w mieście", *Kultura i rozwój*, 1(2). https://doi.org/10.7366/KIR.2017.1.2.03

Santagata, W. (2002) "Cultural Districts, Property Rights and Sustainable Economic Growth", *International Journal of Urban and Regional Research*, 26(1), 9–23

Scott, A. J. (2000) *Cultural Economy of Cities: Essays on the Geography of Image-Producing Industries*. London-Thousand Oaks, CA-New Dehli: Sage.

Smith, R. and Warfield, K. (2007) "The creative city: A matter of values", [in:] Cooke, Ph. and Lazzeretti, L. (eds.) *Creative Cities, Cultural Clusters and Local Development*. Cheltenham and Northampton, MA: Elgar, 287–312.

Stryjakiewicz, T. (2008) "Rozwój sektora kreatywnego w regionach metropolitarnych", [in:] Parysek, J.J. and Stryjakiewicz, T. (eds.) *Region społeczno-ekonomiczny i rozwój regionalny*. Poznań: Bogucki Wydawnictwo Naukowe, 105–119.

Throsby, D. (2001) *Economics and Culture*. Cambridge, New York, Port Melbourne, Madrid, and Cape Towne: Cambridge University Press. Available at: https://doi.org/10.1017/CBO9781107590106 (Accessed on: 30 September 2021).

Törnqvist, G. (1983) "Creativity and the renewal of regional life", [in:] Buttimer, A. (ed.) *Creativity and Context: A Seminar Report. Lund Studies in Geography*, 50, Lund: Gleerup, 91–112.

UNESCO (2004) *Creative Cities Network. Mission Statement*. Available at: https://es.unesco.org/creative-cities/sites/default/files/uccn_mission_statement_rev_nov_2017.pdf (Accessed on: 14 October 2021).

UNESCO Institute for Statistics (2009) *UNESCO Framework for Cultural Statistics (FCS)*. Montreal: UNESCO Institute for Statistics. Available at: http://www.uis.unesco.org/culture/Documents/framework-cultural-statistics-culture-2009-en.pdf (Accessed on: 14 October 2021).

Urząd Statystyczny w Krakowie (2020) Szkolnictwo wyższe w województwie małopolskim w roku akademickim 2019/2020. *Informacje sygnalne*. Available at: https://krakow.stat.gov.pl/opracowania-biezace/informacje-sygnalne/edukacja/szkolnictwo-wyzsze-w-wojewodztwie-malopolskim-w-roku-akademickim-20192020,1,14.html (Accessed on: 14 October 2021).

Villa, N. (2018) *CVSuite Data Dives: The Creative Vitality Index Explained*. Available at: https://cvsuite.org/2018/04/09/cvsuite-data-dives-the-creative-vitality-index-explained/ (Accessed on: 14 October 2021).

WIPO. 2003. *Guide on Surveying the Economic Contribution of the Copyright-Based Industries*. Available at: http://www.wipo.int/edocs/pubdocs/en/copyright/893/wipo_pub_893. (Accessed on: 14 October 2021).

Wojnar, K. (2016) *Polska klasa kreatywna*. Warszawa: Narodowe Centrum Kultury.

Zukin, S. (2004) *Dialogue on Urban Cultures: Globalization and Culture in an Urbanizing World*. World Urban Forum, UN-Habitat, Barcelona, 13–17 September. Available at: http://mirror.unhabitat.org/downloads/docs/3070_67594_K0471966%-20WUF2-2.pdf (Accessed on: 14 October 2021).

Interviews: 1. Interview with a senior official in the municipality who is currently dealing with the cultural policy (21 October 2021).

Notes

1 Wojnar makes a valid reservation about the calculation – the data available from Statistics Poland (study Z-12) does not include self-employed individuals, those working based on freelance agreements and commission contracts (contracts of mandate), all of which are very popular within the Polish creative class. Due to the complexity of the subject, her attempt to appraise the size of the creative class in Kraków (and several other cities) remains the only one available and is, therefore, worth citing. Given the dynamic growth of the creative class over the years (Wojnar, 2016, p. 117), the increasing number of cultural and creative industries (see below), and the general development of Kraków, it can be assumed that the size of the creative class in Kraków has also grown since 2010.

2 REGON register (National Official Business Register) is an all-Poland database of national economic entities run by Statistics Poland, with which all entities conducting economic activity in Poland are required to register. The data in the register includes the allocation of economic activity types to NACE Rev. 2.

3 In one of the most prestigious university rankings in Poland, Perspektywy, the Jagiellonian University again won in the "university" category. Other winners included the Pedagogical University of Kraków (first position in the "pedagogical universities" category) and AGH University of Science and Technology (second position in the "technical universities" category) (Perspektywy, 2021).

4 Landry (2000) also emphasises the importance of soft and hard elements in building a creative environment. For the creative environment to work, a communication and transport network, as well as a financial base that allows investment in new products and services, are needed (Andersson, 1985).

5 This definition aligns, to a great extent, with the definition adopted by Statistics Poland, which can facilitate the statistical analysis of entities belonging to the cultural and creative industries. It includes a statistical framework, as proposed by the ESSnet-Culture group (Bína et al., 2012, p. 44) that includes not only ten cultural domains (e.g., heritage, visual arts, advertising, etc.) but also six functions (e.g., creation, production/publishing, dissemination/trade, etc.).

6 Cultural industries and creative industries are defined differently by various authors, with definitions often overlapping and the use of other terms, such as "creative sector" or "creative economy". The distinction between cultural and creative industries made here is only to clarify the scope of the domain in question. Both industries will be further analysed jointly.

7 Cultural and creative goods and services are goods (material objects) or services meeting human needs, resulting from the activities of cultural and creative entities. They are defined, first of all, by the requirement of human creativity in their production, by being a carrier of symbolic messages and meanings for their recipients and are (potentially) covered with some form of intellectual property protection (Bińczycka et al., 2017, p. 39).

8 One needs to be aware of the reservations concerning an analysis of the REGON database. Its structure does not allow detailed data on the cultural and creative industries to be extracted in the case of some of the subclasses (e.g., 63.91, 73.11), so all the entities registered there are included in the analysis. Some of the data may not be up to date, as changes in the status of a registered entity are often delayed. However, given the illustrative purpose of the data for this chapter, the shortcomings of REGON are accepted.

9 Each domain includes different economic activities categorised according to the NACE Rev. 2 (in Poland: PKD – Polish Classification of Economic Activity), i.e., Advertising: advertising agencies activities; Architecture: architectural activities; Artistic education: out-of-school forms of cultural education; Audiovisual and multimedia arts: retail sale of music and video recordings in specialised stores, publishing of computer games, motion picture, video and television programme production activities, motion picture, video and television programme post-production activities, motion picture projection activities, sound recording and music publishing activities, broadcasting, public and licence television programmes broadcasting, rental of video tapes and CDs, DVDs, etc.; Books and press: retail sale of books in specialised stores, retail sale of newspapers and stationery in specialised stores, book publishing, publishing of newspapers, publishing of journals and periodicals, news agency activities, translation and interpretation activities; Cultural heritage: operation of historical sites and buildings and similar visitor attractions (this class includes operation and preservation of historical sites and buildings); Visual arts: specialised deign activities, photographic activities, artistic creation activities, Manufacture of jewellery and related articles, Manufacture of imitation jewellery and related articles, Retail sale of watches, clocks and jewellery in specialised stores. The statistics include also manufacture of musical instruments that would be classified under Performing arts – this is not included in Figures 10.3 and 10.4 due to the very small number of entities registered in REGON (in 2021: 15) compared with other domains.

10 Since 2004, UNESCO has been awarding the title in seven creative fields: literature, design, crafts and folk art, music, film, media arts, and gastronomy. At the moment, there are 246 cities that make up this network, including four from Poland (apart from Kraków: Katowice – music, Wrocław – literature and Łódź – film).

11 Kraków's metropolitan functions[1]

Jacek Purchla

Metropolitan functions are the key to diagnosing the condition of the city and developing a proper strategy for its development. In thinking about today's Kraków, one needs to talk loudly about the mechanisms of the development of these functions and their variability in time, rather than just about the functions themselves. The question of the metropolitan functions is primarily one about the place of Kraków in Europe's network of settlement, and the nature of the changes that the city is undergoing while increasing its competitiveness. A city is a living organism, and the speed and complexity of the change it is undergoing is a measure of its development.

The discourse on the role of metropolitan cities

Three characteristic issues have come to the fore in the international discourse on the role of metropolitan cities during their development since the 1990s.

The first is the renaissance of the concept of central cities. Large metropolises are currently the decision-making centres that control the globalising financial markets and the services sector. In this sense, they are hubs of information and disposition of a supranational character. In this way, the process of concentration of decision-making centres into the major local hubs is progressing in parallel with the globalisation of the economy. Symptomatically, not only did the IT revolution not weaken the position of the metropolitan centres, it even reinforced their role as communication networks hubs offering easy access to information, the media, and complex services from the realms of culture, science, and education (Purchla and Sepioł, 1997, p. 3).

The second aspect of the discussion results from a claim that is gaining in popularity, namely that the economic power of a state is the sum total of the economic potential of the metropolitan regions construed as the zone of impact of their central cities. Therefore, the great metropolitan centres are the engines of economic growth (Jacobs, 1986).

Finally, the third important aspect in this discussion is the level of creativity and innovation in urban centres. To be successful, besides providing a positive environment for business, a city must offer a positive environment

DOI: 10.4324/9781003252757-12

for people and/or creativity. There are two features characteristic of contemporary large cities: toleration of "aliens" and a lack of tolerance for mediocrity. However, only a few cities become incubators of these new intellectual values. The level of a city's creativity depends on the combination of political and economic factors (Purchla and Sepioł, 1997, pp. 3–4).

The competitiveness of Polish metropolitan centres

The question about the conditions of excellence – that is, those particular conditions that are decisive for the success of the cities and for turning them into centres of politics, business, and primarily of intellectual and artistic creation – is therefore also a question about Kraków. It cannot be separated from a more extensive context and the question of whether Poland has conducted a policy towards metropolitan cities after 1989. I am convinced that there was, and is, no policy that would reinforce the metropolitan functions of Kraków, Wrocław, Poznań, and Gdańsk, and make better use of their potential. Poland is a unitary state. This destroys the polycentric tradition based on a network of multiple strong metropolitan centres and favours Warsaw. In other words, after 1989, the distance between the capital and the remaining "big cities" has continued to increase. From the point of view of the developmental interests of Poland, this is a negative phenomenon. Its syndrome is the centralism present in areas of importance for the metropolitan successes, such as the banking sector, public media, and transport infrastructure (Purchla, 2018, p. 52).

What is the competitive capacity of Polish cities in contemporary Europe? This is how Andreas Billert described the competitive edge of Polish metropolitan centres back in 2012:

> Polish cities not only do not show the slightest traits of modern development, but even the legacy spatial, construction, historical and cultural, social, and economic potential they have is undergoing degradation and destruction. What is decisive today for the development of the post-industrial city is being destroyed in them. In this way, Polish cities have lost their competitiveness compared to other European cities, together with the possibility of building it in the nearest future. Due to the transformation policy, Polish cities, and the Polish state together with them, have been marginalised and reduced to the level of the European Union's 'third world'.
>
> (Billert, 2012, p. 93)

After 1989, Poland lacked a state policy for the largest cities as the engines for growth. The obvious claim that these are the metropolitan centres that generate growth was replaced by the state's fiscal centralism that left the cities with only 10% of the revenue that their local governments generated! The scale of resistance and ignorance of central authorities towards the nascent local governments was particularly visible in the big cities. It is hard to resist the impression that the fathers of the Polish local government reform of 1990 lacked imagination. The metropolitan cities were not treated as the main centres of growth (Błaszczyk, 2013, p. 99) and in creating the local governments, the state primarily wanted to use them for the straightforward administration (and not governance) of bankrupt municipal resources. The mistrust, if not the downright fear of the central administration to give up its competences, remains visible in the budget structure of our local and regional governments. In the "soft" system of central distribution, the municipal government is shorn of efficient instruments for building the metropolitan power of the city (Purchla, 2018, p. 53). In this way, in 1990, the development of Kraków was not based on good law, and without it, the metropolitan potential of the historic capital of Poland cannot be properly used.

The city and politics: a Kraków experience

Development of metropolitan functions is a long-term process. At the same time, it is hard to overestimate the dependency between a city's success and politics. Such has been the experience of Kraków in the last 200 years. The decisions and impulses decisive for the fate of our city came from afar. It is enough to remember that:

- In 1815, in Vienna, the European powers decided to establish the Republic of Kraków (also known as the Free State of Kraków), a decision that became the foundation for the city's brief prosperity in the first half of the 19th century.
- 30 years later, also in Vienna, the decision was made to allow Austria to annex and fortify Kraków. *Festung Krakau* became an important city-forming factor that contradicted with the metropolitan ambitions of Kraków in Galicia, as it strangled the modernising city, stripped it of any chance for metropolitan development, and provincialised it. This is a model example of how the city-forming functions can clash with the capital functions, and an explanation for why Kraków of the late 19th and early 20th centuries – a time especially formative for European urban development – developed no new city centre alternative to the Main Market Square.
- In 1939, the decision to force Kraków into the role of the capital of the General Government was reached in Berlin, with visions of transforming the ancient capital of Poland into a model German city – the Nuremberg of the East.
- In 1949, the decision to build Nowa Huta, the Polish Magnitogorsk, were made somewhere between Moscow and Warsaw. Nowa Huta significantly changed Kraków's functions, urban form, and social structure.

It is only in this broader historical perspective that one can appreciate the independent decisions of President Juliusz Leo and the sovereignty of the local governments who, in creating "the Greater Kraków" in around 1910, made real the vision of a modern Central European metropolis – as the centre of academic and cultural life and an administrative centre, as well as a centre of economic life that was gaining importance. The heterogeneity of Kraków's functional model became the city's forte in the 20th century (Purchla, 2018, p. 54).

Culture heritage as a metropolitan function of Kraków

A key role in this combination of various functions was played by the heritage of the ancient capital of Poland, in its both tangible and non-tangible dimensions. It was no coincidence that in the Concept for the Spatial Management of the Country formulated by Jerzy Buzek's government in 2001, "Kraków was recognised a hub highly saturated with symbolic functions" (Ziobrowski, Jarczewski, Kafka, 2012, p. 78). Beyond doubt, Kraków belongs to those ancient cities of our continent where the past and tradition significantly determine the contemporary development. Moreover, between Warsaw, Berlin, Prague, Bratislava, Vienna, and Budapest, it is the only city of that size with historically developed metropolitan functions to have been degraded to the role of a provincial centre. Today, the cultural heritage of Kraków needs to be construed not only in the national, but also in the universal dimension. The potential of heritage is the natural capital that Kraków brought into the 21st century. It is the first metropolitan function that determines its position in Europe even today. The archetype of the nation's spiritual capital reinforced in the 19th and 20th centuries is decisive for it, as it bolsters Kraków's significant role as the element that integrates Poles, and at the same time, it is crucial for the very high recognition of the city in Europe and in the world.

Kraków's cultural heritage also has its extraordinary tangible dimension: its perfectly preserved historic urban tissue and built heritage of the highest quality with, last but not least, its museum collections. It is the variety, integrity, continuity, authenticity, grandeur, artistic class, and substance of Kraków's cultural heritage that is decisive for the supra-local dimension of this resource: a fact validated by the inscribing of Kraków on the original UNESCO World Heritage List in 1978.

Therefore, it is no coincidence that, especially after Poland's accession to the European Union, cultural tourism has become an important factor boosting the dynamic of the economic growth of Kraków and Małopolska! Success in tourism also means that Kraków has overcome the impact of the crisis caused by the lessons of communism and its aftermath. Today Kraków is "trendy". The change in its image is owed not only to overcoming the environmental catastrophe, but also to the quick liquidation of its aftermath through activity in the field of heritage conservation. That was possible thanks to a particular form of state patronage that is the parliament-sponsored Kraków National Fund (NFRZK). Conservation efforts have thoroughly changed the image of Kraków's city centre as well as Kazimierz – the former Jewish district that in the 1990s was still the symbol of the tragic fate of the heritage of the disinherited in Central and Eastern Europe.

What must be emphasised finally is the social aspect of cultural heritage. For Kraków is the only major historic city within the current boundaries of Poland that survived the tragedy of the Second World War undamaged – it is a symbol of continuity and permanence. Through its heritage, it symbolises the essence of European civilisation best of all the Polish cities, simultaneously remaining "Poland's quintessential home". Through the power of its brand and through the attractiveness of its heritage, Kraków has potential in the game of metropolises. It is precisely this heritage that is decisive for Kraków remaining Poland's second metropolis rather than but one of the 16 regional capitals (Purchla, 2018, pp. 49–51).

Heritage, however, goes beyond just the tangible goods of culture, as it extends to our memory, choices, and identity. Cultural heritage is a category with its own dynamic, a process of continuous interpretation of the past. The notion of cultural heritage reflects both the attitude of the society to the world of values and the very process of their reinterpreting. In Kraków, this process is infinite. For playing the game of heritage here also denotes fulfilling the dreams of the city's metropolitan power. In this sense, Kraków is certainly among Europe's key heritage poleis – "the Europolis of heritage".

Europolises and the polycentric tradition of settlement networks in Poland

The number of criteria defining the "europolises" in the aforementioned Concept for the Spatial Management of the Country from 2001 includes:

- a multifunctional character
- a demographic potential of at least 500,000 inhabitants, with growth perspectives
- a complex structure of employment with opportunities to grow
- being a hub in the transport system
- a developed centre of science and higher education
- a high-quality human environment (natural and anthropogenic)
- large and receptive investment and consumption markets.

The Polish cities recognised as "Europolises" in the document were Warsaw, the Tricity (Gdańsk, Gdynia, and Sopot), Poznań, and Kraków (Ziobrowski, Jarczewski, Kafka, 2012, pp. 74–75).

The vision of Poland as a polycentric network metropolis is also dominant in the Concept for the Spatial Management of the Country 2030, a document adopted by the Council of Ministers on 13 December 2011. Intended to be the Polish contribution to the idea of coherent European space, it is based on the polycentric tradition of the settlement network in Poland. However, that concept absolutely unrealistically increases the number of Polish metropolitan centres to 10–12 (Ziobrowski, Jarczewski, Kafka, 2012, p. 79).

The polycentric arrangements of the Polish settlement network, a product of a long historical process, was, however, practically questioned recently. Krzysztof Nawratek was right to notice that the Polish regional metropolitan centres failed to exploit the opportunity of becoming "an important centre on the European scale". That failure results mostly from the centralist aspirations of Warsaw and its functional hypertrophy, the animosities between the local governments, and the provincial focus of thinking limited solely to the territory of Poland rather than the status quo and potential scenarios for the future (Nawratek, 2008, p. 54).

Let us add here that researchers have rightly emphasised that

> the functional centralisation does not need to denote spatial centralisation and concentration, especially with today's technology in mind. Even France, a flagship example of centralism, has analysed the spatial development of the country and consciously decided to move such institutions as the National School of Administration and the offices of Interpol out of Paris.
>
> (Kokoszkiewicz, 2012, pp. 188–189)

The Polish tradition of the polycentric model of the settlement network, which even back before the Second World War was based on what was known as the five civilisation centres of Warsaw, Kraków, Poznań, Lwów (Lviv), and Wilno (Vilnius), was always closer to the German tradition "where the central offices are distributed evenly around the country, and even the civil servants are employed to serve in the ministries in equal numbers from all the federal countries" (Kokoszkiewicz, 2012, p.189). Sharing of the state functions by the capital cities is also natural in the post-communist countries. It is enough to quote the examples of St Petersburg, Brno, and Košice as the second cities that are home to the high offices of the Russian Federation (the Constitutional Court of the Russian Federation), the Czech Republic (the Constitutional Court, the Supreme Court, and the Czech Public Rights Defender/Ombudsman), and the Slovak Republic (the Constitutional Court of Slovakia), respectively.

The political "incompatibility" of Kraków

So the fate of Polish metropolises depends to a great degree on the "Warsaw distribution list". A pathology that, in the case of Kraków, is aggravated by the inefficiency of lobbying by the local political class, as in this system an independent mayor from outside the power circles in Warsaw is not a lobbyist. And yet, this is the particular situation of Jacek Majchrowski, who has governed Kraków for five terms. The first direct election of the Mayor of Kraków was held in 2002, and in its second round, Jacek Majchrowski,

Professor of Law (Jagielloniensis) and the Voivode (Governor) of Kraków, during the rule of the Alliance of the Democratic Left (SLD) in 1996–97, won against Józef Lassota, one of the former Solidarity mayors of the city. That opened the "era" of Majchrowski who, as "an independent politician", has held the sceptre of Kraków since 2002 without interruption. For the first time, this has given the city a political stabilisation that has lasted for many years, and which coincided with Poland becoming a member of the European Union in 2004. As much as the strategy of the successive Kraków local governments of the 1990s was based on the release of simple reserves, with the city's investment capability being highly limited, the year 2004 opened entirely new potential for development. The EU funds and regulations, a very favourable economic environment, and the overcoming of the barrier of transport inaccessibility of Kraków (notably with Poland entering the Schengen Zone and with the breaking of the state monopoly on air traffic) provided the grounds for a prosperity that rapidly expediated the process of multidimensional change.

A particular feature of the Majchrowski "era" was the political "incompatibility" of the Mayor of Kraków with the successive governments in Warsaw, which resulted in a number of negative consequences for Kraków, especially as the transfers from the state budget, which were envisaged by the system of public finance developed early in the 1990s, accounted for 50% of the municipality's revenue. This effectively makes a large city hostage to central power, a recipient of the clientelism of Polish ministerial silos. The political independence, if not downright "incompatibility", of Mayor Majchrowski not only meant the exclusion of Kraków from the list of cities hosting the UEFA Euro 2012 European Football Championship, but also omitting Poland's second city from the strategies for road infrastructure development.

Examples of weakening Kraków's development potential by the sectoral policy conducted by the centralist state abound. They include the crisis of regional television, many years of blocking the development of Kraków–Balice Airport, which was managed by a company controlled by Warsaw's Okęcie Airport, the chaotic defortification and demilitarisation conducted by the Ministry of National Defence in pursuit of short-term gain and to the detriment of the city, and settling the obligations of the State Treasury towards the Catholic Church at the cost of the municipality and behind its back! Today the central government, its budget, and companies owned by the State Treasury make decisions about where to direct the opportunities for city development (Purchla, 2018, pp. 56–57). The negative impact of the obnoxious centralism on Polish cities is described by Mateusz Kokoszkiewicz (Kokoszkiewicz, 2012, pp. 188–189). Let us add that Polish law allows businesses to move their registered addresses to wherever they want, fictitiously, as this is only on paper. In this way, many Polish local governments were stripped of millions of zlotys of revenue, most of which was pumped into Warsaw. Such a policy undermines the competitiveness of the city and its fate becomes a function of political clientelism. Moreover, the future of Kraków depends on too many actors, as, apart from the municipal government and "the Poland of the ministerial silos" we also have the governor, the regional government, and the local governments of the communes surrounding Kraków, as well as the PKP Polish State Railway in play.

At the same time, Kraków has been undeniably successful. For looking at it as a process, resource, potential, and function, today one needs to address not only the rapid change of the growth model and mechanisms, but also that Kraków exploited the significant change that was the driver of development after 1989. This success is realised to a great extent outside the local government. The constituents of Kraków's power include the scale and class of its heritage, the power of its brand, and its high recognition, as well as its attractiveness to tourists and academic potential.

It is a paradox that the tourist internationalisation of Kraków, and predominantly of the heritage gathered here, goes hand-in-hand with its clear marginalisation in state policies. From the perspective of Warsaw, post-1998, Kraków is but one of the 16 regional capitals and not the country's second metropolis.

Kraków as an academic centre

It was the university function, and not the political one, that was of key importance for the metropolitan character of Kraków in the 20th century. It was in the last 100 years that Kraków returned to its position as a major academic centre, recently exceeding 150,000 students. It is the only large university centre between Warsaw, Berlin, Prague, Vienna, Bratislava, Budapest, and Kyiv that is not at the same time the capital of the state. Today, Kraków gathers 15% of Poland's entire academic potential (which is nearly on a par with the far bigger Warsaw). Kraków is eager to promote the Jagiellonian University: Poland's oldest university and one of the longest operating universities in Europe. Since 1872, it has also been home to the well-deserved Polish Academy of Arts and Sciences (PAU), reborn in 1989 after four decades of dormancy under communism. It is no coincidence either that the National Centre for Science started its operation nowhere else but in Kraków (Purchla, 2018, pp. 186–187). The rapid development of the Kraków research and higher education hub was accompanied by the development of material resources. The largest investment of an urban-building character in the first two decades of the 21st century was the construction of the Campus of the 600th Anniversary of the Refounding of the Jagiellonian University in Pychowice. The campus also attracted Motorola and Onet, who built their thoroughly modern offices in its vicinity, and the John Paul II Pontifical University, which built its monumental library there. The university function not only significantly determines the space of the city but is also decisive for its character and position in the settlement network of Central and Eastern Europe (Wdowiarz-Bilska, Zuziak, 2008, pp. 172–185).

In summing up his long and varied academic experience before the UK's House of Lords, Ralf Dahrendorf, one of the most eminent intellectuals of contemporary Europe, reformer of German universities in the 1960s, European Commissioner for Research, Science, and Education in the 1970s, Rector of the London School of Economics, and the Warden of St Anthony's College at the University of Oxford in the 1980s and the 1990s, pointed to three necessary constituents of the modern system of higher education, namely that it should:

- be accessible to anyone who can and wants to study
- be sufficiently varied to satisfy different needs, from basic research to their practical application, from general education to lifelong learning
- step beyond the surrounding world – of business, local communities, and society as such.

In his book, *Universities after Communism*, Dahrendorf emphasised that after the change of 1989, the countries of post-communist Europe failed to develop any of these necessary constituents. Openness to the civil environment, and especially to the world of business and politics, is a near-taboo subject. Such relationships are treated as tarnishing the autonomy newly regained by universities (Dahrendorf, 2000, pp. 15–16). For this reason, Tomasz Domański is right to note that "as yet the strategies of development in Polish cities and regions have been too insufficiently correlated to the strategic potential of institutions of higher education operating on their premises". The author also pays attention to aspects of the new relationship between the city and the region such as:

- the university being the city's and region's partner in the process of its development
- the university being the provider of a professional workforce
- the university being the vehicle of innovations that are important for the cities and regions
- the university being an independent adviser and objective reviewer [and not sycophant – J.P.]

it is not insignificant either to construe regions and cities through the perspective of universities, thinking of institutions of higher education as an element of the competitiveness of cities and regions and an element in their positioning (Domański, 2011, pp. 15–24).

Therefore, the current role of the universities, unlike the traditional one of the "impenetrable ivory towers", should certainly be based on the intensification of their mission in the context of regional development. This means the inclusion of the universities in the process of creating and stimulating entrepreneurship, which can allow them to become local development catalysts. It is true that the model of a "glocal" university is based on openness, a contemporary value that is becoming the foundation for building its excellence.

A particular role of the universities is to generate new values. Therefore, if today it is beyond doubt that the university is an institution absolutely crucial for the creative economy and that, as Jane Jacobs claims, the city is a collection of chances, opportunities, prospects, and openings of all types (Florida, 2010, p. 288), then our universities must certainly take up the challenge of the game to be played with the environment, in which partner relationships with the city's and region's local governments must play a special role.

Kraków – an ideopolis?

In his acclaimed book, *The Rise of the Creative Class*, Richard Florida hit the bull's eye in stating that economic development at the regional level is fuelled by creative people who prefer tolerance and strongly differentiated locations that are open to new ideas (Florida, 2010, pp. 256–257). The author believes that the core of the creative class are scientists and engineers, architects and designers, people working in education and entertainment, artists and musicians, i.e., people whose economic function is to create new concepts and ideas, new technologies, and new creative content. A factor that attracts creative capital and stimulates the development of high-tech sectors is variety. Therefore, the successful cities of today must possess this "openness to variety" (Florida, 2010, pp. 31, 34, 271). Anna Marszałek is therefore right to note that when a knowledge-based economy becomes the foundation for development, the *ideopolis* becomes the engine for the process of building a metropolitan area (Marszałek, 2012, pp. 58–66).

Does Kraków have a chance of becoming an *ideopolis*, a city generating new ideas in the heart of a learning region? The question about the conditions of excellence – the particular conditions that are decisive for the success of cities and turning them into the hubs of politics, economy, and predominantly of intellectual and artistic creation – is also a question about Kraków. Looking at Kraków, you can risk the claim that the administrative reform of 1998 weakened the potential of the creative class in the city. Today, Kraków is a festive city that is recognised in Europe, yet is it a creative one?

As the Polish state has no coherent policy towards big cities, and yet our metropolises release and multiply their resources in open competition above and beyond the country's borders, then the academic function has become a priority for Kraków and its local government, including in the face of the inevitable globalisation of urban-forming processes. Moreover, the academic and intellectual function of Kraków is strongly in tune with the potential of its heritage! For today's "uniqueness and particularity" of a city is a value that turns into the opportunity to oppose the unified model of the global world. Richard Florida's theory of creative capital and his three T's (Technology, Talent, and Tolerance) lead to the conclusion that economic growth at a regional level is, to a great degree, fuelled by the clusters of the creative people – the "vehicles" of creative capital – who prefer places of variety and tolerance that are simultaneously open to new ideas (Florida, 2010, p. 230).

Thus, universities become the beating hearts of creativity. In the creative economy, any region with a major university running scientific research will have an advantage over other cities (Florida, 2010, p. 302).

The dream of the *ideopolis* and the synergy of the academic circles with business is already making an impact on the spectacular development of the sector of modern business services, which already employs around 100,000 young people from various countries in Kraków. Opening here are not only ordinary outsourcing centres but also hubs of advanced research and innovation. The city has become the sector's leader in Europe, ahead of Dublin. This was possible also thanks to the European Union and its cohesion policy that significantly influenced the city's transport accessibility after 2004. The rapid development of air connections and the construction of a network of motorways and fast railroad connections to Warsaw, Berlin, Prague, Vienna, and Budapest over the past ten years has boosted the importance of the Kraków transport hub. Highly significant for such spectacular development of the sector of modern business services in Kraków was not only the improvement of infrastructure and its competitiveness, but also a radical improvement in the quality of life in the city.

Kraków has an opportunity to become an ideal place: a city generating new ideas and acting as the heart of a learning region. These are the Kraków universities that play the role of catalysts of local development, for their particular role is to generate new values. For this reason, the university is an absolutely key institution for the creative economy, and institutions of higher education become elements of the city and region's competitive advantage and a tool for its positioning. Kraków's post-1989 experience confirms that the grouping of cultural, educational, research, and information functions has played a profound role in the transformation of its model of operation. The cumulation of the forces of these functions triggered synergy effects and released the creativity and innovation potential that was frozen under communism. This is where the accuracy of the new vision of Kraków created by its local government reborn in 1990 should be found. It resulted from the conviction that Kraków is not, and will not be, a global metropolis but can become a creative city. Fernand Braudel used to say that "towns are like electrical transformers. They increase the tension".

Bibliography

Billert, A. (2012) "Miasta w postindustrialnej Europie i w kleszczach polskiej transformacji", [in:] Filar, P., Kubicki, P. (eds.) *Miasto w działaniu. Zrównoważony rozwój z perspektywy oddolnej*. Warszawa: Instytut Obywatelski, pp. 55–112.

Błaszczyk, M. (2013) *W poszukiwaniu socjologicznej teorii rozwoju miast. Meandry ekonomii politycznej*. Warszawa: Wydawnictwo Naukowe Scholar.

Dahrendorf, R. (2000) *Universities after Communism*. Hamburg: Körber-Stiftung.

Domański, T. (2011) "Rola uniwersytetów w promocji polskich miast i regionów – nowe wyzwania strategiczne", [in:] Domański, T. (ed.) *Marketing akademicki. Rola uniwersytetów w promocji miast i regionów*. Łódź: Wydawnictwo Uniwersytetu Łódzkiego, pp. 15–32.

Florida, R. (2010) *Narodziny klasy kreatywnej oraz jej wpływ na przeobrażenia w charakterze pracy, wypoczynku, społeczeństwa i życia codziennego.* Warszawa: Narodowe Centrum Kultury.

Jacobs, J. (1986) *Cities and the Wealth of Nations: Principles of economic life.* Harmondsworth – Middlesex: Penguin Books.

Kokoszkiewicz, M. (2012) "Miasto a prawo", [in:] Filar, P., Kubicki, P. (eds.) *Miasto w działaniu. Zrównoważony rozwój z perspektywy oddolnej.* Warszawa: Instytut Obywatelski 2012, pp. 159–195.

Markowski, T., Drzazga, D. (eds.) (2008) "Rola wyższych uczelni w rozwoju społeczno-gospodarczym i przestrzennym miast'. *Studia Komitetu Przestrzennego Zagospodarowania Kraju PAN,* 121.

Marszałek, A. (2012) "Potencjał naukowo-badawczy uczelni i jego rola w regionie uczącym się (na przykładzie Małopolski)", [in:] Domański, T. (ed.) *Marketing akademicki. Rola uniwersytetów w promocji miast i regionów.* Łódź: Wydawnictwo Uniwersytetu Łódzkiego, pp. 58–66.

Nawratek, K. (2008) *Miasto jako idea polityczna.* Kraków: "Korporacja Ha!art".

Purchla, J. (ed.) (2019) *Kraków: History & Art.* Kraków: International Cultural Centre.

Purchla, J. (1996) *Kraków – prowincja czy metropolia?* Kraków: Towarzystwo Autorów i Wydawców Prac Naukowych UNIVERSITAS.

Purchla, J. (1998) "Metropolitane Funktionen Krakaus und die neue regionale Einteilung Polens", [in:] Purchla J. (ed.) *Metropolitane Funktionen Krakaus,* Vol. 1. Kraków: Międzynarodowe Centrum Kultury, pp. 59–65.

Purchla, J. (2018) *Miasto i polityka. Przypadki Krakowa.* Kraków: Towarzystwo Autorów i Wydawców Prac Naukowych UNIVERSITAS.

Purchla, J., Sepioł, J. (1997) "Metropolie a rozwój regionalny Polski", *Samorząd Terytorialny,* 11, pp. 3–19.

Sassen, S. (2000) *Cities in a World Economy.* 2nd ed. Thousand Oaks, CA: Pine Forge.

Wdowiarz-Bilska, M., Zuziak, Z. (2008) "Krakowskie uczelnie w przestrzeni miasta", [in:] Markowski, T., Drzazga, D. (eds.) "Rola wyższych uczelni w rozwoju społeczno-gospodarczym i przestrzennym miast". *Studia Komitetu Przestrzennego Zagospodarowania Kraju PAN,* 121, pp. 172–185.

Ziobrowski, Z., Jarczewski, W., Kafka, K. (eds.) (2012) *Modele zarządzania gospodarką przestrzenną w obszarach metropolitalnych i aglomeracjach. Kompendium.* Kraków: Instytut Rozwoju Miast.

Note

1 This is an amended and updated version of my article published originally as Purchla, J. (2014) "Metropolitalne funkcje Krakowa/The Metropolitan Functions of Krakow", [in:] Dziedzic, S., Glińska-Holcer, E. (eds.) *35 lat na Liście UNESCO. Materiały z sesji: Dziedzictwo a wyzwania współczesności. 35 lat Krakowa i Kopalni Soli "Wieliczka" na Liście UNESCO. 5–6 września 2013 r. / 35 Years on the UNESCO List. Materials from a session entitled heritage and Challenges of the Present. 35 Years of Krakow and the Wieliczka Salt Mine on the UNESCO World Heritage List, September 5–6, 2013.* translated by Zespół Tłumaczy Przysięgłych Sigillum and Linqua Lab. Kraków: Wydawnictwo "Czuwajmy", pp. 61–72/pp. 73–82.

Afterword

Kraków: Dialectics of history and change

Robert Pyrah

As the essays in this volume demonstrate, the fall of communism was not the full caesura that is often simplistically assumed. Kraków had preserved a strong sense of its historical mission as "the" Polish cultural capital; the difference was the scale of free public discussion on the subject after 1989, the institutional frameworks to act on that notion, and the parallel revival of urban history specifically on and about it, in tandem with other storied cities across Central and Eastern Europe. This book, with the accompanying explosion in post-1989 studies it references, is testament to that underlying continuity in Kraków's sense of self, notwithstanding the turbulence of political and economic transition. And yet, transition itself, as these essays explore, implies a process far beyond economic change, straddling multiple vectors and dimensions, both tangible and intangible. Foremost among these is a wholescale reshaping of mental frameworks of and around cities in the region within reframed "national" contexts after 1989/1991 (Ukraine), chiming with the introduction's reference to Lynch, emphasising values and ideas being equal to form and function in defining city identity. This manifests in Kraków, as elsewhere, in a dialectical negotiation between the future-facing push toward development, variously defined, in spheres of education, culture, and the economy; and the "pull" of intrinsically normative identity narratives framed around a city's history.

This "presence of the past" in discussions of city identity and urban planning, at both national and local levels, is the explicit but also spectral red thread of the case studies assembled, and is therefore the focus of these concluding reflections. In offering them, I propose to raise the following question: if Kraków is a "laboratory of change", to what extent is it *sui generis*, versus being a laboratory of wider processes visible across the region? Given the scope of this short discussion, the answer will inevitably be partial, and it is one I would like to leave open for further reflection. To fast forward to a tentative answer, it is one that in large measure pivots on the peculiarly freighted dialectics of history versus change within this specific city context.

While it is surely a truism that every case possesses unique features, there is substantive *historical content* in terms of tangible and intangible heritage pertaining to Kraków's transition that suggests fundamental structural differences with other cases in the Polish discussion alone, to take a manageable frame of reference. Foremost among these is the astonishing continuity of the physical but also social environments noted by authors in this volume, at least for the Polish population of Kraków, throughout the upheavals of the 20th century. This is not to diminish the enormous losses of the Holocaust, which saw a substantial Jewish population decimated (with a not-uncontroversial cultural revival underway in recent years).[1] In relative terms though, Kraków is a case that lacks the near-total population displacement across all ethnic groups, and near-total physical destruction of Warsaw. Nor did Kraków land across a redrawn border after the controversial post-war settlement of Yalta (1945). This was the case with now-Ukrainian Lviv, formerly interwar Poland's third largest city of Lwów (over 50% self-declared "Polish" population, approx. 30% Jewish, 10% Ukrainian), from which almost all the once majority-Polish population were deported. Kraków also differs sharply from Wilno, another once majority-Polish (and Jewish) city that today is largely emptied of the pre-war Polish and Jewish population and its descendants, and is now Vilnius – the capital of Lithuania.[2] Finally, looking at other Polish cities of comparable size and importance, the case of Wrocław is another instance of key structural difference: formerly German Breslau, it was resettled with Poles and saw almost all its German population displaced, having been drained of its once-thriving Jewish community.[3] These other Polish cases, moreover, bear key structural similarities to each other, but Kraków is a clear outlier in the group.

Crowning such differences is a superstructural narrative of significant force, which Jacek Purchla terms "the enduring power of Kraków's capital city stigma".[4] This doubtlessly, in part, motivates the enormous numbers of internal tourists who, as noted in this volume, visit the city year on year, and for all, the emphasis on the perils and pitfalls of *international* tourists, who are (arguably) often of dubious cultural sensitivity, strikes me as a more important index of the city's identity narratives. Massive internal tourism (Broński quotes the statistics in his essay) reflects the city's disproportionately exalted status in the Polish cultural firmament, with visits being a quasi-obligatory rite of passage for schoolchildren. While these factors may appear to root Kraków's sensibility firmly in the past, as opposed to the superficially forward-pulling dynamic behind, say, forging multiple budget airline connections across Europe, Ewa Chojecka suggests a key nuance worth exploring further. Writing in *Herito*, she suggests:

> Kraków functions colloquially as a *pars pro toto* of national memory [... but] *the resulting threat of unbearable pathos is eliminated by accents of distancing irony and Young Poland's grotesque.* This awareness of cultural continuity, so rare in unstable Mitteleuropa, seems to be an important determinant of Kraków's local memory.[5]

In other words, that same "cultural continuity", which could make for rigidity and small-c conservatism, reinforced by a "rite of passage" status for millions of Poles, are in her eyes tempered by a cultural aspect of substantial mitigating power.

Young Poland was a development roughly contemporaneous with other Arts and Crafts movements in Europe, often overlapping visually in forms deriving from Art Nouveau, and therefore a high point of pan-European "modernism". It sought new forms of aesthetic expression to convey (at the time) evolved sensibilities across a range of artforms: from poetry and drama to stained glass.[6] Particularly through its most exalted exponent Stanisław Wyspiański (1869–1907), a Kraków native, it gained national renown, which further bolstered the city's status.[7] The irony here of course, and an accepted occupational hazard of "heritage", is that of inadvertent ossification – whereby even the most radical of cultural movements, over time, dissipate their radical *content* through museal fixing around their *form*. Some may argue this is the case with Vienna's analogous Jugendstil offshoot, embodied in the rebel artists' creation of the Secession in 1897: today, their gallery is a tourist heirloom in a city shorn of its once vast creative hinterland as part of a much smaller Alpine Republic. This is not to be ungenerous about Austria and its world-class heritage, or its present-day creative industries: rather, it is again to make the point about key forms of social and historical discontinuity, which does not apply at that scale to Kraków's Polish cultural community.

A full examination clearly exceeds the scope of this essay – again, I confine myself to a small number of examples to invite further reflection. But Kraków has arguably succeeded in keeping at least a continuously creative *spirit* alive in certain spheres: examples are mentioned in the essays here, including some nurtured at policy level by the city council (e.g., the creation of a culture district in formerly industrial Zabłocie), but we could also note the "continuous heritage of creativity" in such phenomena as underground fusions of cabaret, jazz, and poetry at the city's legendary club, Piwnica pod Baranami [Cellar under the Sign of the Rams] (e.g., singer-songwriter Marek Grechuta, 1945–2006, Ewa Demarczyk, 1941–2020) during communist times.[8] Again, what matters is less the precise aesthetic content of these creations, which can date quickly – rather, the continuity of spirit behind these efforts. A more recent, but deeply symbolic example is that of the Nowa Huta steelworks, famously installed to help counteract the aristocratic, patriotic, traditionalist spirit of Kraków during communism, and now preserved in repurposed form. Broński, in this volume, discusses the case from the perspective of economics, telling a story that reflects the wider waxing and waning of international capitalism, passing between foreign investors to land in the hands of a global owner – in fact, the world's largest steel conglomerate (Mittal). What is perhaps more interesting for present purposes, however, is how even this and other less visible aspects of the communist urban fabric are being incorporated into the city's discussion of heritage and the built environment, showing a dynamism and adaptability that the outward image of a small-c conservative, former capital often belies.[9]

This notion of inherent adaptability as baked into the city's self-imposed and high-profile negotiation with its past finds analogues elsewhere: in its political history of resistance examined in this volume by Hołuj ("Municipal self-government 1990–2019"); or the relatively recent emphasis on a cultural "experience" economy with engineered value beyond market-led facets, as discussed by Sanetra-Szeliga ("Kraków – an eventful city"). Indeed, a similar lens has been applied to the cultural role of the Catholic Church under communism (here by Hołuj, in "Civil society. From "Solidarity" to urban activism"), for its role as a quasi-political force that gave institutional support to the national cause – most powerfully symbolised by the election to the papacy of the vocally anti-communist Cracovian, Karol Wojtyła (1920–2005; Pope John Paul II from 1978 until his death). Although the Church's role in society and politics today, not least in terms of any "progressive" functions likely merits a different form of scrutiny, one that exceeds the scope here, its force within the *historical* narrative of Kraków's cultural presence of the past, is clear. Seen through these lenses, Kraków's historical identity has a self-conscious dynamism within its cultural DNA. In other words, while its exalted status within the Polish cultural firmament risks a backwards-pulling inclination toward intoxication with an irretrievable past, aspects of the city's cultural heritage, such as they inform the present, are a countervailing influence, since they are *founded* on the idea of creative dynamism. This suggests, at least in theory, an integrative position: forging forward-looking policies on a bedrock of heritage, with a form of progressive licence.

Nevertheless, also on the evidence of these essays, there are important provisos. First, the city still lags behind on certain international metrics, being judged more "artistic" than fully "creative" in some instances (Landry, as quoted in Sanetra-Szeliga's "Kraków. A Creative City"). Second, it does not completely meet a further criterion based around a mainstream western European notion of "tolerance", to judge by perceptions among some minority communities, again quoted by Sanetra-Szeliga (*ibid.*). Furthermore, the Catholic Church's political and social role today, beyond the one it played in vouchsafing national identity under foreign control, does not invite a one-to-one comparison with more secular societies further to the west, which are typically used as the benchmarks of urban cultural development. Another important point concerns the trade-offs noted in various essays here, which to some extent all modernising historic cities need to make between the forces of slapdash capitalism insensitive to heritage or even simple quality, and the urge to "develop".

Yet here, too, the particularly Cracovian dialectic of past–future is visible: notably in the discussion of architecture by Michał Wiśniewski ("Kraków architecture and globalisation"). On the one hand, Kraków occasionally succombs to of the typical aesthetic and developmental pitfalls of globalised capitalism, with anodyne or displeasing developments out of step with their surroundings, e.g., the Unity Tower, or various "big box" shopping centres. On the other hand, Kraków's heritage of cultural vanguardism is reflected in the considerable range of bold, visionary, "evolutionary" architectural projects with high visibility, and of global standing. This is important, as it demonstrates the opposite of "heritage" assuming rigid, historicised garb, from a policy of preserving the past for its own sake to fit the Procrustean bed of self- or externally-imposed formal characteristics. Rather, this is heritage understood as a spirit of cultural innovation, a commitment to quality, and upholding or exceeding mainstream European and global standards. Notable here is the sheer number of initiatives nominated for the Mies van der Rohe Award. These are enumerated in passing by the author but are worth pulling out *in toto* as a remarkable feat over which to pause. So while Kraków does not always get it right, something that it has in common with almost any storied city the world over, there is more than simply the weight of history in the Polish discussion here, and the city's longstanding (1978) status as a UNESCO World Heritage Site pushing for standards. Namely, the city also positively embraces bold, good quality *new* aesthetic forms. These even include the Jagiellonian University's purpose-built, modern campus outside the old city centre. Again, by the example of one of most revered institutions in the country, let alone just the city – we see the notion I am highlighting of dynamism *within* a self-conscious sense of commitment to "history".

At the simplest level of analysis, we can postulate that Cracovian cultural identity, at least in the aesthetic field, may positively allow for progress, insofar as cultural creativity forms part of its self-definition. This squares the circle of small-c conservatism being culturally progressive, but perhaps socially less so by some measures. But as we have seen, to speak of the "dialectics of history and change" is of course also to describe a process (rather than a state) of constant negotiation, often on a case-by-case basis, with our posited notions of the city's self-understanding challenged by the plurality of actors with divergent interests involved in decision-making at the policy level. These, as Purchla and others have attested, can lead to short-sighted planning decisions, even when heritage is interpreted generously as relating to an outward form vs a building's original substance. A recent example (current at the time of writing in early 2022) is that of Polish Railways' (PKP's) lobbying to demolish and rebuild a viaduct and railway bridge built in the mid-19th century close to the city's historic centre, on ul. Grzegórzecka. The bridge had been on the list of protected monuments but was summarily removed in September 2021. This caused a strong reaction from some politicians and the city's storied body known as the Towarzystwo Miłośników Historii i Zabytków Krakowa [officially: Society of Friends of Kraków History and Heritage, but whose literal translation lands closer to "Society of *Lovers* of..."] (founded in 1897, currently with Professor Purchla as its president). Their objections noted the common practice in other European cities to preserve outward form, as, for instance, with the reconstructed Mostar Bridge after the Balkan Wars, and pleaded for the same approach here. Although the case does not speak directly to the progressive dynamism within Kraków's notion of heritage – the Towarzystwo noted it was "a work of exceptional-class technology related to the cultural landscape of Kraków", i.e. they clearly factored in a progressive notion of modern-day function into their notion of preservation.[10] Their apparent failure was described by the author of a press report in his title in the starkest terms as follows: "Once again, cultural barbarism and money won out".[11] Here, then, is another example of the Cracovian "laboratory" assuming contours that are doubtlessly familiar to defenders of heritage in other cities, East and West.[12] Yet once again, the locally specific suggests itself – among other things, through committed agitation by a strongly profiled local group, acting in the name of the city's historic identity and built environment; one that is ready and willing to engage at civil society level to affect wayward policy decisions.[13] The group is manifestly spurred by general, historically evidenced notions of the city's identity and mission, but also on some specific aspects of content – here, a bedrock of innovation and excellence in engineering and architecture.

In short, we have another example of widely understood local notions of heritage (beyond the narrower interpretations relating to preserving the historic centre per UNESCO policy, for example) being peculiarly dynamic in their essence. But we also see, on the evidence of these essays, where these definitions end and where future priorities might begin to evolve. As flagged by Miodunka ("Kraków and its region: mutual relations after 1989"), noteworthy by its absence in generally discussed notions of heritage for Kraków is agriculture. The author comments on the untapped potential to match advances in other areas like research and development, or "business process outsourcing" services. Agriculture may even be one area that the city looks toward in its adaptive notion of heritage, particularly insofar as Kraków has otherwise manifestly absorbed wider European (as well as some global) influences. And these, in turn, now trend towards sustainability: "The challenge for the future lies in the coordination of activities ensuring the coherence and *sustainable* development of the metropolitan area." [Miodunka, emphasis added].

Another notable aspect with arguably untapped potential relates to Kraków having been part of the Austrian-administered crownland of Galicia and Lodomeria during Poland's partitioning. In Kraków's case, Austrian control covered two periods: 1795–1809 and 1846–1918.[14] As these essays have shown, Kraków like other cities has inevitably been subject to the whims of much larger outside forces in politics at a range of scales, from national to imperial, as with its incorporation into Galicia. However, the paradox here is that a past "occupation", placing the city under an increasingly mild jurisdiction (especially after the Austro-Hungarian so-called "Compromise" of 1867, which further devolved government of regions to local magnates), today provides an additional vector of potential (positive) differentiation for the city within the Polish context. In other words, the "Galician" narrative certainly fits Kraków's "unique" historical self-definition in the present-day Polish context.[15] This is all the more potent in the situation this volume's essays clearly describe, where the national government has repeatedly encouraged the pull of resources, funding, even of local tax revenue, to Warsaw.

Belonging to the "Austrian" sphere of influence allowed for greater national self-expression but also offered a flattering narrative of greater "Europeanisation" vis-à-vis the more repressive partitioning powers that ruled other large Polish cities like Warsaw (Russia) or Poznań (Prussia, Germany after 1871). Kraków held Free City's status after the Congress of Vienna, 1815, before being the heart of an Austrian-controlled "Grand Duchy" from 1846. Along with the Galician regional capital of Lwów (now Lviv) it was able to develop cultural institutions, forming the bedrock of "myths" that were, in fact, tangible realities through which (national) cultural consciousness could be expressed and forged.[16] To what extent the concept of Galicia could be activated today around Kraków and its unique identity is moot. To take the somewhat parallel case of now-Ukrainian Lviv: there were attempts in the 1990s to activate this discourse, mainly among a circle of Ukrainian intellectuals (publishing in the now-defunct magazine *Postup*).[17] Within that national context, the "Galician" angle was offered as something *sui generis* to boost the city's prestige inside the matrix of historical memory vs. contemporary evolution; it also reinforced a faultline in the Ukrainian national discussion between East and West that acknowledged Kyiv as capital, but emphasised Lviv the (true) spiritual home of the nation. Its belonging to a "European" past with cultural prestige offered a clear rhetorical boost and differentiating argument to such status. Could something similar be true for Kraków in Poland?

Certainly, Poland's accession to the EU in 2004 is regularly quoted as a major catalyst for Kraków's own development, not only economically, but also rhetorically and symbolically – reinforcing the sense of belonging once again rightfully to the mainstream of European culture and progress. That is certainly a strong factor in the Ukrainian case, which scarcely needs describing: tragically, their "pull to Europe" is today less motivated by prestige, perhaps, than existential survival against an aggressor that uses ancient historical mythologies (one people, Kyivan Rus') to override a democratic will for separate statehood, and to be outside Moscow's political and cultural orbit ("*Euro*maidan" being the emblematic name for the revolution that ousted their pro-Russian president Yanukovych in 2014, the catalyst for Russia's first aggressive moves against Ukraine in Crimea and the Donbas). Kraków's European pull is differently freighted, but shares with Lviv a sense of cultural difference within its own national context. Also analogously, the activation of a "Galician" discourse appears to be relatively marginal in Kraków today, but does have some prominent manifestations in academia and popular culture. In the realm of light commercial kitsch, there are brands (e.g., mineral water) and shops (e.g., tobacco) in Kraków that display the image of Kaiser Franz Joseph I; the International Cultural Centre (MCK) on the market square actively exhibits on aspects related to regional (that is, Galician) history;[18] while "softer" aspects such as Kraków's tourist-baiting horse-drawn carriages and well-developed café and gastronomic culture (occasionally with tuxedo'd waiting staff) as likely noted by savvy tourists, nod very directly in atmosphere and sensibility to Vienna – not Warsaw or Berlin. Whether current developments in Ukraine help reactivate such conscious regional discourses in Kraków remains to be seen – these are of course transnational from a present-day perspective, drawing on longer-standing cultural bonds of experience and practice that traverse political borders. A major barrier to such narratives within Poland appears to be national politics, to judge by these essays, with the centralising force of the present government showing no sign of relenting, and the traditional polycentrism of the Polish urban landscape referenced by Purchla (in "Kraków's metropolitan functions") – which also links Kraków historically to Lwów through Galicia – all but vanished in public discussion and formal policy.[19]

Looking back to look forward, then, appears to be Kraków's *modus operandi*. But it is important also to note the contingencies at work in the story we are telling here. History of course tends to be "read" teleologically. It is all too easy to assume retrospective causality between chains of events, as though their final outcome were inevitable. Hence the importance of seeing the "laboratorium" of developments synchronically, as through these essays. They draw attention to the shifting perspectives and pressures of the time in which they took place. This way of looking exposes the contingencies of the moment, reinforcing how differently things could have turned out with alternative decisions, actions, or circumstances. It also reinforces, once more, the importance of history in the matrix of change for Kraków. To my mind, the city's guiding sense of mission helps explain precisely how it has been able to cement a more or less international profile proportional to its historical cultural stature (e.g., being joint European Capital of Culture, 2000) – despite the enormous hurdles presented, notably in the essays on politics and the economy by Hołuj and Broński. Further, the city's success on a range of measures, such as higher education (per capita far exceeding Warsaw's student population) or culture (festivals and conferences; tourism) was by no small measure *in spite of* central government, not *because* of it. Whether pushing back against Warsaw's centripetal force, with the initiative to become a large centre of "business process outsourcing" that now exceeds even Dublin in size and importance, or in attracting ever-larger numbers of international conferences and festivals, the explanation behind overcoming such odds appears in no small part to be a sense of historic self-importance. In this context, Kraków's widely accepted, apparently by and large stable sense of self is enormously important – but so, too, as I have argued here, is the dynamism inherent in that definition.

This allows the city to embrace certain notions of change within a commonly accepted and UNESCO-sanctioned mission to vouchsafe its historical environment, while also adapting to trends, with noted provisos. The major exception mentioned here is agriculture, an area that, until recently in the wider European discourse, largely sat outside the discussion about *urban* and *metropolitan* identity. After all, these latter categories were the ones by which Kraków has understood itself since at least the late 19th century, as Nathan

Wood's work has shown. Tellingly, his analysis begins with the following quotation:

> Kraków should look after all the wonderful things that the past and has given it with the greatest respect and the most diligent care, and at the same tıme [...] has the obligation to move with the spirit of the times and as well as it can meet the needs, for the good of the people, that well understood progress demands.[20]

Although spoken by Kraków's Deputy Mayor in 1904, the sentiment could almost verbatim apply today. Thus, we close the circle of how change in Kraków depends on the very specific interpretation of its history – but because it *allows* for change, by at least comprising a dynamic self-definition, the same is true vice versa.

Notes

1 A discussion on the "revival" of Jewish culture, especially in and around the historic district of Kazimierz, also on the commercial scene and in festival form, exceeds the scope of this essay but embraces some controversy over the potential disconnection between numbers of Jewish residents and outward forms. See e.g., the press discussion in: Soren Gauger and Duncan Rhodes, Debate: Kazimierz: Revival or Reminiscence?, *The Kraków Post*, 1 June 2008, last accessed 12 April 2022.

2 For a comparative history, see Laimonas Briedis, *Vilnius – City of Strangers* (Budapest: CEU Press, 2009).

3 For broader comparative discussions of Lviv and Wrocław in particular, see the essays in: Jan Fellerer and Robert Pyrah (eds.), *Lviv and Wrocław, Cities in Parallel? Myth, Memory and Migration, c. 1890-Present* (Budapest: CEU Press, 2020).

4 Jacek Purchla, *Miasto i polityka. Przypadki Krakowa* (Kraków: Universitas, 2018), p. 194.

5 "Kraków funkcjonuje potocznie jako *pars pro toto* pamięci narodowej, a wynikające stąd zagrożenie nieznośnym patosem niweluje akcentami dystansującej się ironii i młodopolskiej groteski. Ta świadomość kulturowej ciągłości, jakże rzadka w rozchwianej „Mitteleuropie", wydaje się istotnym wyznacznikiem Krakówskiej lokalnej pamięci." – Ewa Chojecka, "Trzy modele kulturowej pamięci: Kraków, Katowice, Wrocław", *Herito* No. 2 (August 2011). https://herito.pl/artykul/trzy modele kulturowej pamieci-krakow-katowice-wroclaw/ – last accessed on 10 April 2022.

6 Julia Griffin and Andrzej Szczerski (eds.), *Young Poland: The Polish Arts & Crafts Movement, 1890–1918* (London: Lund Humphries, 2020).

7 As an example of the connection, Tadeusz Chrzanowski, "Wyspiański – Kraków – Polska", *Tygodnik Powszechny*, No. 29 (2000): 13.

8 Jolanta Drużyńska, Stanisław M. Jankowski, *Kolacja z konfidentem. Piwnica pod Baranami w dokumentach Służby Bezpieczeństwa* (Kraków: Przedsięwzięcie Galicja, 2006).

9 On the evolution of Nowa Huta in the early post-communist years, see: A. Stenning, "Placing (post-)socialism: the making and remaking of Nowa Huta, Poland", *European Urban and Regional Studies* 7/2 (2000): 99–118; also: Mariusz Czepczyński, *Cultural Landscapes of Post-socialist Cities: Representation of Powers and Needs* (London: Routledge, 2016), pp. 80–81.

10 Mirosław Haładyj, "Kolejny raz zwyciężyło kulturowe barbarzyństwo i pieniądz", *Onet.pl*, 22 January 2022: https://www.onet.pl/informacje/glos24/kolejny-raz-zwyciezylo-kulturowe-barbarzynstwo-i-pieniadz/yg821c2,30bc1058?fbclid=IwAR2zKyAWsUkytUCJ-fs4qyM3aEAyr6mPdp8PGmNtTvZB5AngPcyY_0XrLbk – last accessed on 10 April 2022.

11 *Ibid.*

12 Note that at the time of writing in early 2022, the case was still unresolved.

13 "Its goal is to conduct academic studies in the history, art, and culture of Kraków, promote knowledge of Kraków, reinforce respect for the city's tangible and intangible heritage, and care for their condition and protection. The Society has built, and continues to build, social capital in support of Kraków's history and the effective and efficient protection of its cultural heritage." – "About Us", http://www.tmhzk.krakow.pl/index.php/pl/8-o-nas/114-about-us, last accessed on 12 April 2022.

14 On the artificiality of the region, drawing on historical mythologies and part-facts, see the chapter on Galicia in Norman Davies, *Vanished Kingdoms. The History of Half-Forgotten Europe* (London: Penguin, 2012), but also on its power as a mental geography: Larry Woolf, *The Idea of Galicia: History and Fantasy in Habsburg Political Culture* (Stanford, CA: Stanford University Press, 2012), esp. pp. 383–420. Detailed analysis: Jacek Purchla, *Krakau unter österreichischer Herrschaft 1846–1918. Faktoren seiner Entwicklung* (Wien – Köln – Weimar: Böhlau, 1993).

15 For a wider discussion: Jacek Purchla, *Cracow in the European Core* (Kraków: MCK, 2016).

16 For more, see: Jan M. Małecki, "Lwów i Kraków – dwie stolice Galicji", *Roczniki Dziejów Społecznych i Gospodarczych* 50 (1989), pp. 119–131.

17 Lidia Stefanowska, "Back to the Golden Age: The Discourse of Nostalgia in Galicia in the 1990s (Some Preliminary Remarks)", *Harvard Ukrainian Studies* 27/(1/4) (2004–2005): 181–193.

18 "Mit Galicji" – a major international exhibition in 2014–15, with the following description: "The exhibition presents Galicia as a land of paradoxes. On the one hand, it was a space of development of national identities and cultures, on the other, the ethnic differences between the groups locked within artificially created borders led to numerous tensions". Source: https://mck.krakow.pl/wystawy/mit-galicji-1, last accessed on 12 April 2022. See also the resulting research-led publication, Jacek Purchla et al., *The Myth of Galicia* (Kraków: MCK, 2014).

19 The considerable literature on both cities as "European" includes at least one comparative volume, Jacek Purchla (ed.), *Kraków i Lwów w cywilizacji europejskiej.* (Kraków: MCK, 2003), also published in Ukrainian.

20 Nathaniel D. Wood, *Becoming Metropolitan: Urban Selfhood and the Making of Modern Cracow* (Ithaca, NY: Cornell University Press, 2010), p. 3, quoting *Nowiny dla wszystkich*. 7 October 1904, p. 5.

Names Index

Note: *Italic* page numbers refer to figures and page numbers followed by "n" denote endnotes.

Allen, Danielle 161, 177
Amersfoort, Philippe van 26, 31
Andersson, Åke 198, 202n4
Antohi, Sorin 29, 30
Arato, Andrew 28, 29
Ashworth, Gregory 176

Bajgier-Kowalska, Małgorzata 172, 181
Balcerowicz, Leszek 7, 8, 48, 49
Baldersheim, Harald 47
Bartuś, Krzysztof 88, 104
Bavinck, Maarten 44, 46
Beiersdorf, Zbigniew 87, 104, 157, 167, 176
Berbeka, Jadwiga 77, *77*, 83
Berkowicz, Aleksandra 23, 29
Bernhard, Michael 29
Bianchini, Franco 83
Biedrzycka, Anna 111, 128
Bilińska-Głód, Katarzyna 171, 176
Billert, Andreas 205, 214
Bína, Vladimír 198, 202n5
Bińczycka, Ewa 190, 199, 203n7
Błaszczyk, Mateusz 206, 214
Bobrowski, Michał 194, 199
Bogacz-Wojtanowska, Ewa 172, 176
Bojanowski, Krzysztof 145, 151
Bolsi, Paolo 189, 190, 199
Booth, Peter 74, 83
Borkowska, Agnieszka 60, 65
Borodako, Krzysztof 62, 65, 78, 83
Borowiec, Piotr 6, 15
Botta, Mario 133
Boyle, Robin 74, 83
Brańka, Patrycja 116, 120, 128
Brannan, Tessa 20, 29
Brataniec, Marcin 144, 148, 149, 151
Braudel, Fernand 214
Briedis, Laimonas 225n2
Broński, Krzysztof xiii, 48, 105, 218, 219, 224
Brzosko-Sermak, Agnieszka 93, 104
Buček, Ján 45
Buchowski, Michał 18, 20, 29
Bujas, Piotr 148, 151
Butterfield, Jim 17, 31
Buttimer, Anne 201
Buzek, Jerzy 207
Böhm, Aleksander 136, 162, 164, 176

Castells, Manuel 26, 19
Cęckiewicz, Witold 133, 141
Chlebicki, Michał 25, 26, 29
Chmielewska-Szlajfer, Helena 20, 29
Chmielewski, Jan M. 93
Chojecka, Ewa 218, 225n5
Chrzanowski, Michał A. 82, 83, 189, 199
Chrzanowski, Tadeusz 225n7
Chwalba, Andrzej 11, 13, 15, 18, 20, 29, 156, 176
Cichońska, Izabela 133, 151
Ciryt, Barbara 116, 129
Conrad Korzeniowski, Joseph 80, 81, 197, 198
Cruysen, Adriana van 183, 199
Cymer, Anna 89, 104
Czapiński, Janusz 186, 187, 199
Czapnik, Wojciech 138, 151
Czartoryski, family 171
Czepczyński, Mariusz 225n9
Czerski, Jarosław 140, 151
Czerwiński, Miko 190, 199

Dahrendorf, Ralf 212, 214
Davies, Norman 226n14
Delorme, Andrzej 29
Demarczyk, Ewa 219
Deńko, Stanisław viii, 136, 141, 142, 146, *147*, 151
Dimitrovska Andrews, Kaliopa xviin1
Domański, Tomasz 212, 214, 215
Domicz, Antoni 136, 141, 145, 151
Dreher, Christopher 185, 199
Drozda, Jacek 32, 46
Drużyńska, Jolanta 225n8
Drzał-Sierocka, Aleksandra 83, 85n4
Drzazga, Dominik 215
Dudek, Antoni 6, 7, 15, 19, 29
Dunikowski, Marek 100, 104, 140, 150, 152
Dybała, Bartosz 118, 129
Działek, Jarosław 186, 201
Dziechciaruk-Maj, Bogna 136, 152
Dziedzic, Stanisław 156, 176, 177, 179–181, 215n1
Dzięgielewski, Mariusz 193, 199
Dzierżanowski, Leszek 23, 29
Dziewanowska, Katarzyna 70, 83

Ewý, Jacek viii, 136, 145, *146*, 191

Fabiański, Marcin 99, 105, 135, 152
Faracik, Robert 126, 127, 129
Fellerer, Jan 225n3
Fijałek, Krzysztof 99, 105
Fikus, Marian 136
Filar, Przemysław 214, 215
Firlet, Elżbieta 86, 105
Florida, Richard 182–186, 189, 190, 199, 213–215
Forczek-Brataniec, Urszula 148, 149
Foryś, Iwona 134, 152
Fowkes, Ben 20, 29
Franz Joseph I 223
Frentzel-Zagórska, Janina 18, 29
Friszke, Andrzej 18, 29

Gąciarz, Aleksander 125, 129
Gaczoł, Andrzej 157, 162, 177
Gądecki, Jacek 95, 105, 189, 199
Gajczyk, Marta 134, 153
Galent, Marcin 26, 29
Gałka, Jadwiga *114*, 129
Garton Ash, Timothy xiv, 20, 29
Gauger, Soren 225n1
Geremek, Bronisław 49
Getz, Donald 71, 83
Gierat-Bieroń, Bożena 79, 83
Gilmore, James H. 69, 70, 84
Glaeser, Edward L. 185, 199
Glińska-Holcer, Ewa 215n1
Glondys, Danuta 74, 83
Gołąb-Korzeniowska, Monika 113, 129
Gołaszewski, Tadeusz 87, 105
Gold, John R. 70, 83
Gold, Margaret M. 70, 83
Góra, Magdalena 29
Góral, Anna 172, 176
Gorbachev, Mikhail S. 6, 13
Gordon, Claire 44, 45
Górecki, Mikołaj 75
Grasso, Maria T. 200
Grechuta, Marek 219
Greenwood, Royston 43, 46
Grela, Jerzy 19, 29
Griffin, Julia 225n6
Grycuk, Adrian 60, 65
Gryglewski, Ryszard 10
Gumińska, Maria 29
Gupta, Joyeeta 46
Gurba, Krystian 65, 68n5
Guzik, Robert 119, 121, 122, 129
Gwóźdź, Andrzej 66

Haduch, Bartosz 149, 152
Haduch, Michał 149
Haładyj, Mirosław 226n10
Hamilton, F.E. Ian xviin1
Harańczyk, Anna 50, 65
Hartley, John 183, 199
Harvey, David 27, 29
Hausner, Jerzy 44, 45
Hendriks, Frank 46
Hollanders, Hugo 183, 199
Hołuj, Artur 118, 129
Hołuj, Dominika xiii, 17, 32, 33, 36, 45, 53, 65, 220, 224
Howkins, John 190, 199
Hubert, Wit 25, 26, 29
Hughes, Howard 76, 161, 177
Hughes, James 44, 45
Hyams, Jonathan 182

Ilba, Mateusz *110, 113, 115, 158*
Illner, Michal 44, 45, 47
Ingarden, Krzysztof viii, 135, 136, 145, *146*, 191
Isozaki, Arata viii, *135*

Jacobs, Jane 5, 15, 72, 83, 204, 213, 215
Jagodzińska, Katarzyna 174, 177, 180

Jamry, Tomasz 59, 65
Janczykowski, Jan 166, 167, 169, 171, 177
Jankowski, Stanisław M. 225n8
Jarczewski, Wojciech 207–209, 215
Jarosz, Adam 37, 45
Jarosz-Nojszewska, Anna 66
Jaruzelski, Wojciech 5, 11, 12
Jasieńko, Jerzy 177
Jasieński, Manggha, Feliks 22, 135
Jędruch, Dorota 133, 152
Jeżak, Łukasz 125, 129
John Paul II *see* Wojtyła, Karol
Juchnowicz, Stanisław 22, 29
Jurkowski, Ryszard 147
Juros, Andrzej 21, 30

Kacprzak, Agnieszka 83
Kaczmarek, Tomasz 34, 45
Kaczmarska, Elżbieta 130
Kaden-Bandrowski, Juliusz 16n1
Kadłuczka, Andrzej 161, 167, 177
Kafka, Krzysztof 207–209, 215
Kajdanek, Katarzyna 97, 105
Kaliński, Janusz 49, 52, 55, 66, 134, 152
Kanik, Józef 168, 177
Kantor, Tadeusz viii, 75, 102, 146, 147, *147*
Karpińska, Marta 133, 141, 151, 152
Karwińska, Anna 73, 84, 189, 199
Kersting, Norbert 46
Kisielewski, Bartłomiej viii, 147, *148*, 149
Klaś, Jarosław 152
Klasik, Andrzej 63, 66, 184, *184*, 199, 200
Kliche, Krzysztof 100, 104, 150, 152
Kokoszkiewicz, Mateusz 209, 210, 215
Kołodko, Grzegorz 49, 66
Kołodziej, Joanna 169, 177
Komański, Andrzej 56, 66
Komar, Żanna 169, 180
Konev, Ivan S. 13
Kopeć, Marcin 165, 168, 179
Kopyciński, Piotr 58, 66
Korpal, Grażyna 171, 177, 178
Kowalczyk-Anioł, Joanna 172, 173, 178
Kowalik, Tadeusz 49
Kozłowski, Dariusz viii, 133, *134*
Krasnowolski, Bogusław 157, 159, 178
Krasowski, Robert 7, 12, 15, 20, 30
Krawczuk, Aleksander 193, 200
Kreidler, John 183, 200
Krochmal, Piotr 57, 67
Kruczkowska, Eliza 64, 67
Krzak, Izabela 98, 105
Kubicki, Paweł 26, 29, 214, 215
Kuczyński, Waldemar 15
Kudłacz, Tadeusz 128, 129
Kukliński, Antoni 34, 45
Kulesza, Michał 15, 33, 36, 45, 46
Kumięga, Patrycja 64, 66
Kurek, Sławomir *114*, 129
Kurowska, Anna 186, 200
Kuryłowicz, Ewa 148, 149, 152
Kuzianik, Robert 93

Ladner, Andreas 43, 45
Lahusen, Christian 200
Lanckorońska, Karolina 171
Landry, Charles 182–184, 187, 194, 195, *195*, 198, 200, 202n4, 220
Lankina, Tomila 35, 47
Laskowski, Andrzej xiii, 156
Lassota, Józef 210
Łatak, Kazimierz viii, 138, *139*, 144, 148, 149, *149*
Latko, Pola 25, 26, 29
Lefebvre, Henri 27, 30
Lehtimäki, Marianne 172, 176, 178
Lem, Stanisław 197
Lenin, Vladimir I. 13
Leo, Juliusz 206
Leśniak-Rychlak, Dorota 133, 143, 152
Levitas, Anthony 33, 45
Lewicki, Piotr viii, 138, *139*, 144, 148, 149, *149*
Lidström, Anders 46
Lipton, David 49
Liro, Justyna 134, 154
Lityński, Piotr 122, 129
Loegler, Romuald viii, 99, 132, 133, 136, 137, *137*, 148, 191
Loughlin, John 46
Lynch, Kevin 4, 217

Mach, Zdzisław 29
Maciąg, Kazimierz viii, *165*
Majchrowski, Jacek 209, 210
Majewski, Jerzy S. 140, 141, 145, 148, 152
Maki, Fumihiko 133
Makowski, Grzegorz 23, 30
Małecki, Jan M. 104, 105, 156, 157, 165, 169, 176, 178–180, 226n16
Malik, Cecylia 27
Malkowski, Tomasz 136, 145, 148, 152
Mamica, Łukasz 66
Mandelli, Emma 177
Mańkowska, Maria 133
Mańkowski, Tomasz 133, 138, 152
Marciszewska, Barbara 70, 84

Marcou, Gérard 32, 45
Markowski, Tadeusz 215
Marszałek, Anna 213, 215
Marszycka, Małgorzata 73, 84
Martin-Brelot, Hélène 189, 200
Matyja, Rafał 6, 16
Mayer, Jürgen 142
Maziarka, Katarzyna 65
Mazowiecki, Tadeusz 6, 7, 8, 12, 48
Mazur, Dagmara 60, 66
Mazur, Paweł 90, 92, 97, 99, 103, 134, 135, 137, 139, 146–149
Micek, Grzegorz 60, 66
Michalczak, Janusz 95, 105, 144, 152
Michnik, Adam 20, 30
Miecznikowski, Wojciech 140
Mikulski, Andrzej 134
Miłosz, Czesław 80, 197, 198
Miodunka, Piotr xiv, 109, 222
Misiąg, Wojciech 33, 45
Misiągiewicz, Maria viii, 133, 134
Montalto, Valentina 195, 200
Morawski, Wojciech 49, 56, 66
Moreno, Angel-Manuel 46
Moretti, Enrico 185, 200
Morris, Philip 54
Motak, Maciej 89, 105, 139, 142, 153
Mrożek, Sławomir 75
Murzyn (Murzyn-Kupisz), Monika A. 164, 165, 167, 168, 172, 178, 186, 201
Musiał-Malagó, Monika 116, 118, 120, 128–130
Mycielski, Krzysztof 136, 138, 145, 151, 153
Myczkowski, Zbigniew 162, 179

Nawara, Piotr viii, 141, *147*, 149
Nawratek, Krzysztof 209, 215
Nieć, Melania 66, 68
Niezabitowski, Michał 166, 179
Noga, Zdzisław 105, 177–180
Nowak, Katarzyna 136, 152
Nowakowski, Rafał 9, 16
Noworól, Aleksander 113, 118, 130, 133
Nowotnik, Dariusz 118, 130, 131n3

Obtułowicz, Wojciech 134, 138, 148, 153
Ogiński, Tomasz 145, 153
Olczyk, Przemysław 143, 149
Olechowski, Mateusz 25, 30
Orlewicz, Adam 142, 153
Ost, David 20, 30
Ostrowski, Wacław 173, 179

Pakuła, Marek 141, 154
Pakuła, Marzena 141, 154
Palmer, Robert 69–71, 84, 179
Panek, Tomasz 199
Panicz, Urszula 23, 30
Paprocki, Wojciech 49, 66
Parkinson, Michael 83
Parysek, Jerzy J. 201
Pawłowska, Krystyna 95, 105
Pawłowski, Krzysztof K. 157, 179
Peck, Jamie 185, 201
Piaskowski, Robert 81, 82, 84
Piątkowski, Marcin 49, 66
Pichler-Milanović, Nataša xviin1
Pine, B. Joseph, II 69, 70, 84, 201
Polesello, Gianugo 133
Popera, Karolina 133, 151
Porębska, Ewa P. 147, 153
Porter, Michael E. 188, 201
Pouw, Nicky 44, 46
Priller, Eckhard 30
Profiroiu, Marius 46
Purchla, Jacek xiv, xviii, 1, 5, 6, 8–10, 12–18, 30, 66, 72, 84–88, 99, 105–107, 135, 136, 140, 152–154, 156, 157, 159, 161, 162, 164, 168, 169, 171–172, *173*, 174–180, 204–208, 210, 211, 215n1, 218, 221, 224, 225n4, 226n14, 226n15, 226n18, 226n19
Putnam, Robert D. 28, 30
Pyrah, Robert xiv, 217, 225n3
Pytel, Sławomir 114, 130

Radłowska, Renata 144, 153
Raźniak, Piotr 114, 118, 130, 131n3
Regulska, Joanna 43, 46
Regulski, Jerzy 16, 32, 33, 46
Reklewska, Maria 180
Rembrandt 171
Rhodes, Duncan 225n1
Richards, Greg 69–71, 82, 84
Roche, Maurice 72, 84
Rogerson, Robert J. 189, 201
Rojkowska-Tasak, Halina 165, 168, 174, 176, 177, 179–181
Rolski, Mateusz 49, 66
Romanowski, Robert 56, 66
Ros-Tonen, Mirjam 44, 46
Róziewicz, Magdalena 157, 179, 180
Ruano, José 46
Rudolf, Agnieszka 80, 81, 84
Rutkowska-Gurak, Anna 61, 66
Ryder, Andrew 34, 45
Rygiel, Paweł 136, 153

Sachs, Jeffrey 49
Sakowicz, Marcin 33, 46
Sanetra-Szeliga, Joanna xiv, 63, 67, 69, 182, 190, 201, 220
Santagata, Walter 188, 201
Sapieha, Adam 18
Sarzyński, Konrad 117, 130, 142, 154
Sasse, Gwendolyn 44, 45
Sassen, Saskia 215
Schimanek, Tomasz 30
Schindler, Oskar 146
Scott, Allen J. 190, 201
Seibert, Krystian 86, 106
Sepioł, Janusz 106, 132, 140, 153, 161, 164, 171, 180, 204, 205, 215
Serafin, Dawid 93, 106
Siwek, Tadeusz 48, 67
Skala, Agnieszka 64, 67
Skotarczak, Teodor 88, 106, 135, 153
Skotnicki, Aleksander B. 164, 180
Skrzyńska, Barbara 23, 30
Słodczyk, Janusz 67, 131
Smith, Andrew 70, 84
Smith, Gordon 13
Smith, Richard 182, 183, 201
Smolar, Aleksander 20, 30
Snopek, Kuba 133, 151
Sołjan, Izabela 134, 154
Stanek, Łukasz 140, 154
Stangel, Michał 101, 106
Stec, Anna 117, 130, 142, 154
Stefanowska, Lidia 226n17
Stefański, Wacław viii, 133, *134*
Stenning, Alison 225n9
Stępień, Jerzy 8, 16
Stewart, John 43, 46
Stiasny, Grzegorz 136–138, 145, 146, 148, 153, 154
Stryjakiewicz, Tadeusz 189, 201
Strzałka, Kazimierz 64, 67
Strzeszyński, Jarosław 57, 67
Styrna-Bartkowicz, Krystyna 137, 154
Swianiewicz, Paweł 32, 34, 43, 45, 46
Swinarski, Konrad 75
Szczerski, Andrzej 225n6
Sześciło, Dawid 36, 46
Szmygin, Bogusław 162, 180
Szpak, Jan 105
Szpanowski, Piotr 162, 180
Szulborska-Łukaszewicz, Joanna 78, 84
Szultk, Agnieszka viii, 147, 149
Szymborska, Wisława 24, 197
Szyper, Barbara 172, 176, 180
Theiss, Maria 186, 200
Throsby, David 190, 191, 201
Tismaneanu, Vladimir 29, 30
Tocqueville, Alexis de 14
Tomaszewski, Andrzej 179, 180
Tomczak, Małgorzata 146, 154
Tosza, Elżbieta 137, 154
Tracz, Mariola 172, 181
Trammer, Karol 92, 106
Tridico, Pasquale 49, 67
Trounstine, Philip J. 183, 200
Turowicz, Jerzy 6
Twardoch, Agata 143, 154
Törnqvist, Gunter 187, 201

Urbańska, Marta A. 136, 152

Vetter, Angelika 46
Villa, Natalie 183, 202
Vinci, Leonardo da 171

Wajda, Andrzej 22, 135
Wałęsa, Lech 12
Walicki, Andrzej 17, 31
Walkowiak-Markiewicz, Katarzyna 56, 66
Wallace, Helen 45
Wantuch, Dominika 101, 107
Warfield, Katie 182, 183, 201
Wasik, Dorota 161, 177
Wdowiarz-Bilska, Matylda 211, 215
Węcławowicz, Grzegorz 110, 114, 131
Węcławowicz-Bilska, Elżbieta 113, 129
Weigle, Marcia A. 17, 31
Więcław-Michniewska, Joanna 112, 131
Wiśniewski, Michał xv, 86, 87, 107, 132, 133, 140, 141, 143, 148, 151, 152, 154, 172, 176, 180, 220
Włodarczyk, Małgorzata 132–134, 153–155
Włodarczyk, Marcin 132, 155
Wójciak, Ewelina 57, 67
Wojnar, Katarzyna *185*, 186, 189, 202n1
Wójtowicz, Mirosław *114*, 129
Wójtowicz-Wróbel, Agnieszka 113, 129
Wojtyła, Karol/John Paul II 12, 18, 109, 133, 220
Wollmann, Hellmut 32, 35, 45, 47
Wood, Nathaniel D. 226n20
Woodward, Richard 49, 68
Woolf, Larry 226n14
Woźniak, Michał Gabriel 16
Woźniakowski, Jacek 12
Wróbel, Piotr 138, 152
Wroński, Józef Szymon 133, 155

Wyrozumski, Jerzy 105
Wyspiański, Stanisław 75, 145, 153, 219

Yanukovych, Viktor 223

Zachariasz, Agata 162, 181
Zamorska-Przyłuska, Ewa 138, 155
Zborowski, Andrzej 111, 121, 131
Ziejka, Franciszek 156, 159, 181
Zimmer, Annette 30
Ziobro, Anna 97, 108
Ziobrowski, Zygmunt 86–88, 93, 108, 207–209, 215
Zukin, Sharon 183, 202
Zuziak, Zbigniew 93, 211, 215

Subject Index

Note: **Bold** page numbers refer to tables; *italic* page numbers refer to figures and page numbers followed by "n" denote endnotes.

3T factors 183, 189, 190
41st Session of the World Heritage Committee 161

academia 24, 58, 60, 62, 136, 138, 182, 223
academic centre 51, 58, 65, 136, 156, 171, 186, 207, 211–213
Academy of Fine Arts 171
accessibility 56, **195**
Act on the protection of land 88
activist, activism 23, 26, 28
administrative division 109, **110**, 110
Africa 55–57
agriculture 95, 118, 121, 125; land 87, 126, 127, 222, 224; market 128
Alpine Republic 219
Amsterdam 172
amusement park 141
ancien régime 6, 7, 10
Andrzej Frycz Modrzewski Kraków University 102, 188
anthropogenic pressure 118
Aptiv Technical Centre 58
aquaparks/waterparks 98, 141, 142
architects (local) 150. 171, 185, 213
architecture 132–155, 191, *192*; commercial 141; historical 141; local 133; new 102; office 141; postmodernist 132, 133; public 138; residential 133; religious 133
Art Nouveau 219
Arts and Crafts movements 219
Asia 55, 56
Auschwitz–Birkenau Camp 161
Austria 206, 219; Austria–Hungary 109
authorities 104
autonomy 32, 43, 87, 212
Avignon 74

Baghdad 132
Balice 34, 56; *see also* Kraków–Balice Airport
Balkan Wars 221
Bank Przemysłowo-Handlowy 56, 140
Bergen 74
Berlin 1, 5, 82, 92, 156, 206, 207, 211, 214, 224; East 6
biotech sector 63–64
Bohemians 185
Bologna 74
brand: image-building 14, 37, 73, 79, 120, 208, 211
Bratislava 1, 5, 156, 207, 211
bridges 39, 87, 89–91, 99, 139, 221
Brno 172, 209
Bronowice 96, 144
brownfield sites 65, 96, 98
Brussels 74
Budapest 1, 5, 156, 207, 211, 214
budget 34, *35*, 40, 44; participatory 25; investment 39; state 6, 7, 72, 210
business 38, 51, 53, 55; entities **51**; foreign 100; services 48, 60, 214; service centres 58, **59**, 59, 100, 127

capital: external investment 150, 161; foreign 50, 52, 54, 103, 134, 161
capital city 1, 109, 172, 209, 218
capitalism 8, 219, 220
Catholic Church 18, 22, 156, 210, 220
central administration 111, 206

central cities 204
Central European cities 1–3, 5, 14, 57, 72, 90, 92, 103, 139, 164, 168, 175, 186
centres of business 127
Chamber of Commerce and Industry 62
city centre 13, 14, 97, 98, 100, 103, 117, 136–138, 140, 143, 144, 148, 157, 164, 167, 172, 206, 207, 221
City Council 12, 13, 219
city of festivals 69, 79
city with events 71, *71*
city's cultural capital 70
city's cultural policies 69, 73, 78, 81
city's cultural potential 38, 80, 198
city's culturescape 2, 143, 145
city's identity 26, 62, 82, 150, 151, 164, 217, 222
city's pro-development policy 71, 174
cityscape 141, 142
Civic Committee 9–12, 20
civil activity 21, 23; participation 43; servants 33, 164, 209
civil society 3, 8, 17–31, 37, 57, 161, 187, 222
cluster 62, 68n5, 188; creative 187, 213
Cold War 15
Comarch Capital Group 57
ComCom Zone 148
commercial companies 52, 98, 143
commercial facilities 98, 103
commune 8–11, 19, 32–39, 93, 97, 109, 111–114, *114*, 116–124, 127
Communism 1, 2, 5–15, 81, 134, 156, 159, 161, 169, 170, 174, 175, 211
Communist Party 13, 16n2
communist system 6, 11, 48, 72
commuting 44, 110, 118, 121–122
competition (architectural) 146, 167
Conrad Festival 80, 81, 197, 198
conservation 40, 76, 148, 157, 162, 164, 171, 191, 193, 207
construction market 87, 89, 132, 134
Coordination Plan 99
Council of Europe 44
county 33, 35–37, 111–113, 127
COVID-19 pandemic 44, 53, 78, 85n5, 127, 150
Cracow University of Economics 3, 136, 137, 172
creative arts 191
creative capital 182, 184, 184–187, 213
Creative Cities Index 182, 183, 194–195
Creative Cities Monitor 182, 195–197
creative city 184, 198
creative class 182–186, *185*, 189, 202n1, 213
creative cluster 187
creative industries 62, 63, 182–185, 190, 192, 194, 197, 198
creative milieu 187
creative stock indices 183
creativity 2, 74
Cricoteka Centre for Documentation of the Art of Tadeusz Kantor 102, 146, 147, *147*
Crimea 223
crisis 5, 7, 9, 13, 72, 110, 132, 156; 2003 42
cultural creativity 221
cultural district/quarter 185, 187, 188
cultural identity 82, 221
cultural industries 191, 202n5
cultural institutions 38, 74, 78, 80, 82, 102, 148, 168, 187, *187*, 191, 223
cultural policy 69, 73, 78, 81
cultural sector in Poland 191
Culture Park (CP) 162, 163, *163*, 168, 173, *173*
culturescape 2, 142, 145
Cyprus 92
Czartoryski Princes Museum 102, 148
Czech Republic 209
Czechia 2, 171
Czerwone Maki 91
Czyżyny 27, 39, 54, 96, 100, 144, 147

Damascus 132, 140
Dębniki 89, 95
Debrecen 172
decentralisation 2, 19, 32, 34, 44
decommunisation 10, 13
deconstructivism 136
deindustrialisation 14
density of development 144
depopulation 14, 103, 173
developer, developers 55–57, 95, 96, 116, 117, 136, 167
development strategy 2, 14, 37, 39, 44, 58, 187, 197; Development Strategy 2030 78, 79, 198
Disneyfication 166
Donbas 223
dormitory town 122, 127
Dublin 214, 224
dwellings 57, 89, 94, 96, 144

Eastern Bloc 18, 19, 42
ecology 18, 22, 25, 60
Economic Activity Zones 61, 120

economic growth 145, 175, 204, 207, 213
economic reforms 7, 49
economy 48–68; centrally planned 72; command 2; creative 81, 185, 195, 198, 202n6, 213, 214; experience 69, 70; free-market 7, 14, 53, 87, 140, 161, 166, 175; knowledge based 50, 213; new institutional 48; real socialism 48
EFFE Award 81
elections 6, 8–13, 16n2, 19–24, 32, 33, 48, 50, 209
employment 14, 52, 52–55, 59, 59, 65, 121, 183, 208
environment: pollution 14, 27, 53, 174, 207; protection 113
enterprises: state-owned 50, 51; medium-sized 52, 120, microenterprises 51, 186, 191; private 57
entrepreneurship incubators 61
estate management 87
Euro-Atlantic civilisation 5
Europe: Central and Eastern 58, 82, 208, 211, 217; Western 60, 73, 92, 98, 137, 142, 220
European Capital City of Culture 79
European Capital of Culture, ECoC 73
European City of Culture 73
European Community 49, 161
European Cultural Month, ECM 69, 71, 72
European Union, EU 2, 23, 74, 205, 210, 214; accession 2, 28, 34, 43, 49, 56, 57, 94, 96, 100, 123, 134, 144, 161, 174, 207
Europolis 208–209
eventful city 69–85, 71
expenditure 34, 35, 36, 39, 76
experience goods 70

festivals 69, 79; city, industry 72, 73; literary 79, 80, 197, 198; *see also* Conrad Festival; Misteria Paschalia; Opera Rara; Sacrum Profanum
France 209
free time 70, 125, 189
funds 34, 41, 57, 101, 210

Galeria: Galeria Bonarka 99, 100, 142; Galeria Kazimierz 98, 142; Galeria Krakowska 90, 90, 98, 99, 142; Galeria Plaza 142
Galicia, and Lodomeria 3, 157, 206, 222–224, 226n14, 226n18; Western 109, 131n1
Gallery of Polish Art in the Cloth Hall 102
Gdańsk 5, 10, 59, 205, 208; Shipyard 11
Gdynia 59, 208
genius loci 132, 150
Germany 124, 223; East 5; *see also* Nazi (German) occupation
Glasgow 74
globalisation 132–55
Google Research & Development Centre 58
governance 13, 20, 21, 37, 50, 206
Górka Narodowa 91, 96
Grzegórzki 89, 96, 98, 142

Habsburg monarchy 156
Hanseatic League 156
Helsinki 74
heritage: cultural 2, 15, 18, 22, 65, 72–74, 151, 159, 161, 172–175, 191, 192, 207, 208, 220; culture 3, 156–181, 207; disinherited 164, 208; intangible 156, 159, 170–171, 174, 217; management 3, 172, 176; preservation 157; protection 162, 164, 165; without inheritors 164
historic centre 86, 99, 150, 157, 193, 221, 222
historical centre 14, 87, 90, 95, 133, 162, 168, 169, 173
historical building 96, 103, 138, 148
Holocaust 139, 161, 164–166, 174, 218
horticultural traditions 125
housing associations 94
Hungary 2, 171
hyperinflation 49

IBM Software Lab 58
ICE Kraków Congress Centre 38, 40, 77, 79, 102, 145
ideopolis 213–214
independence 16n1, 156
India 141
industry 14, 48, 50, 52–55, 120
Integrated Territorial Investments (ITI) 34, 41, 112, 123
International Biennale of Architecture (MBA) 132
International Conference on Conservation Kraków 2000 161
International Cultural Centre (ICC, MCK) 148, 159, 171, 223
International Exhibition and Convention Centre EXPO Kraków 77
International Monetary Fund 49

investors: Western 100
Iraq 132
Iron Curtain 6, 132, 156, 159, 175
Ispat Polska Stal company 54
Israel 73
IT services sector 57, 60
Italy 92

Jagiellonian dynasty 156
Jagiellonian University 61, 91, 102, 103, 136, 156, 172, 186, 193, 202n3, 211, 221; campus 95, *103*
Japan 73, 135
Jewish Culture Festival 79, 81, 164
Jewish ghetto 138
Jewish quarter 164–167, 207; *see also* Kazimierz
John Paul II Centre 98, 134
Jugendstil 219

Kalwaria Zebrzydowska 161
Katowice 25, 59, 203n10
Kazimierz 39, 40, 103, 157, 163, 164–167, *165*, *166*, 168, 207, 225n1
Kleparz 167
Kliny Borkowskie 144
Košice 172, 209
#Kraków *passim*; *see also* Bronowice; Czerwone Maki; Czyżyny; Dębniki; Górka Narodowa; Grzegórzki, Kazimierz; Kleparz; Kliny Borkowskie; Krowodrza; Kurdwanów; Mały Płaszów; Metropolia Krakowska; Mistrzejowice; Nowa Huta; Nowy Ruczaj; Podgórze; Prądnik Biały; Prokocim; Pychowice; Ruczaj; Salwator; Wesoła; Wola Justowska; Żabiniec; Zabłocie; Zakrzówek
Kraków 2000 75, 76
Kraków–Balice Airport 56, 210
Kraków Development Agency 103
Kraków Development Strategy 78, 79, 198
Kraków Festival Office 69, 71, 74, 75, 78, 80, 191
Kraków Fortress 147, 167
Kraków Functional Area (KFA) 112
Kraków Metropolitan Area (KMA) 34, 109, 112–115, *113*
Kraków Metropolitan Region (KMR) 9, 10, 109, 111, 125
Kraków Municipal Area 113
Kraków Special EconomicZone 61
Kraków Technology Park (KPT) 61, 191, 194
Kraków Transport Centre (KCK) 38, 99, 168
Kraków Urban Area (KZM) 114
Krowodrza 169
Kurdwanów 91, 95, 144
Kyiv 211, 223
Kyivan Rus 223
Kyoto Prize 22, 135
Kyoto University 64

"laboratory" 1, 50, 72, 175, 217, 222
Landscape Act 164
large-format retail centres/shops 53, 100, 119; *see also* Galeria; shopping centres
Lenin Museum 13
Lenin Steelworks 11, 19, 86, 87, 126; *see also* Tadeusz Sendzimir Steelworks
liberalism 2, 11, 12, 27, 49, 56, 78, 185
Libya 132
Life Science Park 63
local authorities 8, 9, 14
local zoning plans 41, *41*, 42, 93, 94, 101, 103, 118, 126, 150, 162–164
Łódź 9, 10, 25, 124, 162, 203n10
logistics centres 103
Luxembourg 92
Lviv/Lwów 209, 218, 223, 224, 225n3

Main Market Square/Rynek Główny 40, 101, 145, 148, 159, *163*, 167, 193, 206
Małopolska 22, 128, 186, 207; Region 34, 40, 56, 59, 88, 109, 111, 112, 121
Małopolska BiotechnologyCentre 63
Małopolski Garden of Arts 145, *146*
Mały Płaszów 91
mass culture 175
mass events 69, 80, *81*, 162
mass-media 194
Mayor of Kraków 9, 10, 12, 13, 209, 210
McDonaldization 166
meetings industry 62
memory 3, 139, 164, 208; collective 13; national 18; historical 223
Metropolia Krakowska 118, 120, 123; Association 34, 112, 116, 121, 123, 124
metropolis 2, 14, 65, 86, 98, 111, 112, 120, 122, 124, 125, 127, 128, 156, 198, 207, 208, 211, 214
MICE 69, 77, 77, 80
Mies van der Rohe Award 137–140, 143, 145–147, 149, 151, 221

migration 88, 110, 113, 114, 118, 120, 122, 127, 128
Misteria Paschalia 80, 82
Mistrzejowice 95
Mitteleuropa 3, 218, 225n5
MOCAK Museum of Contemporary Art 40, 101, 146, 147, 171, 188
modernism 127, 135, 140, 141, 144, 146, 219; socialist 169
Monument of History 162, 169
movements (civil, urban) 3, 20, 22, 26, 27
Moscow 206, 223
Mostar Bridge 221
motorisation 92
motorway ring 89, 91
multiculturalism 164
multifamily development 143, 144
multipliers 60, 62
multi-screen cinemas 98, 125, 141, 142
Municipal Council 11, 20, 28, 88
Municipal Heritage Preservation Officer 162
municipal investments 25, 39, 40
Municipality of Kraków 24, 32, 36, 40, 55, 61, 79, 123
Museum of Kraków 40, 101, 146
Museum of Municipal Engineering 39
Muzeum Galicja 165
myth 3, 223

National Council 10
National Museum 102, 171
nationalisation 87
Nazi (German) occupation 138, 146, 164, 169
New Delhi 141
New York 188
Nobel Prize 24, 193, 197
non-governmental organisations 21, 22, 26, 28, 62, 77, 80, 191
North America 56
Nowa Huta 11–13, 17, 18, 61, 86, 87, 89, 96, 98, 125, 133, 148, 163, 168, 172, 206, 225n9; steelworks 168, 219
Nowy Ruczaj 95
Nuremberg 74, 206

office buildings 98–100, 140, 141, 150
offshoring 58
Opera Rara 80
Oskar Schindler's Enamel Factory 40, 101, 146, 147, 171, 188
Oświęcim 91, 133; *see also* Auschwitz

outskirts 55, 92, 95–98, 119, 126, 147, 172
outsourcing 58–60, 68n4, 128, 214, 222, 224
ownership 14, 32, 49, 54, 65, 87, 92, 100, 161, 162, 165, 171, 172

parks 95, 188; pocket parks 96
participation 20, 21, 23–26, 28, 43, 69, 74, 195
perestroika 6
Philip Morris Polska SA 54
pilgrimage 38, 133, 156, 161
Piwnica pod Baranami 219
Plaszow, concentration camp 166, 167
Planty Garden Ring 157, 172
Podgórze 91, 138, 145–147, 163–168, 172
Polfa 54
Polish Academy of Arts and Science (PAU) 22, 211
Polish Aviation Museum 102, 147, *148*
Polish Central Engineering Associations (NOT) 100
Polish Investment Zone 61
Polish United Worker Party (PZPR) 13
population density 115
post-communist: city 3, 64; Europe 209, 212
post-industrial city 65, 70, 96, 167, 205
postmodernism 132–134, 136, 137
Poznań 9, 10, 59, 113, 114, 122, 124, 125, 127, 128, 162, 205, 208, 209, 223; Metropolia 113
Prądnik Biały 94
Prague 1, 5, 74, 156, 207, 211, 214
prefabricated concrete slabs (*wielkapłyta*) 86
preservation 162, 164, 171
price of land 118, 128
private entities 94
private property 42, 88, 95
private sector 50
privatisation 7, 48, 49, 52–55
Prokocim 87
Prussia, Germany 223
public: administration 32, 60, 62, 87, 187, 189; finance 32; investments 27, 42, 89, 103, 134, 145, 167, 189, 197; public authorities 17, 25, 26, 28, 32, 37, 166; services 36, 39, 95, 96, 189; space 23, 89, 102, 135, 138
public–private partnership 36, 40
Pychowice 95, 102, *103*, 136, 143, 211

Quito in Ecuador 157

railway 39–41, 90, 91, 98, 99, 101, 118, 120, 123, 124, 128, 131n1, 131n5, 141, 142, 147, 168, 211, 221; fast commuter railway system, SKA 41, 91; railway station (Kraków Główny) 91, 99, 101, 141, 142, 147, 168
real estate market 49, 62, 88, 94, 164
reclamation and revitalisation 132
reconstruction 127, 138, 167
Red Army 5, 13
reforms: economic 7, 8, 20, 21, 49; of the territorial administration 111
Register of Immovable Heritage of the Małopolska Region 88
REGON register 50, **51**, 186, 191, 192, **192**, 194, 202n2, 203n8, 203n9
remembrance 2, 164
research and development centres 58, 188, 222
residential estates: Avia 96, *97*, 144; Nowy Płaszów 96; WiślaneTarasy 96
residential housing 57, 88, 94, 103, 143
restoration and conservation 148
revenue 33–39, **35**, 44, 62, 73, 118, 205, 210, 222
Reykjavik 74
right to the city 27, 28
ring road: second 90, 91; third 91
road system 86, 95, 98
Roman Catholic Church 156, 161
Round Table, Polish 6, 12, 16n2, 19, 21
Ruczaj 144
Russian Federation 209

Sacrum Profanum 80–82
salt mines (Wieliczka, Bochnia) 161
Salwator 89
Sanctuary of Divine Mercy in Łagiewniki 98, 133
Santiago de Compostela 74
Secession 219
second homes 126
Second World War 17, 72, 86, 87, 96, 101, 109, 157, 164, 166, 168, 208, 209
self-employment 186, 202n1
self-government 8, 14, 17–19, 21, 22, 32–44, 50, 62, 72, 111, 159, 162, 174, 184, 220
settlement, network 2, 3, 204, 208–209, 211
shopping centres/malls 53, 90, *90*, 97–99, *99*, 100, 119, 125, 135, 141, 142, 167, 220
Silesia 56, 109, 120, 125
single-family housing 94, 96, 101, 127, 143, 150
Skawina 19, 91, 121, 122, 124–127, 131n4
Slovak Republic 209
Slovakia 2, 171, 209
smog 126
social activism 17, 28, 174
social capital 24, 28, 183, 186, 187
socialist realism 168, 169
Solidarity 5–13, 17–19, 168, 210
Solvay 14, 53, 98, 99
Sopot 59, 208
South America 55
Soviet Union 5
spatial development 86–108, 133, 163, 209
spatial planning/zoning 163, 169
spiritual capital 3, 74, 109, 156, 207
sports hall 38, 39, 148
St Petersburg 209
Stalinist period 18, 22, 168
start-ups 48, 63–64, 68n6, 194
State Agency of Foreign Investment (PAIZ) 50
State Treasury 44, 52, 54, 61, 210
Steelworks 11, 14, 18, 19, 50, 54, 61, 65, 86, 87, 91, 101, 103, 110, 126, 168, 219
Strategy for Culture Development 78, 79
strike 11, 18, 20, 26
study of conditions and directions of spatial development 93
subsidiarity 44
suburban areas/zone 88, 110, 112, 114, 118, 121, 122, 127
suburbanisation 92, 96, 97, 110, 113–122, 127, 128, 143
suburbs 96, 100, 114, 116, 123, 143
sustainable development 78, 82, 128, 197, 222
symbolic functions 207
Symposium of the Conference on Security and Cooperation in Europe (CSCE) 1991 15, 72, 159
Syria 132
systemic transformation 37, 48, 50–57, 64, 65, 121, 144
systemic transition 19, 48

Tadeusz Sendzimir Steelworks 14, 50, 54, 61, 65; *see also* Lenin Steelworks
Tauron Arena Kraków 38, 77, 79, 102
technology transfer centres 61, 63

territorial government 8, 33, 48, 50, 60
Tishman Speyer Properties 99
Toruń 159
totalitarian system 1, 2, 14
tourism 37, 38, 43, 57, 62, 63, 70, 72, 74, 75, 81, 125–127, 173–176, 207, 218, 221; cultural 81, 207; weekend 126, 127
tourist destination 1, 37, 38, 65, 142, 161
Towarzystwo Miłośników Historii Zabytków Krakowa/Society of Friends of Kraków 18, 172, 221
towers (high-rise, office) 100, 133, 140, 141, 150, *170*, 220
trade 49, 52, 53, 125
trade union 11, 18, 20, 26–28
tram 39, 76, 91; rapid 39, 90
transformation 111, 124
transport: buses 111, 123; network 89, 111; *see also* railway; tram

Ukraine 89, 217, 218, 223, 224
unemployment 8, 20, 49, 53, **53**, 134
UNESCO 64, 173, 197, 203n10, 222, 224
UNESCO City of Literature 80, 197
UNESCO Creative City of Literature 79, 182, 193, 197–198
UNESCO World Heritage 94, 101
UNESCO World Heritage List (WHL) 3, 15, 157–161, *158*, 161, 162, 169, 170, 175, 193, 207
UNESCO World Heritage Site 221
UNESCO's Representative List of the Intangible Cultural Heritage of Humanity 171
Union of Polish Architects (SARP) 132, 139
United States of America 60, 73, 137, 142, 189
Unity Tower 100, 150, *170*, 170, 220
universities *see* Academy of Fine Arts; Cracow University of Economics; Andrzej Frycz Modrzewski Kraków University; Jagiellonian University
University Hospital 102, 103
Upper Silesian urban area 109
urban: centres 17, 43, 204; culture 26; democracy 25; development 2, 42, 69, 76, 87, 91, 99, 102, 103, 138, 173, 197, 206; planning 3, 93, 94, 99, 144, 157, 171, 217; policy 71, quality of life 37, 38, 40, 42, 64, 70, 81, 182–185, 184, 187–190, 198, 214; sprawl 118
urbanology 4

Venice 133, 172
Vienna 1, 156, 170, 188, 206, 207, 211, 214, 219, 223, 224; Congress of 206, 223
Vilnius/Wilno 209, 218
Visegrád Group 171
Vladivostok 6

Warsaw 1, 3, 5–7, 9, 10, 22, 44, 56, 59–61, 64, 68n2, 74, 92, 114, 122, 127, 151, 156, 159, 161, 194, 205–211, 214, 218, 222–224
Washington, DC 157
water/water intake 56, 111, **112**, 131n1, 223
Wawel (Hill, Castle) 14, 76, 77, 109, 135, 142, 156, 157, 162, 169, *170*, 171
Wesoła 103
WHL *see* UNESCO World Heritage List
Wola Justowska 143
World Bank 49
Wrocław/Breslau 9–11, 59, 82, 114, 124, 162, 203n10, 205, 218, 225n3

Young Poland 218, 219

Żabiniec 94
Zabłocie 40, 89, 96, 100–102, 146, 147, 168, 188, 219
Zakopane 91, 126
Zakrzówek 27, 95, 133, *170*
Zamość 159
zoning laws 150, 162

For Product Safety Concerns and Information please contact our EU representative GPSR@taylorandfrancis.com Taylor & Francis Verlag GmbH, Kaufingerstraße 24, 80331 München, Germany